THE SELF-

Endorsements

"*The Self-Healing Human* is a glorious, inspiring, practical guide for anyone seeking better health. Today, as science focuses increasingly on drugs, genes, stem cells, and surgical advances, it is refreshing to see Dr. Susanna Ehdin's thrilling vision of the whole person, which focuses not only on our physical body, but on our mental and spiritual sides as well. Well researched and warmly written, The Self-Healing Human deserves a wide readership."
Larry Dossey, M.D.
Author: *Healing Beyond the Body* and *Reinventing Medicine*

"Bravo for *The Self-Healing Human!* By recognizing the power of the mind, body and spirit, Dr. Ehdin brings to light the missing pieces of today's healthcare system. This book opens an underutilized door to self-healing. Evidence-based and excellently researched, this work represents an important shift in the healthcare paradigm."
Mimi Guarneri, M.D., F.A.C.C.
Rauni Prittinen King, RN, HNC, CHTPI
Founders of Scripps Center for Integrative Medicine, La Jolla, California

"An amazing book, gives a truly holistic view that leads us into the new paradigm of self care, includes biochemistry, vitamins and minerals, diet, exercise, personal process, detoxification, consciousness and spirituality. *The Self-Healing Human* is one of the best books on keeping ourselves healthy. It leads us through the broad perspective of our responsibility in self-care, and shows us how self-healing arises out of our basic nature. Some call it the future; in this book, the future is now."
Barbara Brennan, Founder of the Barbara Brennan School of Healing,
Author: *Hands of Light and Light Emerging*

"Dr. Susanna Ehdin has written a progressive and enlightening book on the changing paradigm of how we as humans interact with our own bodies and with the healthcare system. Drawing from her vast knowledge both as an immunologist and as a spiritual healer, Dr Ehdin has created a new understanding of our bodies. For the reader, this book will expand your understanding of the potential everyone has within themselves to keep both the mind and body 'fine-tuned' and healthy. I highly recommend it."
Abigail Shefer, M.D.
Board Certified in Internal Medicine

Praise for the Swedish Edition

"Dr. Susanna Ehdin describes with solid knowledge and in great detail a health philosophy based on the theory that our natural state is to be healthy and that we can strengthen our healing powers to create a long and healthy life. This is revolutionary in our fast-paced healthcare system with its many crises." *Läkartidningen* (*The Journal of the Swedish Medical Association*) # 23, p. 2884–8, 1999.

"Dr. Ehdin uses clear language as she combines large quantities of dry facts with sensual messages in a way that excites her readers and audiences. Some of it we have heard before, but much is new – and it is exactly her grasp of the whole, her ability to summarize the research, that gives the 'aha' reaction." *Prosana* (*The Journal for Doctors in Biological and Nutritional Medicine*) # 4, 1999.

"Many health books may have come before Dr. Susanna Ehdin's *The Self-Healing Human*, but there won't be another one quite like this one for a long time. Dr. Ehdin, whose degree is in immunology, has summarized much of the latest research on how we can feel better and live a longer and happier life." *Hälsa* (Health), July 1999.

THE SELF-HEALING HUMAN

Susanna Ehdin, Ph.D.

Translated by
Susan Larsson
and
Charles Larsson, M.D.

Holistic Wellness Publications

*The best teacher is the one who gets
the students to ask the questions themselves.*

For additional information
or to order books,
please see www.ehdin.com

Copyright © Susanna Ehdin 2002

Holistic Wellness Publications
A division of Holistic Wellness Inc.
Encinitas, California, USA.
All rights reserved. No part of this book may be used
or reproduced in any manner whatsoever without
written permission except in the case of brief quotations.

First edition

Cover photo: Paulina Westerlind
Typeset at Ljungbergs sätteri, Köping, Sweden

Printed in the United States of America by
Central Plains Book Mfg.
ISBN 0-9727856-1-2

To Martin and my brother Peter, with love.

*To all healing powers that
flow through everything.*

Also By Susanna Ehdin, Ph.D.

The Art of Cooking for the Self-Healing Human
(in Swedish)

The Little Book on Health and Well-being
(in Swedish)

HQ – The Human Holistic View
(written together with Martin Ehdin in Swedish)

12 Weeks to a Self-Healing Life
(in preparation, to be published in 2004)

The Self-Healing Human
has been translated into six languages.

To the reader:
The information in this book is not meant to replace your doctor's advice and treatment. People are biochemically individual and there is no standard treatment that suits everyone.

Table of Contents

	Acknowledgments	13
	Prelude	14
1.	The New Health Awareness	17
2.	We are Made of Energy	33
3.	Healing Powers of Vitamins and Mineral	71
4.	You Become What You Eat	103
5.	Intestinal Flora and Fauna	145
6.	Movement Creates Flow	164
7.	The Importance of Emotions	182
8.	The Creative Power of Mind and Thought	221
9.	Healing Detoxification	245
10.	Consciousness and Spirituality	285
11.	The Holistic View – The Foundation for Self-Healing	309
	Postlude – My Path to Self-healing	343
	References	350
	Index	361
	About the Author	368

Chapter Contents

1. The New Health Awareness — 17

The Mechanical Paradigm 18 • Ailing Medical Care 19 • A New Health Philosophy 21 • Spiritual Healing 23 • Bio-balance 25 • Bio-imbalance 26 • Personal Power Over Health 28 • Heal the Whole Being 29

2. We are Made of Energy — 33

Energy: the Underlying Force 35 • Universal Energy 35 • Earth Energy 37 • Life Energy 41 • The Health Triangle 43 • Cellular Energy 44 • Illness and Wellness Processes 46 • Symptom – Mechanism – Cause 49 • Immune System 51 • Our Senses 52 • Influence of Light 53 • Influence of Color 54 • Influence of Sound 57 • Hidden Sights 59 • Eastern View of Energy 60 • Anatomy of Energy 64 • Psychoimmunity 65 • Holographic View of the World 67 • Healing 68 • Near-life Experience 69

3. Healing Powers of Vitamins and Minerals — 71

The Vital Minerals 72 • Vitamins 76 • Vitamin + Mineral = True 78 • Metabolism 81 • Osteoporosis 84 • Create Balance with Food 87 • Stress Depletes Nutrients 89 • Poor Nutrition: A Sad Condition 91 • Smart Minerals 94 • Nutrition Affects the Mind 95 • Toxins 96 • Free Radicals 98 • Antioxidants 99 • Detoxification and Cleansing 101

4. You Become What You Eat — 103

The Digestive System – Our Center of Force 104 • Food for Thought 104 • Changed eating habits 105 • Eat to Live, Not to Survive 107 • Manipulated Food 108 • Toxic Fats 109 • Fat for Life 110 • What About Our Children? 113 • Teen Eating Habits 116 • The Bitter Truth About Sugar 117 • The Role of Insulin 120 • Health Foods versus Sick Foods 122 • Eat Like Stone Age Man 126 • Health and Nutrition 128 • Lifestyle Creates Health 130 • Vital Enzymes 133 • The Food of the Future 135 • Acid-Base Balance 136 • Balancing Food 139 • Food as an Emotional Shock Absorber 140 • Live 120 Years 142

5. Intestinal Flora and Fauna — 145

Digestion 146 • The Intestinal Ecosystem 147 • Intestinal Flora and Allergies 150 • A Bad Stomach Burdens the Body 151 • Candida – A Scourge through the Ages 153 • Food as Medicine 156 • How to Keep Your Stomach Happy 157 • Functional Foods 159

6. Movement Creates Flow — 164

Breath of Life 164 • Breathing Practice 166 • Exercise 169 • Increased Body Awareness 170 • The Body Armor 172 • Dance of Release, Dance of Relief 174 • Healing Music 175 • Micromotion with Sound 176 • Laughter as Exercise 179 • Joy and Enjoyment 180

7. The Importance of Emotions — 182

Emotional Intelligence 183 • The Value of Feelings 184 • Separation of Body and Soul 185 • Molecules of Emotion 187 • Anatomy of a Feeling 189 • Memory and Emotions 190 • Dreams 193 • The Power of Therapy 194 • Living Without Emotional Nuances 196 • Empaths and Psychopaths 200 • Limbic Stress 203 • Power of Touch 204 • Healing Touch 209 • Verbal Abuse 211 • The Muted Child 212 • Health and Emotions 213 • Relationships 215 • Emotional Repression 217 • Living with Feelings 218

8. The Creative Power of Mind and Though — 221

Limited and Unlimited Individuals 222 • The Power of the Mind 225 • Fear of Change 228 • Tension and Relaxation 231 • Powerlessness is Hazardous For Your Health 232 • Reduce Stress 235 • Being Present 236 • Inner Practice 237 • How to Manage Life 241 • Luxuriate in Joy 242 • Personal Transformation 243

9. Healing Detoxification — 245

The Oral Society 246 • Bad Food Habits 248 • Chemical Addiction 250 • Dopamine and Serotonin 252 • The Craving Brain 254 • Sugar Sensitivity 255 • Sugar Dependency 257 • The Caffeine Effect 258 • Stress, Hormones, and Addiction 260 • Autogenous Stimulation 263 • Global Detoxification 265 • Food as Drug and Allergen 267 • Food Allergies 268 • Dairy and Gluten Intolerance 270 • Primary Allergy 272 • Food and Autoimmunity 275 • Food and Mental Imbalance 276 • Our Most Common Toxins 278 • Detoxification of the Body 281

10. Consciousness and Spirituality — 285

The Ingenious Brain 286 • Consciousness and Awareness 289 • The Infinite Human 291 • The Flow 294 • Raised Consciousness 295 • Healing Prayer 298 • Healing Relationships 301 • A Spiritual Awakening 303 • Our Origin 305 • Remembering My True Self 308

11. The Holistic View – The Foundation for Self-Healing — 309

Psychoneuroimmunology 311 • The Female Immune System 313 • The Challenged Immune System 315 • Bio-balance versus Inflammation 318 • Different Paradigms 321 • Integrative Medicine 323 • Medical Freedom 325 • Self-healing 327 • Sleep and Rest 330 • Replenish your Energy 332 • The Laser Effect 333 • Activate Your Self-Healing 335 • Self Diagnosis 337 • The Wholeness

Acknowledgments

I have nurtured the seed for this book for many years and it took me nine months to write. Many people and many thoughts inspired me before and during the course of this project. But I would particularly like to thank the following people:

- Editor Kerstin Bergfors, president Karin Leijon, and publisher Viveca Peterson at Forum, who were most helpful and provided constructive and enjoyable suggestions for the Swedish edition. Thank you for believing in me immediately and signing a book contract right away, based on just a two-page book proposal!
- Translators Susan Larsson and Dr. Charles Larsson, for the tremendous effort you put into the translation of the book. Thank you, Susan, for your speed and great skill. You have the patience of an angel and you managed to make this collaboration both fun and educational. Thanks to Charles for keeping Susan straight on the scientific facts. Thank you to Tim Nicholson, who read every word and whose feeling for the language added linguistic sparkle to every page. And thank you to Erik Larsson for your contribution to the final copy, turning the project into a family venture.
- Dr. Larry Dossey, Dr. Dean Ornish, and healer Barbara Ann Brennan for your great inspiration and support–both in books and at meetings–and for your vision and courage to pursue what you believe in.
- Photographer Paulina Westerlind for the wonderful pictures and design, and for being such a lovely friend.
- Author Gunilla Gerland and journalist Lena af Petersens for sharing your advice and encouragement.
- All those who contributed by participating in interviews.
- Lisbeth Haglund, Barbara Huff, Marie Löfkvist, and Johanna Falk for having introduced me to new horizons of psychology, personal development, meditation, and nutrition.
- Martin and Daniel for your warm support and loving patience.
- Terri Kosmicki, the healing goddess, for all the incredible healing you do and that you are teaching me.

Prelude

Welcome to the world of the self-healing human. We all have a natural power within us that enables us to heal and stay healthy. But we need to become aware of this power—our hidden potential—in order to use it for our well-being. This book describes various paths that we can choose to enlist our physical and mental resources. It presents different lifestyles that will enhance our self-healing power and create good health.

It takes time to build up and care for good health – just as it does to have a loving relationship. Health and well-being are created through the choices we make. Our immune system is part of our whole being; you cannot strengthen your immune system without simultaneously affecting your thoughts, soul, emotions, lifestyle, eating habits, and the biochemistry within your brain. You have great influence over these factors, but you need knowledge in order to make the right choices. Over the last decade, more and more people have become interested in health, healing, and alternative ways of creating well-being.

Everyone has the capacity for self-healing. If you cut your finger, you don't spend time worrying about whether it will ever heal. But with the increasing numbers of people suffering from chronic disease such as diabetes, heart disease, allergies, arthritis, and osteoporosis, good health cannot be taken for granted. This makes it even more urgent to understand the situation and to search for its causes. However, we can choose a different path – one that stimulates self-healing and leads to excellent health.

Over the last decade, researchers have discovered many of the immune system's secrets and its connection to other bodily functions. Today we understand how different factors influence our health. It is with great pleasure that I share with you this new view of health, based on my knowledge and experience, as well as that of other people. In order to present the best possible picture of health and the paths to self-healing, I have chosen to merge information from many fields, summarizing the essence of knowledge and understanding that I have gathered over twenty years of research and studies. The human being has fascinated me for as long as I can remember. My driving force has been a wish to reach behind the façade and understand the soul, the emotions, the functions of the body and the whole. This has been my aim in life, as well as in the process of writing this book.

This book also deals with a new way of viewing ourselves. We are more than just a body that functions like a machine. Our mind and soul interact with our body in a very sophisticated manner. Everything happens with the purpose of creating wholeness in balance. Therefore it is essential to keep the connection with our inner selves alive and to listen to the signals from within – though staying attuned to and understanding these signals requires practice.

We are "beings of energy," made up of both matter and energy. The energy component, however, far outweighs the portion made up of matter. Thus it is more efficient to treat the energy, rather than only treating the matter – our physical being. But our bodies also need the right building materials; we will not thrive without a balanced and nutritious diet. The food we eat affects our biochemistry–our metabolism–as well as the type of bacteria in our digestive systems. Actually, we are an integral part of an ecosystem in terms of chemistry and energy. This interaction is both with the environment and ourselves. This symbiosis–a co-existence of mutual interaction–is the foundation of all life.

Everything–from the air we breathe to the food we eat–has a negative or positive impact on our metabolism. The immune system and the detoxification system take care of internal as well as external toxins. This process requires large amounts of energy; if the system is overloaded, the toxins are deposited in our own body tissues. However, we will not notice this right away; it will be years before the problems are discovered, when the accumulated toxins manifest in the form of cancer, rheumatism, arteriosclerosis, hypertension, kidney failure, and other degenerative diseases. In other words, the lack of symptoms is not the same as being healthy.

We are currently in the midst of a paradigm shift involving a radical change in our view of health. A paradigm is "a pattern or a model." It is the basis of how we perceive the world. The new way of thinking is as great a change for us in the western world as it was when people finally understood that the earth is not flat, but round. Change can be challenging and revolutionary; some people find it easier to accept than others. The process of embracing change has to happen at our own pace. It is part of human nature to change, to grow, and to mature. The process of changing is in itself the very basis of the survival of our species.

A unifying movement is sweeping across the world; a marriage between apparently incompatible aspects is approaching. It is a union of East and West, male and female, body and soul, thought and emotion, life and death. Perhaps this is why the present time seems to be so chaotic. Afterwards, we'll shake our heads in wonder at how these aspects ever could have been separated.

This new way of thinking is about a deeper experience, which cannot be understood by reading or hearing about it. You cannot possibly understand what the color of blue looks like or how the scent of lavender smells by hearing a description. First you have to see the blue sky or inhale the scent of lavender blossoms. And so I invite you to open your senses and other channels, leading to an understanding from within.

This book could just as well have been titled *The Lively Human Spirit* – because self-healing is a natural and spontaneous process in a vivacious person with an optimistic view of life. And that is really what we need in a society at our level of material sophistication – more lively human beings in touch with their own spirits.

1.
The New Health Awareness

The new health awareness is unique because it can spread on its own, without any official plan. People accept responsibility for their own health; they seek knowledge actively and welcome a whole new way of thinking. We have reached a turning point; we cannot evolve much further unless we look beyond the limits of the current materialistic and mechanical view of humankind. Why is this change taking place at this particular time? Because there is enough knowledge and awareness to dismantle the old view of the world, paving the way for a shift in thoughts and views

Self-healing is natural to all life forms. Though practiced for thousands of years, we seem to have forgotten how to do this in our modern society. And sure enough, over the last fifty years more and more people have become ill with an increasing number of chronic diseases. We face a major health crisis caused by the "technological revolution." Bad health accumulates from one generation to the next; if we don't take this threat seriously, we risk extinction. But a shift in perspective will show us what has been there all along.

Our ancestors relied on good nutrition, healing herbs, and help from wise medicine men and women. Many of the ancient healing traditions were based on a philosophy about the origin and cure of disease that was both physical and spiritual in nature. Each person was treated as an individual. Hippocrates, considered the father of medicine, said, "It is more important to know what sort of person has a disease than to know what sort of a disease a person has." Today, we do not focus on the individual, but on disease. We use all of our resources to fight disease, rather than to strengthen our healing powers. We see the body as a sophisticated machine, no greater than the sum of its parts. These parts are also treated separately, as if they had no connection to each other. The soul and the body are also treated as though they were totally separate. With the development of our modern society, we have lost track of our basic self-healing nature. How did this happen? Is there a way out? The new health awareness will bring changes that are greatly needed to return to a state of optimum health.

The Mechanical Paradigm

Today's view of health is the result of ideas imprinted on the western world over the last several centuries. According to the mechanical view, we are made up of matter and the body works as a machine. It began in the seventeenth century, when English physicist Isaac Newton discovered a natural law that applied not only to the sky, but also to Earth. The law of gravity made it possible to understand the universe intellectually without the presence of spiritual principles. This mechanical view was supported by iatromechanics (*iatros* means physician); pumps run the human body, muscles work as levers, and blood vessels and nerve paths are channels for transportation. Everything in the universe could be studied and understood according to the nature of each component.

This was a reductionistic view of life. It was also based entirely on the power of logic and thought. Intuition and emotion were worthless and irrational. Science was the only tool for understanding the individual and the environment. Reductionism relied upon the mathematics of Newton, the philosophy of René Descartes, and the methodology of Francis Bacon. Matter was the basis of all existence, and the material world was perceived as a collection of separate objects pieced together to form a giant machine. While this view was perfect for the emerging mechanical and industrialized society, it doesn't fit today's integrated information technology society.

In the seventeenth century, however, this mechanical paradigm represented a major advance. It paved the way for the great mechanical and technological revolution, and progress in our current society – a revolution made possible by the firm belief that intellect and thought were the only reliable instruments. These new ideas represented liberation from the church's view of the world and its claims of exclusive rights to knowledge. For example, Galileo was almost burned at the stake in the 1630s for saying that the sun was at the center of the universe, and in 1689 the King of Sweden banned philosophical studies that were in conflict with the Bible. But the growing middle class used this new science and knowledge to assert itself, despite the church and those in power. In the wake of this trend, writers, philosophers, scientists, and other intellectuals were greatly appreciated.

The nineteenth and twentieth centuries witnessed vast technological and mechanical advances. Or, as the aborigines in New Guinea put it at their first interaction with westerners: "Your gods must be very powerful, since they can create so many things." This contains a grain of truth, since science and technology have had an almost divine place in our society. Distinguished researchers such as Einstein have reached guru status, and Nobel Prize laureates are in a league by themselves.

Our material progress generated great faith in the future. After World War II, people hailed science and technology as the solution to every conceivable problem. These great expectations may have culminated with the spectacular televised moon landing in 1969. The energy crisis that followed in the 1970s revealed our disappointment in the limitations of technology. Today we are experiencing a similar disappointment in the shortcomings of the healthcare system.

It is interesting to note that most of our institutions and academies were founded under this old mechanistic paradigm. These values laid the foundation of our society; imagine how different the world might be with a new paradigm.

Ailing Medical Care

During the early days of modern medicine, doctors named and classified each anatomical body part and known disease, using the Swedish botanist Carl von Linnaeus' classification of plants as a model. The field of medicine successfully elevated its status by adopting the methodology and precision of the physical and chemical sciences. By the late nineteenth century it was recognized as a science, while traditional folk medicine came to be condemned as superstitious and unreliable.

The pharmaceutical industry evolved in the late nineteenth century from the German chemical industry. Its view was strictly pharmacological; diseases should be treated with drugs–chemicals–that cured the symptoms. This pathological view was based on the revolutionary findings of French chemist Louis Pasteur in 1862. He was the first to prove that a bacterial infection could cause a specific disease. With the discovery of antibodies at the turn of the century, Nobel Prize laureate Paul Ehrlich formulated a new theory for treatment called immunotherapy. Like a "magic bullet," the antibody would seek out the pathologic structure and destroy it. In many ways, this resembled a strategic war against the "enemy." Scientists went on to search for antiserums to cure infectious diseases. When this proved impossible, Ehrlich saw the future in chemotherapy instead, and brought his concept to the pharmaceutical industry.

Since the 1950s, conventional medicine has been characterized by a high tech view of the human body. The idea of the "spare-part human" was born: a person could be repaired by replacing defective parts. This also fostered the belief that stronger and more effective medications could eradicate all symptoms and diseases. Penicillin formed one of the cornerstones of this philosophy. Unfortunately it did not work as planned. Today we have more diseases than ever, many of which are even harder to defeat. We've lost the war against cancer, infection, degenerative, and autoimmune diseases. Antibiotic-resistant killer bacteria can take a life in just hours. Yeast, virus, and bacteria are constantly changing, generating new diseases for which we have yet to find cures.

Today's medical system also applies a pathologic approach: the absence of disease equals health. But the concept of health is so much broader than being free of symptoms. If the treatment doesn't address the cause of the disease, a new and more tangible symptom will soon surface.

The philosophy and organization of our healthcare system come from an outlook deeply rooted in a bygone era. This traditional approach is no longer valid. The result is expensive medical care and sick people, with much unnecessary suffering.

During the past few decades, our culture has programmed us to expect pills or injections to bring fast, effective cures for anything that ails us. We think we can abuse our bodies without consequence – that its resources are infinite or repairable. But, there are also vast financial interests behind a medical system based on the old paradigm. The pharmaceutical industry is one of the four largest businesses on this planet, so who would want change? Doubts about the effectiveness of the current healthcare system may be a reaction to the power and control exercised by the medical community, which has assumed the omniscient role formerly held by the church. Doctors seem to have claimed the right to define sickness and health.

We need greater humility regarding the true nature of health, as well as deeper respect for the needs of the individual. We must leave behind the old symptom-oriented way of thinking and focus on the individual. Rather than lumping people with the same symptom together under one "disease" heading, we need to look at each individual. Everyone is biochemically unique and a specific symptom may have several causes, each of which requires individual treatment.

Western medicine is in trouble because there is no underlying health philosophy with a long-term perspective. Without a well thought-out philosophy, no system will be effective in the long run.

A New Health Philosophy

The opposite of reductionism is the holistic view: everything is connected, and the whole is greater than the sum of its parts. We are far too complicated to be reduced to anatomy – to organs and nerve paths. This view can only take us so far. Medical care is more than technology: it involves trust and results. People only seek help from physicians if they believe they can be helped or in an emergency; otherwise, they turn elsewhere.

A survey reported in the Journal of the American Medical Association in November 1998 showed that 46 percent of interviewees had used complementary and alternative medicine (CAM)[1] during the previous year. People who turned to alternative medicine had a higher than average education. They chose alternative treatments because of such treatments fit better with their views on health and life. A study

---

[1]CAM: A therapy is generally called complementary when it is used in addition to conventional treatments; it is often called alternative when it is used instead of conventional treatment. Conventional treatments are those that are widely accepted and practiced by the mainstream medical community.

published in the July 2000 issue of the Journal of Clinical Oncology revealed that 83 percent of cancer patients interviewed had used at least one CAM therapy as part of their cancer treatment. Today, people in the United States seek care from non-conventional healers (around 600 million visits a year) more frequently than from physicians and spend more of their own money on these treatments (about $30 billion a year).

The National Institute of Health (NIH) established a National Center for Complimentary and Alternative Medicine (NCCAM) in 1998. The first symposium on integrating alternative therapies into the current healthcare system was held in December 1996. Today, Duke, Harvard, Stanford, Columbia, and the University of California, San Francisco all have centers for integrative medicine, and at least two thirds of all medical schools in the United States offer courses in CAM. Complementary theraphy is becoming common at most hospitals: between 1998 and 2000 the number of hospitals offering CAM treatments doubled. In an extensive article about the science of alternative medicine in December 2002, Newsweek summarizes the current status of the field: "What's at stake is not just the status of some individual therapies, but the whole meaning of health care."

We are moving toward a new way of thinking. The present medical system is going to be subject to revolutionary changes. A totally new concept will emerge by combining the materialistic western view with the more spiritual knowledge of the East – and we can only get a glimpse of its scope.

The recent World Health Organization (WHO) Policy and Strategy on Traditional Medicine for 2002–2005 recognizes the great use and need of traditional medicine in the world, even though it differs in various regions. Eighty percent of the world's population still relies on herbs as their major medication and many countries consider traditional medicine a priority for healthcare, but in other regions it is treated as complementary or alternative medicine.

In China, western medicine is already used alongside traditional Chinese medicine (TCM) – because both are needed. The Chinese art of healing is based on a different view of health. Drugs are ranked on three levels; at the bottom are those with specific effects on certain diseases. This is completely opposite to the philosophy in the West. The second rank of medicines has a broader effect, while the top rank gives an overall boost to the immune system and therefore has a positive effect on all medical conditions. Further, these medicines are not toxic. And, on top of this, physicians are not paid if the patient falls ill, since this is a sign of failure.

The eastern understanding of the human body was based on experience of the way energy works in living bodies. This knowledge may be gained through meditation. It is possible to feel energy flowing through the body's centers and meridians (energy channels) in an altered state of mind. Western medicine, on the other hand, based its knowledge on dissecting dead bodies, thereby missing the energy aspect (*qi*). This is neither tangible, nor can it be measured with any scientific apparatus invented so far, which disqualifies it as part of western science. *Qi* can be perceived through meditation, intuition, and your hands if you are trained for it.

It was only recently that the West encountered the ancient knowledge of *qi*. Until the late 1970s, China was completely closed to the outside world, and Chinese *qigong* masters were regarded as state secrets until 1979. But with the change in political climate, knowledge of *qigong* spread throughout the world. Today, a growing number of westerners practice *qigong*, Tai Chi, yoga, and Zen Buddhism. Also, many scientific studies have demonstrated the health benefits of *qigong* and Yoga.

In the West we've focused on IQ
for the past hundred years –
while the East has focused on QI
for thousands of years.

Spiritual Healing

A series of important events has allowed us to share the ancient knowledge preserved in the sacred spiritual traditions of the monasteries. The Dalai Lama, Tibet's religious leader, was forced to flee with a group of Buddhists after the Chinese invaded Tibet in the 1950s. After thousands of years of keeping Tibetan knowledge and wisdom within the country's boundaries, these refugees had no choice but to turn to the outside world. Now they have shared their understanding and spiritual belief, to the great benefit of the West. Lamas have set out in the world to spread their knowledge, and numerous Buddhist monasteries have been founded. The Dalai Lama plays an important role in spreading a message of peace and sharing timeless wisdom.

In the 1960s, the Vatican released its grip on Christian mysticism, a philosophy that perceives the essence of existence as something divine that can only be understood through feelings and perception. Mysticism implies mystery, and mystics turn inward, or meditate, to find "Truth" and "Life" within themselves. The Vatican decision was a major advance, because mysticism as a form of religious practice had long been beyond the reach of non-spiritual people. Hildegard of Bingen (1098–1179) and Meister Eckhart (1260–1327) were prominent mystics who have attracted much attention in modern times. People read their books for spiritual comfort and listen to the beautiful meditative music composed by Hildegard of Bingen. Modern recordings of her music have sold millions of copies – making her a female bestseller from the twelfth century.

One of the most widely read poets in the United States today is Rumi, a 13th Century Persian mystic. In twenty-five years he wrote 70,000 verses of poetry of divine love, mystic passion, and ecstatic illumination. As his translator Shahram Shiva says: "Rumi and his spiritual friend Shams left an undying legacy of the way-of-the-heart triumphing over intellect and logic." Maybe that is what attracts so many people today as we search for our spiritual roots.

Meditation and visualization are other important tools for reaching your internal healing powers. The word "meditate" means moving toward the middle. When you meditate, you shut out outer signals while silencing the mind to attain inner peace and knowledge. The Beatles went to India in the late 1960s to study meditation. After the Flower Power era, several meditation techniques spread around the world. There are many ways of meditating: meditative walking, breathing techniques, Zen Buddhist meditation, using a mantra, or you can meditate with your eyes open while focusing on a candle, a flower, or a spot on the wall. Meditation can heighten your awareness of the moment, putting you in touch with your entire being – body, mind, and spirit. Eastern philosophy has become so popular that trendy hotspots are called the Golden Buddha, Prana, Kharma, Nirvana, and Lotus, and many musicians and actors have converted to Buddhism.

Bio-balance

Our culture relies on the balance between opposites: summer and winter, day and night, male and female, life and death, young and old. Since we are products of the very environment that we have created, health also implies a balance between various levels and concepts. Bio-balance is a new theory based on living with the body in balance. It refers to our internal ecology–our pH, fluids, and molecules–but it also involves our cells and symbiosis with the multitude of microorganisms inhabiting our bodies.

The body maintains a physiological balance through construction and destruction of cells, alternating tension and relaxation of muscles, and a constant flow of fluids throughout its parts. Temperature and pH are both kept at an even level within a narrow range.

Physiological imbalances may upset this delicate balance, which may lead to extensive construction or destruction of cells, excess tension, or a disturbance of the normal flow of fluids and gases. But emotions can also get out of balance – you feel confused, depressed, frightened, frustrated, miserable, or aggressive. The body is highly adaptable, but long-term imbalances can create changes that ultimately cause physical symptoms.

Physical symptoms occur because something in the body needs attention. We need to notice what is happening in our bodies and to our emotions. Ignoring these signals or suppressing them with drugs is the same as ignoring a red warning light on the instrument panel of a car. For instance, before a cold breaks out, we might notice tension in the body, experience fatigue, or have a sense of unease and restlessness. These symptoms indicate something is wrong, that there is an imbalance. We need rest, warmth, and nourishment to allow the body to regain its balance.

If we do not attend to the needs of our bodies and soul, we will create an increasing imbalance: a bio-imbalance.

Bio-imbalance

Today we must face the consequences of the gloomy prognosis for disease in the twenty-first century. A billion people are overweight and just as many lack access to fresh water according to the Vital Signs report from the international research institute Worldwatch Institute. The World Health Organization considers obesity to be the most important hidden health problem of our day. Medications for digestive disorders, cardiac conditions, and high blood pressure sell better than any other in the world. The United States has 5.3 million overweight children according to a study from Center for Disease Control (CDC) in October 2002. This leads to an escalating number of chronic diseases at a far too early an age. For example, the number of children with Type 2 diabetes has doubled in the last twenty years.

Diabetes is becoming a major global problem. By 2010, Europe is expected to have 25 to 30 million diabetics, and Asia (excluding Russia) will have another 138 million. According to a 1998 report from the World Health Organization, the incidence of cancer will double by 2020. Over fifty percent of American women have osteoporosis, and depression is becoming increasingly common. Roughly 18 million Americans meet the diagnostic criteria for mood disorders, having reached an emotional low that impairs their functioning. Three million of them are children. Several reports on the health of children under the age of eighteen refer to the rising incidence of psychosomatic symptoms such as headache, stomachache, and anxiety.

These symptoms have specific causes. Though the human being has existed for three million years, it is only in the last couple of decades that diseases such as cancer, asthma, obesity, allergies, arthritis, and cardiovascular disease have developed on such a large scale. Many factors have changed, including our eating habits, less nutritious food, high sugar consumption, the liberal use of antibiotics, and fast food with chemically manipulated fatty acids. Our modern lifestyle is also more stressful. But are these diseases caused by external stress or is this stressful society the result of our inner imbalance?

Obesity is one of the most widespread problems in developed countries. On average, half the population in western countries is overweight or clinically obese (60 percent in the United States), and weight gain among young people surpasses all existing records. In

1979, 12 percent of Americans were pathologically obese; today this condition affects one third of the population. Physicians do not understand the cause of this phenomenon, though recent data compiled from decades of research by Harvard Medical School and the Harvard School of Public Health strongly indicate that recommendations from the USDA Food Pyramid actually cause obesity. Another report from the Harvard School of Public Health (1996) estimates that 65 percent of cancer deaths are linked to lifestyle factors – food, smoking, obesity, and a sedentary lifestyle. External factors such as the environment, genetics, and biological causes such as viruses account for a mere five percent each. The good news is that you can change your lifestyle, but you need knowledge and motivation.

Over the past few generations we have switched to a new type of food, one that is industrially refined and produced. We are not designed for this type of food since most of our genetic inheritance (99 percent) originates from before *Homo sapiens* reached Europe (40,000 years ago). The human species is metabolically adapted to the nutritional habits we have had throughout evolution. Today's processed chemically manipulated foods cause a slow, internal poisoning. This changes our entire biological system and we become acidified, like our environment. Our hormones and moods are affected and forced out of balance. Poor diet, illegal drugs and/or chemical substance abuse (sugar, alcohol, nicotine, and drugs) have a negative effect on neurotransmitters in the brain, making us stressed out, irritable, and hyperactive.

The society we have created is a mirror image of our altered inner bio-balance, and internal stress causes external stress. One obvious example of the stress we create is pollution. As economic factors overshadow environmental concerns, Earth is being exploited and robbed of its resources. We extract oil and metals. We recklessly cut down rain forests that have grown for centuries. And what do we offer in return? Useless negative waste – the most toxic of which we export to developing countries in need of money. By living this way we are squandering resources that rightfully belong to our children.

The time has come to discuss our inner ecological system openly, for the same kind of pollution is taking place within our bodies. We are out of balance. We need to get rid of the accumulated toxins and pollutants in our bodies that are now manifesting as diseases. We need to clean out mental toxins in the form of negative attitudes, destructive thoughts, and victim roles. This detoxification process will start with the individual and then spread to global proportions.

Oceans and lakes die when they become too polluted and run out of oxygen. But once cleaned up to a certain level, their self-healing system is activated and they purify themselves. We work the same way, since we consist two thirds of water. Once we start to detoxify ourselves, our inherent self-healing system will take care of the rest. In addition, we need the positive energy found in rest, healthy food, and activity. If we want good health we have to take greater responsibility for ourselves.

Personal Power Over Health

For a long time we handed over that responsibility to others. But at some point during the 1960s, we became more aware. We realized that we "create our own reality." No longer are we victims – we can influence what happens to us. By choosing our lifestyle we can choose good health. This means we have enormous control over our own health. Self-healing is a basic phenomenon accessible to everyone, but we need the knowledge that will give us power over our bodies and health. Only we can heal ourselves.

The time has come to reclaim individual and moral responsibility – from the government, institutions, and other authorities. People are more aware of the benefits of taking care of themselves. Security is not found on the outside – we have only to look within ourselves. We must answer the question: "Who am I?" We need to strengthen our own resources in the face of growing threats to our health. Many people suffer from diffuse stress symptoms such as aches and pains, chronic fatigue, stomach problems, or concentration problems. The diseases of our high tech and information society have made their debut. While the medical system cannot cure these diseases, at least their existence is acknowledged. However, this is not good enough. Many of us no longer accept being sent home with a prescription and a pat on the shoulder – not when other solutions are available.

The new approach requires the addition of habits promoting good health – a healthy lifestyle. People are actively seeking knowledge and want to accept responsibility. Self-healing, feedback, knowledge, bio-balance, awareness, empathy, energy, and integration are just a few of the keywords associated with the new health paradigm. The path to good health is one you choose proactively. Everything you do affects your health; your decisions determine whether it will evolve positively or negatively. Women in mid-life were the first to adopt and develop the new health awareness, but interest has gradually spread to men and women of all ages.

Today, new demands arise as people participate proactively in caring for their health. Any healthcare-related business will be affected by our choices. For the past decade, no American pharmaceutical company has been able to survive unless its most popular products are available over the counter. Drugs for colds, pain, allergies, inflammations, and fungal infections all need to be instantly available. The focus is no longer on the physician, who used to prescribe the medications, but on the individual patients, who make their own decisions and buy the necessary medicine or vitamins. Granted, this involves a higher level of responsibility, but people are actively seeking knowledge at an ever-increasing rate. Health information is readily accessible on the Internet as well as in newspapers, magazines, and books on alternative health and science. Our potential for knowledge should not be underestimated.

Health is the natural order of things, a positive attribute to which humankind is entitled – if we govern our lives wisely. If we follow the laws of Nature, we are ensured a healthy mind in a healthy body
                                      Hygieia, Goddess of Health and
                                      daughter of Askleipos, God of Healing

Heal the Whole Being

Beginning in the 1950s, people believed that health differences between social classes could be eradicated by making medical care available to everyone. Now we're in the twenty-first century and nothing has changed. The correlation between high income and better health remains. Owners of small businesses, together with blue-collar workers in general, are less healthy than the average. Women are among those who take care of their health best, and most are middle or upper class. More education on preventive health care will enable more people to take better care of their health, including information on exercise, choosing the right foods, and not smoking – lessons that should be taught from childhood. Schools could be influenced to serve nourishing and tasty food. People can be taught that they deserve good health. Teaching healthy behavior that strengthens self-healing is the only way to achieve a long-term cure for poor health and disease.

The current health culture has its roots in California's warm climate, where it has flourished since the sixties. California is a cultural melting pot where East meets West. Coupled with comfortable economics, a solid platform for new ways of thinking in a number of different areas has emerged. When I was a researcher in San Diego in the early 1990s, I had the privilege of experiencing these new health trends. For me, it also meant an introduction to a fairly new research field called Psychoneuroimmunology. Scientists had discovered that different systems in the body cooperate–across presumed boundaries– to build an integrated whole. The human body is sophisticated and complex, and there are many factors affecting our well-being. The world was turned upside-down when researchers discovered that the separate systems for nerves, hormones, and immunity actually produce the same substances. Over a hundred active substances circulate in our bodies, thus enabling the exchange of information and other vital processes. This is precisely why there is no need to be dependent on external remedies, since we already have everything we need within us.

Faith in miracle drugs ("magic bullets") is gradually being replaced with the realization that we can activate the hidden healing capacity of our bodies. We do this by strengthening healthy aspects instead of fighting disease symptoms. Increasing the body's resistance to remain healthy no matter what is a concept embraced by the Chinese thousands of years ago. This is the principle of self-healing. Recent research on stem cells has shown that they can be made to differentiate into any mature cell in the body. This scientific proof demonstrates the body's ability to repair and heal itself.

The new health awareness puts the individual in the center. We take responsibility, we actively seek knowledge, and we are open to new alternatives, ideas, and thoughts. These new ideas include seeing the whole picture, living in the present, and accepting emotions – which is the same as accepting ourselves. Quite simply, good health deals with increasing our awareness – and this takes time and practice.

For a long time western thinking has relied solely on intellect. Scientific materialism only seeks physical causes for physical phenomena. This makes it difficult to discuss or to get funding to study non-physical causes, thereby slowing the process of integrating old with new.

Change is bound to happen when enough people say and believe the same thing. At that point, the critical mass needed to reach a turning point will be attained. Scientific growth and spiritual growth rarely take place simultaneously, but now the time for a merger is upon us. An alliance between West and East–the belief system that has dominated the western world for the last several centuries combined with ancient eastern knowledge–is the natural progression. So are merging thought with emotion, body with spirit.

Self-healing comes from seeing the human as an integrated whole. The time has come to understand how we function on a deeper level. We have several unknown dimensions, and by exploring them, we can achieve advances in human awareness equal to those achieved on the materialistic level. By integrating wholeness, we can achieve health and well-being. We can heal ourselves.

For some time, we lost track of our true nature. We are, and always will be, a part of nature – where self-healing occurs naturally. It's time to return to what we always knew and practiced for thousands of years – and innately know now.

What is involved in the new health awareness?

Prophylaxis	Strengthening healthy aspects rather than fighting symptoms of disease
Living in the present	A new approach to body and health – we live wisely now, instead of repairing damage later
Self-healing	Using the body's hidden resources
Autonomy	People are seeking knowledge independently
Freely chosen	New knowledge spreads rapidly without anyone controlling it
Energy, qi	Adopting a fresh way of thinking, being open to new things
Presence	Living in touch with oneself and surroundings
Holism	All parts cooperate to make a whole
Emotionalism	Acknowledging the importance of emotions – and of expressing them
Spirituality	Spiritual outlook
Reflection	Listening, learning from others, and drawing personal conclusions

2.
We Are Made of Energy

We are actually "energy beings," consisting of 98 percent energy and 2 percent matter. Becoming healthy always involves a transition from one stage to another, with a higher level of energy and well-being. However, we need to "exercise" our energy if we want to be able to use it, just as our muscles need exercise. But what is energy, really, and how does the body function according to the principles of energy? What are the differences and similarities between western and eastern approaches? And how can we use our life energy to influence our health?

Why is it that in certain situations, people can suddenly acquire superhuman strength? A mother lifts a car all by herself to prevent her child from being crushed to death. A soldier on the battlefield keeps fighting, oblivious to the pain in his shattered leg. You run out of strength during a race, and your can hardly move your legs – but with a sudden burst of energy, you finish the course. Inexplicably, some people recover from serious or life-threatening diseases, as Bernie Siegel recounts in his book *Love, Medicine and Miracles*. Some people have charisma – a strong, radiating presence that attracts others to them.

These are all examples of how energy affects us. It shows that our somewhat one-dimensional view of the human state is no longer adequate. By contrast, sometimes we're in a bad mood; everything feels frustrating, and nothing seems to go right. Our energy level is low at times like this. Or alternatively, we take a walk in the woods and suddenly experience inexplicable joy – and feel absolutely charged with energy. Being in love can fill some people with so much energy that they want to turn the world upside down.

We are complex, sophisticated beings and if we want, we can use our energy dimension, though we don't necessarily have to. We can choose to live entirely in the material world, the world we can study and measure with our five senses. But we cannot avoid the influence of energy – because it is the basis of all life processes.

The body's life processes can be compared with nature. Imagine that you're standing on a lushly blooming summer meadow dotted with green saplings. Look around; everywhere you look there is growth and it's all absolutely quivering with life – from the tiniest patch of clover to the largest oak. Trees, bushes, grass, and flowers, animals, insects, and worms… they all yearn for the sun and the sky. What you see and feel is the living force. Clearly, time spent in nature is good for you.

In nature, there is a continuous cycle involving the interchange of water, air, and energy. The green chlorophyll of the leaves captures the energy in sunlight while the plant absorbs carbon dioxide for nourishment and further growth. Tiny spring seeds grow up into big plants with richly colored flowers that wither in fall, and decompose into the soil. A constant process of building up and breaking down is taking place – in both the body and nature.

The desire to grow is strong, natural, and irrepressible. But we must stop burdening our metabolism with so many toxic substances; otherwise, the breaking-down processes will gain the upper hand and we will die before our time. The physical processes can be poisoned, and the living forces of the psyche can decay, leaving a person in isolation. This means you are out of touch with your life force and your inner emotional life; in other words, you are suffering from psychosclerosis. Many grow old ("die") between the ages of 45 and 50, and are buried at age 75. The sparkle in their eyes dies long before the end.

We must focus on strengthening our life force and boosting our energy level to enable the wellness processes to thrive. If we don't, our bodies will have no time for anything else but countering the toxins and repairing the injuries. This could be compared to the way society spends all its resources fighting disease, with almost nothing left over for wellness – the life force. And so we have a natural starting point for a description of the self-healing human, based on a presentation of the energy concept and life energy.

Energy: the Underlying Force

A prerequisite for the development of all civilization has been our ability to harness energy. In prehistoric times we learned to harness fire and to put to use the things we found lying on the ground. After that we put animals to work, making them carry, pull, and plow for us. Unfortunately we have also used energy from other people – slaves, indentured servants, and serfs. Waterpower has a long history of use in mills and mining. As early as 1500 BC, people in Knossos, on the island of Crete, collected rainwater high up on the roofs, leading it along stone gutters down into large stone vessels filled with clothes, where the water span round and round before being drained off. This was probably history's first washing machine!

Industrialism laid the foundation for our material welfare. We learned to harness the earth's energy – to convert fossil fuels energy and natural forces into useful energy. The nineteenth century brought steam-driven trains and ships, marking the beginning of our global transportation system. The atomic age increased our energy supply – to the point where it was nearly infinite. In the 1970s, people seriously wondered what they would do with their time, once machines took over their jobs. Looking back, the oil crisis was perhaps a welcome wake-up call.

Now we have entered the age of information technology (IT). We are advancing, raising our level of knowledge, and increasing communications tremendously with developments such as the Internet. Knowledge provides individual power and strength, which will bring us into the next age – the human age. Our understanding of the energy concept will gradually evolve, and the way we view and deal with energy will change. Exciting times lie ahead.

Universal Energy

Energy is all about us. The sun shines by day, providing heat and light. While we sleep, storing the biomolecules needed for tomorrow's activities, the stars shine brightly. (Molecules are composed of different elements, or atoms.) The sun's energy is our planet's driving force. Thanks to the sun, life on earth emerged billions of years ago – and it continues to be the life source of all living things. It is no surprise therefore that sun worship became common in many cultures.

What is life? In biochemical terms, it is the ability to reproduce and to change. This is the case, from the tiniest of organisms to complex systems such as human beings. Biochemistry is the chemistry of life. It is the study of organic molecules that both multiply and organize themselves.

Organic molecules are compounds that contain carbon. Carbon compounds are the foundation of all life, not only in our galaxy, but even in other star systems. The chemistry of carbon compounds is cosmic biochemistry – it's dizzying to think that it might be the prerequisite for life even in other galaxies. Here on earth carbon compounds are created and reshaped in enzyme-driven processes. The enzymes are not consumed, but help accelerate the reactions. A human parallel would be those people who help others feel good – without consuming their own energy.

The body consists of atoms that can be found throughout the universe. These are atoms of elements such as carbon, hydrogen, oxygen, nitrogen, calcium, and iron. They bind themselves to the molecules that form all proteins, carbohydrates, DNA molecules, and fats. An element is defined partly by the movement of its atoms, and partly by the force that it exerts on other atoms. The force can be seen as a form of attraction.

Energy holds the atoms together in a molecule; it gets new molecules to form, and it lies behind all creation. Energy is dynamic, taking different forms depending on the surroundings – just as people are influenced and shaped by their surroundings. The way energy is measured makes us perceive it either as waves or as particles. But below the level of the atom there is no difference in energy, shape, or area. It is perhaps on this level that we find our consciousness – which is restricted by neither time nor space. Thus some people believe that our consciousness forms a pattern, which we can use to influence how matter and energy take shape in the material world. This is the same as saying that the world is created by thoughts. Consciousness and thoughts are both abstract concepts that cannot be measured – but they can be evaluated.

Describing the world according to the principles of matter and energy (in the form of particles and waves) is not a new idea. In 1905 Albert Einstein proposed the theory that mass and energy are flip sides of the same coin. Matter is actually a denser form of energy. Vast empty distances separate the atoms that make up all matter, and when nuclear physicists approach the level of atomic particles, quarks, and similar entities, energy becomes crucial to holding the small units of the force field together.

Today physicists use large particle accelerators in which particles can be transformed into waves. But it was not until recently that a group of physicists from Stanford University managed to transform light into matter. The laser experiment resulted in exactly two particles, representing the dualism on which the world is based. Dualism is the theory of two opposing fundamental forces: light and dark, spirit and matter, winter and summer, thought and emotion, positive and negative, desert and rain forest. Alternatively, it can be viewed as two aspects of the same thing, with more unification than division. The more we know and understand, the more the boundaries between spirit and matter fade.

Our ability to discover energy depends on whether we can perceive or measure it. Although today we can measure subatomic particles, sixty years ago we could not. Obviously, that didn't mean they didn't exist, just that we couldn't measure them. Bacteria have existed for almost four billion years, but we did not know about them until the microscope was invented. Similarly, there are several subtle forms of energy that we still cannot perceive with our five senses or even measure with modern scientific instruments.

Earth Energy

Radiation from inside the earth can affect your mood and your health. The earth's radiation resembles giant invisible walls stretching miles and miles up into space. The "Curry lines" weave a grid of regular, diagonal boxes, about four meters apart, all over the earth. But we also find other divisions, and lines of radiation can follow waterways or form spirals. People have known about earth rays for thousands of years – the Vikings deliberately sited their buildings to avoid negative earth rays. Many small cottages built on Swedish farms in the eighteenth and nineteenth century are eight by four meters in size, with their outside walls aligned with the Curry lines. Well into the nineteenth century Swedes designed and built their houses and churches to avoid the negative effects of the earth's radiation. This practice later went into decline, as it was not considered to have any scientific basis. Along with several other "inexplicable" phenomena, the scientific establishment still does not accept earth rays.

Geopathic stress is the name given to local geomagnetic disturbances that have an adverse affect on our health. It is caused by geological irregularities such as cracks and fault lines in the bedrock, as well as by underground running water. The American Department of Health conducted a study in 1977 called "Geomagnetism, Cancer, Weather, and Cosmic Radiation" which showed a worldwide correlation between cancer mortality and horizontal geomagnetic flows.

People, animals, and plants can indeed be affected negatively from being in locations that lie above geomagnetic disturbances or where earth rays intersect. You'll never find a dog taking a nap on an earth ray line. Although it is not the lines that cause the diseases, they shrink our energy field, and the body is also more vulnerable when we sleep. While less important for people who are healthy and strong, the radiation can affect both the mood and the immune system of those who are feeling unwell. Their resistance drops, and they become sick more easily.

About half of all earth rays are positive, however, and places with high positive energy will strengthen your energy level substantially. This may be one reason why nature has such a healing effect. People who spend time in a natural environment every day are significantly healthier than those who only have contact with nature once or twice a week. Many people have favorite places where they feel harmony and inner peace. Nature has a healing energy that can positively affect our self-healing ability. It has even been noted that hospital patients seem to experience better healing if they have a view of greenery from the window, though this could be a placebo effect.

Feng Shui is Chinese; it means water and wind. It summarizes the ancient Chinese philosophy of creating a harmonious relationship with nature and the "powers." The Chinese believe that the earth is a living being, filled with energy. The energy is either yin or yang, with yin flowing along valleys and waterways, while the more powerful yang is found in the hills and mountains. By applying the principles of

Feng Shui, people can furnish their homes to achieve maximum positive energy and harmony. In the western world there are now a great number of Feng Shui experts who help furnish homes, as well as offices for progressive companies, to allow the energy to move freely.

In our daily life we are influenced not only by the earth's radiation, but also by the electrical wiring in our houses and in the busy hearts of our cities. Power industry researchers have measured the magnetic fields along sixty miles of street in downtown Stockholm. The measurements showed as much electromagnetic radiation leaking out of the sidewalks as from major power lines: between 1 and 2.5 microtesla, and in some places as much as 6 microtesla. The strength of the magnetic fields varies with the use of electricity, and the radiation comes from buried heating pipes and power cables (about eighteen inches below the streets and sidewalks). A general limit of 0.2 microtesla has been proposed for low-frequency magnetic fields, and it is feared that chronic exposure to higher values could be a health hazard. According to one report from the National Institute of Environmental Health Sciences, electromagnetic fields may pose a cancer risk, which means that some people might be affected but not others. Research has shown, for example, that children exposed to electromagnetic fields have a greater risk of leukemia.

The World Health Organization recently classified electromagnetic radiation as a carcinogen, and cell phones emit electromagnetic radiation. Research has shown that electromagnetic fields from cell phones affect memory and the immune system. A study of leukocytes in the immune system showed that only one third of the cells survived after three hours in cell cultures next to a mobile phone. In an extensive study of Sweden, which has more cell phones per capita than any other country in the world, Professor Lennart Hardell at Örebro University showed that people who use analog NMT telephones run an increased risk of suffering brain tumors. The major risks associated with magnetic fields include cancer and various neurological diseases such as Alzheimer's. However, the issue remains controversial and as long as researchers funded by cell phone producers publish results indicating the opposite, not much will happen. Also, the effect of the electromagnetic fields varies enormously from one individual to another. Children and older people are often more susceptible. In any case, limiting the time spent with a force field next to your brain is a good idea – whether it's a cordless phone or a cell phone.

There is no doubt that even the weather affects your health. Biometeorology is a new interdisciplinary science studying the effects of different atmospheric phenomena. Rain, wind speed, temperature, humidity, geomagnetic activity, and the number of hours of sunlight all affect us. About one fifth of the population is sensitive to weather, which could explain why people can be happy one day but wake up depressed the next. When the sun shines from a clear blue sky, when it's pouring rain, or when you stand by a waterfall or in the shower – negatively charged ions form, which have a soothing and healing effect. In stormy weather and during thunderstorms, positively charged ions form, which can cause a variety of symptoms ranging from worry, weakness, apathy, aggression, headaches and other pain, to breathing problems. These problems may start as early as twelve hours before the storm breaks out, and indeed you can "feel" bad weather coming. When solid gray clouds cover the sky, I usually refer to it by saying the "lid is on." When this occurs for weeks at a time, people's moods clearly change and you can see their stress level in traffic rising.

Surveys have found, for example, that the number of heart attacks and surgical complications doubles during cold fronts as compared to warm ones. For centuries people have been aware of the harmful effects of winds like the mistrals in France, the foehn winds in the Alps, and the Santa Ana winds in southern California. They are charged with positive ions that lower the brain's production of the soothing neurotransmitter, serotonin. I had the dubious privilege of experiencing the Santa Ana wind first-hand while working as a researcher in San Diego: it had a very negative effect on both my mood and the laboratory experiments. Without even knowing it, we are indeed living a bit dangerously! Yet another reason why it is important to make sure that your life energy is in good shape in order to resist damaging electromagnetic radiation and severe weather.

Life Energy

Western medicine's view of man is based on anatomical studies, while the eastern view is based on observations made during meditation. This means that the body's flow of energy has been observed under an altered state of awareness. You might think that this gives a subjective view of how the body works, but these observations have been repeated countless times. Thousands of years ago, people already knew about the body's energy centers and the meridians for the energy flow.

Something fundamental is missing in the western method of viewing the body as a machine, built of many different components (cells, nerves, organs). This approach neglects human consciousness, ignoring the existence of the unifying factor: our life energy, and its significance for the functioning of the body. It is energy that drives the body's processes, and there is no energy flow to be found when dissecting dead bodies. Obviously, it is only found in living beings and if you don't look for something, you'll never find it. Western medicine has overlooked the most essential element – the energy concept and the importance of the life force to health.

Life energy was first described seven thousand years ago in India. The original source of all life was called "prana" in Sanskrit. Five thousand years ago the Chinese called the energy necessary for all life processes "*qi*" (or "chi"), which translates as both "life" and "breathing." Pythagoras identified the vital energy twenty-five hundred years ago, and believed that this energy led to the body's healing. In the sixteenth century, the Swiss physician, Paracelsus–considered to be the father of pharmacology–described the life energy. He called it *iliaster*, the vital force that creates healing and spirituality. Since then it has been given many different names, especially during the latter half of the twentieth century: orgon, life field, biofield, HEF (Human Energy Field), and UEF (Universal Energy Field).

What is life energy, and how does it affect us? We are composed not only of our physical bodies; you could also say that we exist on three levels. These have been described by different cultures and religions.

Existence on three levels	Daoism	Tibetan medicine
1. The physical body	Essence (*jing*)	Nirmanakaya: matter – duality
2. The subtle body: the emotions and the mind	Energy (*qi*)	Sambhogakaya: motion, radiation, expansion, contraction
3. The causal body: that causes life, that is, the soul and the spirit	Spirit (*shen*)	Dharmakaya: the universal consciousness, the "global brain"

Daoism is the philosophy of the way, *dao*, which is one of the earliest spiritual concepts in China. Dao is the ultimate metaphysical truth in and beyond the thing. Tibetan medicine is based on the Indian Ayurveda philosophy and Tibetan Buddhism, developed in the seventh century. According to these teachings, the first energy level, the outer or physical one, is the most inert form of energy. It is restricted to the physical world. The second is the underlying emotional level, containing awareness of our beings, our needs, and our emotions. This has a non-physical form and can move freely not only within our bodies, but also between people. Our emotional condition also helps us to be in touch with the here and now. And far below–beneath and behind everything–is the life force. Neither the soul nor the spirit is bound in time or space. It lives in our body but can travel in time and to different places, just as we do in our dreams. This is probably the cause of phenomena such as telepathy, in which people with an emotional bond can transmit messages to one another.

These energy levels interact and affect one another. If they do not harmonize, we will inevitably lose energy. If they vibrate on the same frequency, they will resonate, and this gives us a large amount of energy. If our actions and the people around us cause us to resonate with our whole being, we automatically supply our energy reservoir. Our spirit is the strongest, controlling strength. But our physical condition also affects our spiritual status – the strength of the life force. It is difficult for your soul to be healthy if your body is sick and run-down. The body is indeed the temple of the soul.

The Health Triangle

Our natural condition, however, is to be healthy, and the healing force is therefore natural. But in order to heal itself, the body needs a certain quantity of energy – otherwise we wouldn't have the strength to stay healthy. We can increase our energy level in various ways. This can best be illustrated by a triangle with the different sides representing food, emotions and thoughts, and life energy (spiritual life). People can improve their ability to absorb energy (food, nutrients, emotions, thoughts, and life energy, *qi*) and to increase the flow of energy in their bodies.

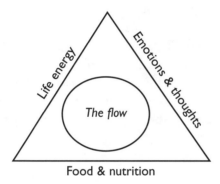

You can raise your energy level by influencing the sides of the triangle. Food is the base that supplies the body with nutrients – the first energy level. The second side is your emotional life and your thoughts, representing the subtle body. The final side is the life energy and life force, which are also found on the third and deepest energy level. It is infinite and needs spiritual nourishment to work. Our physical body affects our conscious body, which in turn influences the spirit or soul. We must stay in touch with and nourish all three levels in order to function properly. This is a prerequisite for good self-healing. In the following chapters I will discuss how to take care of each of these three aspects of energy.

Seen in this perspective, you could say that the body is a materialization of both our soul and our consciousness. The body is an incredible and ingeniously developed living organism in which there is much left that we don't understand – and how incomprehensible, then, is the soul or the spirit? Medical science has mainly evolved during the past century, while some men and women have devoted their entire lives to spirituality for thousands of years. Can we ever "understand" the soul? Perhaps we are not meant to understand, but rather we should get in touch with our soul and our spirit and let them shine through our being; let the spirit lead us in our lives. The organized structure of the body requires a good match between the physical form and the other two energy fields. If we are to function well, there must be a fine-tuned balance between body, consciousness, and soul; between the energy's form and field (body and soul).

What is the artist's mission, if not to let parts of his or her consciousness or soul take shape on canvas or in sculpture? What do musicians and singers do, if not to release spiritual tones from other energy levels, making the audience experience strong emotions? Authors turn inwards to tap the inexhaustible source of creativity. The Danish author Peter Høeg says that his books "write themselves." In many highly advanced cultures that are now extinct, such as the Mayan civilization, artists and musicians were exempt from paying taxes since they were considered to be intermediaries conveying divine strength and spiritual sustenance.

Cellular Energy

A cell is a distinct unit with a membrane separating it from everything external. Cells are one of the smallest functioning units in the body. They have a nucleus containing the genetic material, DNA; they manufacture their own protein; and they produce their own energy supply. Cells have different specialized functions, but each cell communicates with the entire body, forming an integrated information-society. They exist as a whole.

We can never be any healthier than our cells. If the cells have a low energy level, so do we. The mitochondria are the cell's energy factories, and any injury to the mitochondria will affect every organ in the body. Especially sensitive are the tissues that have high energy requirements: the brain, the heart, the muscles, and the hormonal system, as well as the liver, kidneys, and pancreas. A full 90 percent of all oxygen metabolized in a cell is used in the mitochondria's combustion process. Most of the oxygen is converted into water, but about 5 percent goes to help form free radicals. Free radicals are extremely reactive substances which steal electrons from their surroundings. They can cause DNA mutations, oxidation of fatty acids in the membrane, and other damage to the cells.

When the mitochondria are attacked and become injured, the very core of the cell's life is destroyed – its ability to create energy. According to experts on free radicals, damage to the mitochondria is the primary cause of aging. Magnesium deficiency results in increased activity in the cells' free radicals, reducing the cells' ability to function and thereby resulting in premature aging. The most common diseases are caused when cells, tissues, or organs degenerate and atrophy as a result of the action of the free radicals. But the body has developed mechanisms to defend itself against attack of the free radicals: antioxidants. However, there are no mechanisms for repairing damage to the mitochondria's DNA. Indeed they are extremely sensitive and are exposed to permanent mutations ten times as often as the cell nucleus. As mitochondrial DNA is inherited only from the mother, it is essential for young women to be health-conscious and include plenty of antioxidants in their diet.

If the antioxidant protection drops—because of radiation, infection, inadequate nutrients, or an overload of toxic substances—the mitochondria may be exposed to such widespread damage that energy production falls off dramatically. Then the cell can no longer function as it should. Increasingly, research reports are linking specific injuries to the mitochondria's DNA to degenerative diseases such as diabetes, Parkinson's, Alzheimer's, and weakened cerebral and muscle functions.

Many diseases are actually symptoms of a lack of energy because the body lacks energy for its life-sustaining processes. The diagram on the following page gives a very simplified picture of how different energy levels are expressed in the body. Unfortunately we don't know much about the higher energy levels. What is actually involved in having a high energy level all the time? What is it like to feel really healthy? Perhaps we can never know unless we've also felt really unhealthy…

What can we do to influence our energy levels? First we need to understand something about the body's life processes. Different reactions are constantly building up the body and breaking it down. These are

How different energy levels affect the condition of the body

100%	—	Fully vital, highest spiritual and physical energy, often has emotions of joy, happiness, and connection (=flow).
		Vital, strong resistance to illness, physically fit.
		Mostly healthy, rarely has a cold or falls ill.
		Some resistance, but often has a cold or falls ill.
50%	—	Chronic fatigue syndrome, depressed.
		Degenerative diseases.
		Chronic diseases in the final phases.
		Life-support with heart-lung machine, respirator.
0%	—	Death.

referred to as anabolic and catabolic reactions, and are a natural part of our metabolism. The substances you feed your body will either burden it, speeding up the breakdown process, or stimulate the building-up and vital life processes.

The body is influenced in either one direction or the other, depending on how we treat it. Wellness factors stimulate maintenance of a healthy and balanced body. But if the body is exposed to too many negative factors–illness factors–that burden it and steal its energy, illness processes are promoted instead. We will all eventually grow old, break down, and die – but there is little reason to speed up the process.

Illness and Wellness Processes

Unfortunately, illness factors have a tendency to accumulate and intensify over the years. Lifestyle is crucial. Examples of substances that burden the body and cause it to break down in the long run are sugar, caffeine, cigarettes, and chemically processed fat. However, it is not only what you eat but also what you inhale and absorb through your skin that affects your body's processes. Thoughts and emotions are also different forms of energy influencing the body's metabolism. Heavy negative thoughts will make everything move slowly, while happy, optimistic thoughts will make you feel so cheerful that everything seems quicker and easier to do.

It is always a question of balance. Metaphorically speaking, place what you do in the two pans on the scale (see next page), and see how lifestyle and habits affect your health. Indeed, we make choices daily that affect our health in either direction.

What is the state of health in the United States? Over one in three people have allergy-type oversensitivity problems; one in four people suffers from cancer; and cardiovascular disease still causes half of all deaths. Osteoporosis is now a widespread disease affecting not only women, but also men and teenagers. One third of those seeking a physician in primary care have psychiatric or psychosocial problems. An estimated 35–40 million Americans living today will suffer from major depressive illness during their lives. Many people suffer from compulsive thoughts and about 18 million Americans meet the diagnostic criteria for mood disorders, which impairs their function in daily life. During the 1990s anxiety, worry, and sleeping difficulties have become increasingly common. The number of women between the ages of 25 and 34 who experience anxiety, worry, and angst has doubled over the past six years. In that same period, sales of antidepressants have more than tripled. Women between the ages of 35 and 75 consume twice as many antidepressants as men. One fifth of both men and women say that they suffer severe pain. The rapid increase of diabetes among children and adolescents over the past few decades is not genetic in origin. In Europe, Scandinavia has the highest incidence of diabetes among children; over 90 percent of them have no family history of the disease.

Of course there are many reasons for the growing ranks of people suffering from the degenerative diseases of the western world. But, clearly we must redirect our focus to a lifestyle and dietary habits that strengthen health – that support the body's healing processes.

Wellness processes require change. While everyone wants to improve their lives, few are ready to undergo the necessary transformation. Becoming healthy always means a transition from one stage to another, and consequently a certain resistance must be overcome. This may take some mental preparation.

How different substances, actions, and emotions affect the body's life processes in a positive or negative direction

infections, radiation	vitamins and minerals
sugar, junk food	exercise, nutritious food
smoking, drugs	functional foods
empty calories	healthy intestinal flora
hate, bitterness	love, good moods
negative attitudes	genuine emotional expression
resignation, worry, stress	light, sleep, meditation, *qigong*

<—————————————— o ——————————————>
▲

burdens the body   **builds up the body**
reduces energy   **increases energy**

A wellness process requires energy, but once it is underway, the forces released during healing can propel it onward. Sometimes you will have to feel worse for a while; perhaps the body will need to flush old waste products so that long dormant emotions can reawaken. There is plenty of room, however, to correct misdirected processes. A full 98 percent of the body's components are replaced over the space of a year's time; you really are hardly the same person now that you were a year ago! The wellness process is energy-dependent, demanding both strength and willpower.

In fact, we don't know enough about what wellness means. Very little research has been carried out in this regard. What is health?

"There is not just one health, but many 'healths'," said the late Kristoffer Konarski, Associate Professor of Psychosomatics at Karolinska Institute, Stockholm. "Medical care has a reductionistic approach, which means that it views health as the absence of disease. But something is wrong here. Health and disease stand for two completely different dimensions. We have wellness factor versus risk factor, with protective factors decreasing risk factors and increasing wellness factors. For example, quitting smoking reduces the risk factors, but it won't increase the wellness factors. There are eight thousand diagnoses for diseases, but only some ten different definitions of health.

This means that health is a deep, dark wilderness. We've closed the lid, and we tend only to see the illness perspective."

Symptom – Mechanism – Cause

A symptom describes a condition. Behind the symptom is a biochemical mechanism. For example, in the case of a sore throat, the foreign bacteria reproduce – but it is the body's own immune system that leads to fever, swelling, and tenderness. By comparison, when there is a fire, the greatest damage is often caused by the water used to extinguish it rather than by the fire itself.

But neither the symptoms nor the mechanism necessarily provide information about the cause of the problem. That must be found elsewhere. Some energy disorders provide a setting in which diseases may develop. We do not become sick unless the bio-balance is disturbed – either externally or internally.

Dr. Howard S. Friedman, distinguished professor of psychology at the University of California, Riverside, has carried out extensive research on the correlation between personality types and diseases. He has shown that worry and anxiety are linked to almost all diseases. Ordinary worry, though unpleasant, is no threat to health. But serious worry drains our strength and our mental energy. Worry is actually an existential uncertainty – we don't know ourselves, nor do we trust life. We don't believe that everything will be all right and that we will get what we need, and this weakens us at a mental level.

Linking personality with diseases, however, can be misleading. Scientists long believed that people with type-A personalities had peptic ulcers because of constant stress. But research has shown that Helicobacter pylori bacteria–which you can get by eating chicken that is not thoroughly cooked–causes peptic ulcers. Instead of surgery, peptic ulcers can now be cured with a regimen of three types of penicillin and Prilosec. Not everyone gets peptic ulcers, however, so what is the true cause? The body has strong defense mechanisms that need to be disturbed before an infection can take hold. Usually there has to be a disruption in the energy, which in turn can be caused by constant stress, poor eating habits, or repressed emotions focused on the stomach.

We live dangerously! We are constantly vulnerable to dangers and intruders who want to come in and take over our warm, comfortable bodies. Don't forget that the ability to reproduce and adapt to the surroundings is the very basis of life. While it's true that bacteria don't have a brain, they thrive in places with nourishment and heat where they can grow.

Below is an overview of the risk factors that can lead to injury or cause disease. They can hardly be said to have diminished during the late twentieth century. Mad cow disease received considerable attention in the mid-nineties, but prions were actually first discovered among flesh-eating tribes in New Guinea. Prions are small proteins that "rape" other, apparently normal, proteins of the same type, which then become abnormal. This leads to insoluble protein deposits forming in the brain cells, which causes them to die. Oxygen creates free radicals through oxidation, and is therefore our greatest enemy – yet we are dependent on oxygen. But free radicals are also part of the body's arsenal against infections, since hydrogen peroxide has a sterilizing effect.

This is why a strong immune system–and a good energy level–are important for preserving the body's integrity and bio-balance.

Examples of risks to which people can be exposed (in order of size)

people	everything from abuse and mental and physical violence, to accidents and self-destructiveness
parasites	often chronic infections in which the person is the host and the parasite has developed defences to the immune system
fungi	genital, oral, and intestinal fungal infection
bacteria	throat infections, GI disorder
viruses	colds, influenza, polio, HIV
prions	mad cow disease, kuru (New Guinea)
chemicals	heavy metals, PCBs, DDT (interfere with enzyme function and bind to DNA)
free radicals	attack DNA, cell membranes, connective tissue in the skin, and even the defense mechanism (sterility)
radiation	injury to DNA and cells (acts by creating free radicals)

Immune System

The word immunology comes from the Latin *immunis*, which means exempt. If the same epidemic afflicted a city more than once, those who had the illness the first time and survived it were seen as being exempt – or immune. When something foreign–such as a cold virus or bacteria–invades the body, the immune cells, antibodies, and other biotransmitters work together, quickly and efficiently, to eliminate whatever is disturbing the balance. With this interaction the immune system can wage a war on many fronts against a foreign substance or organism. Indeed, it is of fundamental importance for the immune system to be able to distinguish between what belongs to the body and what is foreign.

The immune system has several barriers; the first line of defense comprises the skin, the mucous membranes, and the gastric juices. These provide mechanical and chemical protection (acid environment and enzymes that can break down the cell walls of the bacteria). The second line of defense is inside the body, where cells and soluble active substances are responsible for redness, heat, swelling, and pain. The phagocytic cells, scattered throughout the body's organs and in the blood, engulf foreign particles and render them harmless.

Several factors must cooperate for a virus to cause an infection. It must reach the right area of the body and stay long enough to attach itself onto the right cell. A cold virus needs to land on the mucous membrane in the airways; sticking to the skin is not good enough. Moreover, in order to force its way into the cell, the virus needs to attach to the right receptor. Once inside the cell, the virus quickly reproduces and then abandons the cell, which dies as a result. The viral infection stimulates the cell's production of interferon, which in turn protects surrounding cells from infection. The cellular immune system is then activated to render the virus harmless in various ways.

Our defense against bio-imbalances

Physical:	skin, mucous membranes, cilia in airways
Chemical:	enzymes, pH, antibodies, histamine, interferon
Cellular:	immune system cells and phagocytic cells
Bioenergy:	psychoimmunity (protective energy casing)

The immune system maintains a balance at all times. When there is an injury, substances are released that stimulate the immune system locally and travel to the brain via the blood. Thus the brain is notified that somewhere in the body, the balance is disturbed. Brain centers respond by releasing a stress hormone (cortisol), which then subdues the body's activity to restore the original balance. Like so many other processes in the body, it is regulated in a yin–yang manner.

All of this takes place without our giving it a single thought, though our bodies are working to maintain the balance all the time. So, the body possesses an amazing inherent fund of wisdom and strength, and by making friends with it we can help ourselves.

Our Senses

While the immune system mainly protects us against bacteria, viruses, and allergens, our senses deal with energy waves or chemicals. Our five senses—sight, hearing, taste, touch, and smell—help us receive and classify signals from the world around us. The rods and cones in the retina of the eye receive electromagnetic light and convert it into nerve signals that the brain interprets as pictures. The skin is full of sensors that convert touch, pressure, heat, and cold into electrical signals that are coded by higher cerebral centers. Advanced structures throughout the body can receive impressions from the world around us, convert them to signals, and make them understandable.

Although our five senses work independently, at times the distinction can become blurred – a mixture of the senses is called synesthesia. Any combination of two of the five senses is possible, though the most common is seeing colors when you hear sound. Synesthesia is more common in children than in adults, and women experience it more frequently than men. People with different psychotic diseases, such as schizophrenia, often experience synesthesia, though it is not unusual in healthy people either. American neurologist Dr. Richard Cytowic has carried out studies to see if there are points on which synesthetes agree: for example, does everyone with synesthesia feel that "A" is yellow or that "Monday" is red? Consensus was only found once: for some inexplicable reason, 80 percent of those with synesthesia feel that Wednesday is white!

The traditional view has been to consider the world to be an association of observable objects (particles, fluids, etc.) moving about according to definite laws of force, so that one could form a mental picture in space and time of the whole scheme ... It has become increasingly evident ... that nature works on a different plan. Her fundamental laws do not govern the world as it appears in our mental picture in any very direct way, but instead they control a substratum of which we cannot form a mental picture without introducing irrelevancies.

Paul A. M. Dirac, 1930, on modern
physics and sensory perception

Influence of Light

In the beginning there was light ... Or was it sound? The universe is full of light, cosmic rays, and other forms of radiation that can be interpreted and are transformed into sound. Radioastronomical explorations have revealed a complete orchestra of sounds emanating from the earth, the sun, and the other planets in our solar system. When cosmic radiation is transformed into sound, it creates rhythmic patterns of crackling, hissing, humming, ticking, and drumming sounds.

Light can appear in the most widely varied forms (see below). Radio waves can be miles long, while x-rays are measured in tenths of nanometers. A nanometer is a millionth of a millimeter (10^{-9} meters). Heat is light and closely related to infrared (IR) light, since it lies below the red frequency spectrum. Ultraviolet (UV) light, found in the rays of the sun, is responsible for sunburn.

Light appears in various forms

	The optic window	
	Long-wave light ←———	**Short-wave light** ———→
ultrasound radio TV radar IR heat	ǁ	UV x-ray gamma cosmic

We humans can only experience a tiny portion of visible light in the electromagnetic spectra. We see between 400 and 700 nanometers (the optical window) and can perceive light because specialized cells in the retina can convert it into electric signals. These are sent from the retina, via the optic nerve, to centers deep inside the brain. The signal travels via the thalamus to the visual center, located in the brain's outer layer at the back of the head. The light's signals are interpreted there to form a picture that we can place in context.

Light itself is nourishment. Too much artificial lighting and too little natural light affects the entire body, including our hormones and biocycles. Production of the sleep hormone melatonin in the pineal gland is controlled by light and dark. When there is too little light, as during winters in the northern regions, the pineal gland doesn't shut down production of melatonin in the morning. People become depressed more easily, and develop listlessness and either decreased appetite or weight gain as a result. Daylight is also needed to produce vitamin D, which is necessary for normal metabolism of calcium and phosphorous in the body. Vitamin D3 is formed in the skin by the action of ultraviolet light (photolysis) and is transformed in the liver and kidneys into vitamin D.

Christiane Northrup, M.D. wrote in her book *Women's Bodies, Women's Wisdom* about the difficulty she had becoming pregnant and that her body temperature rose very slowly with ovulation. She decided to take a daily twenty-minute walk in the middle of the day. After one menstrual cycle, her body temperature began to rise quickly with ovulation, and after two cycles she became pregnant.

It is now possible to get bright light therapy for depression, either in special white rooms or by buying a phototherapy lamp for home use. The added light raises energy, improves productivity, and increases learning capacity. Moreover, people sleep better as a result.

Influence of Color

The Egyptians used color therapy as long as forty-five hundred years ago. They appear to have had a well-developed interest in color in their advanced sun cult. Early in the eleventh century the learned Persian physician Avicenna let the sun, filtered through clear colored boxes, shine on his patients. Avicenna recommended that people with nosebleeds should not be placed in red light, while people suffering depression should avoid blue light. This connection lives on in our expression for depression, "feeling blue," and in the "blues," in the melancholy music of the African American slaves. During the course of history many people have been interested in the effect colors have on us, including Goethe and Rudolf Steiner.

In 1903 the Danish physician Niels Finsen won the Nobel Prize for his discovery that skin disease could be cured by exposure to radiation with sunlight or ultraviolet light. Finsen also found that red light helped prevent the ugly scars left by smallpox, chicken pox, and measles. But color therapy, like herbal medicine, has been forgotten, and is rarely used in conventional medicine. One example, however, is that premature infants suffering from jaundice are now treated with deep blue light, which corrects the condition after a few days.

Lasers are routinely used in precision surgery today, but it is not generally known that radiation with a lower intensity laser affects healing processes of the body and mind. An efficient way of raising your energy level is to get a dose of colors from a low-intensity (or a low-energy) laser. This provides a monochromatic light, meaning that a single pure color is emitted. In nature you'll find monochromatic colors in a peacock's feathers, on shiny green beetles, and on the head of the male grasshopper. But with laser technology you can produce colors with incredibly high resolution and purity – you could almost call them "super colors."

Low-intensity laser therapy has proven to be especially effective in dental care, for healing wounds, in veterinary medicine, and for treating musculoskeletal problems. This relatively new method was developed in the early 1970s, and today it is used in Russia and at several European centers. Professor Tiina Karu at Moscow University Laser Institute, a pioneer in the field, has studied the effects at the cellular level.

The Swedish company Biolight has developed an appliance with light diodes in which a combination of wavelengths and pulses increases the blood flow and reduces pain and inflammation. The effects have been demonstrated in both clinical studies and through molecular biology technology.

"Six hours after treatment, a significant increase in the activity of several genes is achieved, stimulating production of growth factors and collagen," says Jan-Åke Gustavsson, professor at the Department of Biosciences, Karolinska Institutet, Stockholm, Sweden.

What happens with exposure to monochromatic light? The mineral silicon absorb the light's energy in the tissues or cytochromes (a type of molecules) in the mitochondria absorb the photons, causing them to produce energy. This stimulates the cells to increased oxygen consumption, greater energy conversion, and higher enzyme activity. In other words, we humans can convert the energy of light into biochemical energy!

Clinical studies have shown clear results when treating chronic oral and dermatological wounds and inflammations. Among other things, researchers have observed severe bedsores healing 35 percent more quickly. This opens up completely new therapeutic possibilities, of interest to both doctors and dentists.

Psychologist and architect Karl Ryberg, author of *Living Colors*, has had great success treating his patients with monochromatic light sessions. During treatment you intuitively select the colors you most wish to receive. Colors have a major effect on the mind. Cerebral cells also respond quickly to this light, resulting in reprogramming of the brain, which initiates various processes in the body. This is why patients experience a broad range of healing effects after just one treatment.

This form of color therapy is effective for worry, anxiety and insomnia, as well as with more non-specific problems such as extreme fatigue and depression. It has even helped people with migraine headaches, asthma, and ulcers, and after a few sessions patients with rheumatism become problem-free. How is this possible? As impurities and waste accumulate, the body ages. It stops forming new bone and connective tissue. Low-intensity laser radiation stimulates cartilage cells to divide, accelerating processes outside the bone and connective tissue. However, some damaged tissue needs additional nutrients to return to optimal levels.

Low-intensity laser treatment with monochromatic colors is highly effective and is set to become an important method of treatment in the first decade of the twenty-first century.

Influence of Sound

Vision is our predominant sense, occupying about 60 percent of our conscious attention. But the ear perceives a much broader frequency range than the eye. The eye reacts to approximately a doubling of the light frequency spectrum, from red to purple. The ear perceives about ten times as great a frequency range and is able to distinguish between very high- and low-pitched sounds.

Sound consists of a series of vibrations or oscillations in particles or objects. It is a form of energy that propagates through the air by means of alternating compression and decompression of the air molecules. The number of oscillations per second is called the frequency and is measured in hertz (one cycle per second). Sound waves move at different speeds through different materials: 340, 1500, and 5000 meters per second through air, water, and steel, respectively.

The volume of the sound is determined by the degree of movement of vibrating atoms and molecules. Thus, the more air molecules vibrate, the stronger the sound, and the height of the sound wave is measured in decibels (dB). Human physiology only allows us to perceive a small part of nature's vast sound spectrum. The lower limit at which we can perceive sound is 20 dB, while the pain threshold is 120 dB. People can die if exposed to sound over 150 dB, proving just how significant the effect of sound and vibrations can be.

Sound vibrations can affect individual cells. Research findings from sound therapists and biologists show that the different frequencies of the musical scale change the color and shape of red blood cells. The C note makes cells longer, E makes them globular, and A changes the color from red to pink. Cancer cells are often much larger than healthy cells and die at 400–480 Hz (A – B above middle C). Thus it could be possible to use sound therapy as a tool in strengthening healthy cells or destroying those that are diseased.

Instinctively, we know which sounds are good and which are bad (noise). The ears of the fetus are fully developed halfway through the mid-point of gestation, after which it can both hear and react to sound, especially to music. Infants can distinguish between harmonious and dissonant music from a very early age, preferring the harmonious kind. Harmony is a wave frequency with a special mathematical relationship to the fundamental tone.

Geometric symmetry and harmony as well as the relationships between sound, scales, and octaves can be found throughout nature, from the perfect six-sided cells of the bees to the spiral-patterned snail shell. Artists and architects have long used the "golden section." The human body and the face can also be divided up using harmonious proportions that follow the laws of music. Research has shown that the faces of people considered beautiful in our culture follow certain harmonious measurements. Some people say that sound and music are an expression of cosmic laws, and even the human body complies with these laws.

In fact, the human body can be compared to a musical instrument: each atom, molecule, cell, tissue, and organ constantly emits energy at different frequencies. At the same time we can receive energy in many different forms. The human organism can be seen as a manifestation of a state of vibration – an intertwining of matter, sound, and light.

Crystals are inorganic but never "dead," since they can transmit and strengthen energy. There is a special relationship between sound waves and the fixed, geometric molecular structure of crystals.

A quartz crystal is made up of billions of molecules of silicon dioxide arranged in a specific three-dimensional pattern. Unlike gases and liquids, in which sound is transferred as movements of free molecules, sound waves and other vibrations press the entire molecular structure together in crystals, thereby releasing an electric charge. The frequency of the incoming vibrations determines the frequency of the outgoing electrical voltage. This can be read as small electrical shocks, which are an example of the well known "piezoelectric effect." This is used, for example, in old-fashioned crystal pickups, telephone microphones, and gas lighters. Conversely, electric energy connected to a crystal releases mechanical energy that can produce sound.

Crystals can be seen as energy converters. Some people feel that this is the basis of their healing function, that they focus and balance different energies. Imagine that crystals respond to acoustic energy and convert it into amplified electromagnetic energy. The electromagnetic balance in living cells is maintained partly by quartz (silicon dioxide), which is a very common crystal in nature.

Hidden Sights

Traditionally, we have tended to believe that only our senses can inform us about the surrounding world. But the models we use to understand the world are constantly changing. Perhaps even the current model of the five senses is a somewhat restrictive view of human capacity. In his book *A Hidden God*, cancer researcher Stefan Einhorn, M.D. wrote: "We cannot achieve knowledge of everything with our five senses, and what we can experience intellectually is thereby a pale copy of the 'true reality,' which at the base is unity."

Science only studies phenomena as they manifest themselves. But this excludes our own consciousness, which has no objective manifestation; instead, it is the object of all manifestation. Indeed, there are good reasons for being open, even to things that don't seem to be as obvious and tangible as those we ordinarily encounter.

Communication is the exchange of information and energy. A full 90 percent of communication between two people takes place non-verbally. This means that what we say accounts for just 10 percent of the message, while the rest is conveyed by the way we say it–our tone, gestures, posture, the nuances in our voices–and a variety of signals of which we are totally unaware.

It is easier to understand someone who is on the same wavelength. This means that your energy has a similar frequency. Two people who have been together for a long time begin to resemble one another, as is often seen in the loving relationship shared by elderly couples. They have synchronized and coordinated their energy through the years. This can also be seen in employees who increasingly adopt their supervisor's dress, posture, expression, and mannerisms. Successful sales representatives quickly mimic their customers' gestures and signals to help the client feel secure and well received. Indeed, we use such energy information in non-verbal signals – intentionally or otherwise.

How can we become more aware of other people's energy? In order to feel this energy you cannot be closed off from your own core; you cannot fence off your spirituality. Experiencing empathy requires you to be in touch with your emotions and thereby your energy flow. You cannot learn empathy with your intellect; you must have your own spectrum of emotions in order to sense the emotional state of others. At the same time you become more self-assured and more confident in your own identity. If you are sensitive to the energy of others, you can also interpret that information as comprehensible words or symbols. Life becomes easier to understand.

Eastern View of Energy

The Chinese words *yin* and *yang* mean the shady side and the sunny side of a hill. The yin – yang concept has existed for 3000 years and refers not only to the two opposites, but also to how they fit into one another. They represent opposing forms of energy, and consequently there is a charge between them. Yang is considered to be active, while yin stands for the passive resting state. Some organs of the body have yin properties and others have yang properties. The Chinese believe that the body's health depends on a balance between the two states.

Society, companies, and people can also be analyzed in terms of yin and yang. Yin suffers when there is too much yang, or externally aimed activity and persistent work. With time this can have significant consequences; you have to stop to recover your yin and restore your balance. Good yin activities include long walks in nature, hot baths, massages, relaxing music, meditation, or hugging and cuddling with your beloved. Anything that stimulates serotonin is yin, while anything that stimulates the release of dopamine is yang.

It is fairly common these days for companies to run into problems because of their overly dominant yang. What should they do? They become fearful, devoting even more energy to work, thoughts, and structures, which only serves to further reinforce their yang. The company would be healthier if it had more yin – people need to sit back, listen to good advice, and above all, trust their intuition. Generally speaking, women are often better at yin than men. Men also have yin forces, of course, but they are not encouraged in the same way as in women. The global financial crisis is probably due to the fact that yang has been dominant far too long, which is why we now should come into a yin phase.

It's the same way with health. As we travel through life we find ourselves in phases in which yin or yang dominate. That is completely natural. But if you live your life dominated by yang forces, an imbalance gradually arises. It leaves its mark in the temple of the soul, our body, and manifests itself in the form of symptoms or illness. Life would be better if we approached it with the idea of balancing yin and yang forces – side by side. We need them both.

The Chinese name for universal energy is *qi*, and it flows in our bodies through the twelve meridians, the *qi* channels. They branch out throughout the body into a total of 72,000 energy meridians, including blood vessels. Chinese and Tibetan medicine see illness as a blockage in one or more of the *qi* channels, which prevents enough energy from being released. The vital force doesn't reach out to the sick part of the body, just like when a cable breaks and there is a power outage. The blockage can be reversed using acupuncture, acupressure, massage, breathing exercises, or *qigong*.

However, you must have energy to be able to receive it, just as a radio must first be turned on before it can receive radio waves. Indeed we need to exercise our energy to maintain it at a high level. Tai chi, yoga, and *qigong* are good ways of raising energy levels and increasing contact between body and soul. Yoga has become increasingly popular in the United States over the past five years. Yoga classes are everywhere and stars like Madonna and Gwyneth Paltrow practice it every day.

Qigong involves slow movements following a specific pattern helping to process and improve energy flow in the *qi* channels. Some movements are considered to have a healing effect on different diseases and may be administered as "medicine" by those trained in the art of traditional Chinese medicine. Medical *qigong* works by activating and regulating the energy meridians and the acupuncture system. It is a powerful method of affecting the energy flow in the body.

Gabrielle Gauthier-Hernberg is a physician and instructor in medical *qigong*. After a few months of therapy her problems with asthma, allergy, and eczema disappeared.

"Our energy system is like a highly sophisticated computer," she says. "The energy is the software, and the system's structure (anatomy) is the hardware. The best way to affect it is from the inside, via thoughts and meditation. In medical qigong, you enter another state of consciousness and gain access to a vast energy supply. Certain frequency ranges are especially stimulating for the life processes. Quite simply, you replace the old consumed energy and replenish it with new life-supporting energy."

To feel the energy, hold your hands in front of your chest and rub your palms together for a minute. Then separate your hands and try to find the distance between them at which you can feel energy (four to eight inches). Your palms will tingle a bit and it feels as though you are holding a ball of energy between your hands. It could even be difficult to bring your hands together, as though they are separated by an invisible wall. (The exercise works best when your hands are dry and warm.)

According to Gauthier-Hernberg, the general public–and companies in particular–have become very interested in *qigong* in the past few years. "It is part of a general awareness of health in which being healthy is the natural condition. Wellness programs and a holistic approach are popular, since taking good care of your employees is important." Attitudes are changing. The body is no longer seen as consisting merely of matter, but to a large degree of living energy.

In one study of the effect of *qigong*, thirty-one asthmatics completed 80 hours of *qigong* training over a two months period. The patients were assessed before and after by physicians at the Department of Pulmonary Medicine and Allergology at Karolinska Institutet, and a significant increase in pulmonary function was noted. Over half of the participants were able to cut back on their asthma medications or discontinue them entirely.

The goal of Chinese acupuncture is to balance the energy among the organs in the body in order to maintain equilibrium. Acupuncture can also be used for relieving pain related to surgery and childbirth. A thin needle is inserted between one and four millimeters into the skin in one of the body's hundreds of acupuncture points. Its analgesic effect is the result of the release of endorphins, the body's own equivalent of morphine. Anecdotally, the analgesic effect of acupuncture was discovered in prehistoric times, when people fought with bows and arrows. It was often necessary to twist the arrows to get them out, and the injured warriors sometimes experienced pain relief in the process.

The concept of *chakra* is spreading in the western world. It even pops up in the James Bond movie *Tomorrow Never Dies*, when media mogul and villain Elliot Carver shows his instruments of torture: one for each *chakra*, inserted to cause maximum pain and an excruciating death. While these implements of torture may or may not exist in reality, they show that there is widespread knowledge that the *chakra* represents bundles of nerves.

Chakra is a Sanskrit word and means wheel. According to some eastern religions, we have seven *chakra*, or energy centers, arranged in a vertical line, stacked one on top of the other, from the genitals to the crown of the head. The *chakra* can be viewed as transformers for our life energy, and they are closely linked to the body's glands (se below).

The body has three major energy centers: the head, the heart, and the abdomen. Our *qi* is centered at the spleen *chakra*, two finger-widths below the navel, and just as deep. Focus on that point to come into balance: use this method when you find yourself in an unbalanced setting, and your breathing will automatically slow down. The heart *chakra* is a very strong potential energy center, and the source of our abilities to love, forgive, and show compassion. The head, of course, is an important energy center, since the central nervous system is located here. Inside the frontal bone is the neocortex, the new brain, which we use for planning, thinking, and coordinating our activities. The brow *chakra* is associated with awareness, intuition, insight, and wisdom. It is also considered to be the location of the "third eye," the one that cannot be seen but that people use for intuitive "vision."

Each of the seven *chakras* carries a message about life and about us. We can view the *chakra* system as an archetypal description of the de-

Chakra	Gland	Hormones (a selection)
7. Crown	pineal gland	melatonin
6. Brow	pituitary gland	growth hormone, prolactin, oxytocin
5. Throat	thyroid, parathyroid	thyroxine, triiodothyronine, calcitonin
4. Heart	thymus gland	thymus hormones (thymosin)
3. Solar plexus	pancreas	insulin, glycogen, somatostatin
2. Sacral	ovaries or testicles	estrogen, progesterone, testosterone
1. Root	adrenals	adrenaline, noradrenaline, cortisol

velopment of the individual in seven well-defined stages. For example, the base represents the roots (the family) and basic security, the solar plexus is associated with ego identity, while the crown stands for spirituality and higher awareness. As you pass through each *chakra* level (level of awareness) on your path to spiritual maturity, you gain increased strength and self-knowledge.

Anatomy of Energy

Energy medicine involves the knowledge of how we handle and control the force or energy available to us in our bodies. Remember, we are actually energy beings – not just physical beings. This takes us into the realm of physics and quantum chemistry, but ultimately, when everything is reduced to the smallest component you reach the energy level.

Caroline Myss is a journalist, theologian, and doctor of energy medicine who has worked together with neurosurgeon and researcher Norman Shealy for fifteen years, studying the effect of stress and emotions on the development of diseases. In her book *Anatomy of the Spirit* she claims that our life experiences leave their marks on our bodies. "Our biography becomes our biology," as she puts it. Healing is an active, inner process involving a personal audit of attitudes, habits, memories, and values. Becoming healthy means you must accept changes in your life, and that requires effort in the form of energy and willpower. Myss believes that our relationship to energy and power is the very core of our health. Our lives are built up around symbols for energy and power: money, authority, titles, and beauty. We are constantly being called upon to be conscious of our energy sources and symbols – so that we don't give our energy away to others. Becoming healthy and staying that way is easier if we untangle our relationships with these factors, and then listen to the messages coming from our bodies and our intuition.

Energy anatomy deals with a new way of relating to our surroundings: the ability to receive and process matter and energy, simultaneously. The body emits a broad spectrum of electromagnetic and acoustic radiation, which can now be demonstrated in scientific experiments. For example, the electric activity of the brain (as measured by EEG) creates a constant magnetic field and we are vulnerable to disturbances in the electromagnetic field. Magnetic imbalances affect biological cycles, such as our sleep cycle, making it harder to get the deep sleep we need to become truly rested. A good tip is to avoid electrical appliances in the bedroom or to disconnect them at night. We can also counter this by using an "earth magnet" to help balance the brain's electromagnetic field.

We can also perceive radiation emissions from another person, though this usually happens unconsciously. Caroline Myss believes there are two types of people living on earth right now. One type relates to everything on a physical (material) level, using the five senses to tackle its surroundings with physical energy (money, power, sex, etc.), while the other tries to handle both the physical and energy-related impressions simultaneously. This means that people of the second type are receptive both to what a person says and to the energy signals and emotions they transmit. While most people have this ability, the question is whether we develop and use it. Some people, however, have a greater talent than others for "reading" and registering energy. For example, Myss has intuitively made many medical diagnoses, 90 percent of which have subsequently been confirmed by physicians.

Psychoimmunity

We are constantly exposed to different types of energy; how this affects us depends on what we absorb. Closest to the body is the bioenergy field consisting of both subtle and scientifically measurable energy. This energy is a result of the body's life processes, which constantly emit energy. The bioenergy field is made up of chemicals such as ammonia, salt crystals, carbon dioxide, and evaporated water. But it also contains electromagnetic, acoustic, and subtle energy fields. As a result, the body is surrounded by an ubiquitous cloud of ionized particles. It usually extends two to five inches out from our skin, and has a clearly defined outer limit.

The condition of our bioenergy field reflects our physical and mental state of health. The bioenergy field expands when we are healthy, but contracts with illness. It is also affected by the earth's radiation and by the magnetic fields surrounding power lines, computers, and household appliances. You could also view this field as a protective layer–an energy barrier–that helps us fend off unwelcome energy. It is actually the first defense against intruders, and it is a stronger defense than the physical immune system. I call it psychoimmunity: it is mental and subtle (in terms of energy), and a weak barrier can have actual physical consequences.

The purpose of the barrier is to prevent energy from leaking out, either freely from our beings, or when someone tries to steal our energy. Most people never even know they are losing and gaining energy through this field, since they don't grasp the significance of life energy. As a result we've overlooked an important part of the body's function.

One example of the effects of energy flow is the sudden fatigue we experience in the company of certain people; we could be losing energy to them. We've all run into "energy vampires" who consume our energy; they haven't learned to produce their own energy, and thrive on the emotions and energy of other people. They have to manipulate and control their surroundings to make sure they satisfy their energy needs. By training your energy, as in medical *qigong*, you not only learn to open yourself fully to get in touch with nature's energy, but also to close off your energy field afterwards.

Just as you must check your house for energy leaks, you need to learn how to manage your inner energy. A large amount of energy is needed to heat a drafty house. If too much of our life force–our energy–slips away, we become more susceptible to illness. Becoming aware of these things can be difficult for people who grew up in families with clearly-defined outward boundaries, but vague inward limits; in these families, limits between individuals are not respected either mentally or physically.

We fight over energy and try to steal it from one another, when the supply of energy is actually unlimited. Many relationships between people are all about power play; one person tries to emerge victorious – to usurp the energy of the other person. This explains why people are attracted to individuals with a high energy level and strong radiation. They want part of the good energy. Once you realize that you can meet your own energy needs from within and from the abundance in the universe, you can ignore these power plays. Fundamentally, this concept deals with knowing how to handle and control energy.

Try to become aware of how other people affect you and your energy level. Whose company makes you feel better, happier, and stronger? Do some people around you make you feel tired, less successful, or perhaps sad? What happens if you avoid them for a week; how are your energy levels affected? Or try holding up an imaginary shield in front of your chest when you meet "energy vampires," just as you would don a lead apron to avoid exposure to radiation. You could also imagine a huge rose in front of you and they will get "lost" among the petals. While you cannot stop others from trying to manipulate your energy flow, you can act to make sure you aren't affected. This is what it means to have healthy boundaries. Far too many people are unaware of their own boundaries or the boundaries of others, and energy flows in and out. Boundaries are very important for developing your identity. And the more clearly you define your identity, the more genuine intimacy you can handle.

Holographic View of the World

A hologram is a three-dimensional photograph made with a laser that was first designed in 1965. Karl Pribam, Stanford University neurophysiologist, said in 1969 that a hologram is a good model for the brain's processes. In 1971, physicist David Bohm–a disciple of Einstein–proposed the theory that the entire universe is organized holographically. Barbara Ann Brennan is a physicist who worked at NASA and is now a healer and teacher. In her fascinating book *Light Emerging* she says that we are entering the holographic age, involving several fundamental changes in the way we perceive the world. The holographic model is based on the following conditions:
- Our reality is found in the energy that our senses perceive, rather than in objects we define as real.
- Everything is tied to everything else.
- The whole is larger than the sum of its parts.
- Each tiny part contains the whole.
- Time is not limited to the present; we have access to every moment.

The effects of our actions are thereby not limited by either time or space.
- Individuation and energy are the basic principles of the universe. Each element in the universe is the result of either wave motion or individual energy particles. We consist not only of our bodies (matter); we also have an energy component – waves, like those found in light. We can use our light component to heal our bodies faster.
- Awareness creates both reality and our perception of reality. This means that we perceive reality according to our expectations, which in turn are based on our system of beliefs and our heritage.

What does this mean in concrete terms? All creation comes from the life energy of the universe – our thoughts, senses, emotions, consciousness, and matter. Our health is the result of our true essence as expressed through these different levels, and this even applies to our physical bodies. Our health and our diseases are created through this process, and thus *we are our health*.

Illness occurs when we become disconnected from our deeper essence, the soul. Disharmony and energy loss occur, leaving room for infections or degenerative processes in the body. This energy imbalance is manifested in a bio-imbalance. The three energy levels in our bodies are not synchronized but rather they are displaced in relation to one another. They must be brought together to form a whole in order to heal. This will make you "whole."

Healing

Healing means becoming whole. In order to achieve healing in the body the parts must be brought together into a whole. It is common in modern society for us to be separated from our spirit. If our daily activities are inconsistent with our soul (our mission in life), whether we are aware of it or not, the seeds of imbalance and illness are sown. If we aren't in touch with our souls, perhaps a healer can help.

There are many healers in history, people who lay on hands, of whom Jesus of Nazareth is perhaps the best known. But how does it work? Physicist and healer Barbara Ann Brennan describes how researchers have shown that the magnetic pulse coming from the hands of a healer has a frequency of 8 Hz. Robert Beck is a nuclear physicist who has traveled all over the world performing EEGs on healers. He found that during healing sessions their brain wave patterns were between 7.8 and 8 Hz. The earth's magnetic field varies between 7.8 and 8 Hz; these are called Schumann waves. Beck found that during a healing treatment the healer's brain waves pulsated at the same frequency as Schumann waves. The right and left halves of the healer's brain are synchronized at this wavelength. Healers are believed to be able to transfer this healing energy to patients by making contact with the earth's magnetic field – a considerable source from which to retrieve healing energy! Barbara Brennan expresses this as: "The more grounded you get, the more you can heal humans."

What happens in the body with healing? Stanford-trained Dr. Leonard Laskow writes extensively about it in his book *Healing with Love*. Two thirds of the body is water, and when energy is added it is the water structure that changes fastest. Water consists of two hydrogen atoms connected at an angle with an oxygen atom in the middle. When energy is unstructured, the two atoms stand at an angle of 105 degrees to each other, but when water absorbs energy the hydrogen link extends outward to 109 degrees. This changes the physical properties of the water, including its pH, solubility, surface tension, and ability to absorb light. It also splits more easily into charged atoms called "ions." Healing creates a field that structures the water in the body, changes its ionization, and even its pH value. This also affects the vital bioprocesses of the enzymes.

Anyone can develop the ability to heal. We all carry an inner energy and the ability to heal ourselves as well as others.

Near-life Experience

Everything we feel, think, and do affects our health. Health is neither static nor stationary. You might feel one way when you wake up and completely different at bedtime. So, you can influence your health at any time, no matter where you are in the process. It is never too late. But you must choose to do so – for no one else can do it for you.

A cold is a signal that you are out of balance. Perhaps you slept too little, or ate incorrectly, and this affected your body negatively. An improper diet may also include foods that cause symptoms of allergy or poisoning, resulting in constant irritation of the immune system. This makes us more susceptible to infections. Or maybe you've been under too much stress, neglected your emotions, or repressed your energy with negative emotions. Recurrent colds could be the result of a nutritional deficiency, food disharmony (allergies) or perhaps because your work or the people around you don't really fit with the "real" you. You may need to get in touch with your soul and try to define the meaning of your life.

Most people carry on with the more physical and material aspects of life for the first twenty to thirty years; getting an education, a job, a home, and a life partner. Not until then do they begin to consider existential questions. A crisis often acts as a catalyst, causing people to question and possibly change their lives. Crisis, illness, and divorce stir us up, giving us the impetus to break away from the routine and create something that better suits who we are.

Some people must even need a near-death experience to understand this and take control of their lives. Why not have a "near-life" experience, instead? Get in touch with your innermost self–with the life force–and let it flourish throughout your essence.

> *Self-healing humans*
> *have realized that they are a part of the universe.*
> *What they do for themselves*
> *They also do for their surroundings.*
> *What they do for their surroundings*
> *They also do for themselves.*

How will we use this understanding of energy? We can never know in advance what is "useful" and therefore useable. When Michael Faraday carried out his electrical and magnetic experiment around 1830, one of his students wondered if it could be useful. Irritated, Faraday replied: "What good is a newborn child?" Who could have guessed that Faraday's electromagnetism was to form the basis of our entire technology-oriented society? Similarly, today we do not know where our changing views of the energy concept, health, and the human being as an energy being will take us. Perhaps our great great grandchildren will know...

3.
Healing Powers of Vitamins and Minerals

Our bodies require vitamins and minerals. Since we cannot produce the minerals essential for life, we must include them in our diet. It is important for our food to be rich in vitamins and minerals such as zinc, iron, and magnesium. But what is the specific role of vitamins and minerals in our bodies? Nutritional deficiency and stress have a negative effect on the mind and emotions, though this can be countered by balancing nutrients properly. Detoxifying the body is important, but can we improve this process?

The seeds of life may have been activated when the sun's rays oxidized chemical compounds in the primordial seas and created pantothenic acid, a type of vitamin B. Pantothenic acid is needed to bind amino acids together, and to create the DNA making up our genes. Over the next billion years, many more molecules were formed–fats, amino acids, vitamins and minerals–and these in turn helped generate countless forms of life. These life forms, including human beings, came to depend on what is essentially the same group of nutrients. When the first life forms took to the land, they brought part of the sea with them. The liquid found outside an organism's cells, which comprises one fifth of total body fluid, has a mineral content similar to that of the prehistoric ocean.

Free radicals are thought to have played a central role in the development of life on Earth. Free radicals are characterized by reactive oxygen, which wants to steal electrons. They are formed when cells use oxygen to oxidize nutrients for their energy requirements. About three and a half billion years ago, free radicals triggered chemical reactions that led to the formation of the first and simplest forms of life. But since oxidation with free radicals can also be destructive, different antioxidant defenses soon developed, such as vitamins C and E.

Evolution often proceeds in a zigzag pattern, rather than in a straight line. For example, some 25 to 70 million years ago, our ancestors lost the ability to produce vitamin C. Nevertheless, some human species survived and ultimately *Homo sapiens* developed from them – probably because they lived near the equator, where food rich in vitamin C was abundant. Meanwhile, most other animal species–from insects to mammals–continued to produce vitamin C. (Based on studies of the vitamin C production of animals, several researchers believe that the daily requirement for a human being is 2–13 grams – depending on age, stress, and diseases.) According to a new theory, our ancestors' loss of the vitamin C gene might have accelerated their development. Vitamin C is an important antioxidant, and without it the body forms far more free radicals. An overabundance of free radicals may have led, in turn, to a large number of DNA mutations. Although this may have contributed to aging and disease, it may also have created a number of biological variations that were passed down to these early humans' offspring – one of which came to be *Homo sapiens*.

The Vital Minerals

Minerals account for a full five percent of our body weight, about eight pounds in a 150-pound person. This is a considerable amount – over twice as much as the weight contribution from carbohydrates. Aside from this, the average adult male consists of 17 percent proteins, and about 15 percent fat. The remaining two thirds is water.

Minerals are actually more important than vitamins, since they cannot be synthesized by living matter. They are the spark plugs of life's chemistry – the energy efficiency of living organisms depends on them. They also carry our energy; without them we lose our "charge" and feel less vital. Minerals, in the form of charged ions, play a central role in the body as components of enzymes and hormones, and by modifying enzyme function. Their action is very specific and accelerates vital life processes.

In the past few decades we have learned more about the importance of maintaining balance in the mineral levels throughout our tis-

Health-promoting effects of important minerals and trace elements

Phosphorous Works in tandem with calcium to form and maintain strong bones and teeth. Boosts effects of other nutrients. Found in cell walls.

Iodine Needed for thyroid hormone production and metabolism.

Iron Crucial for formation and functioning of red blood cells. Important for brain function.

Calcium Necessary for developing and maintaining bones and teeth. Aids enzymes, muscles, hormonal function, blood coagulation, and nerve signal transmission.

Potassium Regulates heartbeat and fluid balance and helps muscles contract. Needed for hormonal balance and nerve signal transmission. (Sodium works in a similar way and is just as important.)

Silicon Required for bone formation, healing of wounds, elasticity of skin and blood vessel walls, and three-dimensional structure of collagen.

Cobalt Stimulates formation of red blood cells.

Copper Needed for normal formation of red blood cells and connective tissue. Works as a catalyst, storing iron and releasing it for use in hemoglobin. Essential for formation of myelin around nerves, and for hormonal function, especially for estrogen.

Chromium Necessary for metabolizing glucose and regulating blood sugar levels.

Magnesium Activates over 100 enzymes, and helps nerves and muscles function. Needed for an open mind.

Selenium Component of an important antioxidant enzyme. Essential for normal growth and development.

Sulfur Needed for muscle protein and hair. Participates in body detoxification.

Zinc Essential part of over 200 enzymes involved in digestion, metabolism, reproduction, and woundhealing. Important in the skin and for the brain's normal perception.

(Source A. Schauss, Minerals, Trace Elements, and Human Health) sues, organs, and cell fluids. This is necessary for good health. The way in which we absorb minerals from food depends on several factors, including age, healthy intestinal flora, secretion of gastric acid and enzymes, absence of intestinal disease, and fiber content in food. Different people therefore react differently to food and dietary supplements.

Since we cannot produce minerals ourselves, we must include them in our diet. We are therefore dependent on the ability of plants to absorb and bind the earth's minerals. In a study during World War II, researchers analyzed the dental records of seven thousand American marines. They found that soldiers from the Midwest, where the soil is very fertile, had far fewer cavities than soldiers from areas where the earth was eroded or low in nutrients.

During the twentieth century farming conditions changed as small farms gave way to large-scale operations using synthetic fertilizers. The result has been a depletion of the soil and a decrease in the nutritional value of food. For example, a one-acre plot will yield a ton of tomatoes – but at the same time 1000 pounds of nutrients are taken from the earth, and these must be replenished. Conventional artificial fertilizers containing nitrogen, phosphorous, potassium, and calcium are deficient, since crop cultivation requires sixteen minerals (according to Soil Science of America). Plants need enough nourishment to resist infection, just as we do. Moreover, crops such as tomatoes, cucumbers, and strawberries are grown in greenhouses on a fiberglass matrix containing nutrient medium. Is this really a good solution?

In his book *The Healing Power of Minerals, Special Nutrients and Trace Elements*, botanist Paul Bergner shows that on average, the total content of calcium, magnesium, and iron in cabbage, lettuce, tomatoes, and spinach has dropped in the United States from 400 mg to 70 mg over the past eighty years. This means that the same food contains only one sixth of the minerals it provided in the early twentieth century. An extensive study conducted in Chicago in 1993 by B. Smith compared the content of thirty-six different minerals in pears, apples, potatoes, wheat, and barley. Organically grown crops had about twice the mineral content of "ordinary" commercially available vegetables. Studies in Sweden have shown that organic vegetables have a higher dry mass, which results in higher nutritional value and better taste. But conventional agricultural research shows little interest in the issue.

"Only a tiny fraction of research grants are allocated to studying organic foods and how they differ from food cultivated with artificial fertilizers," explains Bengt Lundegårdh, researcher at the Swedish University of Agricultural Sciences in Uppsala. However, research shows that the quality of plants grown using artificial fertilizers is deteriorating. These plants cannot absorb all the necessary minerals, and this leads to heightened absorption of nitrogen, and thus to an increase in biomass. Indeed, conventionally-grown food products give a higher yield in terms of quantity. But the amount of essential amino acids does not increase correspondingly, and the plants end up with a higher level of simple carbohydrates. Research has also shown that the immune system of plants grown on a nitrogen-rich fertilizer in a natural ecological environment deteriorates. These plants then contain fewer antioxidants and bioflavonoids. At the cellular level, the plants' immune system and detoxification mechanisms (P-450, glutathione, etc.) are actually the same as those of humans and animals. The plants provide us with energy in the form of nourishment, and when we reduce the quality of the plants we are also gambling with our own health.

The vegetables we buy in the supermarket may not necessarily be inferior; it all depends on their growing conditions. Although we can pick from a much wider variety than ever before, we have little or no control over quality, pesticides, antibiotics, or the biological effects of additives. So even a healthy diet does not ensure that you are getting the vitamins and minerals you need.

> *When shopping for food consider quality rather than quantity. For two weeks try avoiding food with low nutrient value and empty calories; eat nutritious food instead. Buy organic fruits and vegetables and other organically-grown products, and see if you can taste the difference. For example, in my experience organic bananas and organic whipping cream taste like they did when I was a child – much better! Organic carrots are crisper and have a better flavor than ordinary carrots. Go to an all-organic grocery store and botanize among flavors and colors! Talk to your grocer to get the quality of food products that you want. Note the difference in the way you feel after two weeks. You should at least be more aware of both nutritional content and flavor.*

Vitamins

The word vitamin comes from the Latin vita, which means "life." Vitamins are contained in many enzymes, which accelerate nearly all reactions in the body. As a result, they are important in regulating our metabolism. There are fat-soluble vitamins (A, D, E, F, and K) and water-soluble vitamins (B, C, and H).

Vitamin A deficiency can lead to night blindness, a fact that has been known for 3500 years: the ancient Egyptians recommended eating rooster's liver to see better in dim light. Vitamin A and beta carotene deficiency increase the risk of certain types of cancer by up to 800 percent.

The vitamin B group consists of vitamins B_1, B_2, B_3, B_5, B_6, B_{10}, and B_{12}, all of which play an important role in most of the body's activities. Vitamin B_6 takes part in almost one hundred different enzymatic reactions in the body. A mild vitamin B deficiency may result in headaches, fatigue, poor appetite, anxiety, depression, constipation, and reduced energy.

Vitamin C is needed to increase resistance to infections. Throughout history, thousands of people have died of scurvy, which is caused by vitamin C deficiency. This condition resulted in the death of thirty thousand soldiers during the American Civil War. Medieval Europe was greatly diminished by the Black Death—a form of bacterial infection—and pneumonia, resulting from scurvy. In all, twenty-five million people died, a quarter of the continent's total population.

Vitamin D is important for calcium metabolism, and a shortage can lead to skeletal changes known as "rickets." This condition was especially common among the poor during the days of coal-fired heating in England.

Vitamin E prevents blood clots and the formation of scar tissue and is therefore important in surgery. It is also important for reproduction, since vitamin E regulates the balance between progesterone and estrogen. The body also uses vitamin E to fend off viruses.

Of all these vitamins, the only one our bodies can produce for themselves is vitamin D, which is generated by exposing the skin to sunlight. Healthy intestinal flora can produce vitamin K and certain B vitamins. All of the others must be supplied by our diet. The vitamin content in our food may deteriorate through the use of synthetic

Health-promoting effects of vitamins

Vitamin A Important for vision; required for cell membrane function; important for the skin; strengthens mucous membranes; improves the immune system; aids digestion; balances the sex hormones; required for the liver to detoxify fat-soluble toxins; lowers elevated cholesterol.

Beta carotene An initial stage in vitamin A, it has the same effects but also works as an antioxidant, protecting against cellular damage (especially to cell membranes and DNA).

Vitamin B There is a whole group of B vitamins, which are required for important body functions such as cell division; digestion; antioxidation; immune system, nerve and hormonal function; and metabolism of fat, protein, and carbohydrates.

Folic acid Required for metabolizing protein and therefore vital during pregnancy; needed for normal absorption of nutrients through the intestine; crucial to cell renewal in the tissues; necessary for healing processes, healthy hair and skin, and important in the formation of white and red blood cells.

Vitamin C Strengthens the immune system and boosts resistance to colds, influenza, infections, and cancer; required for protein synthesis; counteracts early aging; contributes to maintaining healthy gums, teeth, bones, and collagen.

Bioflavonoids Also known as vitamin C2, required for proper absorption and use of vitamin C; also an anti-inflammatory and an antioxidant agent.

Vitamin D Improves uptake, transport, and use of calcium and phosphorous, which are important for bone and tooth formation; maintains a stable nervous system and normal heartbeat; important for the thyroid and blood coagulation.

Vitamin E An important antioxidant. Preserves cell membrane integrity, supports prostaglandin synthesis, and improves cell oxidation.

Vitamin F Essential fatty acids needed for general health and specifically for cells, contributes to keeping the cell membranes pliant and creating electric charges between the areas inside and outside the cell membrane; influences growth, vitality, and mental state; required for healthy, elastic skin and strong teeth; important for cell oxidation, and necessary for hormone formation in inflammatory processes and maintaining normal blood pressure.

Vitamin H		Biotin, needed for formation and oxidation of fatty acids and for amino acid metabolism. Healthy intestinal flora produces enough to cover our needs.
Vitamin K		Necessary for blood coagulation and to prevent bleeding; strengthens the walls of the liver and blood vessels; important for strong bones. Healthy intestinal flora produces vitamin K.

(Source P. Wilhelmsson, Healthier life with the right diet + vitamins and minerals)

fertilizers in agriculture, and by harvesting fruit and vegetables prematurely so that they can be transported across the country – or around the world. Food preparation can also lower vitamin content, and enzymes are rendered inactive by heating.

Vitamin + Mineral = True

Vitamins, minerals, and trace elements cannot function independently and are always considered in relation to one another. When there is an excess or deficiency of any individual mineral, at least two others are affected. For example, a vitamin C deficiency could result in too much copper being stored in the body. This in turn leads to a shortage of iron, selenium, and potassium. Too much vitamin D can lead to a copper deficiency, which results in an accumulation of iron.

Minerals and vitamins are in an interactive relationship in which they either work as synergists that cooperate and reinforce one another, or antagonists that counteract and weaken each other's effects. This means that each mineral and vitamin has both a synergistic and an antagonistic function, which is why the balance between them is so crucial.

Nutrients work synergistically within the cells. For example, both copper and iron must be present for them to be integrated by hemoglobin (the oxygen-binding substance in red blood cells). Calcium, phosphorous, and magnesium work together to ensure a strong skeleton. Vitamin C increases iron uptake, while vitamin D increases calcium uptake. Antagonism can be found in the mucous membranes of the intestine and in cells. Over-consumption of calcium leads to decreased absorption of zinc, iron, phosphorous, and magnesium. Only with optimal nutrient levels in the body can all the nutrients be used efficiently.

Clearly, this is an entire science in itself. If you are considering taking large doses of vitamins and minerals, it may be a good idea to consult an expert or perform a tissue mineral analysis.

Between 1935 and 1945 many vitamins became available in their pure form at a low price. Researchers were interested to see whether increased intake of vitamins could prevent or protect against new diseases. Interest in this field faded, despite many encouraging findings, probably as a consequence of the development of sulfa drugs and other antibiotics. The "magic bullet" had been found, which like a smart missile homing in on its target, would destroy diseases instead of preventing them. Since then, the importance of good nourishment for maintaining health and preventing illness has been more or less ignored by the medical establishment and by government health authorities.

Over the past five to ten years, however, there has been a reversal, with an ever-growing interest in the relationship between diet and health. Two-time Nobel Prize laureate Linus Pauling was among the first to recognize the crucial role played by vitamins and minerals in good health. Pauling coined the term orthomolecular medicine, where *ortho* means "right" or "correct." The essence of orthomolecular medicine is correcting molecular imbalances in the body. He first turned his attention to psychiatry, feeling that many mental illnesses might be corrected through heavy supplementation of specific nutrients and molecules. This would help the brain achieve its optimum molecular environment. This theory has not yet been adopted by mainstream psychiatry, though in the past decade a correlation has been established between nutritional deficiency and mental disturbances. For example, a deficiency of vitamins B_3 and B_6 leads to changes in the perception of reality, usually in the form of illusions, which often develop into hallucinations. Schizophrenics usually have a severe deficiency of vitamin B_6 and zinc, but food allergies are also common (see p. 271). Likewise, vitamin B_{12} deficiency can result in obsessive-compulsive behavior. A common cause of neuroses is malnutrition related to overconsumption of industrially produced and refined food, leading to several B-vitamin deficiencies.

Canadian physician and researcher Abram Hoffer has followed in the footsteps of Linus Pauling. Hoffer published his findings in 1955, showing that high doses of vitamin B_3 reduce cholesterol. His first book, *Orthomolecular Nutrition*, was published in 1978. The underlying idea is that people can fight, heal, and prevent physical and mental illness through treatment with optimum doses of nutrients. Though orthomolecular medicine can be considered "alternative" in its approach, it is based on biochemical principles concerning the body's requirements for normal function. It is actually fundamental to medicine and recapitulates the popular view of the 1930s – that nutrition is crucial to health.

As a medical science, vitamin and mineral therapy is in its infancy. The first hesitant steps were taken in the early twentieth century, with the discovery of individual vitamins. During World War II people began to calculate the minimum dose needed to prevent serious nutritional deficiency diseases in young soldiers. Today there is newfound interest in the effect of vitamins and minerals on the body. As people recognize that inadequate nutrition may be a contributing factor to illness, they increasingly choose nutrient supplements as a form of prevention.

Since both the nutritional content of food and dietary habits have deteriorated, most people probably need a multivitamin supplement to meet these requirements. A nutritional analysis of the body can be a good place to start, since both too few and too many minerals can be harmful. For example, too much copper can result in depression, weight gain, PMS, and pain at the front of the head. Zinc is necessary for the immune system's ability to combat viruses, but excess levels can increase susceptibility to bacterial infections. Too much iron can contribute to migraine headaches, arthritis, and cancer.

A reliable tissue sample can be taken from the hair and tested with a "hair mineral analysis." A piece of hair is cut from the hairline at the neck and the chemical content of minerals, trace elements, and metals (including mercury and lead) is analyzed. The test is a good indicator of metabolism in the body's cells during recent months and any deficiencies can be corrected using a customized dose of vitamins and minerals. In the United States, many nutritionists and physicians use hair mineral analysis to help people achieve better health. Hair mineral analysis is based on twenty years of clinical research.

"The importance of hair mineral analysis is that it not only helps prevent single nutrient deficiencies, it also plays a role in correcting metabolic disturbances and preventing diseases," says Dr. David Watts of Trace Elements Inc. in Dallas.

There is a correlation between the levels of minerals and vitamins and the nervous, endocrine, and immune systems. Researchers have identified two types of metabolism–fast and slow–as a measurement of whether oxidation in the cells is fast or slow. By carefully classifying tens of thousands of hair mineral analyses, Watts noted that the two types of metabolism can be divided into four sub-groups, each with different requirements for vitamins and minerals.

Metabolism

When the nutrient components of food are burned in the cells using oxygen (oxidation) energy, water, carbon dioxide, and waste products are formed. Oxidation is what happens when the surface of a cut apple becomes brown. It can be prevented by drizzling fresh-squeezed lemon juice, which is actually Vitamin C, on the cut surface. The term metabolism is used to describe how well nutrients are used at the cellular level. Cell metabolism is regulated by both the nervous and endocrine systems, affecting the efficiency of nutrient absorption, retention, and excretion.

Just as fingerprints differ from one person to another, our metabolism is also unique. We are quite simply biochemical individuals, a characteristic that researcher Roger Williams was one of the first to discover. Williams demonstrated that children in the same family had significantly different needs for nutrients. Even adults of the same age and build, living in a similar environment, showed significant differences in nutritional requirements for maintaining good health.

The body's energy consumption is regulated by the hormones and the nervous system. The sympathetic and parasympathetic nerves are the two parts of the autonomic nervous system that take care of our internal organs. A fast metabolism, which means that the sympathetic nervous system dominates, is linked with increased activity in the thyroid and the adrenals. The latter produce the stress hormones adrenalin and noradrenaline, resulting in rapid oxidation. The thyroid

Effects of the autonomic nervous system on internal organs

Effect on the body	Sympathetic (stimulating)	Parasympathetic (calming)
saliva secretion	decreases	increases
skin	sweats	dries
breathing	increases	decreases
heartbeat	accelerates	slows
digestion	inhibited	activated
adrenals	increased secretion of stress hormones	decreased quantity of stress hormones

produces hormones that affect mood, calcium metabolism, and body temperature. In a slow metabolism characterizing parasympathetic dominance, on the other hand, there is decreased activity in both the adrenals and the thyroid. This results in slow oxidation.

We are born with either one or the other, and it will control and affect all our life processes including digestion, nutrient absorption, energy level, and the diseases to which we are predisposed. But it also affects how we perceive and react to the world around us – in other words, it affects our emotional life.

Our genetic makeup also controls which minerals we absorb from food. This process starts as early as the embryonic stage, when our metabolism determines what we absorb from our mother's blood. People with a fast metabolism tend not to absorb—or even lose—calcium and magnesium, and they accumulate phosphorous, sodium, and potassium. The reverse relationship applies to people with a slow metabolism. Indeed, a slow metabolism results in higher levels of calcium and magnesium, while a fast metabolism leads to higher sodium and potassium levels.

Thus we inherit a certain composition of minerals and trace elements from our parents, but we can then be nourished with greater or lesser imbalances, which in turn affect our susceptibility to diseases. If we don't do anything to balance this, these inherited patterns will worsen over the years, as we find it easier and easier to accumulate certain minerals while suffering an increasing deficiency of others. For example, someone with a fast metabolism may tend to be stressed, which can eventually result in heart problems. A person with a slow metabolism almost always resists iron absorption.

Our metabolism is also affected by several other factors in the course of our lives, such as nutrition, exercise, infections, medicine, and emotions. A hair mineral analysis gives a mineral snapshot showing the type of metabolism we have right now – for it can change. Most people are born with fast metabolism, since that enables us to develop and grow. Usually, it remains fast up to puberty, after which it slows down, especially among girls. A fast metabolism is more common in adult males, while a slow metabolism is more common among women of child-bearing age. Sex hormones are anabolic (building) hormones, and when they decrease during menopause metabolism once again becomes faster. This means that the body becomes faster, while the cognitive ability gradually slows down. Old people often find it difficult to maintain calcium and magnesium, and therefore become more anxious and find sleeping difficult. A calcium deficiency makes it difficult for us to fall asleep, while magnesium deficiency makes us wake up very early in the morning.

When there is a balance, people with a fast metabolism are energetic, industrious, curious, evocative, laugh easily, enjoy fast sports, and look for active jobs. When these people have a bio-imbalance they perspire easily, their blood pressure rises, and they put on weight around the abdomen (looking "apple-shaped") and shoulders. In these circumstances they have a tendency to become egotistical workaholics. They may be worried and anxious about the future, and turn to calming drugs (alcohol, cigarettes, sweets), yet look for an energy charge (coffee, candy, snacking).

People with a slow metabolism who are in balance are calm and stable and take things in stride. They are methodical, caring, and sensitive to emotions. They enjoy endurance exercise, and they have a long-range outlook on life. If they have a bio-imbalance, people with a slow metabolism can have problems with low blood pressure and slow circulation, as well as weight gain around the thighs and hips (to give a "pear-shaped" look). They may tend to suffer from depression, low self-esteem, and dwell too much on the past. They also have a tendency to eat too rarely or too little, and can therefore suffer from eating disorders.

But we don't need to get stuck in one type of metabolism or the other; we can change several times during the courses of our lives. This can be seen, for example, in a person's weight, mood, energy level, and the occurrence of certain symptoms related to type of metabolism. If the change is brief it can pass without our even noticing it. Changing from rapid to slow metabolism depends on several factors, such as rising age (up until middle age), chronic stress or repression of emotions, vegetarian diet, poisoning with heavy metals, estrogen therapy, osteoporosis, poor digestion, and acidification (low pH). Changes of metabolism in the other direction are caused by the excretion of toxic heavy metals and from recovery following mental or physical exhaustion. But the change can also be triggered by acute stress or from entering menopause (also applies to men in penopause).

During a healing process people often change their type of metabolism many times. This is the body's way of accelerating cleansing. Going from slow to fast metabolism increases hormone secretion from the adrenals, which in turn stimulates the thyroid. This increases the detoxification capacity of the liver and kidneys. Put simply, the purpose of this process is to enhance the body's detoxification ability.

Osteoporosis

It is important to understand that although the symptoms of an illness may be fairly constant, the underlying mineral composition may differ. Osteoporosis is considered today to be one of the major diseases afflicting one in every two women, as well as many men and young people – even children. Osteoporosis is a symptom with several causes. Bone mass decreases and is demineralized, leading to an increased risk of fractures. Researchers estimate that if your calcium intake falls short by as little as 40 mg per day, it can result in an annual bone loss of 1.5 percent. The decreased bone density, however, is not detected in x-rays until there is a 30–50 percent reduction. Osteoporosis is a major, costly, and growing problem in developing countries, and the healthcare system invests heavily in treating menopausal women, especially with estrogen.

There are two completely different causes of osteoporosis, which must also be treated differently. Type 1 osteoporosis is associated with a negative calcium balance resulting from low calcium intake, decreased uptake, or increased excretion. This is caused by an increase in the adrenals' hormone production resulting from physical or emotional stress, often over a prolonged period of time. This can also happen to women with a fast metabolism when they reach menopause. The symptoms include higher body temperature, increased perspiration, worry, sensitivity to noise, muscle spasms, sleep disturbance, and irritable moods. Type 2 osteoporosis is characterized by appropriate intake of calcium, and decreased or normal excretion. The calcium wanders out into the body's soft tissues; you feel tired and chilled, with cold hands and feet, low blood pressure, and poor reflexes. Calcifications of the lymph nodes, gall bladder, and renal pelvis are common. Vitamin D deficiency, which is especially common in the elderly, is also a factor in type 2 osteoporosis.

The body is constantly walking a fine line between breaking down and building up. People who are in balance maintain a healthy bone structure. The skeleton is heaviest between the ages of 30 and 40, after which it slowly starts to decalcify, though this can also start much earlier. Once decalcification starts about 1 percent of bone mass is lost annually. During the first five years of menopause women lose between 3 and 5 percent every year. After that bone mass decreases by about 1.5 percent annually. Osteoporosis is often treated with estrogen, though this has adverse effects and results vary for different women.

Dr. John R. Lee sets out the progesterone hypothesis in the book *What Your Doctor May Not Tell You About Menopause*. He says osteoporosis can be treated with natural progesterone (a sex hormone produced during ovulation, which is important in helping the fertilized egg to attach to the wall of the uterus, as well as for a properly-functioning pregnancy). If the estrogen hypothesis is true, then there should be no reason for losing bone mass before menopause – when estrogen levels are normal. Progesterone, however, starts to decrease several years before menopause. Losing bone mass so quickly in early menopause indicates that estrogen is only a contributing cause – the true answer can be found in how these two hormones affect the osteocytes, or bone cells.

Bone can be seen as mineralized cartilage; it is living matter and is constantly undergoing change. Osteoblasts are bone-forming cells that are transformed into osteocytes, or bone cells. These are surrounded by a hard network of collagen and calcium which form the actual bone. Osteoclasts destroy the bone cells and leave a hole in the bone structure. Osteoblasts get into these holes and create new bone cells. This process is constantly taking place throughout our lives.

How is it affected by the hormones? Estrogen decreases the osteoclasts' function somewhat, while progesterone increases the function of the osteoblasts. Between 1980 and 1989 Lee treated women with osteoporosis who had entered menopause, using a program including diet, mineral and vitamin supplements, mild exercise, and of course, progesterone. The treatment resulted in a 15 percent increase in bone mass after three years, compared with only a few percent in women on estrogen therapy, and a 5 percent reduction in the untreated group. This means that progesterone's function of building up bone mass is more important than estrogen's function in preventing the bone from breaking down.

Silicon is essential for bone formation, since the highest silicon levels are found where incoming calcium hardens the growing bone. Researchers believe that silicon contributes to the matrix that forms the gridwork for appropriate mineralization of bones and teeth. Silicon directs calcium to locations in the body where it is most needed. Consequently anyone taking calcium supplements should also take silicon. In addition, the silicon level in tissues always declines prior to leaching, resulting in osteoporosis. The silicon leaves the skeleton first, followed by magnesium, and then calcium.

But the highest silicon concentration is in the skin, hair, and aorta. Much is also contained in collagen and consequently silicon is important for maintaining the skin's elasticity, preventing dry skin, and premature wrinkles. It is also needed for healing wounds and repairing injuries to the tendons, ligaments, and cartilage. Silicon deficiency leads to decreased elasticity in the walls of the blood vessels of laboratory animals. In patients with hardening of the arteries, reduced silicon levels can be detected in the walls of the blood vessels, and during aging too, levels of silicon in the skin decrease. A Finnish study found a correlation between lower levels of silicon in drinking water and a higher rate of cardiovascular diseases. And yet silicon levels in the Finnish study were about 5–8 milligrams per liter, compared with drinking water in areas with low mineral content (as low as 0.20 milligrams per liter). So look for the silicon content in your mineral water!

No daily requirements for silicon have been defined, and silicon may well be a neglected factor in osteoporosis. Today's processed and refined foods provide a low silicon intake, even though silicon is right behind oxygen as the most common substance found on earth. Grain loses 98 percent of its original silicon content when it is ground and refined. The best sources for silicon are brown rice, soybeans, leafy vegetables, algae, beets, pepper, and whole grain.

For some time we have been told that milk gives strong bones. Yet even though Sweden and United States have the highest consumption of milk in the world, we have the highest incidence of osteoporosis! Today about 75 percent of our calcium intake comes from dairy products, while we would be better off getting it from beans, fish, and green leafy vegetables, and consuming only 5 percent from dairy products. The Bantu women of Africa eat no dairy products, yet they get 150–400 mg of calcium per day from their food. Though this is only half the quantity of calcium consumed by western women, osteoporosis is essentially unknown among Bantu women over the age of sixty.

For a healthy skeleton you need exercise, a wholesome diet, balanced vitamins and minerals, and an appropriate hormonal balance.

Create Balance with Food

The different components of food affect the way the body burns fuel. We feel best when our food is adapted to our metabolism type:

Proteins — Accelerate metabolism as long as the body can digest (break down) the proteins into amino acids. Undigested proteins slow the metabolic process.

Carbohydrates — Simple sugars increase metabolism while complex (slow) carbohydrates lower it.

Fats — Slow down metabolism.

Water — Hard water (high content of calcium, magnesium, copper, and iron) lowers metabolism, while soft water (high content of sodium and potassium) increases metabolism.

With fast metabolism, protein and fat intake should be 30 percent each, and carbohydrates should be limited to 40 percent. Fruit, vegetables, and grains are good carbohydrates. However, don't forget that whole grain contains phytic acid, which binds calcium and transports it out of the body. You can deactivate the phytic acid by soaking it in lukewarm water (about 90–100° F). If your metabolism is slow, your diet should include 40 percent protein with a lower fat content. Carbohydrates should comprise 40 percent of your diet, and roots, beans, whole-grain products, and brown rice are all good choices. In either case, you should avoid sugar and candy.

Drinking water can also be a good source of minerals – assuming it has any. Make sure there are minerals in the mineral water you buy, or you will spend too much for too little. The mineral content in some carbonated water is so low that drinking dechlorinated tap water would be healthier, as the late Swedish environmental activist Bengt Danielsson pointed out. It is interesting to note that two of the world's largest soda producers use purified water with minerals added to it – rather than selling the best spring water available. Mineral water from France and Italy is usually high in calcium and magnesium, "hard water," which is good for people with fast metabolisms. Mineral water with high sodium and potassium levels, "soft water," is better for people with slow metabolisms, since those with fast metabolisms already have high sodium and potassium levels.

The quality of tap water varies all over the country, but by adding coral sand to regulate the pH, it can be made less acidic and the mineral content is even enriched. Coral sand is very high in calcium, and even your cut flowers will be happier and last longer if you add some to the water in the vase. It is also interesting to speculate how the mineral content of tap water might influence entire populations in different regions of the country as hard water has a slowing effect, while soft water speeds up metabolism.

Vitamins and minerals can also be classified by their effect on metabolism. Metabolism can be increased by the minerals iron, phosphorous, sodium, potassium, and selenium, and by vitamins A, C, E, B_1, and B_3, and can be slowed by minerals such as zinc, copper, calcium, and magnesium, and by vitamins D, B_2, and B_{12}. In simplified terms, people should choose their vitamins and minerals to stimulate or slow down their metabolism. We can balance our metabolism by taking the appropriate vitamins and minerals to match our current nutritional status.

Stress Depletes Nutrients

Modern society exposes us to many stressful experiences, and if we cannot cope with them our metabolism can become imbalanced. There are many stress factors, including loud noise, lack of time, excessive exercise, unpleasant experiences, no time to process emotions, and high demands on performance. Our emotions greatly influence the way in which we perceive stress and our physical response. But the body is also exposed to other stress factors, including disease, ongoing viral or bacterial infections, toxic minerals or chemicals, as well as the harmful side effects from medicines.

How do stress and trauma affect the body in purely chemical and physiological terms? All reactions involve some stress, which in turn requires a special response from the nervous and endocrine systems. The brain interprets impressions and generates signals to which the body responds. Specific vitamins and minerals are required for these systems to function by producing neurotransmitters for the nervous system and hormones for the endocrine system.

"Stress is the body's non-specific response to any demand placed on it," says Hans Selye, a pioneer in stress research. In the seventies, Selye defined four stages of stress that have been linked to different emotional conditions: the alarm phase, the recovery phase, the resistance phase, and the fatigue phase. The reaction is less extreme or protracted if you are in biochemical balance.

The first reaction to an unexpected or distressing experience is the *alarm phase*. The sympathetic nervous system triggers a signal telling the body to defend itself, a "flight-or-fight" response. The body reacts by consuming a series of vitamins and minerals (listed in the figure on next side). An adult who is in balance and feeling secure may be able to handle the situation quickly. However, children, or adults with low defenses or who are in a state of imbalance or exposed to repeated stress without the opportunity to unwind, could become "stuck" in this stage. This leads to a constant state of tension, and the feeling that something unpleasant is just bound to happen. Steady exposure to stressful situations will sooner or later lead to a nutritional deficiency. Unless you are able to handle the stress appropriately, the acute stress keeps the body in a state of shock, resulting in continuous consumption of vast quantities of vitamins and minerals.

If the body does not have time to recover, the alarm phase is usually followed by the resistance phase. The acute incident is intellectualized rather than being processed emotionally. This may take place on a conscious or a subconscious level. In the former case, the individual rationalizes the events to find an explanation that fits your earlier pattern of experiences. The brain sorts its impressions to make the world comprehensible. Subconsciously, this can become a survival strategy. For example, children often blame themselves when their parents fight. Children believe that if they change, the situation at home will become calmer and work better. The subconscious is completely removed from the conscious (what you know) and can lead to behavior that seems to be completely unrelated to the original cause.

After years or decades in the resistance phase, you gradually enter a *chronic resistance phase.* This transition is barely noticeable when it occurs. You may experience increasing fatigue, with the manifestation of various mental and physical symptoms. Recovery from stressful experiences becomes increasingly difficult, and an aversion to activities and social situations develops. Nutrients are constantly metabolized

The consumption of vitamins and minerals during the different phases of the stress cycle

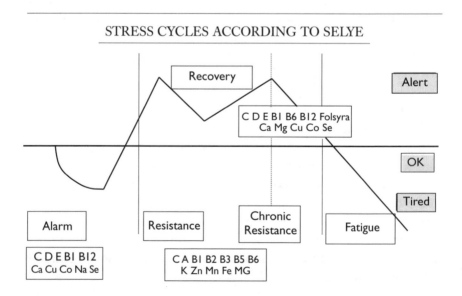

and your physical reserves become depleted. It also becomes harder to get in touch with the original emotion that triggered the reaction. The energy, the memory of the traumatic event, becomes encapsulated in your inner self. However, adding the necessary nutrients will help you get in touch with and process the previous event. Minerals supply the energy needed for emotions to be experienced and handled correctly. This helps you resolve problems without resorting to drugs such as alcohol, painkillers, or antibiotics to alleviate the symptoms. Such substances result in the breakdown of even more vitamins and minerals, taking you even farther away from recovery. Metabolism of headache pills (acetylsalicylic acid and acetaminophen) requires all of the steps in liver detoxification (see p. 281).

If instead you gradually calm down after the alarm phase and process the emotions that follow a stressful incident you can move on to the *recovery phase*. This can also happen after spending time in the resistance or chronic resistance phases. You might attend a course or some form of therapy, become inspired and gain energy by processing the situation. This may give you relief, releasing the locked up energy that consumed your resources when you weren't even aware of it. Recovery results in consumption of the nutrients shown below this box.

Without the physical resources or mental fortitude needed for recovery, you will eventually proceed to the *fatigue phase*. You probably experience obvious physical symptoms, feel very tired and find most socializing stressful. Taking the vitamins and minerals needed in the recovery phase will break this pattern.

Poor Nutrition: A Sad Condition

Nutritional deficiencies can also be purely physiological in origin, resulting from not enough food, or food lacking in adequate nutrients. But what are the implications of a deficiency of these nutrients – regardless of whether the cause is stress, emotions, or poor diet?

All enzyme and endocrine systems in the body require vitamins and minerals, and these systems control both physical and mental functions. The entire body is affected by a lack of nutrients – both physiologically and psychologically. Many important vitamins and minerals are also linked to different psychological conditions. As a result of stress and poor eating habits many people today have a deficiency of B vitamins, and minerals such as magnesium and zinc.

The entire B-vitamin group has a strong affect on personality. People with a vitamin B deficiency may become depressed and their perception of reality may be altered. They can even become aggressive or even worse – become schizoid or callous. Different types of intestinal infections can cause vitamin B deficiency – and sufferers may not even be aware of them. A healthy intestinal flora actually plays a critical role in the formation of B vitamins. Unhealthy intestinal flora leads not only to the formation of gases and poor breakdown of food, but also to psychological problems such as depression, aggression, and changes in the general state of consciousness. Stress causes fairly rapid changes to intestinal flora that is not in optimal health.

Almost 80 percent of the population has a mild or severe deficiency of magnesium, a common mineral found predominantly in bones and muscles. This deficiency is caused partly because our diet does not include food with enough magnesium and partly because junk food and soft drinks deplete the body of nutrients. Because of its phosphoric acid content, every time we drink a glass of Coke we lose 150 mg magnesium, which is half the minimum daily requirement. Also, magnesium is a small molecule that can easily be lost in the urine when people are under stress. In contemporary society everyone is under stress. People usually don't eat enough magnesium-rich food – whole-grain products, vegetables, and fruit. Nor does our food contain as much magnesium as it did in the past, though nuts of all types are still one of the best sources.

Stress hormones–adrenalin, noradrenaline, and cortisol–are released in response to stress, making us more alert and better able to cope with danger. Paradoxically, in magnesium deficiency the stress response increases damage to the cardiovascular system, and thus provokes even more body stress. This creates additional magnesium deficiency, making it even harder to deal with the stress, which again amplifies the deficiency, etc. During particularly stressful periods people can lose over half their magnesium supply.

Magnesium deficiency lowers the irritation threshold and people tend to worry about things more easily. In order not to alter the Ca-Mg balance it also causes calcium to move from the bones to soft tissue. Surplus calcium is stored in muscles, joints, and connective tissue.

But calcium and magnesium can also travel from the bones to the body's soft tissues as a defense against acidification (too low a pH). The soft tissues can become acidic as a result of stress, chronic muscle cramps (producing excess lactic acid), or poor diet. The result is that people become not only magnesium-deficient, they also feel tired. This means that you can be very tired while at the same time there is a constant inner activity making it difficult for you to relax. People don't sleep well or think in a calm and balanced way, and there is a tendency to palpitate. The individual becomes over-tense in response to situations that would not seem so stressful if magnesium levels were correct.

Zinc deficiency is also very common. At least sixty zinc-dependent enzymes have been identified in the brain. Without enough zinc, the brain cannot comprehend its environment properly, preventing people from viewing the world from a neutral stance, with appropriate nuances. Zinc is important for proper operation of the immune system and healing of tissues and scars. A lack of zinc will show up on the nails as white dots on more than two fingernails. Additionally, zinc deficiency leads to impaired taste and loss of appetite. PMS is another common symptom of zinc deficiency. Many women note a difference in their emotional reaction during the days prior to menstruation; they may become oversensitive and cry easily, or get angry over minor details. The emotional response can be normalized if the zinc deficiency is corrected.

A sodium deficiency is associated with indecisiveness. Sufferers find they can get nothing done and they become less social. It is often accompanied by a potassium deficiency, since the two are paired. However, low sodium with a high potassium level can result in mood swings with unmotivated emotional outbursts and repressed anger.

Iron deficiency (defined as the lack of iron reserves) is especially common in young people, particularly women. With iron deficiency you become less strong-willed, it is harder to complete projects, and you may not have the strength to stand up for your opinions. Important neurotransmitters in the brain require iron to help control concentration and for mental acumen. Iron deficiency leads to problems concentrating and a feeling of fatigue.

Smart Minerals

The zinc content of the adult body is two grams – half that of iron and 10–15 times more than the body's copper level. The highest concentration of zinc and iron is found in the brain. Zinc deficiency is associated with a poorly functioning accumulation of DNA, RNA (which transfers the genes' message to protein), and protein during the development of the brain. As a result, zinc deficiency during pregnancy can result in apathetic children, who may be mentally underdeveloped and have learning disabilities. The hyperactive child may have a deficiency of both zinc and vitamin B_6, as well as an excess of lead and copper.

In a study of 615 school children in California, one group was given a multivitamin and mineral supplement containing 100–200 percent of the recommended daily intake, and the other received a placebo (ineffective sugar pills). In the first group, 45 percent of the children had an IQ increase of over 15 points compared with the placebo group's increase of 4.4 points.

When Elisabeth Cagan became coordinator of New York City's school lunch menu, she gradually replaced junk food with nutritious food. From 1979 to 1983, 600,000 school children participated in this "experiment" and the result was an improvement in both academic and athletic performance. In addition, mobbing and criminal behavior decreased. Researchers at the Massachusetts Institute of Technology in Boston have also found that reducing intake of junk food leads to higher intelligence.

According to a survey of the eating habits of Swedish middle school and high school students, only 70 percent received the recommended daily intake of nutrients. A full 15,000 rarely or never ate breakfast or lunch. Instead they ate ice cream, candy, and chewing gum more frequently than those with good breakfast and lunch habits. Students who are tired, cranky, and have low grades have different eating habits than students who feel more alert and have high grades. Fortunately, the study has led to a revolution in the food served in Swedish schools. It began in the north of Sweden, in Kiruna in 1993 when senior dietitian Lena Hammarberg started a two-year program for school food service personnel intended to fuel a desire for change. They learned to use more vegetables and prepare varied salads and appetizing vegetarian dishes. Not only did the students feel better, the municipality also saved about $80,000 annually. The successful "Kiruna model" has spread to other municipalities further south. Most enthusiastic about the new diet are the preschool children. Actually it is remarkable that the "green" school food revolution began in Kiruna – which has plenty of hunting and fishing but almost no tradition of eating vegetables!

Nutrition Affects the Mind

Professor Alexander G. Schauss at the American Institute for Biosocial and Medical Research in Tacoma, Washington, has been studying the relationship between nutrition, brain function, and behavior for over twenty-five years. He has published numerous books outlining his research into the correlation between nutrition and mental illness. Anorexia and bulimia have spiraled over the past decade and Schauss has reported a connection between these diseases and zinc deficiency. Zinc deficiency gives a loss of taste and appetite, as well as over-consumption of certain foods. This can cause pregnant women to experience an urgent craving for food they previously found uninteresting.

Women between the ages of 12 and 25 are in the high-risk bracket for both zinc deficiency and anorexia, which can be caused by stress, diet, and changing estrogen levels. Anorectic behavior often has its origins in highly stressful situations such as puberty, starting college, or marriage. Princess Diana's anorexia, for example, began just before her marriage. Schauss feels that zinc deficiency may be one of the reasons why young girls keep slimming even after reaching the culturally accepted weight. Zinc deficiency causes a change in their perception of reality, and they do not see how thin they have actually become. Schauss has successfully treated eating disorders in teenage girls through a regimen of zinc therapy, normalizing food and exercise habits, and counseling for the entire family.

Even alcoholism is believed to have a correlation with a deficiency of zinc and vitamin B_6. Alcohol also depletes levels of magnesium, a mineral with a calming effect. All in all, this can give rise to a vicious cycle with mood swings, tantrums, irritability, hyperactivity, and learning disabilities – and should be treated by changing the diet to achieve balanced nutrition.

Copper is often called the female mineral because it is important for estrogen production. High levels are associated with caring and conscientious behavior. Zinc is called the male mineral, as it is important for semen and testosterone production. But it is also crucial during pregnancy as daughters born to zinc-deficient mothers show a higher degree of aggressive behavior and learning disabilities. Excessive iron levels also lead to aggression, especially in people with a fast metabolism. People with a slow metabolism become dominant instead.

To sum up, nutrient deficiency affects people mentally. This fact is worth considering, given the huge and quickly expanding expenses for antidepressants: sales have more than tripled in five years.

There are two aspects to consider in the relationship between mental health and diet and nutrition. Mental illness can be caused by nutritional deficiency or imbalance, and people with mental problems, depression, and similar conditions often have digestive problems, resulting in a decreased absorption of nutrients. This is important as an estimated 35-40 million Americans living today will suffer from major depressive illness during their lives. Stress and depression impair your ability to use the vitamins, minerals, trace elements, and other nutrients found in food. Decreased appetite is common in people who are depressed or grieving. Because they don't eat as well, they consume fewer nutrients. A negative cycle is created – sometimes without the person being aware of it. From this perspective, it is worth noting that few studies on mental health include questions on dietary habits. Instead, only psychological or psychosocial explanations are given for this complex problem.

Toxins

In addition to nutritional deficiency, body functions are also affected by accumulations of toxic environmental metals such as lead, mercury, cadmium, and aluminum in cells and tissues. This inhibits or disrupts the normal function of other minerals in enzymes and neurotransmitters. Disturbing cellular energy production and the function of the nervous, endocrine, and immune systems impairs psychological protective mechanisms, and also increases sensitivity to stress.

The poisons found outside our bodies are called exotoxins, from the

The effect of toxins on the body, and protective nutrients

Toxic substance	Effect on	Protective nutrients
Aluminum	Abdomen, bones, brain	Possibly magnesium and silicon
Arsenic	Cell metabolism	Selenium, iodine, calcium, zinc, vitamin C, amino acids with sulfur groups
Lead	Bones, liver, kidneys, heart, pancreas, brain, and nervous system	Zinc, iron, calcium, vitamin C, vitamin E, amino acids with sulfur groups
Cadmium	Kidneys, heart, brain's blood vessels, appetite and smell centers, development of cancer	Zinc, iron, calcium, vitamin C, vitamin E, amino acids with sulfur groups
Mercury	Nervous system, appetite- and pain centers in the brain, immune system, cell membranes	Selenium, vitamin C, pectin, amino acids with sulfur groups

(Source A. Schauss, Minerals, Trace Elements, and Human Health)

Latin exo, which means outside. But even substances from within our bodies can be toxic if they are present in sufficient quantity. They can be natural products of our metabolism, free radicals, or waste from intestinal bacteria. These are called endotoxins, since they are found on the inside (*endo*). The body's endotoxin levels depend on what we take into the body. Everything, from the air we breathe to the food we eat, affects our metabolism – positively or negatively.

The body's immune and detoxification systems are intended to fight toxins from inside and outside. However, this process is high on energy consumption, and when the body becomes overloaded it cannot handle the toxins and they are deposited in the tissues. Ultimately, it is the endotoxins that pose the greatest problem, in combination with exotoxins. For example, mercury leaking from amalgam impairs detoxification by inhibiting important enzymes. If the body is unable to detoxify its own estrogen, it could result in breast cancer.

Good health is not synonymous with being free of symptoms – it takes years of accumulating toxins and the resulting bio-imbalance before the symptoms appear in the form of cancer, rheumatism, osteoporosis, hardening of the arteries, high blood pressure, kidney failure, and other degenerative diseases. Medical care systems aimed solely at symptoms make relatively inefficient use of resources.

Free Radicals

The air we breathe contains about 20 percent oxygen. It fills an important metabolic function by taking electrons (e-) from the sugar or fat molecules that are used as fuel. Chemical reactions entail dividing, gaining, or losing electrons from one atom or molecule to another.

Oxidation in turn creates free radicals that cause us to pulsate electrically. A cell may be attacked by between ten and a hundred thousand free radicals every day. Cells are at risk of oxidizing from the contact with free radicals and the breakdown process begins with the oxidation of polyunsaturated fats. A chain reaction may be initiated, damaging cell membranes and leading to hardening of the arteries. Research has shown that essential fatty acids, such as those found in olive oil, lower the risk of cardiovascular disease and cut the risk of breast cancer in half. Olive oil makes the cell membrane more resistant to the attack of oxidation from free radicals, which could otherwise lead to fatty acids becoming rancid, a step in the development of cancer.

Most common diseases are caused by the breakdown of cells, tissues, and organs as a result of oxidation. Many factors interact to cause chronic disease, but free radicals play a prominent role in the development of over sixty serious diseases, including cancer, asthma, diabetes, skin disease, arthritis, cataracts, hardening of the arteries, inflammatory bowel disease, multiple sclerosis (MS), and Parkinson's disease.

Elastic connective tissue is highly vulnerable to injury from free radicals, leading to scarring and wrinkling of the skin. Free radical attacks also cause hardening of the eyes' lenses, hardening of the inner ear, and stiffening of arteries and joints. In the 1950s Denham Harman,

Free radicals	Absorbed by antioxidants
Superoxide	copper, zinc, histidine, lysin, manganese
Hydrogen peroxide	glutathione, vitamin C, selenium
Hydroxyl	mannitol, lipoic acid
Singlet O$_2$	beta carotene, vitamin A, vitamin E
Peroxyl	beta carotene, zinc, vitamins C and E, glutathione, ascorbyl palmitate
Hypochlorite	taurine

(Source P. Wilhelmsson, Healthier life with the right diet + vitamins and minerals)

Professor Emeritus at the University of Nebraska, was the first to suggest that free radicals might cause aging in the body. For several decades his theories received little attention, but today they are "hot stuff." Much has been written on the subject of free radicals and antioxidants. Books on how to prevent aging have received considerable attention over the last five to ten years.

But free radicals are not just undesirable troublemakers: they also have a protective role to play. Cells in the immune system produce free radicals to neutralize foreign matter.

Free radicals can harm the body in many ways, but the most serious is that they can break down the cell's genome, which contains the code for proteins for the body's functions. According to researcher Bruce Ames at the University of California in Berkeley, an expert on free radicals, the DNA molecules of each cell are exposed to about ten thousand attacks a day. Failure of the body to counter these attacks increases the risk of cancer. Consequently the body has developed a protective system–antioxidants–to prevent oxygen from stealing electrons from the wrong sites. Above is a table of the most common free radicals and the antioxidant nutrients that absorbs them.

Antioxidants

Antioxidants first came to public attention in the 1990s. Their role is to intervene when free radicals attack the cells from both outside and within. Antioxidants can share or absorb electrons without being transformed into free radicals themselves, and can reset the balance in tissues and cells by donating electrons to molecules that are falling apart. This prevents free radicals from stealing electrons from the molecules around them. Antioxidants thereby hinder aging and degeneration. Free radicals can be viewed as offensive weapons, and antioxidants as defensive ones; the balance between these is controlled by a number of complex systems.

The body defends itself against attacks by free radicals with a group of antioxidants including vitamin C, bioflavonoids, beta carotene, vitamin E, and glutathione. Since these substances work as a team, supplementing with one or two doesn't help; you need them all for antioxidation to be effective.

This is why a 1996 Finnish study on the significance of vitamin E and beta carotene in heavy smokers showed an even higher rate of lung cancer in men taking beta carotene. When the beta carotene absorbed the free radicals and became toxic there was no Vitamin C to replenish it since riboflavin was missing (vitamin B_2). Research studies are always based on testing the effect of one variable (or individual substances), while many substances often collaborate in the body – sometimes in such a way that there is a cascade effect. The study was later repeated with more antioxidants added, and the results were positive.

Antioxidants can be thought of as a ladder – all of the "rungs" are needed in order for it to work. Bioflavonoids help vitamin C donate an electron to the free radical. Beta carotene is then a necessary bridge in transferring a new electron from vitamin E, which in turn is replaced with an electron by (reduced) glutathione.

But other substances also function as antioxidants, including vitamin B_2, enzymes such as superoxide dismutase (SOD) and coenzyme Q10, the minerals selenium, silicon, zinc, copper, and manganese, as well as sulfur-containing amino acids such as L-cysteine, methionine, and taurine. There are also herbs with antioxidant properties, such as Ginkgo biloba, salvia, rosemary, and Japanese green tea.

A sure-fire method of getting enough antioxidants is to eat fruits, whole-grain products, and vegetables at least five times a day, and to drink green tea. According to Bruce Ames, this would cut the risk of developing cancer in half.

Detoxification and Cleansing

Supplying nutritious food isn't enough; we must also help eliminate waste in different ways. Most of the body's waste products leave via breathing and the skin – therefore exercise, breathing, and drinking plenty of water help cleanse the body. But it is also important to eat a diet that keeps the body clean and decreases acidification, thereby assisting the detoxification process.

All substances that burden the body's detoxification system or increase the number of free radicals can accelerate aging, and play a role in degenerative diseases and processes. These substances include drugs, sugar, caffeine, alcohol, cigarettes, pharmaceuticals, saturated or trans fats, electromagnetic radiation, and chemical environmental toxins. The more negative factors, the greater the negative impact on the body.

The body's most strenuous activity is ridding itself of undesired substances. Detoxification is mainly based on building up molecules, and not–as one might think–on breaking them down. Each day a large proportion of our energy is spent creating new molecules, and a full 80 percent of these are used for detoxification. By minimizing the toxins and attacks from free radicals to which we are exposed and optimizing nutritional intake we can have a positive influence on our health and the healing processes.

A daily supplement of vitamins and minerals helps meet these needs. You can assist detoxification by taking bioflavonoids together with vitamin C (0.5–1 gram), vitamin E (100–400 IE), beta carotene (25,000 IE), and selenium (100–300 microgram) daily.

It is better, however, to take a multivitamin and mineral tablet that gives a broad spectrum of nutrients, including amino acids, folic acid, and biotin. Best of all is to take the supplements recommended in a hair mineral analysis to avoid disturbing your personal balance. Infections related to copper deficiency actually become worse with a zinc supplement, and the antioxidant coenzyme Q10 is better for a fast metabolizer.

Reaching a ripe old age is no fun if you don't stay relatively healthy. Very old people (age 100–110) usually don't die from any of the major diseases such as cancer or cardiovascular diseases. They die because they don't recover from what would be considered a minor physical injury or infection in a younger person. They are literally worn out before the age of 110.

But limiting calorie intake while following a diet of high-value food (high in vitamins, minerals, enzymes, and trace elements) may help you live a long life. According to calculations a person who follows this regimen could run a marathon in less than three hours at the age of 90–equivalent to what a 70 year old does today. Indeed you can become physiologically–and mentally–much younger than your chronological age by eating a high-value diet.

Many older people suffer from a deficiency of basic, important nutrients, which makes them more susceptible to infections, confusion, and early dementia. A few years ago immunologist Ranjit K. Chandra, from Memorial University in Newfoundland, showed that supplementing with eighteen common vitamins and minerals dramatically improved immune system function in a group of older people. It also cut the occurrence of infectious disease in half. His discovery was considered to be an important breakthrough by the medical establishment.

But why does it take so long for old truths to be accepted? Obviously a garden becomes more lush and beautiful, and plants grow better if we feed them with lime and fertilizer. Why don't we have that view of ourselves? We are in constant need of nutrients and energy to be able to function, since our cells are constantly dividing. The body renews itself all the time, day and night, and if we fail to supply the appropriate "building material" we are compromising our health.

Just as vitamin C and vitamin D deficiencies lead to scurvy and rickets, you can easily imagine that imbalances between important nutrients also cause other diseases. Deficiencies of antioxidants, vitamins, minerals, and essential fatty acids can contribute to the development of cancer, inflammation, and pathological changes in the blood vessels, joints, skin, intestinal mucous membrane, brain, skeleton, genitals, teeth, and in the mouth. It is an interesting thought to keep in mind while reading the following chapters of this book about the importance of food and the intestinal flora.

All truth passes through three stages.
First it is ridiculed.
Second, it is violently opposed.
Third, it is accepted as self-evident.
A. Schopenhauer (1788–1860)

4.
You Become What You Eat

We need a certain amount of energy to utilize the body's natural healing ability. One very important source of this energy is food: its nutritional content and the efficiency with which the body absorbs nutrients are therefore highly important to the process. Is it true that the food people in the developed world eat creates diseases? Why? And what food should we eat to be healthy – and stay that way? Research has shown that degenerative diseases and premature aging can be avoided by carefully selecting what you eat and how you treat your body. You could live to be 120!

The sun's energy is a prerequisite for life on earth. No biosystem could exist without it, and we are not an exception. Our life processes depend on this energy to function.

But how do we gain access to the sun's energy? We need the molecules—the fat, proteins, and carbohydrates—found in food to extract energy for the body's life processes. What happens to food in the body is the opposite of what happens in plants, which convert electromagnetic energy into chemical energy (photosynthesis). Plants capture the energy in sunlight with their chlorophyll and use the energy to convert water and carbon dioxide into oxygen and sugar molecules (starch).

When we eat fruit, salad, or vegetables, our metabolism breaks down the plants' fat, starch, and carbohydrates, thereby releasing energy. The energy is stored in the bonds between the atoms forming the molecules, and is released during oxidation (metabolism using oxygen). For example, glucose, a common sugar molecule, consists of six carbon atoms linked together in a ring. Oxygen and hydrogen atoms are bonded to these carbon atoms. Glucose metabolism consumes oxygen, and the end products are carbon dioxide and water. We inhale oxygen and exhale carbon dioxide, which the plants then use in photosynthesis when they capture the energy radiating from the sun. And so the circle closes on one of the earth's many cycles.

The Digestive System – Our Center of Force

We eat in order to function, to feel vital, and to gain energy. But it is not until the food is broken down that we can tap into the sun's energy for the body's life-sustaining processes: building new cells, repairing injuries, sending nerve impulses, causing the muscles of the heart to contract, and detoxifying the body. The stomach and intestines serve as the center of force from which we obtain nourishment and energy from food.

Our life force and healing ability depend on a certain energy level, which is necessary for body and mind to function well. We must have nutritious food, healthy intestinal flora, and good absorption of nutrients through the intestinal wall in order to harness sufficient energy. Digestion and absorption of nutrients are complicated biological and biochemical processes that are sensitive to external and internal influences: diet, stress, exercise, and emotions. It may take some time to put things right when either mind or body should become out of balance. A preventive dietary approach supporting the body's self-healing is preferable to burdening the body with an incomplete or incorrect diet. The returns are substantial: a well-functioning mind and body that coexist in harmony.

Food affects metabolism and thus the amount of available energy. Fat slows the body's energy production, while protein speeds up the process. Complex or "slow" carbohydrates (starch) break down slowly, so it will take longer for the blood sugar levels to rise. Simple or "fast" carbohydrates–glucose, lactose, and saccharose–can be quickly absorbed by the blood, causing a faster rise in glucose levels. Slow carbohydrates also lower the speed of our metabolism (though not as much as fat), while fast carbohydrates accelerate it. By carefully choosing our foods we can influence our own metabolism.

Food for Thought

The chemistry of the brain is affected after each meal. Food works as a drug, influencing both our mood and our physiology. Researchers at MIT have shown that the slow carbohydrates in whole-grain products stimulate production of serotonin, a neurotransmitter that creates a sense of well-being and inner peace, and improves concentration and sleep. Indeed, it is a good idea to eat slow carbohydrates in the evening when you want to enter a calmer phase.

Meals that are high in animal protein (meat and fish) increase the level of two other neurotransmitters, dopamine and noradrenaline, which make people more alert, attentive, and aggressive. So the recommended daily allotment of protein is best eaten at breakfast and lunch to achieve optimal alertness. Of course high levels of the central neurotransmitters, dopamine and serotonin, are also desirable, and can easily be attained by eating a balanced diet and leading a balanced lifestyle.

Sleep is very important for proper neurotransmitter production. People with sleeping problems can be helped if they follow the usual recommendations for jet lag: get enough daylight, eat protein in the morning (egg, fish, beans, soy protein, or cottage cheese), carbohydrates in the evening (potatoes, brown rice, or whole-grain pasta,) and avoid caffeine. You may enjoy a cup of coffee at three or four in the afternoon, though, since caffeine has a neutral effect and does not alter the daily rhythm.

Proteins are based on combinations of varying numbers of the twenty-two amino acids. Amino acids are important elements in several neuropeptides, which function as neurotransmitters between the cells of the brain and the body. Increasing interest is being focused on the effects of various amino acids on the human body. Recent findings on amino acids by a group of physicians and researchers are presented in the book *The Healing Nutrients Within*. Melatonin, for example, improves sleep, reduces anxiety, and slows aging of the body. Tyrosin boosts energy, works as an antidepressant, and counteracts stress and chronic fatigue syndrome. Phenylalanine acts as a pain-reliever. Obviously amino acid deficiencies can have serious consequences for health.

Changed Eating Habits

In the long run, poor-quality food or inadequate nutrients will undermine your health. Certainly not all foods supply energy; some actually consume more energy than they provide. Just how good is the quality of food in contemporary society? For fully 99 percent of human evolution we were hunters and gatherers. But after two centuries of industrialization, our food has undergone major changes, with a radical shift in diet over the past fifty years. We consume more processed foods, chemically-treated fats, and over two thousand (!) artificial additives – yet we receive fewer nutrients. Large-scale agriculture and synthetic fertilizers are responsible for a drop in the mineral content of our soil since the early twentieth century. The nutritional quality of food has deteriorated as a result. Everything has been speeded up. We no longer "raise" cows, pigs, and chickens; we fatten them up for the market. The focus is on quantity – not quality.

Our food is too high in calories and too low in nutrients. We've more than doubled the consumption of high-calorie food, while consuming only half as many whole grains, roots, and fruits during the past century because of industrially produced and processed products. We eat more sugar, fat, and white flour than ever. The result: we are becoming both overweight and undernourished.

Our over-consumption is understandable, since our food contains fewer nutrients per calorie than ever before. Blood sugar levels yo-yo up and down in response to the overload of fast carbohydrates, as the body craves more food to balance nutritional deficiency, low blood sugar, and hormonal fluctuations. But should this trend of eating high-calorie, low-nutrient food continue, our energy will be sapped and we will continue in a downward spiral.

It's like the emperor's new clothes – although people appear to be well-nourished, with rounded cheeks and bodies, they are actually undernourished, lacking essential nutrients for the brain, body, and immune system. It's not really a question of optimal performance, but rather of sufficient nutrition for maintaining reasonably good health.

More and more young people are growing up on empty calories. Teenage girls get a quarter of their calorie intake from candy, soft drinks, and cookies. The survey "Youth approaching the year 2000" showed that over 70 percent of today's teens eat candy every day, though only half eat fruit or vegetables at least every other day. The number of overweight or obese young women (age 16–24) has more than doubled since 1981. Many young people survive on hot dogs, pizza, hamburgers, and convenience food heated in the microwave, accompanied by chips, French fries, crackers, ice cream, and candy.

They are becoming the empty generation – growing up on a low-nutrient, high-calorie diet. This food, with its few poor nutrients, provides a short-lived and false feeling of satisfaction. These changing eating habits are reflected in increased stress, allergies, morbidity, restlessness, mental problems, difficulty concentrating, and even aggression, in children and adolescents. The World Health Organization (WHO) warns that girls under the age of ten shouldn't eat hamburgers or other fast food, since it increases the risk of getting breast cancer as an adult. Growing evidence indicates that eating habits during the first ten years have significance for health in later life. WHO recommends that parents encourage their children to avoid low-fiber, high-fat foods.

A proper diet should provide nutrients – not drain the body. What is really worrisome is that some foods today are actually poisonous, burdening the body's detoxification system. Reduced glutathione is crucial to detoxification, but the substance is lost when the body eliminates foreign chemicals. This results in a significant loss of energy. When the body detoxifies its own metabolites, however, glutathione is recovered instead. While consuming toxic and unhealthy substances cannot be avoided, it should be kept to a minimum. More importantly, our food should not rob us of nutrients, vitamins, or minerals.

Eat to Live, Not to Survive

We should choose food that promotes the body's life processes, since we eat to live – not to survive. It's reasonable to assume that the fresher and more appealing the food, the healthier it is to eat. What is good food? Our senses help us decide, and we use sight, smell, and taste to find our way through a jungle of products. Don't allow your senses to become dulled, for we rely on them as much today as during the Stone Age. Studies have shown that colorful dishes are far more appealing than brown or black food. We have the strongest and most favorable reaction to yellow and red – a stroke of luck for McDonald's.

It feels better to eat perfect eggs with shiny yellow yolks from healthy chickens than insipid, pale thin-shelled eggs produced by stressed chickens in overcrowded broiler farms. Unfortunately, unless we become informed and start to demand better products, we are at the mercy of food producers. They can manipulate us by feeding their chickens yellow dye (beta carotene), resulting in yolks that look healthy, even though they are not.

Our food selection is limited to what the industry produces. But, consumer behavior can also influence the availability of healthy food – which will only increase as awareness grows. As demand for organic products rises, more will become available. Indeed, food producers have no choice but to respond to consumers' demands – provided consumers are adequately informed.

Manipulated Food

"Space food" was supposed to be the trend for the future in the sixties and seventies. New processed food products were developed for astronauts to bring with them on their missions. I'll never forget my first freeze-dried ice cream in 1980 at Kennedy Space Center in Florida – that's about as futuristic as it gets. At the dawn of the computer age, advancing technology spurred researchers to develop tablets containing all the nutrients we need. In his book *Detoxification and Healing*, Dr. Sidney MacDonald Baker says he learned in medical school that fiber was a worthless part of food. Instead, everyone was supposed to look forward to the day when, like the astronauts, we could get our nourishment from highly processed foods providing all the right ingredients for physical well-being. Today we know that the fresher and less processed our food, the better we feel.

The goal of the food industry has been to produce the most food at the highest possible quality. The last goal, however, has not always been possible to achieve. Efficiency measures, growth hormones, antibiotics, pesticides, and large-scale operations do not exactly result in quality products. In addition, sugar or digested cornstarch is added to most industrially-produced foods. No pharmaceutical company can launch a new medicine without proving that it is beneficial and non-toxic at the right dosage. But food can be processed and marketed with no requirement that any nutritional content remain. Artificial substances and flavoring may be added and nutrients removed without considering the effect on humans. Small wonder that food allergies are becoming increasingly common.

The vegetable oils introduced in the 1950s are one example of how the food industry manipulated food. The industry developed a method that employed a heating process and strong chemicals to press oil from seeds. These new "salad" or "cooking" oils kept for months, since the linolenic acids–the fatty acids that go rancid most easily–were removed. The problem was that the oils removed were those with nutritional value, while those that remained were nutritionally worthless or toxic. At the time, no one knew that linoleic and linolenic fatty acids are needed for the body's production of prostaglandin hormones. This was discovered in the 1960s – yet these products remain on the market today. They are commonly used for producing chips and candy since they are less expensive than natural healthy oils.

Milling flour is another example of food manipulation. The hull and bran are removed from the grain, while important vitamins, minerals, and other nutrients–including useful fiber–disappear in the process. This may extend product shelf life, but no one seems to pay attention to the decreased nutritional value. Flour has also been bleached to make it whiter. Historically, white flour was associated with higher status, since only the wealthy could afford it. Others had to settle for less processed whole-grain rye or wheat flour, baking into coarse, dark bread rather than the refined white bread.

White sugar is another refined and chemically treated product. Sugar beets and cane are very high in minerals and nutrients, but nearly everything useful disappears in the refining process. Oddly enough, sugar is classified as a food even though it contains very few nutrients and gives only a quick energy boost. For the same number of calories, sugar provides 98.5 percent less nutrients than rolled oats.

Toxic Fats

Toxic or unhealthy oils in food are one of the biggest health problems of our time. Unlike proteins and sugars, which are broken down and pass through the liver–our detoxification center–the fat we eat enters the blood directly without being broken down by the body. Thus we become the fats we eat. If you eat a lot of chicken fat, the composition of your fat will resemble that of chickens.

The consumption of salad and cooking oil has more than doubled over the past 40 years. These oils are produced by heat-pressing and extractions with chemical solvents similar to those used in dry-cleaning (hexane). Polyunsaturated vegetable oils are changed to solid form through hydrogenation, a process through which fatty acids become saturated and inflexible (straight) that changes the form of the fatty acids from natural and flexible to the unnatural and rigid "trans" fats. As a result, these processed fatty acids are not appropriate for use in hormone production or as a building material for cellular membranes. Trans fatty acids make rigid cellular membranes, which age faster and function poorly.

Today, most foods with vegetable oil–salad oil, ice cream, cookies, candy bars, mayonnaise, bakery products, chocolate–contain trans fatty acids. Many studies have shown that the consumption of trans fatty acid, and margarine in particular, elevates the risk of cardiovascular disease. The harsh chemical processing also leaves unhealthy residues, like the highly carcinogenic benzopyrene. Recent studies have linked margarine consumption to a higher incidence of allergies and cancer in children.

H.J. Heinz has a new product on the market: chocolate-flavored French fries! The purpose is obviously to increase the consumption of French fries by young people, but the news is hardly encouraging considering that two out of three 13-year olds have hardening of the arteries. This new product will give children a chance to commit "nutritional suicide," according to Dr. Barbara Rolls, nutritionist at Pennsylvania State University.

A diet high in sugar and fats stimulates the liver to produce more unhealthy LDL cholesterol than the body can remove. The excess cholesterol is deposited in blood vessel walls, resulting in hardening of the arteries. Invariably this leads to a poorly functioning cardiovascular system. So it is indeed crucial to eat healthy fats.

Fat for Life

For over thirty years we've been taught to avoid fats, but this isn't strictly true. The body needs fats – healthy, natural fats as opposed to the newly invented chemically processed fats. Fatty acids are essential for healthy skin, they lubricate the joints, and they are crucial for brain function and hormone production. I would like to introduce the concept of "fat for life."

We need good fats to store energy, build the waterproof membrane that surround cells, and to form a group of hormones – the prostaglandins. Produced in the membrane and released directly, these serve as important local messengers. Essential fatty acids were recently discovered to have an effect on protein kinase C, an important enzyme that controls special functions outside the cell.

Which fats should we eat? Linoleic and linolenic acids are essential fatty acids – we cannot form them ourselves so we have to include them in our diet. Like vitamins and minerals, they are necessary for our growth and health. A deficiency of these fatty acids can result in impaired hormone production, pathological skin changes, problems in the reproductive system and the adrenals, and vulnerability of the brain.

Linoleic and linolenic acids are transformed into other fatty acids with medicinal properties. Linoleic acid is transformed into omega-6-fatty acids (such as GLA and AA) and linolenic acid is transformed into the healthy omega-3-fatty acids (such as EPA and DHA). Omega-3-fatty acids have been shown to reduce inflammatory reactions, prevent blood clots, and protect against degenerative diseases. Omega-3-fatty acids are also plentiful in fatty fish from the cold northern seas: herring, mackerel, salmon, and sardines.

An excellent source is flaxseed oil, which has the highest concentration (about 60 percent) of the thin and pliant linolenic acid. Isn't it remarkable that the two fatty acids that we cannot form ourselves are the most flexible! They are also the best raw material for the protective cell membrane, which is needed to maintain normal cell function. Flaxseed oil gives the skin a lovely glow. Flax oil is used in oil painting precisely because of its "fine glow." Flaxseed oil is also part of the traditional diet of the Ukraine, where many people live to a very old age. Fresh-pressed, unprocessed flaxseed oil is loaded with antioxidants. A teaspoon a day of cold-pressed flaxseed oil is recommended for good health. If liver function is a problem, a capsule of EPA/DHA should be taken instead. You can find them in health foods stores and pharmacies.

Linoleic- and linolenic acid are the raw ingredients for prostaglandin production. Prostaglandins affect the contraction of smooth muscles and are extremely helpful during childbirth. They have also been used to initiate abortion. Inflammation also stimulates their production, and prostaglandins play an important role in regulating the immune system. Excessive or faulty production, however, may lead to menstrual cramps and PMS.

Olive oil (cold-pressed virgin olive oil) is another suitable source of healthy fats. It contains phytosterols, which are anti-inflammatory and lower the body's absorption of cholesterol. Replacing the saturated fat in your diet with healthy, cold-pressed olive oil reduces the level of harmful LDL in the blood. This may well contribute to the lower incidence of cancer, degenerative disease, and cardiovascular disease observed in Mediterranean countries where large quantities of olive oil are used in preparing food. Rapeseed oil has a similar effect.

All oils contain the antioxidant vitamin E. Virgin olive oil contains additional antioxidants and is considered especially beneficial. Read the label to find out what type of fat is in the food before you buy it. If you are unsure whether food contains toxic fatty acids – don't buy it. Consuming beneficial oils is an inexpensive way of improving your health since unhealthy fats result in many problems. And an added benefit: good fats are associated with good moods.

It is important to consume omega-3- and omega-6-fatty acids in the right proportion. When our ancestors were hunters and gatherers, over ten thousand years ago, fats accounted for 20 percent of the food's energy content. They were evenly distributed between omega-3- and omega-6-fatty acids. Today, we eat up to fifty times as many omega-6-fatty acids as omega-3s. Fat now provides about 40 percent of total calorie intake, a doubling (!) over the last century.

An omega-3-fatty acid deficiency is easily recognized since it gives dry skin, though the symptoms may vary: cracked skin on the fingertips, dark spots in different shades on the face, mixed skin that is oily and dry at the same time, rough elbows or lower legs, dry and brittle hair, dandruff, scalp sores or hair loss, and soft or brittle fingernails that split. These symptoms (plus internal problems) usually improve dramatically with a supplement of flaxseed oil, fish oil, or other sources of omega-3 fats. Indeed, moisturizers, special shampoos, conditioner, or cosmetics are of little use when the problem is an omega-3 deficiency.

It has long been known that the highest levels of essential fatty acids are found in the brain and the eye. At age two, over one fifth of the child's brain (dry mass) is composed of essential fatty acids. In the 1970s, Canadian researchers showed that rats' learning ability was directly proportional to the level of omega-3-fatty acids in their brains. Now we know that omega-3 and omega-6-fatty acids are especially important in the development of the brain and the eye. New research shows that fatty acid deficiency is associated with dyslexia, learning difficulties, and hyperactivity. Around five percent of the school children (mostly boys) have these problems and they frequently have difficulties with motor function, concentration, or being perceived as "disruptive" in school. Omega-3-fatty acid deficiency in particular is linked to hyperactivity. Studies have shown that diet supplements with essential fatty acids can help these children function better. It is also very important that mothers take omega-3- and omega-6-fatty acid supplements during pregnancy and while nursing, since the nutrients comprise the building material for the growing embryo.

What About Our Children?

How has development of the embryo been affected by the changing eating habits of the past decades? Studies have shown that the mother's health and nutritional status before and during pregnancy are paramount. According to major epidemiologic studies, women whose diet is poor before pregnancy give birth to smaller infants, and the babies are not in the best of health. A correlation was noted that 50-year old men with elevated cholesterol had a smaller chest measurement at birth. Low birthweight, relative to the duration of pregnancy, is associated with an increased tendency for cardiovascular disease. This is significant even for apparently well-nourished westerners, since two thirds of the average calorie intake of the modern diet consists of empty calories that provide no nourishment – just growing power. A diet with too many fast carbohydrates sharply raises the mother's blood sugar, stressing the pancreas of the fetus during development and increasing the risk of diabetes later in life (for example, gestational diabetes). The risk of diabetes also increases if the mother does not eat enough protein late in pregnancy, because of inadequate growth of the fetus' pancreas.

Children need a good environment in the womb to develop physically and mentally – in line with their biological potential. The genes must receive the proper signals from the environment at the appropriate time in order to be turned on and activated. If environmental conditions are changed, the biological functions may change unconditionally for the remainder of the individual's life. This means that diseases can be transmitted from one generation to another in a way that is not caused by genetics. By changing the environmental conditions of the fetus, the natural programming can be modified during development. This can radically change the newborn's potential for good health.

In the thalidomide disaster of the late 1950s, pregnant women who took the drug gave birth to children without arms or legs. This sparked awareness of the embryo's sensitivity to substances ingested by the mother. Since the 1970s, pregnant women have been recommended to avoid drinking alcohol, smoking, and taking drugs (including prescription medications) since these may harm the unborn child. Recently Professor Christopher Gillberg at Göteborg University reported a correlation between smoking during pregnancy and children born with ADHD (Attention Deficit Hyperactivity Disorder). Smoking during pregnancy may also be associated with SIDS (Sudden Infant Death Syndrome), also known as "crib death." Coffee may also be harmful during pregnancy. The risk of miscarriage is three times higher than average among expectant mothers who drink more than three cups a day. This may be the origin of the long-held folk belief that strong coffee can be an abortive.

Some prenatal care providers have begun to recommend that pregnant women avoid sugar and other fast carbohydrates after observing that mothers who consume too much sugar give birth to children who are addicted to sugar. These addicted children have hypoglycemia (low blood sugar) and sometimes require glucose solution soon after birth. Children of mothers who eat more slow carbohydrates, especially late in pregnancy, escape the problem of hypoglycemia.

About 135,000 American women suffer each year from gestational diabetes, which often disappears after giving birth. To avoid such unnecessary complications women are encouraged to eat a healthy diet and take vitamin and mineral supplements. Research has shown that female diabetics are twice as likely to suffer early miscarriage and at increased risk of having children with birth defects. High blood sugar is the cause. Since elevated glucose is more common the older we get, and women are now tending to have children later in life, these problems may well increase. Most of these women don't even know that their blood sugar is too high or too low (hyper- or hypoglycemia).

During the past twenty to thirty years, the birthweight of newborn children in developed countries has risen, and teenagers are taller than ever before. This might be linked to higher sugar consumption, which increases insulin production in the body. Besides regulating blood sugar, insulin is also a growth hormone.

Juvenile obesity is becoming a problem in a growing number of American households. According to a Center for Disease Control and Prevention study released in October 2002, statistics show that twice as many children are obese today (5,3 million) compared with twenty years ago. Ten percent of children between the ages of two and five are overweight or obese, and 15 percent of children aged six to nineteen. A number of other diseases are also on the rise as a result of this trend toward obesity, including a tripling of gallbladder disease and a fourfold increase in sleep-related breathing disruptions. Type 2 diabetes—which leads to complications such as stroke, blindness, heart disease, kidney failure, dysfunctional blood circulation, and even amputation—affects an estimated 300,000 youngsters in the United States. The condition is becoming so common among youngsters that it's no longer called "old age diabetes."

Half of all adults and one fifth of all children in the United States are so overweight that they are at risk of seriously harming their health and reducing their lifespan. Taken together, these are shocking statistics, and unless we take serious action against sweet, fattening junk food, many young lives will be lost.

The incidence of allergies in children has also risen sharply. Twenty years ago only 2 to 3 percent of children were affected, while now over 40 percent have some form of allergy. Every third person in the western world has allergy problems; unfortunately there is no indication of a reversal in this trend: indeed, the number of sufferers is even expected to increase. Allergies are the 6th leading cause of chronic disease in the United States, costing the health care system $18 billion annually. New studies show that external environment factors might be less significant than "inner ecology," as Polish or Estonian children have fewer allergies than Scandinavian children even though air pollution is worse in Poland. For example, allergies among children in eastern Europe increased following the fall of the Berlin Wall in 1989 as western eating habits were adopted.

There is a clear correlation between sugar consumption and tooth decay in children. Candy, ice cream, and cookies create harmful bacterial flora that eats holes in teeth and produces tartar. Since Swedish schools dropped the mandatory fluoride program, children have had more cavities. Pediatric dentists have noted a sharp rise in the number of cavities among two- and three-year olds. Since there is a correlation between the number of cavities during childhood and susceptibility to degenerative diseases in adult life, this is not good news. It is crucial that strong measures be introduced to help our children get a healthier start in life. When I was young, children were only allowed to eat candy on Saturday, but now many indulge in candy, ice cream, and cookies every day of the week. Though the problems may be of our own making, we can also find the solution.

Teen Eating Habits

Consumption of fast food with empty calories–like soft drinks and hamburgers–is common among children and adolescents. Soft drink consumption exceeded milk consumption of 1967, and many children are raised on soft drinks. Considering the health consequences, this is alarming.

Nutritionist and behavioral scientist Johanna Falk says: "Today's teens are stressed. They have a hard time sitting still, and they are constantly fidgeting. When you have a hamburger and a Coke you are eating sugar and white flour, which quickly raise blood sugar levels, as well as caffeine, which provides a temporary kick. Coca-Cola contains large amounts of phosphoric acid (with the same low pH as vinegar), and together with the phosphorous in the meat this combination counters the beneficial effects of the minerals calcium and magnesium. This causes a drop in these 'calming minerals' and results in hyperactive behavior. Infants born with an addiction to sugar may display jitters and it is difficult for them to maintain correct body temperature. These may well be the same effects we see in teenagers."

This is worth considering, since psychosomatic problems are on the rise among school children. A full 40 percent of girls and 25 percent of boys between the ages of 12 and 16 have headaches once a week. The body gets used to its blood sugar kicks and demands more. Dependency may be the result. Popular hamburger chains know this, and some even add sugar to French fries, mayonnaise, and hamburgers – just to build up a loyal, addicted clientele from an early age.

Another problem is the rising number of young people who are either underweight or overweight. Consider the absurdity of this fixation on appearance and the demands it places on young people. Many female TV or movie stars have been under fire from the media because they were considered too thin. To be accepted you have to look "just right" – but how do you know what's normal if everyone is dieting? At any given time, 35–40 percent of adult American women and 20–24 percent of the men are trying to lose weight (according to The National Institute of Diabetes at NIH).

Most of it is linked to nutritional deficiency. Young people today aren't eating properly and they aren't getting enough nutrients. They are under too much stress and rarely sit down to enjoy dinner in peace and quiet. Stress consumes large amounts of B vitamins. Much of the B-vitamin surplus is formed by normal intestinal flora, and to maintain this beneficial flora our diet must contain plenty of fruits and vegetables. This isn't the way it should be; our children and teenagers deserve a better start in life.

The Bitter Truth About Sugar

One reason for our high calorie intake is that just about everything we eat contains sugar – not just candy and cookies, but ordinary food too. Ketchup, for example, contains more sugar than chocolate, and there is even sugar in toothpaste. Most of the sugar we eat is hidden (about 85 percent). Its many guises include glucose, inverted sugar (syrup), lactose, dextrose, fructose, brown sugar, unrefined sugar, or maltose (found in beer). Americans eat around 156 pounds of sugar per person per year. An average American consumes more than half a ton of sugar every ten years, a considerable quantity with serious health consequences – even when no immediate symptoms are noted. Sugar is like smoking; you don't realize the consequences until years later when the body begins to protest.

How can something that tastes so sweet and good be harmful to the body? In truth, sugar is a drug – just as addictive as nicotine and heroin as it effects the brains opoid system. A high consumption is harmful to the body. Several research studies have shown that sugar has direct and indirect negative consequences (see below). It impairs the immune system, elevates blood pressure, and raises cholesterol. The higher the sugar content in food, the more chromium is secreted – and this can manifest itself as the chromium deficiency found in many diabetics. This in turn makes it difficult for other minerals to function properly. Chromium is also promoted as an agent for reducing the desire for sweets.

Sugar hinders absorption of the calcium and magnesium we need for essential life processes. Calcium builds up bones and teeth, while magnesium is required for enzyme activation and energy production.

Documented negative effects of sugar

- causes excessively high or low glucose levels (hyper- or hypoglycemia).
- affects the structure of proteins (via formation of AGE-complex) and thereby impedes their capacity to be absorbed and the ability of blood proteins to transport substances.
- raises lipid and cholesterol levels.
- accelerates the aging process, resulting in wrinkles and gray hair.
- causes anxiety, hyperactivity, irritability, and concentration difficulties in children.
- causes depression.
- causes yeast infections (candidiasis).
- contributes to osteoporosis.
- contributes to hardening of the arteries and cardiovascular problems.
- causes headaches and migraines.
- increases the risk of developing Parkinson's disease by a factor of three in heavy consumers of sugar compared to moderate consumers.
- causes tooth decay.
- affects the embryo's growth when consumed during pregnancy.
- correlates to development of degenerative diseases (diabetes, dementia, kidney failure).
- inhibits the immune system and promotes chronic inflammation.

Sugar also depletes minerals from bones and tissues, contributing in the long run to osteoporosis. Studies of people from developing societies have shown that changing to western eating habits leads to deterioration of their bone structure and the condition of their teeth. You might wonder why this association is not a topic of discussion, since osteoporosis is one of the most common diseases in our time. On some islands in the South Pacific, almost all adults over the age of 40 have become diabetic as a result of their "improved lifestyle."

By medical definition certain forms of refined sugar have a poisonous effect, stealing nutrients from the body, and therefore should not be permitted in foods. If sugar were a new product today, it would probably not be approved as an additive in ordinary food. It is a stimulant – not a food. Paradoxically the food industry is the biggest user, though sugar is also an ingredient in many medications. The industry began to add sugar to food during the years between World War I and II (individual consumption more than doubled). Consumption of "caloric sweetener" has increased 40 percent since the 1980s, when the industry started to add more HFCS (high fructose corn starch), which is less expensive and easier to handle.

Why is eliminating sugar so difficult? Because it affects blood sugar, hormone levels, and transmitters in the brain. It is all too easy to become addicted to sugar as a mood enhancer in the form of candy, ice cream, cookies, soft drinks and baked goods. But this temporary energy surge makes you feel ill, tired, and anxious. It is a mental and physical dead end.

Sugar causes premature aging for many reasons. Elevated blood sugar leads to spontaneous glycosylation (combining with glucose) of proteins, which takes place independently of normal enzymatic control. This also happens when the surface of meat browns as it is heated. These AGE-complexes (advanced glycation end-products) are characterized by brown or fluorescent pigments. This also causes the yellowish tinge in the whites of older people's eyes. The older you get, the more AGE collects in the tissues, which contributes to deteriorating organ function.

AGE-receptors are found in both immune system cells and in nerve cells in the brain. AGE-complexes also circulate in the body. They are toxic because they increase oxidative stress (the oxygen's free radical attack) on the cells. This prevents the cells from functioning properly, accelerating both aging and tissue degeneration. AGE-complexes are deposited in the blood vessel walls, and with time impair vascular function. The body tries to rid itself of AGE in different ways, which can exhaust the immune system and contribute to kidney failure. Diabetics often have chronically elevated blood sugar, which encourages the formation of AGE. But when AGE-complexes are prevented from forming in animals with diabetes, these vascular changes are also prevented, and so are unhealthy changes in the retina of the eye, the kidneys, and the nervous system.

It is well known that smoking accelerates aging of the skin and internal organs. Cigarettes also contain reactive glycosylation products that can quickly react with proteins in the body and form AGE-complexes. People who both smoke and consume large quantities of sugar place a huge toxic burden on the body.

The Role of Insulin

The major diseases of our western culture – obesity, heart disease, diabetes, high blood pressure, and elevated cholesterol – share a common denominator. They are actually not diseases but symptomatic manifestations of a fundamental insulin imbalance.

As a hormone, insulin is of central importance since it affects the body in so many ways. When you eat carbohydrates, glucose is absorbed into the blood. This prompts the pancreas to produce insulin that is then secreted into the blood. The insulin binds itself to receptors on the surface of cells so that they can absorb glucose, which is required for energy metabolism. Glucose can also be incorporated into energy stores in the form of glycogen found in the liver and muscles. This energy is readily available when needed. Elevated insulin levels also lead to increased storage of fat, contributing to obesity.

Eating the fast carbohydrates found in pasta, white bread, candy, and ice cream leads to soaring blood sugar levels, followed by a rise in insulin levels. However, the concentration of blood sugar quickly falls to a lower level than when you began eating. Soon the body starts to crave food again, in order to raise its blood sugar levels, and in the end glucose and insulin levels yo-yo. This is obviously detrimental because it throws our metabolism off balance. After a few years the cells' insulin receptors become exhausted, resulting in chronic insulin elevation. This causes the cells to become insulin-resistant, and the system can no longer function properly, regardless of how much insulin the pancreas produces. Ultimately, the result is skyrocketing blood sugar levels and a diagnosis of type 2 (adult onset) diabetes. Studies on mice have shown that cells may respond inappropriately to insulin if it has become glycosylated by the constantly elevated blood sugar levels (formation of AGE-complex).

Excess insulin also raises blood pressure by forcing the kidneys to retain salt and fluid. Insulin stimulates cell growth in the blood vessel walls, making them thicker and more rigid. It also increases the level of noradrenaline, an adrenaline-like substance which stimulates the heart and causes blood vessels to contract. It also encourages fat to be stored in lipid cells, causing obesity. Eating fat does not necessarily make you fat; it is the combination with a fast carbohydrate that causes weight gain. If you spread butter on a slice of dark wholegrain bread, the body will absorb little fat compared with spreading the same amount of butter on a white roll or English muffin.

But there's more. Insulin stimulates the liver's production of LDL, the bad cholesterol that thickens arterial walls. At the same time, it also stimulates the formation of hard plaque, which can lead to clogged arteries. This puts you in the high-risk zone for a heart attack.

Changing diet by eliminating sugar intake as far as possible reduces the insulin surplus and resets the cell's insulin sensitivity to a normal level, thereby reversing much of the damage. Glucose, blood pressure, cholesterol, and triglyceride levels respond quickly to a healthy change in diet. The alternative is angioplasty, an expensive surgical procedure to dilate the arteries, which is often only temporarily effective, as the arteries just clog up again. It only costs a tenth of the amount to go to a health spa and change your dietary habits – and you save on expensive medications too. During World War II sugar was rationed, and the number of diabetics fell dramatically. Problems with bedsores almost disappeared. Given the right nutrients, the body will heal itself. Lifestyle changes are especially important, since all these modern diseases tend to come in groups.

Many people report that their sense of taste changes completely after they stop eating sugar. It's like quitting smoking; suddenly food has a different taste. Added sugars tend to coat food, and flavor improves if the natural taste or sweetness of the ingredients is exposed instead. Corn and carrots are sweet: try some fresh-squeezed carrot juice, and you'll see. Part of our flavor perception is lost when our taste buds are overexposed to unnatural refined sugar.

Is there anything that tastes good that is all right to eat? Certainly – but make different (better) choices. Eat all the fruit and berries you want. What could taste better than a juicy piece of ripe fruit? Enjoy nuts – almonds, cashews, pine nuts, walnuts, pecans, hazelnuts, and Brazil nuts all contain healthy minerals. Dark chocolate with at least 70 percent cocoa is also great. You can make terrific ice cream with banana, avocado, and frozen or unsweetened raspberries in a mixer, or with whipping cream and crushed berries or fruit in an ice cream machine. Bake delicious berry or fruit pies using whole-grain flour or old-fashioned rolled oats in the dough; try meringue topping. Browse through new cookbooks, use your imagination, and discover a new way to eat!

Health Foods versus Sick Foods

Every fourth person in North America today suffers from degenerative diseases. Had they all suffered from one and the same illness, every effort would be made to find the cause. But with symptoms varying from hyperactivity and learning problems in children to diabetes and inflammatory bowel disease in adults and arthritis in the elderly, the common denominator can be difficult to pinpoint.

The past decade has seen growing recognition of the role played by food in the development of disease. Inappropriate eating habits are considered to be the underlying cause of over half of all types of cancer, as well as most cardiovascular, neurological, and gastrointestinal diseases. Just as people have long discussed "health food" we can now talk about "sick food," meaning food that unquestionably leads to degeneration, the development of disease, and premature death.

In the movie "La Grande Bouffe" a group of men form a pact to eat themselves to death. A cynic might say that is exactly what we are doing – only it takes longer.

Modern grocery stores are lined with shelf after shelf of colorful cans, cartons, and packages. Is it any wonder that the Rausing family, which discovered a clever method of packaging foods, has become one of the richest in the world? The food is processed, modified, flavored, and packaged – but what is actually left? Does it help us feel more alive: does it give us the energy we need?

In his international bestseller *Fast Food Nation*, journalist Eric Schlosser describes the industrialization of our food and its enormous effect on society during the past few decades. The book penetrates behind the cheerful, well-polished façade of the US fast food industry to reveal what lurks there, where maximizing profit is the main objective. The world's first fast food restaurant, McDonald's, opened in 1948 in San Bernadino, California. It introduced the innovative concept of producing food by applying the same assembly-line principles found in the automotive industry. The first hamburger restaurants were located at the edge of the community where land was cheap, and as cars became more common, McDonald's conquered the country and the world with a new lifestyle. This lifestyle has also completely transformed the food handling process into large-scale industrial production. Before the Chicken McNugget was introduced in 1983, most chickens were sold whole. Today, 90 percent of chickens in US supermarkets are sold in parts; a large portion is fried in vegetable oil, which contains unhealthy hydrogenated fats or trans fats – one of the greatest risk factors for cardiovascular disease.

Food processing is the largest manufacturing sector in the US economy. Over 90 percent of grain products are processed and around 40 percent of milk, fruits, and vegetables are processed. You can no longer trust your senses when evaluating food, thanks to the processing and flavorings used in the food industry. Beef flavoring, for example, is added to chicken burgers. Traditionally, good tasting food has always guaranteed good nutritional content. Unfortunately, this is no longer the case, now that food is so easy to manipulate.

The food industry sees food as a source of raw materials from which substances can be developed and combined in a way that convinces the consumer to buy their particular (artificial) product. Food is no longer nourishment – it is diversion, entertainment, and emotional comfort. You eat and drink to look young and sexy for the moment. A constant parade of new products appears to tantalize our taste buds. Tens of thousands of new products are launched in the United States each year, whereas in the 1920s, only a few hundred appeared on the market every year. The past thirty to forty years have seen a radical change in our eating habits, probably because the type of foods available has changed.

But when over 60 percent of children's dietary habits are adopted from TV and 78 percent of toddlers influence their parents' food purchases, you might wonder who is really in control of our eating habits. The food processing market is highly concentrated; the fifty largest food manufacturers account for more than half of food manufacturing value – with no guarantee for variety or quality.

Eating habits in the United States – Changes in consumption from 1965 to 1997 (a selection)

- Use of shortening, salad, and cooking oil has doubled.
- Rye flour consumption is down by over 50 percent while wheat flour increased almost 40 percent.
- Breakfast cereals have almost doubled.
- Use of whipping cream has quadrupled.
- Cheese consumption has doubled.
- Poultry consumption doubled, while red meat and eggs decreased by one fifth.
- Fish consumption increased by one third.
- Vegetable consumption (fresh and frozen) has increased 25 percent.
- Carbonated soft drink consumption has doubled.
- Consumption of fruit juices has more than doubled.
- Coffee drinking is down 25 percent.
- Consumption of sugars and sweeteners increased 30 percent (to 3 lb per person per week).
- Money spent on candy and soft drinks increased approximately 35 percent.

Source. United States Department of Agriculture (USDA)
and Food and Agriculture Organization of the United Nations (FAO)

The food industry is clearly profit-driven, but its philosophy is not defensible in the long run. The high level of food processing doesn't benefit the environment or our health. Half of our energy supply comes from fast (empty) carbohydrates: around 20 percent from soft drinks, candy, ice cream, and sugar; a few percent from alcohol, and the rest from refined white flour in the form of bread, cookies, and other baked goods. Is it any wonder that we are putting on weight and that swelling ranks of people suffer from degenerative diseases? Inadequate nutrition weakens our bodies and cheats our children of a healthy start in life.

Why isn't modern, processed food good for us? Dr. Boyd Eaton, from Emory University in Atlanta, says it is reasonable to assume that we are metabolically adapted to those food habits we developed throughout our evolution. Eaton is also a medical anthropologist and a leading expert on evolutionary nutrition. He believes that 99 percent of our genetic inheritance predates the emergence of Homo sapiens, and 99.99 percent of the genes were formed before the development of agriculture some ten thousand years ago. Seen from a different perspective, we were hunters and gatherers for 100,000 generations. Only the last five hundred generations have subsisted on agriculture, while the last ten generations have lived since the industrial revolution. But only two to three generations have grown up with processed, industrially-produced food. Our human genes, formed over millions of years of evolution, do not thrive on the modern diet. This diet is quite unlike that of our ancestors, with an overabundance of dairy products, refined fat and sugar, cereal products, and alcohol. This burdens both the body and the immune system in numerous ways, paving the way for disease. You can't fool your genes!

Studies of primitive cultures that do not eat refined food have confirmed this. Dr. Staffan Lindeberg at Lund University studied the people living on the island of Kitava near New Guinea, who did not have any so-called lifestyle diseases. He attributed the fact that they hardly ever suffered heart attacks or strokes—even though over 80 percent smoke daily—to their dietary habits. The islanders ate mostly yams, fish, fruit, potatoes, and coconuts. They were slim, with a body mass index of about eighteen to twenty (body mass index, or BMI, is calculated by dividing weight in kilograms by height in meters squared). Their weight showed a linear decrease from the age of about twenty to thirty, unlike people in the developed world. If men and women in their fifties had the same BMI as the people of Kitava, they would weigh about 35–40 lb less!

The results in Lindeberg's study are quite consistent with other studies of health in traditional cultures where nutrition is unaffected by western diet. This does not depend on genes, however, since primitive people who begin eating the modern diet are more likely to get diabetes and cardiovascular disease than northern Europeans are. As one geneticist put it, changing our diet so that it suits our genes would be a much more efficient way of eliminating cancer, arthritis, diabetes, obesity, cardiovascular disease, and other chronic diseases than using sophisticated gene therapy.

Eat Like Stone Age Man

You can eat as much as you like – as long as you eat the right food! Stone Age people had a far more varied diet than we have today. Fruit, nuts, legumes, and vegetables accounted for 65 percent of their calorie intake and gave them 100 grams of fiber every day – five times the current recommended minimum level. Their diet included such large quantities of vitamins, minerals, and antioxidants that today we can only get as much by taking diet supplements. Modern research has shown that people who eat plenty of fruit and vegetables have a much lower incidence of degenerative and chronic disease.

During the Stone Age, 35 percent of calories were in the form of protein – which is two times more than is currently recommended. Their protein came from low-fat fish, game, nuts, and plants. Today skinless chicken and some fish are equivalent low-fat sources of protein, while beef from cattle raised mostly on grains has high levels of fat. We would also improve our health by eating more fatty fish such as salmon, sardines, herring, and mackerel, which contain high levels of beneficial omega-3-fatty acids.

Nuts and legumes are a good source of high-class vegetable protein and were plentiful in the Stone Age diet. The fat content of nuts has given them an undeserved bad reputation, but they are one of the original foods. Their fats are well-adapted to our genes, though canned salted nuts and beans should be avoided. Peanuts may also induce allergies because of aflatoxins (poison produced by molds).

A full 65 percent of our energy intake consists instead of "new" food – grain, milk, sugar, sweetener, alcohol, and processed fats. Grain and bread are "only" 10,000 years old, and are less harmful if you eat them in the form of whole-grain products. But bread and pasta are often made from white flour, which are filling but do not provide adequate nourishment. Moreover, some people are allergic to wheat (gluten), and there is also some correlation with headaches, depression, and digestive problems (see section on candida, p. 153–156). Cavemen did not drink milk either, since animals were not yet domesticated. Dairy products can harm body functions by introducing too much saturated fats as well as proteins that are incompatible with our own (like casein).

Yet we live longer than the cavemen. They died of infections, injuries, and complications at birth that are readily handled by modern medicine. Today's killer is food, according to Boyd Eaton.

Doctors Barry Sears and Robert C. Atkins, as well as French expert Michel Montignac, advocate "Stone Age food" like this in their widely popular books. We should eat food that contains slow carbohydrates, with a low glycemic index. The glycemic index–or GI for short–measures the level to which blood sugar rises during a set period of time. A scale has been established with white bread rated at 100, potatoes at 85, bananas at 75, pasta at 50, whole-grain pasta at 40, and beans at 25. Fructose is sweeter than sugar but has a low GI (20) and therefore makes a good healthy sweetener in moderate amounts (as the liver is affected). Food with a low GI is best: slow carbohydrates such as beans, fresh fruit, lentils, and whole-grain pasta. Blood sugar will rise more slowly, and last longer than with fast carbohydrates. This gives us more energy and helps people stay focused longer. Many migraine and PMS sufferers also respond well to this type of diet.

If you have eaten food with very fast carbohydrates (which most food has today) for a long time, you will need to go on a diet to allow your pancreas and digestive system to recover. In the first phase, avoid all white bread, white rice, sugar, candy, coffee, and alcohol – in short, all fast carbohydrates and avoid combining them with fat. The second phase is less rigorous, but try to stick to slow carbohydrates. Montignac recommends salads, vegetables, fruit, olive oil, herbs, beans, fish, eggs, meat, and even cheese.

Let food be your medicine and medicine be your food.

Hippocrates

Health and Nutrition

We seem to have forgotten that it is the individual's susceptibility that determines whether illness takes hold, and how it develops. It is a myth that colds, infections, and influenza are only caused by the presence of a virus or bacteria. Will plants grow if you spread seeds on a wooden floor? It isn't the seed that makes the plant, but the combination of seed plus fertile soil. The same is true for bacteria; they won't grow without "soil" – a culture media, or the nutrients in our bodies. Consequently, it is the body's nutritional deficiency that lays the foundation for colds, infections, and disease. If your immune system is substantially impaired, a multitude of microbes may take over your body, but with good nutritional status, your immune system will also be strong. It is also well known that disease and epidemics run rampant in a substandard nutritional and hygienic environment.

Western medicine was revolutionized in the 1860s when chemist Louis Pasteur demonstrated that bacteria transmitted infections. The pathology-based approach took over, and all attention focused on killing intruders – fungi, parasites, and bacteria. The discovery of sulfa and antibiotics in the 1920s and 1930s affirmed and cemented this approach, as interest in reducing susceptibility to illness through diet and large vitamin supplements waned.

The first really significant report published by the medical establishment on health and nutrition came in 1988, when the US Department of Health and Human Services established the importance of food in the development of disease. The report described changes in health among Americans during the previous twenty-five years: "Our leading health problem is no longer infectious disease, or diseases related to malnutrition, but those associated with over-consumption of food and nutritional imbalances." People were encouraged to eat less fat and more fiber. This report was a milestone, reflecting a radically changed attitude to health. But the significance of essential minerals and trace elements was completely overlooked, as was the negative effect of sugar.

In point of fact, the leading US health authority was already forty years out of date. Weston Price, a Canadian dentist and pioneer in nutrition medicine, published *Nutrition and Physical Degeneration* in 1938. He studied the dental and skeletal structure of people who ate different types of diet in over fourteen cultures, ranging from the islands of the South Pacific to Africa, Switzerland, and the Scottish Hebrides. The incidence of tooth decay increased from an average of 0.5 to 32 percent when people shifted from traditional food to a "modern" diet. Worst affected were Australian aborigines, who went from having no caries at all to cavities in 70 percent of their teeth. Price also studied general physical and mental health. Even in this area he observed a deterioration when people began eating modern processed food.

There seems to be an unwritten forty-year rule about communicating scientific medical discoveries to the general public. On countless occasions, resistance to change and issues of prestige have dogged medical advances. As long ago as 1851, Dr. Ignaz Semmelweis showed that if physicians washed their hands before delivering babies, the mortality rate in childbirth would drop by ten percent. But rather than being congratulated, he was dismissed from his job, ignored, and suffered premature death in a mental hospital. It would take between thirty and fifty years before doctors began to accept handwashing as routine. In 1753 Sir James Lind proved that citrus fruits cured scurvy (caused by vitamin C deficiency). Yet one hundred thousand sailors were to die from scurvy before the British navy started provisioning ships with citrus fruits in 1795. In 1955, Dr. Abram Hoffer showed that high doses of vitamin B_3 (niacin) lower cholesterol, yet it took forty years before his findings were accepted and used as a leading anti-cholesterol drug. Two-time Nobel Prize winner Linus Pauling long recommended providing optimal nutrition to treat mentally ill patients – but psychiatrists did not listen. (Pauling is best known for having recommended large daily doses of Vitamin C, an antioxidant, to prevent colds and disease.)

Why does it take so long for health and medical care authorities to adopt and publicize scientific findings? Could it be that a generation shift is needed for new knowledge to be accepted and established? It would seem that the most educated people are the most conservative and afraid to change.

Pasteur was far ahead of his – and our – time when, toward the end of his life, he summarized his view of the origin of disease. He noted that the physical condition of the person with an infection was often crucial to the infection process. But he also believed that the patient's mental state could affect the course of many diseases. Pasteur concluded that successful treatment often depended on the physician's ability to restore physiological conditions that promote natural resistance. What the father of bacteriology, Pasteur, stated over a century ago is something that modern medicine has lost sight of in its battle against disease and epidemics.

> *Age-related diseases are not caused by age –*
> *they are caused by an inappropriate way of life.*
> H. Tilden, physician and author

Lifestyle Creates Health

Our lifestyle is defined by factors such as what we eat; how we live, exercise, and manage stress; and our close relationships with other people. These are all factors that reinforce health and that we can influence. This is especially pertinent considering that the biggest threat to health today is premature aging. Signs of this include chronic pain, lack of energy, and a fatigue that will not disappear no matter how much we rest. We can counteract and prevent these processes through lifestyle choices.

A plethora of books and reports studying fitness and well-being have been published in recent years in an effort to examine the concept of health. Diet is one of the most important factors. The China Project is the first major study in the history of medicine to explore the relationship between diet and disease. The main conclusion is simple. The most suitable diet for promoting health consists primarily of a variety of high-quality vegetables. They should be prepared as little as possible and contain a minimum of fat, salt, sugar, and processed carbohydrates. The survey indicates that this diet can prevent the majority (80–90 percent) of all forms of cancer, cardiovascular disease, and other degenerative diseases associated with premature aging. Based on these findings, a group of U.S. researchers have proposed a national action program to combat the cancer epidemic in the western world.

Although supported by the American Institute for Cancer Research and the World Cancer Research Fund, this trailblazing project was negatively received.

"Despite sixty-six years of solid research, the medical establishment now feels that I–to put it mildly–am controversial," says Colin Campbell, professor of Nutritional Biochemistry at Cornell University, and head of the Cornell-Oxford-Beijing study.

Perhaps this is because the study challenges the foundation of the current drug-based approach to medicine. Yet it is no wonder that we become ill and age prematurely when over half the energy intake in our western diet consists of fat and sugar.

The Chinese have long understood the significance of diet for health. Their doctors developed and refined methods of preventing and treating disease that not only included diet but were actually based on the choice of food and herbs.

Cancer is caused by a number of factors, but it is definitely linked to the body's aging process. A ten-year study of the dietary habits of 500,000 Europeans and the incidence of cancer clearly shows that fish, fruit, chicken, and vegetables can protect against various types of cancer. Men who often eat fish have a lower probability of developing prostate cancer, the most common form of cancer in men.

But what if we reversed the reasoning? We seek the cure for serious diseases – when what we really should do is eat a pure, organically grown and unprocessed diet consisting of fish, fruit, berries, vegetables, and, if desired, low-fat meat. Otherwise, we will get cancer, diabetes, and a number of other lifestyle diseases. Throughout the evolutionary process, humankind has developed with a certain type of food. Since our genes have hardly changed since the Stone Age, quite simply we need to eat a diet that agrees with our genes.

Even cardiovascular disease can be reversed through lifestyle changes. Dr. Dean Ornish at the University of California, San Francisco, has shown that a combination of dietary changes, exercise, and support groups resulted in 80 percent of patients healing to a point where they did not require angioplasty or bypass surgery. This saves both human suffering and vast sums of money; if a drug were to achieve the same results it would be headline news. This is particularly thought-provoking, considering that in 2002 cardiovascular disease became the leading cause of death in the world. Many insurance companies therefore support such efforts now offered in hospitals across the United States.

Even after years of abuse, it's never too late to change your lifestyle and significantly improve your health. The body has an amazing ability to repair itself and by acquiring good habits you can actually rejuvenate it. In terms of aerobic capacity, six months of moderate and steadily increasing exercise can reverse the damage of thirty years of aging. Women who start exercising in their forties and walk briskly for thirty minutes a day, four times a week, soon have the same low risk of myocardial infarction as if they had been exercising all their lives. When you eat more fruit, fiber, and vegetables, the blood's sensitivity to insulin changes within two weeks, reducing the risk of diabetes almost immediately. Women who eat as little as 250 g of fish a week halve the risk of myocardial infarction. Even ninety year olds experience pronounced improvement through exercise and dietary change. We may believe that it is only natural to exercise less as we grow older, but actually, older people who exercise also live longer. For every percent of added muscle mass, we can add eighteen months to our lives. Regular exercise is paramount for good health.

Our biological age does not at all have to be the same as our chronological age. Your body can be much younger—or older—than the age on your driver's license. Our biological age is heavily influenced by lifestyle and accounts for two thirds of our state of health after we reach our thirties or forties. Thus how we age does not depend on the number of years that we've lived, but rather on how we have lived and our attitude to life. International studies have shown that for people who live beyond the age of 100 and remain healthy, the critical factor is a strong sense of meaning and purpose in life.

The same modalities that counter stress also slow biological aging: rest, massage, meditation, and an optimistic outlook. One of the healthiest and most long-lived populations in the world inhabits the Japanese island of Okinawa. It has been studied for 25 years. Of course the results point to the significance of diet, but most intriguing is the islanders' relaxed lifestyle and strong sense of cohesion, where people care about and take care of each other. Perhaps this is something for us in the West, as we continue to set new sales records for medications that treat anxiety and depression.

Lifestyle is thus paramount to good health. Depending on which professor or nutritional expert you speak to, lifestyle accounts for 65–99 percent of health. Yet, healthcare authorities devote far too little (essentially nothing) to helping people improve their lifestyle. Behavioral medicine, which studies methods for changing lifestyles, is a rapidly growing field of research in the United States, and its development is fueled by the public and the media. Lifestyle change is a rapidly expanding field.

What we need is more information and greater awareness of how we can propel our physical condition in the proper direction. The theory is simple: food supplies nutrients for the body's processes, and if we change the food we eat we can stimulate other processes in our bodies, and thereby promote the healing, constructive, reparative, and purifying processes. It is preferable to the slow breakdown of our bodies caused by inappropriate diet and the need to treat the damage with medications.

Vital Enzymes

Enzymes are now being used in everything from diet supplements to exclusive skin lotions, and you can buy fresh-pressed green wheatgrass juice–packed with living enzymes–from your take-out counter. Enzyme supplements speed up the self-healing process; build up your strength and help you achieve top performance.

Enzymes are small proteins that are essential for digestion, metabolism, and immunity. They act as catalysts, accelerating the cell's reactions and improve energy production without being consumed themselves. Magnesium activates over one hundred enzymes that help nerves and muscles to function, while zinc stimulates over two hundred enzymes necessary for digestion, metabolism, fertility, and healing wounds.

Although the pancreas produces its own digestive enzymes, we also need enzymes found naturally. However, these enzymes from natural sources are heat-sensitive and become inoperative when food is heated or processed. As a result, modern processed food contains fewer and fewer vital enzymes. Enzyme deficiency causes poor digestion and nutrients absorption; with insufficient enzymes, the load of toxins in the body increases and protection against infections and chronic disease decreases.

Symptoms of enzyme deficiency include abdominal gas and cramps, fatigue after eating, food allergies, and heartburn – all extremely common conditions in today's world.

There are almost three thousand different enzymes and they have wide-ranging effects. The most important digestive enzymes are the amylases, lipases, and proteases, which break down starch, fat, and protein respectively. Enzyme therapy is a powerful new treatment method that strengthens digestion and immunity, and "cleanses" blood vessels. It reduces pain, cramps, swelling, and inflammation, and increases blood flow.

"The great advantage is that these are natural drugs with absolutely no adverse effects and this form of therapy has been proven to be effective," says Peter Wilhelmsson, naturopath and nutritionist at the Functional Medicine Clinic in Falun, Sweden.

The therapeutic effect of various enzyme combinations has been demonstrated in several double blind studies.

- Enzymes can kill viruses and break down the bacteria's cell walls.
- Proteolytic enzymes reduce swelling and inflammation, which could help patients with rheumatoid arthritis.
- Enzymes also help reduce body weight and accelerate healing of sports injuries.

Enzyme production in the pancreas depends on hydrochloric acid production in the stomach, which deteriorates with age. Because people produce half as much hydrochloric acid when they are sixty as they do at twenty, many would benefit from a hydrochloric acid supplement. However, this is not true of people with type O blood, who often produce large amounts of hydrochloric acid and might actually run the risk of developing peptic ulcers if they were to increase their levels.

Modern life takes its toll. Stress, too much "dead" and enzyme-deficient food, and a deficiency of hydrochloric acid all have a negative effect on body function. In major studies, cats fed only on cooked meat and pasteurized milk have been shown to suffer from allergies, arthritis, eczema, fur problems, and impaired fertility. Increasing the amount of raw food in our diet–the basis of the "Living food" movement–and taking enzyme supplements are good for us. Many proponents of alternative medicine also claim that enzyme supplements prevent or help to combat cancer and cure various chronic diseases. Enzymes and hydrochloric acid tablets, which are available in health food stores, should be taken together with meals. We can act to help our bodies function better. Enzyme therapy–from pineapples, wheatgrass juice, sauerkraut, fresh ground beef, or diet supplements–is an exciting health trend that is here to stay.

The Food of the Future

In his book *Eat, Drink, and Be Healthy*, Professor Walter C. Willett, a nutrition expert from Harvard Medical School, points out the fallacies in our food pyramid, which was not developed by a healthcare authority, but by the USDA – which has an interest in promoting grain and dairy product consumption. Dr. Willetts states that our diet should consist mainly of vegetables and non-processed foods. He recommends a brand new food pyramid based on extensive research, giving clear examples of how it can serve as a foundation for preventing disease and generating lasting health.

There are many advantages to be had from eating greens. Plants and plankton contain "phytonutrients" which are important for the body. Phyto comes from Greek and means plant. Healthy phytonutrients are contained in certain plants where they serve an important biological function. As our knowledge on the subject grows, this promises to occupy an important place in the concept of health.

Phytohormones, "hormone-like" molecules found in certain herbs, are so similar to our own hormones that the body is able to make use of them to help maintain health and vitality. These are becoming increasingly popular as a focus of medical research. So far about 5000 herbs and plants in our diet have been identified as having a hormonal effect.

One such plant is the soybean. The active substances are called isoflavones and they stimulate progesterone and hormones in the estrogen group. The fertilized egg needs progesterone to attach itself to the endometrium to avoid being rejected. Isoflavones are also the precursors for several other hormones needed to keep important body functions in balance. The Japanese eat soy in large quantities and have almost no breast cancer. Their language does not even have a word for hot flashes, associated with female menopause in western society.

Wild yams have a strong effect on progesterone and thereby have a secondary effect on estrogen. The active substance is called diosgenin. People on the Trobriand Islands in Polynesia eat a diet with an abundance of yams and though it is known that the women there are highly sexually active, which is culturally accepted, they do not suffer any sexually transmitted diseases. Eating a diet containing plenty of fruit and vegetables (preferably raised organically) is the basis of good hormonal balance. A high-fiber diet also counteracts the harmful effects of sugar.

Food not only serves as nourishment but also as a source of pleasure and stimulation. Every now and then, take your time over your meal. Light the candles, put flowers on the table, and arrange the food attractively with colorful vegetables. In some countries people even garnish their food with flowers. Admire the food on the plate. Taste it thoroughly on the first bite, and let your entire body experience the taste and smell. Chew your food thoroughly and don't wash it down with drink. Digestion is facilitated by a good flow of saliva. For optimal digestion, eat no more than 80 percent of your stomach's capacity. Enjoy the peace and quiet and don't talk the meal to death. Use all your senses to experience and appreciate the food. Feel how the food delivers well-needed energy; then lie down to rest and digest the food. How do you feel afterwards?

Acid-Base Balance

Acidification is a problem not only in nature, but also in people. What does this mean and what can we do to prevent it? Everything we do affects our pH – diet, stress, breathing, and emotional reactions. Using several buffering systems, the body strives to maintain a narrow pH interval and does not tolerate an excess of acids or bases.

When everything works as it should, the body uses oxygen to metabolize food, thereby forming water, carbon dioxide, and waste products. Depending on diet, these waste products may be more or less acidic or alkaline. Food is potentially acid-forming when the substances remaining after the food is metabolized are acidic. Common acids include folic acid, phosphoric acid, and sulfuric acid. If the remaining products are alkaline, the food is "base-forming," and common bases are calcium, magnesium, sodium, and potassium.

The rule of thumb is that fruit and vegetables give an alkaline reaction while all other foods give an acidic reaction. About 75 percent of the food we eat should be base-forming and 25 percent acid-forming. Acid-forming foods include beans, fish, meat, eggs, pasta, rolled oats, coffee, cocoa, ketchup, pepper, mustard, sugar, and asparagus. Base-forming foods include corn, lemons, grapefruit, fresh fruit in general, raisins, avocado, leafy vegetables, and especially raw vegetables. Raw fruit becomes acid-forming when sugar is added, as does other food to which sugar is added. Alcohol, medications, tobacco, and vinegar are also acid-forming. Eating alkaline food when under stress, however, can cause acid-forming substances to be produced.

During the body's natural processes–breathing, heartbeat, and muscular activity–acids are constantly formed and released into the blood. Stress, heavy exercise, and emotions such as fear, anger, and anxiety also produce acids. Each acid that enters the body as food must be neutralized using alkaline substances in the body, especially the calcium stored in bones, joints, and blood vessels. A constant surplus of acid produced by eating foods such as sugar, soft drinks, and hamburgers, can lead to decalcification of the skeleton over time. The acid-base balance is affected by genes, diet, stress, and digestion, but also by the weather. Cold weather makes the blood more acidic, whereas warmth makes it more alkaline.

During illness we almost always have a surplus of acid (acidosis), which means varying degrees of acidification. Symptoms of excess acid include edema, abnormally low blood pressure, insomnia, inflamed joints, hard and foul-smelling stools, difficulty swallowing, and tooth sensitivity to vinegar and acidic fruit. Acidification is caused by the impaired working of the liver, kidneys, or the adrenal glands, which in turn may be caused by inappropriate diet, obesity, or malnutrition. You can get an approximate measurement of your pH using litmus paper, preferably before a meal or at least one hour afterwards.

Saliva should be between pH 6.6 and 7.2, while urine is more acidic and should be about pH 6.4–6.8. The results may be affected, however, by your most recent meal and you should take a number of measurements at different times.

Eating plenty of vegetables and fruit can reset the acid-base balance. Concentrated green "super food" such as alfalfa, barley grass, or algae help the body become more alkaline. Drink plenty of mineral-rich water and take agents that contain bicarbonate as an effective way to add alkaline substances. Improving digestion is also important; poor digestion will make you acidic – even with a base-forming diet.

While there are many advantages to eating plenty of fruit and vegetables, there is a risk of nutritional deficiency if you follow a strictly vegetarian diet. Cultivated food may contain fewer minerals that before because of soil depletion – figures show a 25 percent reduction of calcium, magnesium, and trace elements over the past thirty years. Mineral deficiency is also a risk because vegetarian food is rich in phytins (found in beans, legumes, and grain), which bind to zinc, calcium, and other minerals and transport them out of the body. Zinc deficiency, which is not uncommon among vegetarians, results in a compromised immune system and increased susceptibility to infections.

Absorbing nutrients from plants is also more difficult. If legumes are not cooked long enough the trypsin inhibitors will not permit the protein to be broken down sufficiently to allow absorption. Methionine deficiency may result, which can impair the body's detoxification system. Also, be sure to get sufficient protein to get the full spectrum of amino acids. Understanding the theory behind vegetarianism is essential for an adequate diet.

Balancing Food

Tibetan medicine is rooted in millennia-old traditions and is said to have evolved from the science developed at the universities of northern India over several centuries. In its current form, however, it dates back to the eighth century. It is strongly influenced by Buddhism, with its profoundly conceived philosophy of health. According to this thinking, diet is of central importance to health. An unbalanced diet can block the channels through which life energy flows. Blocking small channels causes only small health problems, while blocking large vital channels–such as blood vessels or intestines–may have serious health consequences. A moderate balanced diet tailored to the individual is therefore recommended. In principle, healthy people should be able to eat most foods, in moderation. But in an unhealthy state, diet and lifestyle must be corrected according to the type of person.

Tibetan medicine divides people into three "humors": wind, bile, and phlegm. Wind is light and dry, bile is hot, and phlegm is chilly, viscous, and heavy. Even if your metabolism matches the wind group, the other two must also be balanced in order to achieve health. This classification also serves as the basis of the Indian ayurvedic art of medicine, which also divides people into three groups: *vata, pitta,* and *kapha.* For more information about this subject, contact an Ayurvedic health counselor or read books such as Deepak Chopra's *Perfect Health.*

The macrobiotic diet originated thousands of years ago from Far Eastern philosophy. Based on the principles of yin and yang, the expanding and contracting forces of the universe, the word "macrobiotics" was first used by Goethe's family doctor and comes from the Greek, in which *macro* means big and *bios* means life: big life. It is a balanced approach to food – the diet is not only a taste sensation, but it is intended to fortify health and prevent illness.

Macrobiotic food usually consists of grains, fish, fruit, berries, algae, legumes, and vegetables, while sugar and chemical additives are avoided. Fresh seasonal ingredients are preferred in order to avoid altering the nutrients by freezing or canning them. Great care is exercised with food preparation, and priority is given to raw fruits and vegetables. At the same time the food should be adapted to the individual's age, job, sex, climate, and situation. The macrobiotic approach is as much a philosophy of life as a diet, with consideration being given to the development, environment, and individual needs of humankind.

Sugar and other sweeteners, strong spices, dairy products, coffee, alcohol, and tropical fruits are examples of foods and beverages that are considered to be extremely *yin.* At the other end of the spectrum are salt, aged cheese, game, meat, eggs, and poultry, which are extremely yang. In the middle are the balancing foods – leafy and root vegetables, legumes, seaweed, and nuts. Fruit and oils have more yin charac-

According to Tibetan medicine the body is composed of these seven components

1. *Nutrients.* The nutritional quality of food is the core. The body is built–and maintains health–thanks to this core, and it is important to have good (100 percent) absorption.
2. *Blood.* Supports life, and is necessary for all life processes. Maintains communication between structure and function (the body and its activities).
3. *Meat.* Represents growth and formation of the body.
4. *Fat.* Maintains the body's tone (physical fitness) and acts as a lubricant.
5. *Bone.* The body's solid base.
6. *Bone marrow.* Necessary for body strength.
7. *Regenerative fluids.* Facilitate reproduction and new life.

ter, while rye, rice, corn, and wheat are more *yang*. The goal is either to eat balanced foods, or to create a balance between *yin* and *yang*. That's why a schnapps (extremely *yin*) goes so well with salted herring (extremely *yang*)!

Food as an Emotional Shock Absorber

Food is an emotionally charged subject that can be even more personal and difficult to talk about than sex. Unusual eating habits may be perceived as deviant behavior, and provoke strong reactions. Being vegetarian is now relatively acceptable, but when I stopped eating sugar in 1994 I could never have imagined how provocative people would find my decision. Turning down a sweet desert is viewed as being almost akin to renouncing motherhood and apple pie.

Why is food such an emotionally charged subject? Because ever since we nursed at mother's breast, food and eating have been intimately linked with deep emotions. Many adults today were brought up under a system which believed that infants should be fed every four hours and should conform to a standard growth chart norm. As recently as the 1990s, some medical textbooks advised the mother to block the baby's nose to interrupt nursing at the appointed time. Indeed an entire generation of children was trained to deny their need for food. Children were left crying of hunger in their cribs rather than deviating from the schedule. This seems strange to us now, as it is now recognized that children have individual needs and should be treated accordingly. Undoubtedly, many adults still suffer from this today – though the cause is long forgotten.

In one case, the parents were so unsure of their oldest daughter's needs that they gave her a bottle every time she cried. She grew rather chubby. When daughter number two arrived, the parents did not want to repeat their mistake and instead allowed her to cry. When they grew up, the first child had constant problems with obesity while the second was always extremely thin. Quite simply, she "forgot" to eat at regular intervals, while her older sister could never keep food in the house – because she ate everything in sight! Her response to emotions was a compulsion to eat. Not until these sisters processed their emotions in body-oriented psychotherapy could they disentangle themselves from the eating habits they had learned.

Unfortunately we don't just eat to satisfy physical hunger: we often have to contend with an emotional hunger too. Do we eat to console ourselves, to fill a hole, or to repress emotions that we do not wish to recognize? The subconscious motivations are many, and the chips, candy, and soft drinks industries all profit from this –while we besiege our bodies with empty calories. The sweet taste seduces, providing momentary pleasure – while a new need for more is insidiously conceived.

Even for people who know they are eating incorrectly, it isn't so easy to change habits. Researchers estimate that it takes eight weeks to break physiological dependency. It is far easier to contend with psychological dependency.

You should therefore be very particular about the foods to which you allow yourself to become accustomed. There is much to be gained from taking a long hard look at habits before you become too attached to them.

You are what you eat. How are you today? Abandoned, respected, punished, or loved? In other words, the food you give yourself says something about how you treat yourself. Stop and think about your emotional relationship with food. Do you skip lunch when you haven't worked or studied enough? Do you reward yourself later with a chocolate bar in the afternoon? Do you want to sink your teeth into a thick juicy steak when you're really angry? Do you ever feel so restless that you could eat a whole bag of cheese doodles or peanuts just to calm down? Is it hard to stop drinking alcohol or eating on the weekend when you relax after a stressful week's work?

Live 120 Years

We age because we "rust and boil." Oxidation makes the cells rust and glucose makes some of our tissues look like roast meat (through the process of glycosylation of proteins). We also become moody because of oxidation of fatty acids (lipids) in the cell membrane. Therefore a diet rich in antioxidants is important to prevent free radicals from attacking. Bruce Ames, an expert on free radicals and antioxidants, believes that this century will bring a substantial increase in life expectancy. It will become increasingly common for people to live beyond the age of a hundred.

According to Professor Roy Walford from the UCLA School of Medicine and one of the leading US experts on aging, maximum life expectancy is a full 120 years. But achieving this requires a balanced, nutritious diet and reduced caloric intake. Walford was in charge of food during the Biosphere project, when he lived together with seven others in a closed ecological system in the Arizona desert for two years. The food may have been a bit monotonous, but it was nutritionally balanced. All the participants lost weight, their blood lipids and glucose levels decreased, and their blood pressure fell. Walford maintains that eating food with a high-quality nutritional content and reducing calorie intake by 20 percent will allow us to function as 60 year olds at the age of 100 – internally and externally. He set out his fascinating results alongside some appealing recipes for future 120-year olds in the book *The Anti-Aging Plan*.

You may wonder why anyone would want to live so long. The important thing is to maintain vitality for as long as you live, so that you can enjoy life to the full. You don't have to go to extremes to enjoy a healthy lifestyle and achieve vitality of both mind and body. The longer you live, the more experience you acquire and the wiser you become.

> *Living ascetically or unilaterally*
> *is good for self-discipline,*
> *but only a well-nourished spirit*
> *is capable of wisdom.*
> Buddha

Food for better health – the essentials

- Food should have high-quality nutritional content (high nutrient value per calorie). This means avoiding empty calories found in foods such as chips, candy, sugar and sugar products, products with white flour, etc.

- Try to avoid toxins and foods that cause allergies or negative reactions; these foods burden the body's detoxification system, thereby stealing large amounts of energy.

- Eat mainly slow carbohydrates, such as beans, brown rice, muesli, whole-grain products, and whole-grain pasta, which also provide essential fiber.

- Your meals should consist mainly of roots, vegetables, and various types of greens. Eat plenty of raw and grated vegetables, including roots, every day. Steam or stir-fry vegetables if they must be heated.

- Try to avoid industrially produced food, including convenience foods. We derive the most benefit from foods that are natural and unprocessed.

- Eat all the fruit you want when it's in season, as long as you tolerate it well. Ripe fruit is preferable. Most people feel best if fruit is consumed at least half an hour before meals or three hours afterwards.

- Include high-quality protein in your diet every day (beans, nuts, fish, lentils, and tofu). Reduce your intake of animal protein and try to eat meat from wild game or naturally-raised, antibiotic-free animals, and organic eggs from free-range chickens.

- Make sure you meet your daily fatty acid requirements from consuming unprocessed fats such as olive oil, canola oil, and flaxseed oil. One tablespoon of olive oil and one teaspoon of flaxseed oil (cold-pressed) daily are recommended.

- Avoid food with trans fatty acids (margarine, vegetable cooking fat, and hydrogenated oils as well as many vegetable oils) and saturated fats (animal fat, coconut butter, etc.). You can use butter for frying.

- Season food with garlic, ginger, and herbs.

- Drink half a gallon of water a day, though not during meals.

- Reduce your intake of coffee. Drink decaffeinated coffee, and plenty of green tea.

- Try to buy locally grown, organic food and eat according to the seasons.

5.
Intestinal Flora and Fauna

The intestinal tract is the body's living fermentation vat and contains about two pounds of bacteria. Usually the bacteria that make up our intestinal flora exist in a mutual relationship (symbiosis) with us and produce substances required for good health. The kind of food we eat has an effect on the quantity of nutrients we obtain and on the composition of the intestinal flora. But it is of key importance whether these nutrients are absorbed, for you are not just what you eat – but more so, what you absorb. Stress, worry, and antibiotics wipe out the normal flora, with a profound effect on nutrient absorption. Eating "functional foods" can positively influence our health by favoring or stimulating beneficial intestinal bacteria, or by adding substances required for a healthy body.

We live in constant close contact with billions of bacteria found on our skin, in our mouths, noses, genitals, and intestines. These bacteria are a necessary part of our environment. Bacteria are made up of a cell surrounded by a cell wall. They reproduce through cell division, and their numbers can be doubled in just fifteen minutes. Unicellular yeasts (fungi), which are much larger than bacteria, also colonize our bodies. A change in the environment of the bacteria and fungi may lead to more harmful forms of bacteria taking over, and the yeasts may become more aggressive. Fungal infections can cause problems of the skin, mucous membranes, genitals, and digestive tract. We have to make sure we cultivate the right "pet bacteria" in our systems.

The intestinal bacterial flora is a crucial link in the production and conversion of hormones, vitamins, and other nutrients. Bacteria in the small intestine produce the essential vitamin B_{12}, while vitamin K, needed for the coagulation of blood, is formed in the large intestine. Bacteria compete with one another for nutrients and niche. During the course of evolution the bacteria in the body have adapted to humans and their dietary habits. It is thanks to our bacterial flora that the growth of new undesired guests–harmful bacteria–is inhibited.

A sound gastrointestinal (GI) system is the basis of good health. Today we have partial knowledge of how bacteria affect digestion, but much remains to be learned before we fully understand this complicated and hidden activity.

Digestion

After food is chewed and swallowed it enters the stomach, where some mechanical processing takes place. At the same time, enzymes and hydrochloric acid begin to break down the food's components. But this stomach activity merely serves to prepare for the actual digestion process and the absorption of nutrients, which will take place in the small and large intestines.

The upper part of the small intestine is called the duodenum, and into it empties a duct coming from the pancreas and gall bladder. The acidic contents of the stomach are neutralized here through the action of carbonates originating from the pancreas. The duct is also the source of the enzymes that metabolize fat, starch, and protein. A total of 0.5 to 2 liters of pancreatic juice is secreted daily, which together with fat-soluble bile salts breaks food down into molecules small enough to be absorbed through the intestinal wall. Calcium is absorbed mainly from the duodenum – the more acidic the pH, the better the absorption. At best, 30 percent of the calcium we consume is absorbed, but a deficiency of gastric acid decreases absorption to as little as 4 percent. Insufficient gastric acid is more common in older people.

The small intestine is about two and a half meters long, but may be two to three times longer when at rest. The strong muscles surrounding the wall of the small intestine push the intestinal contents forward with undulating movements that follow one another at regular intervals of approximately two minutes. Intestinal villi in the walls of the small intestine absorb the food's nutrients and other substances, including any toxins, and transfer these to the blood. Next, the nutrients travel through the liver, a detoxification station and storage site, and then continue throughout the body – to cells in muscles, organs, and other tissues. Each and every cell requires nutrients from our food to keep functioning.

Following a four- to five-hour transit through the small intestine, the contents are portioned out to the large intestine. Here the intestinal contents move more slowly while the intestinal wall absorbs water and salts. The large intestine is just over one meter long, and the journey generally requires about twelve hours. The mucous membrane (intestinal epithelium) is somewhat thicker than that of the small intestine and also lacks intestinal villi. As in the small intestine, the cells of the mucous membrane are constantly renewed. Our health depends on the flourishing bacterial life found in the large intestine since these bacteria form the crucial vitamins B_1, B_2, B_6, and K, and folic acid. But bacteria can also produce waste substances that irritate the intestinal wall and become directly toxic if absorbed by the blood. Depending on what types of bacteria colonize our intestines, their actions may be either helpful or harmful.

The composition of intestinal bacteria is affected by what we eat, which in turn influences how we feel. Thus the digestive system can be viewed as an independent organ that cooperates with the rest of the body. The digestive process within the intestine should not produce unpleasant, foul-smelling fermentation products. When in good health, the intestine empties at least once daily, and stools are not overly hard. Food should pass through the body in twenty to twenty-four hours to prevent over-fermentation or rotting. The more fiber, whole grain, vegetables, and fruit in our diet, the quicker the journey. Meat and fish take longer to pass through the body – up to twice as long if too little fiber and too much fat are consumed.

The Intestinal Ecosystem

A multitude of small bacteria live in our long intestinal tract; at least 100 trillion, which is more than the number of cells in the body. Women have about 1.7 pounds of bacteria in their intestines and men about 2.2 pounds. By comparison, the brain weighs 2.2 pounds.

The intestine may be viewed as an independent organ and ecosystem. The bacteria live and grow depending on the nutrients they receive and their ability to compete for their niche in the ecosystem. The majority of intestinal bacteria (99 percent) cannot survive in the presence of oxygen. Hundreds of different types of bacteria live in the intestinal lumen or the intestinal mucous membrane. Their main source of energy is soluble or insoluble carbohydrates (starch or polysaccharides). The normal flora includes a number of lactobacilli, the most common of which is *Lactobacillus plantarum*. Another common bacteria is *E. coli*, which plays an important role in the intestine, although it creates problems elsewhere. It is a common cause of urinary tract infections. Normal bacterial flora is crucial to health because it prevents disease-inducing bacteria from growing and burdening the body with their toxins.

Intestinal bacteria also play a significant role in hormonal metabolism. Hormones from the thyroid, gonads, and adrenal cortex are excreted from the liver into the gall bladder and transported a short distance into the intestine. There they are absorbed again by the gastrointestinal mucous membrane and transported to the liver. During their passage through the intestines, the hormones can be quantitatively and qualitatively affected by the bacteria, thereby influencing the products that return to the liver. Some of the changed hormones may have an undesired effect on the body. Yet again, this underscores the importance of healthy intestinal flora to good health.

The intestinal wall is about as thin as an eyelid, so there is no great barrier between the contents of the intestines and the surrounding body. Since the intestine is the organ that comes into contact most with foreign substances, the greater part of the immune system is logically also in the abdominal cavity. This area harbors around 80 percent of immune cells, which can be rapidly recruited to neutralize the harmful effects of foreign substances. Further, the abdominal cavity contains a rich network of nerves and blood vessels, and more neurotransmitters are found in the GI tract than in the brain. Some researchers call it "the second brain."

Intestinal leakage permits larger molecules to pass through the intestinal wall and enter the bloodstream. These large molecules tend to mobilize the immune system, since the white blood cells view them as foreign. The risk is especially great when dealing with protein fragments. When digestion functions properly these proteins are broken down into individual amino acids prior to being absorbed through the intestinal wall. But if protein fragments leak out into the blood they can imitate the effect of other substances from the body and cause a change in behavior. They may imitate the endorphins produced by the nervous system to block pain. Because the source of these substances is external they are known as "exorphins." They can affect mood, memory, behavior, and ability to think by interfering with the brain's sensitive system of chemical signals.

It may seem surprising that the intestines and digestive process are so closely linked to the body's immune and nervous systems. But related they are, and if the integrity of one system is destroyed, inevitably the others are also affected. The result will be a spectrum of symptoms from all three systems, including pain, fatigue, inflammation, and abdominal discomfort.

The normal intestinal flora also plays a vital role, teaching the immune system to tolerate harmless substances such as food. It is crucial for the right bacteria to become established in the intestines after birth. Professor Agnes Wold, from Göteborg University, is investigating the role played by intestinal flora in health and illness. A considerable change in the intestinal flora of infants in developed countries has been noted over the past few decades. Dr. Wold believes this is the result of improved hygiene. The environment has become too clean for the common E. coli bacteria, allowing skin bacteria such as staphylococci and clostridia to flourish. Researchers believe that this significant change in children's intestinal flora underlies the steadily increasing incidence of allergies in developed countries.

"Intestinal flora is a fascinating field in which the cause of allergies can be found," says Hans Wigzell, Professor of Immunology and President of Karolinska Institut in Stockholm, Sweden. "Our diet, with more mass-produced, sterilized, and preserved food than ever, has numerous effects on the flora. In certain cases it can actually be harmful."

The change in intestinal flora may also be due to the widespread use of antibiotics. Diarrhea caused by antibiotics is a growing problem in health care. When normal intestinal flora is wiped out, more harmful bacteria may replace them. Chronic diarrhea is the most common cause of death in developing countries. It can result from the common practice of treating acute diarrhea with antibiotics, which further impairs the intestinal ecosystem. Professor Wold's research group is currently experimenting with administering "probiotics" (friendly intestinal bacteria) to Pakistani children with chronic diarrhea. Rather than giving antibiotics, they strengthen the intestinal ecosystem by adding helpful lactobacilli (see Functional Foods, p. 159).

Intestinal Flora and Allergies

You might wonder what we're doing wrong, when humans–who have walked the planet for three million years–have developed such a high incidence of allergies in such a short time span. The environmental and dietary factors that are responsible for allergies serve as a major focus of allergy research. Professor Bengt Björksten, from the Center for Allergy Research at Karolinska Institutet in Stockholm, believes the key lies in dietary changes: the major change in the intestinal flora of children is responsible for the steadily growing incidence of allergies in developed countries. Intestinal flora is essential for normal immunity.

Today we eat a completely different type of diet than our ancestors: frozen and refrigerated foods, sugar, and a wide variety of convenience foods. A new study presented at the European Respiratory Society showed a correlation between the number of McDonald's restaurants and the incidence of allergies in 13 and 14 year olds in the countries studied. Obviously this is not proof of a link, but McDonald's is a symbol of our western lifestyle.

Björksten's group has shown that Estonian children have a different intestinal flora with more lactic acid bacteria than Swedish children. Comparisons have shown that these differences between Estonian and Swedish children are already present when they are only five days old, and as a result different fatty acids are produced. The modern diet contains an overabundance of omega-6 fats compared with omega-3 fats, and researchers believe that this aids in the development of allergies. Asthma is uncommon among the Eskimos, who have a high intake of fish oil (omega-3s). An Australian study found that children who ate a diet containing fatty fish also had a substantially lower risk of asthma.

A major Swedish study of the children of anthroposophists (followers of Rudolf Steiner) showed that half as many of these children had allergies compared with their friends who were the same age, lived in the same place, breathed the same air, and drank the same water. The anthroposophic children ate a vegetarian diet consisting of biodynamically grown food, with plenty of acidic vegetables. These children rarely received antibiotics or vaccinations. Every fifth anthroposophic child was born at home, which seems to have an effect on the intestinal flora that makes it easier for the child to resist allergies. Natural childbirth is also better for the child's immunity than a sterile cesarean section. Those children who grew up with an anthroposophic lifestyle had far more strains of lactic acid bacteria in their intestines than the other children; the more strains of this particular bacteria, the stronger the immunity. Current research shows that expectant mothers who eat lactic acid bacteria can reduce the risk of having a child with allergies by 50 percent. To sum up, lifestyle seems to control the intestinal flora, which in turn influences the development of the immune system.

A Bad Stomach Burdens the Body

Ideally we should live symbiotically with our intestinal bacteria throughout our lives. Yet people have different intestinal flora depending on their age, lifestyle, eating habits, and other factors. Unfortunately in today's world abnormal intestinal flora is all too common, and people suffer the consequences in different ways without knowing why.

A "bad stomach" makes it difficult for your body to absorb nutrients from food. Stressful living conditions and depression may impair the ability to use the vitamins, minerals, trace elements, and other nutrients found in food. This often results in poor appetite, which may lead to an inadequate diet that indeed provides even less nourishment. A vicious cycle is created – sometimes unbeknownst to the sufferer.

The use of medications to treat GI problems is rising steadily. Many people suffer from digestive tract problems such as pain, bloating, heartburn, food intolerance, and poor digestion. A recent study involving 1000 adults in central Sweden over a period of a few years showed that about half suffered from GI problems. This is a lot and the situation has to be taken seriously. The significance of nutrients and intestinal flora for physical and mental health receives far too little attention at present.

The intestinal tract is a fermentation vat in which the types of bacteria depend on what we eat – for we aren't the only ones to be fed; billions of intestinal bacteria must also have nourishment. When there is an overgrowth of bacteria that release toxic products, a burden is placed on the body. And these bacteria can also create a deficiency by consuming our vitamins and other nutrients. The harmful bacteria work as parasites, slowly leaching the body's nutrients from within. This can manifest in many different symptoms, from aches and pains, concentration difficulties, and mood swings to frequent colds and allergies. These symptoms result from substances produced by the bacteria that affect the body's functions and certain neural pathways.

Abnormal intestinal flora may be the result of many underlying factors. All too often, penicillin wipes out normal intestinal flora, and an excess of refined sugar and flour products fosters the overgrowth of yeast. Modern society places us under more stress than we can tolerate; we eat too fast, without chewing properly. Do we choose our food to benefit health, or merely to satisfy hunger? The widespread use of chemical laxatives can destroy the intestinal flora, causing chronic stomach problems.

Infected food can also cause stomach problems. For example, *Campylobacter* can lurk in chicken, *Listeria* in blue cheese, and *Salmonella* in meat and eggs. If our normal flora is compromised, the field is left open to these bacteria to cause a spectrum of symptoms ranging from nausea, vomiting, and diarrhea to peptic ulcers. Infected food isn't restricted to restaurants; it can even be found in our own kitchens. Bacteria thrive wherever it is damp and dirty, and the cutting board or kitchen sponge can be ideal breeding grounds.

The bacteria from the normal flora can also cause disease and inflammation – if their ecological microenvironment changes. This microenvironment can be affected by an altered pH, nutritional deficiency, low-fiber food, or changes in the normal flora caused by antibiotics. More aggressive bacteria and fungi have evolved from the high use of antibiotics – including "killer bacteria," multiresistant bacteria, and chronic fungal infections.

In our culture we prefer not to discuss anything between our navel and our knees. Though we all have a stomach, intestines, and biological processes, these are still considered "unmentionable." Constipation is the direct or indirect cause of many diseases. Recurrent constipation can result in colds, headache, skin problems, and lack of energy – all of which can be prevented by eating a high-fiber diet, drinking plenty of water, and avoiding food that irritates the intestines.

Constipation is the most common cause of "bowel pockets" (diverticula). Part of the intestine is distended and fecal matter is trapped in these pockets, which can result in inflammation. The infected area is coated in phlegm to avoid harming the intestine. With time, the old stool and the mucous membrane harden into a rubbery, black lump (intestinal plaque). These can remain in intestinal pockets for decades, irritating both the intestine and the immune system.

Since most of us eat a less-than-ideal diet, intestinal plaque is quite common. Intestinal cleansing is a good method of strengthening your self-healing ability, though it may not suit everyone. Substances with a cleansing effect that oxygenate the intestine are also available. Remember, though, that intestinal cleansing removes both good and bad bacteria, so the good ones have to be replenished.

In the old days, enemas–though hardly pleasant–were commonly prescribed by doctors. Better methods are now available, and more and more people are undergoing intestinal cleansing – even Princess Diana was a fan. Intestinal cleansing may be viewed as a preventive health care measure that allows you to feel better. Not only does it settle your stomach and improve functioning; there are other unexpected benefits for the rest of the body. Blood circulation improves and you become more alert. Warmth returns to previously frozen hands and feet. Eyes become clearer, and the condition of skin, hair, and nails improves. Your face becomes less oily – it really is a rejuvenating cure! Why? Because "old junk" in the intestine invariably affects the skin and mucous membranes, which is why the condition of skin and hair reflects intestinal health.

Candida – A Scourge through the Ages

Candida was mentioned as a health risk as far back as the time of the ancient Greeks. *Candida albicans* is a harmless yeastlike fungus that is part of the body's natural flora. Its job is to break down undigested food. But if over-stimulated by too much undigested junk food this benign organism can transform into a parasitic variation with long myceles. It attaches to the intestinal wall, increases intestinal permeability, and can be spread via the blood. The parasitic form excretes waste products which burden the entire body and disrupt the liver's detoxification process.

There are many different varieties of candida fungus that can "set up housekeeping" in various locations in the body. People with colds commonly get a white fungal coating on their tongues. Heavy overgrowth of candida (candidiasis) can cause a wide range of problems, including acne, worry, weight loss, fatigue, mood swings, headache, heartburn, PMS, depression, eczema, allergies, irritability, migraine headaches, stomach problems, dry mucous membranes, abdominal pain, muscle pain (including fibromyalgia), menstrual disorders, genital problems, diarrhea, hemorrhoids, weakening of the immune system, frequent recurrent colds, and poor circulation with cold hands and feet. The symptoms arise in so many different places because the fungus itself produces a variety of substances that affect the body's functions, hormones, and neurotransmitters.

Candida can produce "false estrogen," leading the body to believe that it already has enough estrogen. Since this causes natural production to be inhibited, it may lead to menstrual disorders. If blood sugar levels are high the fungus also produces ethanol (alcohol), which can make you feel a bit tipsy, even if you haven't touched a drop. Another by-product is acetaldehyde, which is closely related to formaldehyde, and can be recognized because it produces bad breath. It can also cause a number of physical problems including the inhibition of collagen production, fatty acid oxidation, and blockage of normal nerve function. In other words, candidiasis is a very serious illness.

People can have candidiasis without knowing it and more virulent varieties can be transferred through kissing, sexual contact, or sharing a toothbrush. Just how many people have candidiasis is hard to say, since the severity and symptoms vary. Statistics show, however, that one in every three people (!) in the developed world has or has had some type of the parasitic form. Candidiasis is spreading faster than ever in response to the increased stress in modern society, as well as the abuse of antibiotics, pills, steroids, and too much refined sugar and white flour. Consumption of both antibiotics and candy has doubled since the 1960s and 1970s.

The incidence of genital fungal infections has climbed at an alarming rate since the arrival of sulfa drugs and antibiotics. Women of childbearing age (20–45) today take antibiotics twice as often as men in the same age group. Three of four women have had at least one genital fungal infection at some time during their lives, and many suffer from recurrent infections. Candida may also be related to the growing problem of incontinence in older women because it leads to dryness of the mucous membranes in genitals and even the mouth.

During the late 1980s, two of the most frequently discussed illnesses in the United States were oral candidiasis and AIDS. There are many indications of a correlation between the two epidemics. Candida problems are very common in AIDS patients. Fungal infections compromise the immune system; an impaired immune system allows aggressive forms to flourish. Fungal infections are therefore also common in patients receiving immunosuppressive drugs for organ transplants.

Strong cravings for foods like sweets, pasta, and white bread are common in people with candidiasis. Frequently they have bad breath and a white coating on the tongue. Candida can be diagnosed with simple, reliable saliva tests or by employing phase contrast microscopy of the blood, as well as other measurement methods that rely on yeast metabolites in the urine. The more aggressive form of candida can be activated in a person with an impaired immune system (as a result of stress, oral contraceptives, nutritional deficiency) and frequently following a course of antibiotics. The individual's health must be compromised in some way in order for candidiasis to break out. Antibiotics only worsen the situation by killing large portions of the normal, healthy bacteria flora, disrupting the balance, and creating ideal conditions for nasty yeast to proliferate.

The aggressive form of candida can be eliminated gently by depriving the fungus of nourishment by modifying the patient's diet – quite simply, by starving it to death. No more fast food or junk food; from now on, just healthy, high-fiber, nutritious food. There are many ways of treating fungal infections, so consult a professional rather than experimenting on your own. Though not everyone with fatigue, headaches, or mood swings has candidiasis, it is important to get checked for it just because it is so common.

Dr. Stephen B. Edelson developed a successful treatment method at his Center for Environmental and Preventive Medicine in Atlanta. He prescribes a modified diet supplemented with lactobacilli, which has been shown to eliminate candida from the intestines. This is followed by administration of biotin and olive oil until the benign form of candida returns. The entire process may take up to six months, depending on how long the patient was ill. Following this vitamins A, B_5, and E, and zinc help vitalize the intestinal mucous membrane. More than half of those treated with this regimen have recovered, including many whose problems had been thought to be "incurable."

Food as Medicine

Sufferers from rheumatoid arthritis (RA) experience marked improvement when they change their dietary habits. In a Finnish study, forty-three RA patients were randomized into two groups. The control group ate ordinary food, while the test group ate "living food," a form of vegan diet rich in lactobacilli. After one month the group with living food had experienced a change in intestinal flora and a significant improvement in their RA symptoms.

Ann Wigmore developed the "living food concept." She suffered from arthritis, migraines, and intestinal cancer. At the age of fifty she felt like a sick, old woman. She recovered fully after changing her lifestyle and diet, eating only uncooked food: fresh fruit and vegetables, sprouted seeds, and fermented grain. Feeling healthier than ever, she began teaching other "incurable" patients. She believed that the body can heal itself from any disease if it receives living, enzyme-rich, easily digested nourishment. Ms. Wigmore has received many prizes and awards for her pioneering efforts. It is a direct result of her work that fresh sprouts are now common in grocery stores.

Maija Ruisniemi, a Swedish nurse, also focused on the concept that some foods create the intestinal health needed for healing. She formulated a dietary protocol for different digestive problems, based on eating plenty of fresh uncooked fruits, berries, and vegetables, tailored to the individual's needs and symptoms. Ruisniemi conducted a pilot study of twenty people with GI problems, and after only two weeks of treatment, nineteen were completely problem-free.

People who have digestion problems shouldn't eat protein and starch in the same meal. In other words, don't eat rice, pasta, or potatoes, with meat; choose salad and vegetables instead. This facilitates digestion, and speeds the passage through the intestines. Vegetables can be paired with rice or pasta; your stomach can handle that combination. Fruit passes through the stomach quickly; it should be eaten half an hour before or three hours after meals to prevent it from remaining in your stomach and fermenting.

How to Keep Your Stomach Happy

We all want our stomachs to work well and be happy. A poorly functioning stomach can ruin your day and bring you down – nothing is fun anymore. A well functioning digestive system requires a healthy lifestyle, and this is based on a balanced diet. Fiber is central for proper functioning of the intestinal mucous membrane and for avoiding constipation. Children should eat raw vegetables and whole grain products (unless they are gluten intolerant) to ensure proper development of the GI tract, thereby laying the foundation for good health in adulthood.

Not only do fruits and vegetables contain fiber, they also stimulate growth in the intestine's beneficial lactobacilli, which in turn is a prerequisite for the stomach to thrive and be "happy." Both Nordic health pioneer Are Waerland and well-known English cancer researcher Denis Burkitt have long maintained the importance of high-fiber food for health. When Burkitt worked as a physician in Uganda he noted that Africans who ate traditional food had a completely different disease spectrum than those who ate western food. Those eating traditional foods with high-fiber content did not suffer from the diseases that afflict us such as heart disease, diabetes, hemorrhoids, or intestinal inflammations.

As long ago as the 1970s, Herman Adlercreutz, Professor of Clinical Chemistry at Helsinki University, came to the conclusion that fiber is key to the health benefits of vegetarian food. He found it especially interesting that in Finland, where people ate traditional sour dough rye bread, cancer involving the genitals and reproductive glands appeared to be less common than among European populations which ate white bread. Initially his theories were rejected since fiber was considered unnecessary. Subsequently Adlercreutz demonstrated that substances isolated from rye fiber, soy protein, and several other vegetables could have an effect on sex hormones and inhibit cancer growth. These active substances are isoflavonoids and lignin, though eating the original food is preferable to the isolated or synthetic substances.

Certain bacterial strains in our intestines live on fiber and produce cancer-inhibiting substances. Adlercreutz's research has shown that after we take antibiotics, these anticarcinogens disappear for over three months. Taking antibiotics twice a year leaves you without this cancer protection for over half the year. Soybeans contain cancer-protective substances that do not need these bacteria; they can be absorbed directly by the body. Many studies published since the 1970s show that intake of fiber, flaxseed, soy protein, sesame seeds, and green tea prevents the occurrence or growth of prostate and breast cancer in people and animals. Until official recommendations on dietary changes are available, anyone interested can learn from research findings and develop new eating habits that stimulate health and self-healing.

Pay attention to your stomach and intestines over the next week. Rather than focusing on taste, allow the feel of the food in your stomach to motivate your dietary choices. Pay attention to the way you react to everything you eat. Does your stomach prefer a certain type of food? Does it become full of gas and bloated, is it fast or sluggish, because of what you eat? Try listening to your stomach; go to the toilet when it wants to – and not when it suits you. How does your stomach feel at the end of the week?

During the following week, try changing some of the eating habits that your stomach didn't like. Add something new. Try increasing the amount of fiber by eating more fruit and vegetables every day. Does your stomach feel better after a bowl of oatmeal each morning than after toast and marmalade? Avoid ice cream, cookies, and candy for a few days – what does your stomach think about that? Eating habits aren't written in stone; you can change what you like – as long as you are motivated. Your stomach may help you find the way...

Functional Foods

Tomorrow's pharmaceutical companies are already here. These companies work with "functional foods" – foods that have a documented effect on health, that are both preventive and healing. Indeed, functional foods boost health, thereby increasing the self-healing ability. They are natural substances, without any chemical additives, and they must have a specific scientifically proven health-promoting effect.

Functional foods fall within the no man's land between food, medicine, and naturopathic preparations. Japan was the first country to adopt special legislation for health foods, but now many countries have followed suit. There are clear advantages to the functional food concept. It gives a framework for more research on food and health, promoting knowledge and interest in the health effects of foods. In addition, people are becoming increasingly interested and aware of the concept of nutritious food.

The American market for functional food is estimated to be about $25 billion, with a potential of up to about $200 billion, according to *Functional Foods in the United States*, a report published by Sweden's technical attaché. Eating functional food has become a new lifestyle; evidently half the household food budget is spent on food that claims to have health benefits. Yet another indication of public interest is the growing health food market, which is expanding by 17 to 20 percent annually.

The types of functional foods are many – ranging from yoghurt and kefir, and fruit drinks with healthy bacteria, to high-fiber food and garlic.

Foods that encourage growth of healthy bacteria are known as prebiotics. The food contains fiber that can be dissolved by the enzymes in our intestines as well as fiber that cannot. It used to be believed that insoluble fiber only provided bulk to help food pass through the intestines and prevent constipation, but now it has been found to provide nutrients for beneficial intestinal bacteria, and to stimulate their growth. Insoluble fiber has been shown to reduce the quantity of harmful bacteria considerably. It also has a beneficial effect on the pH in the intestines, increasing absorption of essential minerals and counteracting the negative effects of sugar.

The insoluble fiber found in polysaccharides and oligosaccharides provides nutrients for bifidus bacteria. These bacteria produce fatty acids, which are essential nutrients for epithelial cells of the intestinal mucous membrane. Since epithelial cells are constantly being renewed, they need a steady supply of nutrients. Butyric acid is the most important of these fatty acids. An inadequate supply of butyric acid to the epithelial cells may lead to inflammation of the colon and possibly cancer. The fatty acids produced by the bacteria also play a role in hormone production, and the ecologically correct intestinal bacteria produce substances that act as antibiotics and inhibit the formation of cancer cells. During the metabolism of amino acids, harmful bacteria can form phenols, indoles, and amines, which may be carcinogenic. However, bacteria living on starch and polysaccharides (slow carbohydrates) prevent or restrict production of these toxins.

Polysaccharides are common in many oriental herbal medicines that improve the immune system. It is quite likely that they too work by stimulating better intestinal flora, thereby promoting health, self-healing, and the life force.

So don't forget to eat fiber every day! High-fiber foods include not only fruit, roots, and vegetables, but also beans, lentils, oatmeal, and whole grain products. White cabbage, for example, contains a hefty 20 percent fiber. Our cousins, the gorillas, eat over two hundred different plants and over one hundred types of fruit in the wild. At least one third of their calorie intake derives from fatty acids produced by intestinal bacteria. Only a small percentage of their energy comes from dietary fat – whereas we derive much of ours from the food we eat, which contains 18 percent saturated fats.

Rather than taking antibiotics, which kill bacteria, people should take probiotics by adding healthy intestinal bacteria. Lactobacilli, bifidus, and other strains of bacteria adhere to the intestine and counteract harmful bacteria, thereby promoting healthy flora that strengthen the intestine. The term "probiotics" is used because they strengthen good bacteria rather than "fighting" bad bacteria (like "antibiotics"). Grocery stores carry many probiotic products, including yogurt, kefir, acidophilus milk, and fermented vegetables containing live bacteria. The bacteria adhere to the intestinal wall and produce several healthy substances, while blocking adhesion of disease-inducing bacteria.

ProViva is a product developed by three research groups from different departments at Lund University–internal medicine and surgery, microbiology, and food technology–working in collaboration and is now available in Europe. It contains *Lactobacillus plantarum*, a bacterium found naturally in some foods which has been shown to cure chronic irritable bowel disease. It also stimulates production and increases the amount of fatty acids in the intestines. Supplementing infant formula with *Lactobacillus reuteri* (Reuteri) and zinc reduces diarrhea and improves iron levels. Japanese researchers at Hiroshima University found that yogurt containing Reuteri was the only one out of twenty that had an antibacterial effect on *Streptococcus mutans*, which causes tooth decay. Taking probiotics is preferable to antibiotics, since the latter can create problems by inducing resistant bacteria. I highly recommend taking probiotics every day.

Some foods work as natural antibiotics. Garlic has a well-documented antibacterial and antiviral effect and can therefore be beneficial against colds and infections. Ginger is an overall health enhancer with anti-inflammatory and analgesic effects. It is just as effective as nonsteroidal anti-inflammatory agents, but not nearly as harmful, since it protects the gastric mucosa.

Grapefruit seed extract has proven to be highly effective against over eight hundred different strains of bacteria and hundreds of types of fungi, viruses, and parasitic infections. Grapefruit seed extract can be used internally after it has been diluted in water. It contains bitter and astringent substances that also strengthen the liver and intestines. Tea tree oil originally comes from an Australian tree and contains on the order of one hundred active substances. It is also a natural antiseptic that counters many bacteria and fungi. In a Swedish study of thirty patients with mild skin eczema and mild psoriasis, 75 percent recovered completely or improved considerably after treatment with the oil. However some may get a rash from the tea tree oil. Be careful not to overuse natural antibiotics – it is often preferable to bolster the natural protective mechanisms.

Cabbage contains anticarcinogens that protect against cancers, including breast cancer. They mainly work by interfering with the early changes associated with the development of cancer. It is therefore recommended that you eat kale, cabbage, red cabbage, brussels sprouts, and cauliflower regularly.

Soy protein has an inhibiting effect on breast and prostate cancer. It contains a form of estrogen that competes with natural estrogen. This

The gastrointestinal system benefits from:

- Balanced diet. Food with high nutritional content per calorie – plenty of fruit, roots, grains, vegetables, and whole-grain bread. Eat more tofu, miso, and soy protein. Products with lactobacilli are also recommended (i.e., yoghurt, kefir, bifidus milk, fermented vegetables).
- Fluids. Drink plenty of fresh water, six to eight glasses a day, but avoid drinking with meals.
- Movement. Improve digestion with regular exercise and deep breathing. This stimulates the intestines and facilitates cleansing.
- Mental balance. If you've ever suffered from a stomachache after eating when you're stressed or angry, you know that mental balance is important to normal stomach function. Excessive stress and worry can easily result in an upset stomach. A well-functioning GI system is needed for mental well-being.

lowers the estrogen level in the body, thereby lowering the risk of breast cancer as well. Soy products such as soybeans, soy milk, tofu, and soy protein powder also lower the level of bad cholesterol in the body, though you need 25 grams of soy protein daily to achieve this effect.

Ancient Babylon was the cradle of civilization over thirty-five hundred years ago. It was a wealthy cultural capital with a sophisticated cuisine. Sweet fruits were grown and candied in honey. People ate broiled meat and cookies with fruit, almonds, and nuts sweetened with grape juice. The country's medical arts were also held in high esteem and would later provide inspiration to both Greek and Arabic medicine. There was a rich man living in Babylon, and although he was in the best of health, he felt listless, bloated, and often suffered from headaches. He was served the most delicious of meals, yet he lost interest in life and suffered, even though there was nothing wrong with him. Agreeing to visit a man who knew all about healing the sick, he received a prescription carved in cuneiform characters on a clay tablet that has been preserved to this day. It says: "Eat boiled meat and boiled fish instead of fried and broiled food. Eat more fruits and vegetables instead of sweet desserts and candy. Drink plenty of water. Get out of your sedan chair and walk!"

Throughout most of the course of evolution we have lived in and close to nature. We've lived in the woods, in fields, on mountains, and by rivers, and we have lived on the food provided by nature. As a result we have evolved alongside nature for hundreds of thousands of years. We are a part of it and it is a part of us. We are composed of the same elements.

Perhaps it is time to change the way in which we view ourselves. We are actually hosts for billions of bacteria. This is far more than the number of our "own" cells in our bodies. These bacteria compete for nutrients, and depending on what we eat, can bring either benefit or harm. Clearly, we need both bacteria and a good diet if we are to thrive.

We are–and always will be–a part of nature and we must also live according to the cycles of nature. To flourish we must supply the appropriate nutrients to both our bodies and our bacterial flora. If we don't, we lose our balance, suffer diseases of nutritional deficiency, and age prematurely.

This view will help us to understand where we have gone wrong in recent generations. What good is it to be able to journey to the moon if we cannot understand and live according to the conditions that once shaped us and still apply to us?

6.
Movement Creates Flow

Movement is necessary for life – because life itself pulsates with energy. Increasing the flow in our bodies stimulates a number of vital functions that benefit health and activate self-healing. The body's energy flow can be increased in many ways: through song, dance, music, laughter, exercise, or sexual relations and orgasm. These all affect breathing, which has a great influence on the flow, balance, and relaxation within the body.

Our bodies and our lives are filled with harmonious and regular rhythms, such as ovulation in women, or the changing of the seasons. The body's rhythmic activities include brain waves, heartbeats, breathing, nerve impulses, and peristaltic waves in the intestine. Waking and sleeping are an external expression of our biochemical rhythms. We achieve a healthy harmony when our rhythms are fully integrated, but being out of sync disrupts our well-being. Rhythmic imbalance can be harmful to the body. Because we can directly influence the rhythm of our breathing, it is breathing which holds the key to integrating the body's rhythmic movements into a harmonious relationship.

Breath of Life

Breathing is essential to life and is intimately associated with existence itself, with the living space we occupy and with our emotions. No wonder the words "spirit" (soul) and "respiration" (breathing) are closely linked in most cultures. The Holy Spirit stands for one aspect of God, and God's breath blew symbolic life into the first man. Death is also said to come with an exhalation of breath; as breathing stops, the spark of life departs from the body.

According to the western view, the purpose of breathing is to oxygenate the blood, with all the purifying and life-giving processes this entails. In eastern thought, the body is also considered to be an energy system. This view casts a different light on the significance of breathing. It is the supplier of life energy, granting both physical and spiritual purification.

Breathing is therefore also used for religious purposes, for making contact with other dimensions. The ancient traditions of India and China apply breathing techniques for healing and medical purposes.

Few of us pay any attention to the breathing process, nor do we notice ourselves tightening certain muscles in our stomachs and chests. We hold our breath from tension, or release sighs of pleasure. When frazzled or frightened, we commonly take rapid shallow breaths – or even stop breathing altogether. Some may hold their breath while standing in a crowded elevator – as if breathing less made us occupy less space! Breathing tells the story of our true feelings, and we can also consciously control how we feel through our breathing. It is impossible to be stressed out and at the same time breathe calmly. Increasing our awareness of breathing techniques is therefore an essential step toward developing the self-healing ability.

It makes a difference whether you breathe through your mouth or your nose. Nasal breathing serves to filter particles through the hairs and mucous membranes, and simultaneously heats and moisturizes the air. This doesn't happen when you breathe through your mouth. To help prevent infection, then, it is best to inhale through your nose and exhale through your mouth.

There are many ways of supplying increased energy to the body's life and healing processes. Although most people recognize the importance of exercise for general well-being, breathing technique also plays a role. About a pint of blood circulates through the lungs per minute with "chest breathing." Abdominal breathing, however, allows twice as much blood to be oxygenated, so breathing becomes calmer. Deep breathing also improves circulation, reduces pressure within the chest, and facilitates the return of blood to the heart. Healthy, oxygenated blood contains about 25 percent oxygen that is free to be delivered to the body's cells.

Breathing is the primary means of ridding the body of waste. No less than 70 percent of waste products are eliminated when we exhale, while 20 percent exit through the skin, and a mere 10 percent via urine and feces. In other words, a good supply of healthy air is needed to

Pause a moment to think about your breathing; does your stomach move when you inhale, or just your chest? If you change your breathing so that it becomes deeper and slower, how does it feel? Take an occasional break and breathe deeply for a few minutes. Consider how different situations or people affect your breathing.

cleanse the blood fully and allow proper elimination of waste products. Abdominal breathing of clean well-oxygenated air is therefore essential to good health. For example, Dr. Alice Dohmar at Harvard Medical School has shown that regular relaxation with deep breathing results in a 57 percent reduction of severe PMS symptoms.

More blood flows through the brain than through any other organ. Moreover, it is the site with the greatest turnover of chemical substances. Protein is continuously being produced for mental activity, and people who are mentally active have high levels of protein production in the brain. While the brain barely comprises 3 percent of body weight, at rest it uses a full 20 percent of the oxygen supply. Its energy requirements are so high that it dies if deprived of oxygen for just a few minutes, and function suffers even when the oxygen supply is decreased. Older people are particularly sensitive because of impaired blood flow caused by hardening of the arteries. Significant intellectual revitalization can be achieved in the elderly by increasing the concentration of oxygen. Younger people may also benefit from this, and trendy California sports "oxygen bars" where people go to inhale oxygen – to improve their thinking ability and rejuvenate their bodies!

In summary: the greater the volume of air you move through your lungs, the more your nervous system is nourished. Therefore deep breathing can be viewed as key to a long and healthy life.

Breathing Practice

While breathing movements are not entirely under voluntary control, within limits they may still be consciously modified. Nevertheless, we can rest assured that our breathing won't fail us whether we are awake or asleep. Inhalation is mainly controlled by the sympathetic nervous system, while exhalation is generally more passive and affected by the parasympathetic nervous system.

Inhalation is also the active phase of breathing. Some eastern views hold that inhalation can be compared to yang energy, which represents our active side and the masculine principle. Exhalation is the passive opposite of inhalation, and is therefore represented by yin energy or the feminine principle. The body's yin and yang energies can be balanced by practicing controlled breathing. Holding your breath allows you to retain a "charge" in the "now." The empty space between inhalation and exhalation is as important as the actual breathing. As in classical music, the pauses are as important as the notes they separate. Beethoven claimed that it is the pause that makes the music.

Opera singers and musicians who play wind instruments use abdominal breathing, as do practitioners of yoga and Ayurvedic medicine. By synchronizing your breathing with your heartbeat you will improve your performance and generally feel better. Such breathing also fosters harmony. In a study of physical performance, people with a pulse and respiration rate equally divisible by a whole number–for example, twenty-five breaths for every hundred heartbeats instead of every eighty-seven–achieved much better results. Such synchronization of pulse and breathing can be automatically achieved with proper breathing technique involving abdominal breathing, which makes use of the diaphragm's up-and-down movements.

The diaphragm is the contoured layer of muscle above the liver that separates the abdominal cavity from the thoracic cavity. When the diaphragm contracts, the space surrounding the lungs increases, while the abdomen expands. A "flat stomach" is therefore impossible with proper breathing technique. You should also stretch your spine rather than slouching, since that restricts chest mobility. Diaphragmatic breathing also stimulates the organs of the abdominal cavity, which increases intestinal peristalsis and facilitates the emptying process. Moreover, because the diaphragm is linked to heart rate via the brain, diaphragmatic breathing leads to natural integration with the pulse. Infants naturally breathe using their diaphragm, while most of us need to relearn this technique.

Breathing and emotions are intimately intertwined. Shallow chest breathing is often a sign of emotional repression. Repressed sorrow restricts breathing, while conversely breathing deeply can release the sorrow. By taking repeated deep breaths you can energize your body.

Cleansing breathing is a method of deep rhythmic breathing that helps release repressed emotions. Its purpose is to encourage the body's natural flows and facilitate circulation, thereby allowing the body's energy to move freely. Cell renewal is encouraged and the body is revitalized. As we clear the body's blockages and open its natural energy flows, we can progressively stimulate our self-healing ability.

Chronic stress, striving for the perfect flat stomach, and ignorance of proper breathing techniques can all result in incorrect chest breathing. The body has a difficult time ridding itself of carbon dioxide, which is an unnecessary burden. It is therefore important to be aware of how we breathe, and take the time, frequently and regularly, to practice proper deep breathing techniques.

1. Stand with your feet shoulder-width apart and your arms at your sides. Center yourself by focusing your awareness on the qi-point (two finger-breadths below the navel). Inhale through the nose while slowly moving your arms straight out from your sides until they are stretched above your head.

2. Quietly exhale through your mouth while moving your hands down in front of your body. Bend your upper body from the hips and let your arms hang down toward the floor. Breathe out by using your abdominal muscles to press out every last bit of air. If possible, touch the floor with your hands. Hold your breath for a few seconds.

3. Slowly straighten your spine, vertebra by vertebra, while inhaling slowly through your nose. Lift your arms straight out from the body's sides and up above your head until the palms of your hands meet. Hold your breath for a short time.

4. Exhale through your mouth while slowly lowering your arms. Let your upper body fall forward with a loud, exhaling sigh. Relax for a moment and repeat the exercise from the beginning. (Note: Be careful if you aren't used to this type of exercise!)

If you hold the tip of your tongue against your palate right behind your front teeth while inhaling through your nose, you will connect the energy flows in the front and rear part of your body. Exhale through your mouth as usual.

Exercise

Movement is fun and natural – walking, dancing, swimming, running, or bicycling. Just look at the way children love to be forever on the move. Be sure to find an activity you enjoy; exercising should make you happy and bring pleasure. My favorites are "salsa aerobics" and NIA (Neuromuscular Integrative Activity) – a mixture of free dance, combat sports, and tai qi. Moving to rhythmic music makes exercising easier and more fun. If you find your chosen activity is heavy, boring, and negative you become tense, and that impairs the flow in the body. Exercise relaxes us, reduces stress, and improves sleep. It is rarely a problem to continue exercising once you've gotten started – your body will want to keep moving.

Exercise can provide many benefits. Blood and lymph circulation improve, and the energy flow increases, strengthening the heart and maintaining blood vessel elasticity. The lungs operate with greater vigor, which increases the exchange of oxygen and carbon dioxide. Exercise facilitates the secretion of waste products through breathing and via the skin through sweating. Intestinal movements are stimulated, countering constipation. And of course burning more calories prevents weight gain. Moderate exercise even improves the body's defense mechanisms against infections.

Exercise is also an excellent mood enhancer. Just twenty minutes of jogging results in secretion of beta-endorphins into the brain, promoting a sense of well-being and optimism. It alleviates depression, and studies have shown that regular exercise may be as effective as antidepressants, thereby obviating the need to take medicines and so avoiding their potential adverse effects.

In our modern society, exercise has almost become a separate culture, with special clothing, exercises, rituals, and equipment. Although membership in health clubs and athletics organizations is on the rise, we still have to learn how to make exercise part of our daily lives. Not much muscle power is needed when we have cars, elevators, and buses to take us where we want to go. Think about how to make exercise a natural part of everyday life. Take the stairs instead of the elevator, and whenever possible walk rather than taking the bus or car. Lugging groceries home from the store or carrying small children also count as exercise. If you want to increase the body's self-healing ability, it helps to keep exercise simple – as the natural part of life that it really is.

Long walks are good for your health and for putting your thoughts in order. Feeling upset or frustrated? The soothing effect of a thirty-minute walk on mind and body always helps. As you walk, the rhythmic swinging of arms and legs affects electrical activity in the brain and is considered necessary for optimum nervous system performance. It stimulates the brain and accelerates spontaneous healing of various physical injuries. Dr. Andrew Weil recommends walking as the best form of exercise in his book *Spontaneous Healing: How to Discover and Embrace Your Body's Natural Ability to Maintain and Heal Itself.* The risk of injury is minimal and you can walk just about anywhere. Research has shown that walking twenty minutes twice a day is just as effective as running thirty minutes, three times a week.

When you walk it is also easier to be aware of your breathing. Remember to think about breathing with your diaphragm, and take deep long breaths. This increases oxygenation and thereby the flow in your body. Long walks coupled with abdominal breathing are an excellent way to exercise, doubling blood oxygenation and boosting energy enormously – and they accelerate spontaneous healing of various injuries. Add walking poles to increase your heart rate and oxygen uptake even more. "Pole walking" is the trendy new sport that can be practiced anywhere.

Increased Body Awareness

At some time in their lives, 80 percent of all Americans will experience back problems. Formerly most people did not encounter these problems until between the ages of thirty-five and fifty. In this age group the body is no longer capable of compensating for tense muscles, and the result is pain, stiffness, and joint problems. Now problems appear as early as age twenty-five – even though hard physical labor is no longer common. What causes these problems to occur earlier, and what can we do about them?

The poor diet of our modern food culture is partly responsible. Eating inappropriately has a number of negative consequences. Our brain needs a continuous supply of between 100 and 150 grams of glucose, distributed evenly throughout the day. To provide this glucose to the brain, our own muscles and tissues need to be broken down, resulting in the production of lactic acid, which leads to muscle tension and compromised circulation. This process is associated with local acidification and inflammation which the body attempts to neutralize with calcium. This may result in calcification of the muscles, which harden, stiffen, and become shorter. The body compensates by using other muscles, causing pain elsewhere. The source of calcium is the skeleton, which can thereby become decalcified over time. A vicious cycle is established, as more muscles become stiff and painful, and the risk of osteoporosis increases. The process is so gradual that people become accustomed to the problems. Quite simply, the body adapts to its own breakdown, which can become a chronic condition. Excessive exercise may lead to the same problems – with improper diet.

Young people with these diet-related problems who work at ordinary jobs soon suffer overuse injuries. The incidence of occupational injuries in this age group has risen dramatically in recent years. Alarmingly, they cannot handle what we would describe as a normal workload. Why would a twenty-year old experience the same type of overuse injury after a year on the job as a forty- to forty-five year old first suffers after many years of similar work? Although diet plays a major role, today's young people are also in worse physical condition. Too much time is spent watching TV and playing computer games, and the situation is aggravated by cutbacks in physical education requirements in school.

"The trend is for younger and younger patients to seek help for increasingly serious problems," says chiropractor Catarina Johansson, who has extensive clinical experience with sore joints, stiff muscles, and physical pain. "The typical example is that of a twenty-one year old woman complaining of neck and shoulder pain, and constant headaches. She has a cup of coffee and a cigarette for breakfast, eats a roll in the morning and a light salad with fat-free dressing for lunch. When her blood sugar level is low in the afternoon she has a cookie with her coffee. By half past four she is in acute need of another boost in blood sugar, which she satisfies with a chocolate bar. When she gets home, at best she eats a light snack. People like this don't understand why they lack stamina, why they are tired and become ill, and why they hurt all over. Why? Because they have a significant nutritional deficiency. Simply put: if they have to drive one hundred fifty miles and tank up with only a gallon of gas – how can they expect they'll ever get there?"

The chiropractor's most important treatment is to release blockages caused by "subluxations" in vertebrae and joints; as long as pain is present, you don't want to do anything that causes more pain. Sore muscles are massaged and stimulated with acupressure. The chiropractor gives the patient instructions on how to follow a stretching program at home for contracted muscles, and provides advice on diet and exercise. The focus is on educating "the physician within" so that patients learn to care for themselves.

The Body Armor

Other factors also contribute to stiff muscles and sore bodies. Our emotional and thought patterns–both conscious and unconscious–reside within the body. They shape the body and can cause tightness and stiffness. We may harbor pain, shame, or fear of rejection which may stem from our time in the womb, birth, early infancy, or childhood. Muscles express our fears, thoughts, and emotions. This is known as "muscle armor" and it affects both our voice and our posture.

Fear usually leads to a defensive stance with shoulders raised and hunched forward. Some people resemble turtles, with their shoulders raised well above jaw level. They withdraw into an imaginary shell for self-defense. Others may have a crooked spine with only the right shoulder raised. This portrays the dominant right half of the body, common in people who are completely controlled by their intellectual and rational side. People who strike the ground with their heels when walking are often displaying a sign of anger. This may lead to compensatory muscle tightening elsewhere in the body. Sucking in your stomach and tightening your buttocks in a defensive posture invariably leads to tense muscles in the genitals and the neck. It is not uncommon for women to have tense pelvic muscles. Since these muscles are 90 percent autonomic it may be difficult to recognize where your body is tense. Pain and problems in the lower back may be caused by such stress. In many cases people are unaware of these tensions and the repressed emotions they may represent.

Even after a strenuous workout the body may still be closed off physically. If muscle armor blocks certain parts of your body, no amount of exercise will help, because there will be no chance for the flow to begin. We have to become aware of these closed and "silent" parts of our bodies if the life energy is to flow freely. This energy is needed to remove dead waste products and supply new nutrients to build healthy cells. Various types of massage help loosen tension in muscles and connective tissue, increasing blood flow so breathing can begin after the "closed" areas are reopened. Stretching exercises, yoga, and *qigong* also activate both our circulation and our energy flow.

The neck connects the head (the conscious being) and the body (the unconscious). "Repressed" experiences may cause recurrent neck problems or throat infections. Many people are so closed off that their voices don't reach down into their bodies. Their speech is monotonous because they lack the resonance of the body's "soundbox"; this makes for tiresome listening in the long run. Sound and movement exercises can help bring the voice down into the body and release your inner voice. Vocalizing stiff body parts (emotions) can be an effective way of aerating your body armor.

Breaking ingrained movement patterns is another good way to relax tense muscles. This can be accomplished using the Feldenkrais method or the Alexander technique. Feldenkrais classes are especially popular because they are so simple, relaxing, and refreshing, allowing the brain to unwind and bringing the mental and physical parts into balance. "Rolfing" is another approach to dealing with body armor by softening hardened connective tissue, thereby increasing flow and helping different parts of the body find their natural balance spontaneously.

A beautiful fairy tale tells of a brave knight protected by the finest suit of armor. One day its weight became more than he could bear, yet he could not take it off, no matter how he tried. Then he met a wise old woman who told him to let go of his sorrow. The brave knight cried and cried; he cried so hard that his salty tears caused the armor to rust. By the time he ran out of tears, the entire suit of armor had rusted away. He was free at last, and could happily go forth in the world.

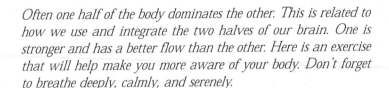

Often one half of the body dominates the other. This is related to how we use and integrate the two halves of our brain. One is stronger and has a better flow than the other. Here is an exercise that will help make you more aware of your body. Don't forget to breathe deeply, calmly, and serenely.

1. Stand with your feet shoulder-width apart and your arms hanging at your sides. Focus on the qi-point right below the navel and take note of how your body feels.

2. Stand with both feet on the floor but move the center of gravity to your right foot and let the body move with it to the right. Stand here a while and think about how the right half of your body feels. Is it warm or cold, compact or thin, stiff or soft? Review that half of your body from head to foot, and look at the color of your legs, arms, trunk, throat, and head.

3. Now transfer the center of gravity to your left foot so that your whole body moves to the left. Observe in the same way how this half of your body feels. Note whether there are any differences between the right half of your body and the left.

4. Move the center of gravity back to both feet and see how it feels now. Have you become aware of anything in your body that you didn't know before?

Dance of Release, Dance of Relief

Throughout the ages dance, like song, has been a natural part of our culture. People have danced for joy, for sorrow, at ceremonies, and as a means of social interaction. Small children move to music spontaneously and rhythmically, and young people love to dance. But as the years pass, we have fewer natural occasions for dancing – unfortunately, for dance benefits both the mind and the body. Dance engages our entire being: our bodies, emotions, and consciousness. This outstanding form of exercise strengthens the body and the immune system. Dance is also linked to joy, releasing beneficial substances within the body and counteracting the effects of stress.

Dance increases physical awareness, and helps us get in touch with dormant parts of our bodies and souls. Just like our voices, the rhythmic movement of dance can aerate our body armor. Gentle movements help us recognize tensions and fend them off before they cause damage. Dance provides an outlet enabling us to "voice" our emotions through body language – without saying a word. Free body movements, inspired by music, can channel unconscious emotions and thereby dissolve blockages. Dance permits the release and free flow of life energy in quantity. The body can be used to accelerate the healing process through the unvoiced expression of pain through movement. This concept is integral to dance therapy, a subject taught at universities around the world. Gabrielle Roth has brought the joy of free movement to many people with her rhythmical exercises – imagine doing the "chaos dance" together with 5,000 people at a convention in Los Angeles!

The growing popularity of hot-blooded dances such as the Spanish flamenco and the Latin American tango and salsa may be a sign of our increasing tolerance of emotional expression. Uptight North Americans could probably benefit from the Latin beat and expressive dance.

Healing Music

Music moves us on many levels. It flows past our logical and analytical filters and directly touches our emotions. Chords, melodies, and tones can awaken memories and stimulate the imagination, in turn creating physical reactions. Different types of music meet different needs; you can listen to soul, classical, rock and roll, opera, or new age music depending on how you feel – or how you would like to feel. Upbeat music at sporting events raises the morale of the fans. Rhythmic drums stimulate completely different emotions than the gentle melody of the flute. Even when performed in a foreign language, an aria can convey emotions that inspire the audience to devoted ecstasy. Listening to Billie Holiday helped me through a period of sorrow. Nothing makes me cry the way her voice does; in its raw nakedness it conveys the pain, sorrow, and longing she experienced during a hard life.

For thousands of years, people have used music as a source of joy and well-being. In ancient Greece and Rome, philosophy students favored music that inspired health, purity, and a stable personality. Shamans, medicine men, and medicine women have used music to heal people throughout the ages. Music has also been central to religious ceremonies, to reach the divine and honor the holy. It is used to achieve ecstasy and contact with spiritual beings. Music has served as a metaphor, an expression of beauty and divinity in the mystical focus of the world's many religions.

How does music affect us? Sound consists of vibrations or oscillations in particles or objects. It is a form of energy that propagates via the air through alternating condensation and attenuation of air molecules. The volume is determined by how much the vibrating atoms and molecules move. An air molecule that vibrates faster creates a louder sound. In the nineteenth century people became interested in the effects of music on the body. Researchers measured its effect on pulse, breathing, circulation, and blood pressure. They found that a certain type of music alleviated pain. The therapeutic ability of music has gradually come to be recognized for both its mental and physical healing effects.

Research has confirmed that resonance is the very basis of music's healing ability. The acoustic principle of resonance applies not only to music but also to the body. Resonance occurs when a sound source emits sound energy waves into the surroundings. Objects with the same frequency of vibration as the source of sound are set in motion, whereby resonance occurs. When the sound enters the body, resonance takes place at atomic and molecular levels. Sound waves are easily reproduced within us thanks to the body's high water content. This is highly relevant for the therapeutic effects of sound. Vibrations are created in living cells, in a process which can be compared to a deep energy massage. This can help restore health by supplying energy, thereby metaphorically "shaking loose" tension and blockages.

Micromotion with Sound

Sound is actually movement – but at the level of atoms and molecules. Indeed we can exercise on a micro level using song and music. In this sense the body is like a musical instrument; it works as a sounding board and is affected by the pitch, volume, and harmony of sound. Different tones stimulate different parts of the body. Our mood and our bodies are affected by singing, making noise, or playing different types of music. Singing can make you feel happy, exhilarated, and warm. In many countries, drinking songs enhance the party atmosphere, and choir singing is also very popular.

Making noise is a powerful way of attacking the blockages and tensions in the body. It's easy. Open your mouth and make "droning" noises. Explore various pitches and sounds at different volumes and let the microvibrations loosen your tense blockages. It's the same principle as dissolving kidney stones using ultrasound, except that the sound is on another frequency. You don't need any expensive equipment; just make your own sound to dissolve closed-in tensions and unconscious blockages. In many cases you will experience relief. You might also be surprised at the loud sounds the body can produce – if you just let it happen. This is a great experience to try in the bathtub, as two thirds of the human body is made of water. Close the door, light some candles, and hold your own private "concert."

Pain, like false notes, can be viewed as misplaced and locked-up energy. Try to locate and focus on the pain or tight muscles and then create sound from that site. By producing sound at the same frequency as the pain in a particular area, the soreness will disappear. I have a friend who always warns her physician and dentist that she screams out loud when she feels pain – a highly effective and direct method of getting rid of it.

Why do we speak? Recent research suggests that we actually were communicating by singing and humming – like the birds – before sounds were transformed into words. The creation of language was a milestone in the history of humankind. Each inner experience was given an audible equivalent that could be communicated to others. As a result it was long believed that words had a power to match the image created in the external world.

Healing mantras and repeated hymns have existed throughout the ages. The word "mantra" means "tool for thinking" (from the Sanskrit *man*, to think and *tra*, a tool). A mantra is a sound or phrase that is repeated continuously. Often it consists of the names or properties of a mythological god or higher force. As you repeat a mantra a mental image appears, and equivalent properties are awakened within. Mantras are sound formulae with the ability to alter matter – they are power words.

Repeating mantras gives your molecules the same micromassage we discussed before, though it can also directly affect higher cerebral centers. Indian mantra-yoga teaches that there is a small energy center in the nasal cavity called *bija-chakrat*, which is the center for all sound. The palate works as a soundboard inside your head, sending the sound's vibrations to the brain's higher mental and emotional centers by way of the *bija-chakrat*.

In ancient cultures the mantra "*om*" or "*aum*" was considered to be the oldest holy sound. Jungian psychologist Joseph Campbell writes in *The Power of Myth* about the metaphysical aspects of "aum" during meditation. "A" symbolizes birth and corresponds to inhalation. "U" represents what is to come and corresponds to holding your breath after inhalation. "M" symbolizes the state of dissolution, which corresponds to exhalation.

Mantras can also be sung as holy songs, psalms, and hymns providing spiritual contact and mental inspiration. Each religion has its own mantras; for example, Christian mantras include "En Emoi Kristus" (Christ Within Me) or "Ave Maria" (Hail Mary); Hindu mantras are "Hare Krishna" ("O Energy of the Lord, O All-attractive Lord) and "Shanti, Shanti" (Peace, Peace); Jewish mantras include shalom (peace) and Barukh Atah Adonai (Blessed Art Thou Oh Lord); and Buddhist mantras include Tare Tutare Ture Svaha (Liberate, Liberate Please Liberate, Please Free Me From The Outer, Inner, And Secret Hindrances) and Namo Amitabha (I Turn To Buddha To Find The Light). Throughout the ages people have repeated these mantras with their magical, mystical words.

The voice is based on breathing, which in turn is influenced by our inner energies and tensions. Consequently the human voice reflects the body's health on every plane of existence – physical, emotional, spiritual, and mental. Just as we each have our own unique sound, birds too have unique songs that make it possible to identify not only the species, but even the individual bird. The voice changes, however, as does the condition of the inner energy.

The voice is the link between the internal and the external, with an effect in either direction. By improving the way you use your voice, you can improve the way you feel.

Laughter As Exercise

"Laughter works like inner jogging," says Dr. William Fry, professor at Stanford University in California, a leading expert on the physiological effects of humor and laughter. It takes just ten seconds for laughter to double your heart rate, compared with ten minutes of rowing. We use 75 percent more energy when we laugh than when we are at rest. Laughter affects the muscles in our face, neck, chest, shoulders, and diaphragm – the very muscles we use during ordinary physical exercise. At the same time it massages vital internal organs. A good belly laugh stimulates circulation and increases oxygen uptake capacity.

Laughter also has a beneficial effect on breathing. The air pushed out through the throat with an outburst of laughter can reach speeds of 60 mph, expelling residual air rich in carbon dioxide. This increases the exchange of oxygen-rich air in the lungs.

When laughter fades, the pulse drops below normal and a pleasant sensation of relaxation and contentment spreads through the body as muscles relax. Laughter also works as an anesthetic since it releases the body's own endorphins in the brain. Researchers studying stress have found that laughter and humor boost the immune system. Situations seem less threatening if you can find the humor in them. Less stress hormone is released, and the immune system is not weakened. Laughter also provides relief for worry and anxiety – it's impossible to laugh and worry at the same time!

A bus full of tourists once broke down in the Egyptian desert. They had neither water nor survival gear, and realized it would be impossible for help to arrive in time. A clergyman in the group invited those who wanted to prepare for death to join him in prayer. Another passenger invited those who would prefer to laugh and have fun to join him. When rescuers finally arrived only a few survivors greeted them – they all came from the part of the group that had chosen to laugh and have fun. Clearly a good laugh can extend your lifespan. Spending time with people who have a sense of humor and enjoy laughing is good life insurance! Follow the good example of children: on average they laugh forty-seven times a day, compared with adults, who only laugh thirteen to seventeen times a day.

> *We take health for granted when everything is in working order, but illness bothers me deeply. I try to find a balance between pleasure and displeasure – having fun is perhaps the very best formula for good health. The inability to feel free is perhaps the worst.*
> Hans Wigzell, President of Karolinska Institutet

Joy and Enjoyment

Nothing stimulates the body flow as much as the emotions of joy and euphoria. Warmth and happiness permeate the body and promote an overwhelming sense of presence and connectedness. To achieve this state it is essential to do things that bring happiness every day. Maintaining the flow is far more difficult when you feel down or pessimistic. Positive actions that cheer you up and make you happy help nurture your self-healing ability!

Falling in love is also a very effective stimulant for the energy flow. It jump-starts your pulse, hormones, and other neurotransmitters, which is highly vitalizing. Sometimes, however, all you need to experience a similar effect is to exchange a glance with the right person, or chat with an optimist.

Just about everyone agrees that sexuality is important. But what are the health-promoting effects of sex? An active sex life helps you live longer – at least if you are a man. An English study of 918 middle-aged men between the ages of 45 and 59 who were followed over a ten-year period showed that their mortality rate was halved when they had intercourse at least twice a week, compared with those who had sex less than once a month.

An orgasm, which normally lasts about ten seconds, gives the body a "hormonal shower," strengthening it both physically and mentally. During sexual arousal a state of tension builds throughout the body: muscles contract, blood pressure rises, heart rate climbs, and blood flows to the genitals. This tension is released with orgasm, after which the body relaxes completely. During orgasm your pulse rate is comparable to that following a six-mile run – and indeed it is pure exercise. The heart muscle becomes stronger, circulation improves, and the formation of cholesterol and other fatty deposits is prevented. This is consistent with results from another study: middle-aged men who enjoy regular sexual activity have a lower risk of heart attacks than those who have sex less frequently. The endocrine system is also stimulated in men and women, and beta-endorphins—which both relax and cause feelings of joy—are released. These endorphins also strengthen the immune system.

An active sex life also has a beneficial effect on your appearance. According to one study of thirty-five hundred subjects in ten countries, people with a good, active sex life look younger and stay in better shape. Thus we conclude that an active and satisfactory sex life benefits our self-healing ability and helps achieve a longer, more vital life.

Relationships become what we make of them. In a relationship with great intimacy and emotional contact the energies flow freely, promoting good health. Research shows that people who have close relationships live much longer. The true challenge is to keep love and the positive flow alive even in a long-term relationship. Dynamics and movement play a significant role in the relationship between two people – just as energy entails movement. There are many different ways we can enhance our energy flow.

7.
The Importance of Emotions

Can anger make us sick? How important are emotions to our health? Emotions have been pushed to the background in our society for a long time; they have been considered irrational and unreliable. Not until the nineties were they restored to their rightful place with the acceptance of the concept of emotional intelligence – EQ. Now it is "intelligent" to be in touch with our feelings. The old dichotomy between body and soul no longer exists. Instead, emotions are now seen as being the bridge between the two. We are well on the way to fully recognizing the importance of emotions for us as spiritual and intelligent beings. This change is so significant you could call it a revolution – a silent revolution.

Emotions play a key role for us as humans. They are a driving force, a motor that can provide immense strength. Sometimes emotions get in the way, complicating life and making it difficult to get a handle on things. On these occasions, some people then prefer to avoid contact with their own feelings, or the feelings of others. Emotions can also be a source of joy, pleasure, and euphoria. Imagine a relationship without emotions – it just wouldn't work! We cannot ignore their fundamental role in our lives, yet they have long been given a low status.

As an illustration, there are few words to describe different emotional states. How many synonyms do you know for the word "love"? The lower the priority, the fewer the number of words. The word emotion comes from the Latin *emovere*, in which the e stands for out and *movere* means movement. The English word emotion was used from the early seventeenth century to describe a heightened or agitated mental state. Not until the mid-nineteenth century was the word associated with feelings and passion.

Emotions are abstract and subjective in nature. They have been considered vague and diffuse, worth less than the intellect, and more primitive. Emotions have been described as irrational and as an expression of lack of control. We have even classified people as being either emotional or intellectual, where the former label is largely applied to women. Only in recent years have we begun to understand the crucial role emotions play in our lives.

Emotional Intelligence

In the late 1980s, two American researchers, John Mayer and Peter Salovey, formulated the theory of "emotional intelligence" and defined it as being aware of ones feelings, being able to deal with them, being able to motivate oneself, being able to empathize with the feelings of others and to handle relationships. In 1995, author and psychologist Daniel Goleman popularized and established the concept EQ in his book *Emotional Intelligence*. The book described the importance of emotional skills for success at work, in love, and socially. Millions of copies of this elegant summary of early research into the importance of emotions were sold worldwide.

People with a high EQ advance faster in their careers and build up a network of contacts around them. They become better leaders and problem-solvers. Evidently a high EQ is more crucial than a high IQ for success in life – at work and in personal relationships. This may be because approximately 90 percent of all communication is conducted by non-verbal means. People who have learned how to interpret social situations and emotional signals have a clear advantage.

People who are emotionally intelligent are skilled in different emotional areas and are in touch with their own feelings. A high EQ means that you know what you are feeling – when you feel it. Emotional skills and competencies are therefore an important part of personal strength. You can handle your emotions, control your impulses, and motivate yourself. You are empathetic and can perceive emotions in others. The key to empathy lies in the ability to interpret non-verbal language, including gestures, stress patterns, facial expressions, and energy signals. These skills are fundamental in creating and maintaining relationships. We like those people who send out emotional signals that make us feel good, and avoid those who make us feel bad.

From an early age, people learn to develop a range of emotions and emotional intelligence in their interaction with others. Although parents play a particularly important role during childhood, emotional intelligence can still be developed later in life. Feelings can be released and channeled through various methods of creative expression (art, dance, song, music, theater, etc.) and in relationships between people. According to Goleman, it takes several months of regular training to modify your behavior. Spending one motivational weekend isn't enough; it requires a complete change in attitude.

> *If you were to classify the competencies found in an effective leadership, you would find that only 20–25 percent consist of IQ. The other 80 percent involves "soft" skills or personal leadership. An emotionally intelligent person possesses self-control, integrity, patience, motivation, initiative, optimism, and empathy.*
>
> Daniel Goleman

The Value of Feelings

We depend on our feelings to be able to interact with other people. However, they are also crucial to the survival of the species, as Charles Darwin established this in his little-known book *Expression of the Emotions* (1873). He studied people all over the world and found that they share common emotional facial expressions, some of which are even identical with those of certain animals. For example, when a wolf is angry or feels threatened, it uses the same muscles that we do to bare its teeth. The physiology of emotion has been preserved throughout evolution and across species. Darwin realized that emotions must play a central role in survival.

This is a reasonable assumption, for during the development of the human brain, emotions existed before reason. The brain stem, which controls the body's survival functions (breathing, metabolism, reflexes, etc.), was the first to evolve. Next came the limbic system—the seat of our emotions, passion, and memory—like a ridge encircling the brain stem in the central part of the brain. From this the cortex and neocortex, the "thinking brain," developed. The neocortex is the folded, gray tissue that makes up the outer layer (3 mm thick) of the brain, and we use it for strategic thinking and long-term planning. Thus rational thought developed from the area of the brain responsible for emotions. The two regions have close neuronal links and are continuously exchanging information; the more sophisticated our emotional life, the more we are able to use this thinking capacity. These two areas stimulate one another.

To a great extent, western society has ignored this connection. For years, emotion was almost considered a dirty word. One study of corporate leaders from the 1970s showed that they thought their work required "brains but not heart." They were afraid to show their feelings to their subordinates, and their ideal was somewhat like Spock in "Star Trek" – super-intelligent but lacking emotions. Many movies are still produced that almost obsessively present these emotionless machines. Murder, violence and abuse are commonplace and the hero is often cold and removed from other people and their reactions. In fact, we are seeing emotionally disturbed people being elevated to hero status. The movie *Forrest Gump* was a welcome exception. Gump was a sympathetic hero with a very high EQ who succeeded despite his low IQ.

Because the field of EQ is so neglected, we live in a society that is emotionally undeveloped. Indeed, within us there is great potential for development that is largely neglected. This approach, which rejects emotions, is based on the mechanistic view of humankind that separates feeling from thought and body from soul.

Separation of Body and Soul

French philosopher René Descartes was one of the most prominent thinkers of the seventeenth century. He believed that man had a soul, separate from the body, and its main function was to think. This concept was completely the opposite of Aristotle's (300 B.C.), whose theories had governed our view of nature for two thousand years. Aristotle was a vitalist (from the Latin *vita* which means life) and theologian, who believed that life has a purpose. He held that the body exists for the sake of the soul, and its parts carry out those tasks for which they have been designed. A human body, Aristotle realized, was no more the sum of its parts than a work of art is.

But enlightenment philosophers and scientists rejected the view of the "old world." By separating reality into its components, they held, it could be understood using mechanical principles. Descartes believed that all natural objects are machines controlled according to these principles. His view was supported by contemporary discoveries of blood circulation and the definition of the movements of muscles based on mechanical principles. The mechanical view of the world covered everything from nerve function to the movement of the planets.

Descartes also formulated theories on bodily functions and human nature. One anecdote tells how in order to be allowed access to cadavers for dissection, he promised the Pope that he would not to devote his studies to the soul or the emotions. This gave the church sole rights in this area, further securing its position and the separation of body and soul. The church was extremely powerful. In 1633 it had forced Galileo renounce his belief that the sun – and not the earth – stood at the center of the solar system under threat of excommunication. The growing field of science could no longer contradict the church, and its domain remained unchallenged.

Descartes also believed that emotions merely served as a transition between external stimuli and the body's response to such stimuli. Emotions made the response less rational; only reason and analysis could be trusted. Like Plato he believed that rational thought is the only reliable source of knowledge. This contributed to the general view that both emotions and intuition were unscientific. According to Descartes the major difference between humans and animals was that the latter were merely soulless machines, whereas man had not only a body but also a mind that was capable of reason. Since animals had no souls they also lacked feelings, and consequently Descartes and others had no compunction about dissecting live animals.

Individual people are responsible for developments in the world, and their personalities shape their view of the world. It is interesting, therefore, to study the personality of Descartes, the man who advised and taught European royalty and other aristocrats of his time. In *Private Myths*, one of England's foremost Jungian psychoanalysts, Anthony Stevens, describes the philosopher's life and how something as irrational as a dream inspired his rational philosophy. Stevens writes that as a result of early emotional disturbances, Descartes developed a schizoid personality with manic-depressive tendencies. He was socially isolated, deeply introverted, and lived within his private world of intellect and imagination. He left a chilly and unemotional impression on his contemporaries, avoided all close relationships, and never settled down. Descartes not only lacked the ability to empathize with people and animals, but also felt cut off from all physical reality, including his own body. His perspective was elevated to scientific dogma, to his well-known "methodical doubt;" not only should man doubt everything –he should do so systematically! Based on his perception of the world he claimed that body and matter are completely separate from mind and soul.

Descartes' scientific and philosophical theories have influenced generations of thinkers. If we are able to understand the origins of our contemporary society it should be easier to embrace the new vision of the world, which stands in sharp contrast to the rational, mechanical philosophy of reason. Totality, context, intimacy, meaning, and emotion as the mediating link between body and soul – that is a true paradigm shift!

Molecules of Emotion

It has taken a long time to connect the body with the soul and the emotions with the mind – and for good reason. Defying a religious edict is likely to have dire consequences! Also, we need to overcome the mechanical view in order to bring about change. We are neither robots nor machines, but far more complex individuals. Only recently have people begun to understand the concept of "emotions" and their deep significance for our health.

It is hardly surprising that it was a woman who contributed to the revolutionary new view on the interrelationship of the body, emotions, and consciousness. For over thirty years, Dr. Candace Pert, a neuroscientist at Georgetown University in Washington D.C., has studied the signals of the nervous system and their significance for the working of the body. In her groundbreaking *Molecules of Emotion – Why You Feel the Way You Feel* she describes how emotions establish the crucial link in facilitating communication between body and soul. The emotions are composed of biochemical molecules that are the bridge between mind (thoughts, senses, breath) and matter (the body). They are omnipresent, moving between and influencing both. Indeed, the emotions are not of lesser value. Rather, they represent the exchange of information between the different parts of the body. The emotions are quite simply central to an organism's exchange of information. Seen in this perspective it should be obvious that the old classification of body and soul was dangerously flawed.

Have you ever wondered why you sometimes have strong feelings and at other times you don't? What is it that "speaks" when something happens to the body and you become aware of it? Most of what happens in the body takes place automatically, with an innate mechanism. But sometimes things go wrong. Unpleasant memories and experiences can be driven out of our consciousness – but where do they go? Could it be that unborn–that is, unexpressed–emotions can cause disease?

Candace Pert has answers to these questions. As long ago as 1973 she was part of the team that discovered opiate receptors in the body. At that time researchers knew that morphine and heroin have a relaxing and analgesic effect, and they searched for their receptor sites in the brain. After the opiate receptor was located, other researchers discovered the body's own endorphins. These create the same pain relief and emotions of joy and pleasure as, for example, morphine, thereby laying the foundation for a new view of humankind. We can anesthetize or stimulate ourselves using the same mechanisms as drugs do. It seems that morphine can attach itself to these same receptors simply because it is so similar to the endogenous endorphins.

Emotions can be said to have their biochemical equivalent in short amino acid chains, peptides, and their receptors on the cell's surface. Peptides were first called "neuropeptides" because they were found in the brain – since that was where scientists looked for them. Later, however, researchers found such peptides throughout the body, with more in the gastrointestinal area than in the brain. This explains why you can feel something within your body, like the feeling of having "butterflies in your stomach."

Some peptides affect us in many different ways, while others are very specific. For example angiotensin causes thirst, and prolactin stimulates milk production in the mother who is about to nurse her child. Oxytocin is a peptide that leads to a calm and serene feeling in both people and animals. Nursing mothers produce larger amounts of oxytocin, and levels also climb after intercourse. Most of the effects of the peptides are the result of autonomic nervous system activity, which regulates responses such as sleep, thirst, hunger, and body temperature.

Our emotional state and mood are indeed shaped by the different neuropeptides and their receptors. What we experience as an emotion is also a mechanism that activates a special neural pathway simultaneously within the brain and the body. This leads to a certain kind of behavior as well as physiological changes. Even our facial expressions change and we are able to read emotional reactions on people's faces. Most changes in the brain and mind are subconscious, and we are not even aware of what we are processing, remembering, and learning.

But we can consciously influence the autonomic nervous system. Through visualization exercises in a relaxed state we can increase the blood flow in one part of the body and thereby raise the temperature. This enables us to control it – but we cannot do so in our normal waking state.

Anatomy of a Feeling

The limbic system, necessary for emotional experiences, is located at the center of the brain. As long ago as the 1920s, Wilder Penfield found that stimulating patients electrically in the limbic cortex (about 2.5 cm in from the ears) evoked a broad spectrum of emotions. The patients reacted either with joy, anger, or sorrow, accompanied by appropriate physical expressions such as laughter, trembling, or tears. Blood pressure and body temperature were also affected. Consequently scientists considered it proven that emotions originate in the brain.

In the 1940s and 1950s Paul MacLean formulated the theory of the "triune" brain – the most primitive part (the reptilian brain), the old limbic system, and the new mammalian brain. The limbic system is considered to be the seat of our emotions. One part of this area is referred to as the "amygdala" and experiments have shown that this area is the gateway to all emotional experience. Another part is called the "hippocampus," which is crucial for learning and memory. Almost every type of peptide receptor can be found in the limbic system. Through this peptide network we can access various moods, memories, or developmental stages. Strong emotional experiences help us to remember, and without the hippocampus we cannot learn anything new.

This peptide network extends far beyond the limbic system to the organs, tissues, muscles, skin, and endocrine glands (which produce hormones). So, emotional memories are stored in many parts of the body, not just the brain, and there is a constant two-way communication between mind and body. Thus our emotions work as a mobile brain that maintains flow and transmits vital information.

Memory and Emotions

American Nobel Prize laureate Eric Kandell has shown that the molecular basis for memory consists of biochemical changes occurring at the receptor level. When a peptide binds to its receptor a change occurs within the cell membrane. This can make it easier for an electric signal to move across the membrane, or conversely, may prevent it from doing so. It also affects the neural pathway that will be used.

This process takes place not just in the brain but also throughout the whole body. There are receptors in the nerve bundles (ganglia) located near the spinal cord, on the pathways leading to all body organs, and on the surface of the skin. These receptors form the basis of the psychosomatic network. They convey what will become a thought, which rises to awareness, and what will remain an unprocessed thought pattern deep within the body. Candace Pert maintains that because memory is coded or stored on the receptor level, emotions unconsciously control the memory process. Grief, guilt, shame, love, and anger may be stored in the body unconsciously. Though the body has a memory, sometimes the memory process also takes place at a conscious level.

There is a connection between memory and emotions. All peptides are found in the autonomic nervous system, which serves as the basis for the emotional connection to our body's autonomic pattern. The autonomic nervous system is the key to understanding how the emotional memory works, though its significance for memory is subtler than researchers previously believed.

Our emotional state at the time when a memory is created affects both how we learn and how we recall a memory. Psychologist Donald Overton has shown that rats that learn a task while drugged solve the problem best when they are under the influence of the same drug. This means that we remember positive emotional experiences much more easily when we are happy; we remember negative emotional experiences best when we are in a bad mood. If you hurt yourself, for example, the pain might awaken old memories that had been completely forgotten. Emotional memories are stored for a long time, since we need them to be able to survive; if we remember dangers, we can also avoid them – when the need arises.

However, too much stress can disturb memory function. When the stress hormone cortisol is secreted in a stressful situation the hippocampus is prevented from using blood sugar, and this impedes the formation of a memory. This explains why it is nearly impossible for someone who has experienced a highly stressful incident (trauma) to remember it. It also explains why stressed people experience short-term memory loss. High cortisol production also affects the function of other neurotransmitters, resulting in confused thoughts and impaired concentration.

People who experience emotional or physical stress use up large quantities of magnesium. This mineral aids neural metabolism and helps prevent brain damage caused by inadequate blood supply. Magnesium's primary role here is to prevent calcium excess within the cells, and in patients with Alzheimer's the brain is so magnesium-deficient that its antagonist, calcium, may reach toxic levels. Magnesium deficiency can therefore result in memory loss.

We've all experienced forgotten memories that suddenly reappear when set off by some taste, smell, view, or touch. The taste of creamy vanilla ice cream can make the memories of far-away sunny childhood summers suddenly return like yesterday. Similarly, like dusty snapshots, the scent of rain-washed asphalt can evoke forgotten memories. A particular association may trigger strong emotions and bitter tears, without any direct connection to present events. These surfacing memories, sometimes referred to as "repressed memories," can be either positive or negative – though it would be more correct to call them "unconscious memories," because they have been submerged so long that they no longer exist in our consciousness.

When speaking about consciousness, Candace Pert is referring to the entire body. An unexpressed emotion travels along the neural

Most people's childhood memories are highly emotionally charged. My earliest visual memory is of the house we lived in until I was two years old. When my three-year-old sister and I came home from the playground there was a large yellow excavator standing outside our house. For some reason it frightened us; we didn't dare to go inside. It may just have been digging up the street, or perhaps we were lost. We walked down the street, crying, until a neighbor helped us go inside. I still remember how unpleasant it was and how vulnerable I felt. Those events that have awakened the strongest emotions of fear, anger, or joy linger longest in the memory. What are your earliest childhood memories?

pathways, starting at the periphery and moving inward, up the spinal cord, and into the brain. An emotion cannot be expressed until it reaches our higher cerebral centers. If we fail to express our emotions, energy is expended to hold them back. This process takes place either consciously or subconsciously. Inhibitory molecules and impulses keep the emotions and information "down." Protein molecules adhere to receptors and prevent them from coupling to peptides. As a result, unexpressed emotions are stored throughout the body: in the skin, internal organs, intestines, or in nerve bundles surrounding the spinal cord.

This explains how unexpressed emotions may cause illness. When you block your emotions, you also block the flow of neuropeptides needed for proper cell function. The receptors become clogged and the flow of peptides and nerve signals malfunctions. These cellular level blockages are reflected at organ level too. In time, this may lead to impaired physical function and disease. A bio-imbalance has been created.

How are unconscious physical memories and unexpressed emotions processed? It may be of some comfort that the body tries to do this for us automatically. When it is unsuccessful, various physical symptoms may draw our attention to different parts of the body or emotions. The body also tries to equalize these imbalances while we sleep. Pay attention to the signals, and don't shortchange your body of sleep.

Part of being a healthy person is being well integrated and at peace, with all of the systems acting together.
Candace Pert

Dreams

Are dreams a way of processing unexpressed emotions? What happens in the body when we dream? The electrical activity of the brain changes during our dreams. It can be measured using an EEG (electroencephalogram), with electrodes connected to the different areas of the scalp corresponding to different parts of the brain. When we dream the brain's EEG changes from the usual, slow waves with high amplitude to increased, rapid low-amplitude electrical activity. This is called REM (rapid eye movement) sleep because the eyes move quickly, even though muscle tension in the rest of the body drops. Dream-sleep comprises about a quarter of total sleeping time for adults, and is necessary for our mental health.

Candace Pert believes that during sleep different parts of the body exchange information, which reaches our consciousness as a story. The information is translated into characters and incidents retrieved from the language of the waking consciousness, which can be expressed symbolically or in more concrete terms. Examples of symbols found in dreams include the snake for sexuality, water to represent emotions, and travel as a metaphor for change. Although there are some universal or "archetypical" symbols, it is important to learn to recognize and understand our own personal symbolism in order to garner information from our dreams. They are an essential source of increased self-knowledge. Our dreams are still neglected and unfortunately their significance for the body's self-healing ability remains undervalued. Perhaps this will change as we accumulate further knowledge of what happens during sleep.

Every night our body resets our psychosomatic network to enable it to function the next day. It strives for homeostasis – balance at a physiological level. Failing to unwind before bedtime after a stressful day may result in uneasy sleep, since the body needs to release its tensions. When the body adjusts its cycle of peptide receptors during the night, the emotions' molecules are released to regenerate the feedback system. Dreams contain not only incidents but also emotions. You can feel these emotions in the dream, and they can even make you laugh or cry in your sleep. Strong emotions not confronted during the day are stored at cellular level. During sleep part of this stored information can be released and rise to our consciousness as a dream. Remembering dreams and processing them emotionally can be a healing exercise for body and soul.

The Power of Therapy

The important thing here is to dispose of unconscious, repressed emotions stored in the body by allowing them to travel up to the brain where they enter consciousness. This allows them to be expressed through words or emotions. Unexpressed emotions are stored in our bodies and can be considered "unconscious." Getting in touch with tense or painful parts of the body in different ways and letting them "speak" allows a release process to take place. This may feel as though we suddenly gain access to a large quantity of energy. More energy is left over when we no longer need to tie it up in blocked emotional expression. Only then can we achieve our full potential. Think of it like a bad relationship that saps energy; leaving it behind suddenly makes more energy available. Energy attached to negative emotions is released when you let them go. This also makes it easier to get in contact with our inner flow.

Interpreting the signals sent out by mind and body can be difficult. Professional help may be needed to integrate and express experiences. Sharing feelings with a knowledgeable person while receiving support and help processing such sensitive experiences can be invaluable. So much can be gained from another person who will accept and listen to your attempts to express your emotions, verbally and otherwise.

Nonetheless, successful therapy does not require the unconscious to become conscious. The unconscious part of the body is omniscient and powerful. Healing and change may occur without a person's knowledge and understanding. Hypnosis, yoga breathing, and various energy-based therapies (from bioenergy to chiropractic and massage) can achieve change at the subconscious level. The main thing is to allow change to take place.

To sum up, the subconscious is vastly larger than the conscious, and is likely to always remain so. We could not tolerate total awareness, all the time. Consciousness can be likened to the top of a volcano: the greater the release, the less the burden on the body. Once you remove the blockages, you can retrieve a multitude of benefits from your subconscious, with its intrinsic wisdom and knowledge.

Removing emotional blockages allows our joy and our positive emotions to flow. Why? Because unshed tears of sorrow cover the joy of life like a transparent membrane. Because anger chokes positive flow and sexual energy. And fear inhibits love. Or as pioneering body therapist Marion Rosen said: "Because love is what we are most afraid to show. We hide it behind all the other emotions for fear of being rejected."

Bodywork therapy has always been a key component of psychological processing. We speak not only with words but also with our body language. Freud, the father of psychoanalysis, began experimenting with free association while administering massage to a patient. (In the early twentieth century, treating physicians at health spas commonly performed massage on their patients.) But it was not until the late twentieth century that body-oriented therapies began to be generally accepted.

George Downing, internationally recognized therapist and teacher, was one of the pioneers in the development of body-oriented psychotherapy. In *The Body and the Word* he explains why the body should be included in therapy. First, the physical dimension is ever-present in our relationships. Even before an encounter we unconsciously prepare our bodies, readying them for action. The body becomes a form of meeting place–a theater–where we interact with others in playing out our unique life drama. One aim of the therapy is to affect and alter physical reaction patterns through bodywork. In addition, the very earliest preverbal layers of childhood are accessible through the body. Memories from the first two years of life are stored in a format other than words, and it is important to be able to access them, since some of our most basic conflicts arise at that time. Body-oriented therapy enables us to bring repressed conflicts and experiences to a conscious level, after which they can be resolved by through verbal expression. This permits unconscious emotions to reach the surface and be synthesized, thereby alleviating physical tensions.

At birth we are completely at the mercy of our guardians – our parents. Our view of the world and our physical patterns are shaped by the treatment we receive in early life. The development of our emotional intelligence depends entirely on the people who surround us. However, we are not condemned to retain every reaction pattern learned in early childhood. Preverbal therapy enables us to modify early behavior and develop a larger and more mature range of emotions.

Stop a moment and think about how you are feeling right now. Check your emotions and your breathing. Is any part of your body tense? What is your reaction to what you have just read? How are you breathing: with your chest muscles, or with your abdomen? Relax your muscles, take a few deep breaths and listen to your inner being...

Living Without Emotional Nuances

Not everyone wants to get in touch with their emotions. Some people actually prefer to manage without emotions. They prefer the distraction of a drink, candy, or a cigarette, to avoid dealing with their feelings. This may be the result of a condition called "alexithymia." The term was coined in 1967 and derives from the Greek *a-lexis-thymos*, which means "no-words-for-emotions." People with alexithymia do not lack emotions, but rather they have difficulty expressing them. They rarely cry, but when they do tears flow copiously without their knowing why. They find it difficult or impossible to distinguish between different emotions. As an example, they may not be able to distinguish between love and sexuality, thus complicating their relationships with others.

Understandably, these people make every effort to avoid emotions. Just as people who cannot swim stay away from water, people incapable of handling emotions stay away from them as well. You must learn to swim–to experience, handle, and express feelings–so as not to drown in a sea of emotions.

The late psychologist Kristoffer Konarski, Sweden's first associate professor in psychosomatics at Karolinska Institutet, conducted research in this field. He studied the relationship between affect (emotion) and health. First he explored the connection between heart problems and alexithymia and then he went on to examine psychosomatic problems in general. Psychosomatics is a holistic concept in which people are simultaneously viewed as physical, mental, and social beings. This view also holds that disease processes and health processes take place concurrently, but it is the balance between them that decides the state of health.

Alexithymia in psychosomatic patients was first described in 1963 by two French psychologists. They found that these patients all had impaired thought processes, lack of imagination, and few dreams. This syndrome came to be known as *pensée operatoire* (operatory thinking). In the 1980s the concept of "primary alexithymia" emerged, referring to a halt in emotional development. Individuals suffering from this condition remained on a preverbal level: their emotional development arrested some time before the full development of language at the age of three. This may occur in people with an emotionally deprived background whose parents failed to provide sufficient contact or were violent. To develop emotional nuances human beings require a background of immersion in a deeply emotional environment.

Konarski formulated a theory to describe the process of normal human emotional development. Divided into three levels, it can be applied to everyone. At the first or embryonic level we learn to distinguish between fast and slow. Since the fetus shares blood circulation with its mother, it learns to recognize whether she is calm or stressed by her heartbeat, breathing, and the quantity of stress hormones. Level two begins at birth, when infants learn to feel emotions of pain or well-being (cold, hunger, pain, satisfaction after nursing). Level three involves a spectrum of more specific emotions: joy, anger, sorrow, and anxiety. Before moving from one level to the next you must pass through and reach full development in the previous stage. According to this theory people cannot feel angst if they cannot feel pain.

All emotions are based on the first physiological differences that the embryo experiences – provided that embryonic differentiation occurs within a deeply emotional environment. Progress requires perception of the differences compared with the earlier situation, and further that the emotions at the prior stage have been understood, accepted, and confirmed. You must be confirmed on one level before continuing to the next. This allows the inhibiting energy linked to the emotion to escape. If the emotion is not differentiated, the energy remains in the body and can gradually manifest itself in various disease processes, mental problems, etc. Clinicians note that different emotions may have different physiological connections. As an example, the lungs, stomach, and heart display a variety of reactions to anxiety. Researchers have found that people with pain, asthma, or cardiovascular disease often have a history of interrupted emotional development. Such people may find life to be extremely stressful and difficult. They constantly try to adapt, respond, and understand, often by focusing on the outside world.

People who have alexithymia become "pseudonormal." They have learned an external behavior to compensate for their lack of an internal compass. They prefer to retain control at all times to avoid discomfort. They don't want to feel emotions, which they consider to be too strong or difficult to handle. For them, feeling normal means feeling as little as possible – and that's how they like it. They insulate their emotions with food, chips, candy, and alcohol. According to both Konarski and Goleman, these problems are on the rise in western society, with more time than ever devoted to TV and the pursuit of wealth than to interaction with other people.

Nonetheless, emotional development does not have to stagnate for life. Verbal psychotherapy is not particularly effective in dealing with alexithymia, since the patient lacks nuanced emotions. If you can't feel anxiety you can't effectively discuss it or process it either. Expressive art therapies such as psychodrama and therapy using dance, mask, and images are useful alternatives. Patients with nonspecific pain usually channel "negative" experiences as pain. Therapists try to teach them emotions such as anger, sorrow, and anxiety. Once equipped with the tools for expressing emotional nuances, their need to find expression in pain diminishes.

Another phenomenon, "secondary alexithymia," describes individuals who are emotionally differentiated but who have experienced total collapse following external trauma. For example, the emotional structure can collapse as a result of wartime experiences. During crisis intervention with children from Bosnia it was found that traditional psychotherapy did not work. Instead therapists tried to re-teach the children emotional nuances based on Konarski's three-step theory. Apparently this was very successful and the children found a fresh start by relearning emotions.

At an experimental day care center in Halmstad, Sweden, a curriculum was developed to rebuild emotional skills step by step. The Swedish branch of "Save the Children" published a handbook for this project, which could potentially help many children. Konarski believed that health-promoting actions should start at a very early age. He called the program an "emotional fluoride rinse" which could prevent future disease processes.

Unprocessed emotional impressions can be expressed as illness. At some time during childhood people may decide to shut off their emotions. Perhaps the people around them did not accept them.

I have a vivid memory of my decision to stop crying at the age of six. I was walking on a fence and fell, hurting myself, but I refused to cry. Although I remember this clearly, I also know that crying was rather unpopular in my family. My decision was a result of my childhood environment, which did not welcome true emotional expression, preferring instead heroic stoicism.

At the age of twenty I decided not to become angry but to rechannel this emotion elsewhere, in reaction to having experienced too much destructive anger for too long. Burying anger in successful research projects was effective, but in the long run the body suffers when emotions are repressed. The results may vary from clenched jaws and teeth-grinding to headaches, sleeping problems, recurrent throat infections or gastrointestinal problems, depending on which part of the body is the weakest link and where you unconsciously choose to somaticize your emotions.

People can also pattern somatization on family traits, which means that certain physical symptoms are inherited from one generation to the next. This means that people experience pain in the body where it is "allowed." This is an unconscious agreement within the family specifying which emotions are acceptable and which are not. The repressed emotions must then find another escape route. Are any symptoms commonly found in your family?

Empaths and Psychopaths

At one end of the emotional spectrum are the psychopaths (or "apaths") and at the other are the "empaths," who live in close contact with their own emotions and the emotions of others. Psychopaths can lie, steal, abuse, manipulate, and even murder without experiencing guilt. When they gain power over others they can become dictatorial. Caligula, Stalin, Hitler, and bin Laden are just a few examples of such people. Milder versions of this personality type can be found in gangs, politics, business, and families ("domestic tyrants"). Psychopaths also have a tendency to intellectualize, since they cannot rely on their emotional resources. Empaths can use their emotional intelligence to gain power. They willingly cooperate to bring out the best in other people. Such personalities become outstanding, highly-appreciated leaders. Most people fall somewhere between these two extremes.

Psychologist and researcher Claude Steiner describes an emotional literacy training program in his book *Achieving Emotional Literacy*. He also developed a scale for measuring emotional awareness. People who are closed off are completely unaware of their emotions. They may display emotions that others around them may notice, but they personally remain unaware of them. And they are also incapable of feeling the emotions of others.

At the next level of Steiner's scale are people who experience emotions as physical perceptions. They somaticize their emotions, and it is common for them to take pain medications for headaches or other physical problems of an emotional origin. At the primal stage, people become aware of their emotions, but these are perceived as an elevated level of disturbing energy that they cannot understand. They know no words to express these feelings. People in this group are more prone to depression, impulsive acts, or uncontrolled anger and emotional outbursts than those whose emotions are "frozen."

The only way to bridge the verbal barrier is to be in an environment that is receptive to emotions. This increases your emotional awareness and fosters rapid progress. Various emotions and their intensity become distinguishable, and people can verbalize them to others. They can identify basic emotions such as joy, love, shame, hate, and anger. They realize that they can feel several emotions at the same time. Jealousy, for example could be a mixture of rage combined with less in-

Scale of emotional awareness (according to Claude Steiner)

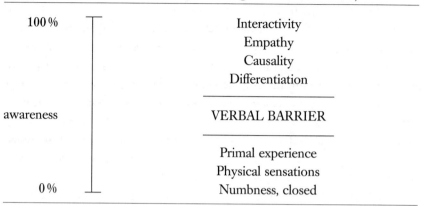

tense feelings of shame and unrequited love, though someone else may perceive this emotion as fear combined with intense hatred.

Once we understand our emotions we begin to discern their cause. We can see which incidents triggered the emotions and why we feel them. No longer are we dealing with something confusing or incomprehensible, but rather something tangible and concrete. At the empathy level, our emotional awareness becomes structured and subtle. We grow introspective and realize that people around us experience similar emotions in a similar way.

"Empathy is a form of intuition about emotions," says Claude Steiner. "It may feel strange initially, like relying on an emotion that approaches clairvoyance. It has been suggested that empathy is a type of sixth sense, which can perceive emotional energies as the eye perceives light. If so, the empathetic ability utilizes an intuitive channel directly connected to our consciousness and separate from the other five senses. Perhaps it is the equivalent of the sixth chakra, which sits in the forehead."

It can be highly stressful to be empathetic in an emotionally closed community. It is important to learn the appropriate use of high emotional consciousness – to cooperate with other people. This entails understanding how people will react to different emotions. Emotional interaction is the most sophisticated level of awareness. It enables you to perceive your own emotions and those of others – and anticipate how two different people might react in a certain emotional situation. This elevated form of emotional intelligence is crucial when meeting new people. It is also essential when falling in love, since you must be able to comprehend both your own and the other person's emotions in order to nurture a budding romance!

Inadequate emotional skills result from failure of the sixth sense to develop during childhood. Some people are empaths from birth; they are highly sensitive. Others are emotionally "tone-deaf." But this is not predetermined at birth nor is it the result of an emotionally impoverished childhood; emotional skills improve with training and people can acquire a higher empathetic awareness.

The first step is a willingness to give and receive touch and praise. Equally important is the ability to set limits for undesirable touching. Treating yourself with positive touches, kindness, and appreciation builds self-esteem. Next we work on becoming aware of our own emotions and those of others, in order to recognize different emotions and their nuances, and to learn how to cope with them.

A major step is to begin trusting our intuition, which enables us to accept greater responsibility for our emotions and their effects. It becomes easier to apologize and accept apologies for past mistakes. We can open our hearts and forgive those who have hurt us. But it is also about being able to convey our needs, feelings, and reactions to other people. We must be direct and honest in our approach, for this is the only formula for a successful relationship. By definition this means accepting emotional responsibility.

The more emotionally secure people are, the more self-assured they are about their identity and limits. This makes it easier for them to build close relationships with others because, paradoxically, healthy limits are a prerequisite for closeness.

Being in touch with your feelings brings you in touch with yourself. Emotions are necessary for developing your identity, for knowing who you are, and what is good for you. Simply put, your emotions are your tools for a healthy lifestyle.

Limbic Stress

Even if most of us no longer live under the pressure of finding food and shelter each night, it is still easy to switch into survival mode as a result of emotional stress. Society today dictates that we must be effective and successful high achievers with financial stability. This can create a vicious cycle involving highly destructive emotions. When emotional worry leads to overload in the limbic brain, it can dominate higher brain functions. This is called limbic stress. The reptilian brain takes over and stunts positive emotions such as love and joy. You are trapped in a fight-or-flight reflex that originates in early human development.

We have blamed the substantial increase in violence and murder over the past ten years on drugs and violence on television and in the movies. However, little coverage has been given to the research showing that solitude and isolation can be a contributing factor in murder. Dr. Anneliese Pontius, a psychiatrist at Harvard University, has propounded a radical theory according to which certain "loners" may have a neuropsychiatric disturbance that can cause violent behavior. Such people experience an "electrical short circuit" within the limbic system, the area that is responsible for all basal functions such as emotion, memory, and aggression. Pontius studied twenty inexplicable murder cases and found that the murderers, who were social loners, had suddenly experienced a psychotic seizure during which they committed the crime. The seizure could last an entire day and the individual might even take a bus trip home without remembering anything of the events. After the seizure, however, they were all very remorseful. Because the majority cited an incident that made them remember something painful or stressful, Pontius believes that these "emotional seizures" were triggered by external stimuli. All of them had had more or less stressful experiences, but had never talked about them because of their social isolation.

Pontius' theory of a triggering cause for limbic seizure is backed by the findings of Paul MacLean, the man behind the triune classification of the brain. MacLean concluded that since separation and isolation from the flock is the worst thing that can befall a mammal, then social isolation could very well be a strong factor causing disruptive behavior. It can "kindle" psychotic impulses from the irrational limbic system. The reptilian brain, the oldest and most primitive portion, represents a low stage of development. Reptiles care about no one; who could possibly be more of a loner?

Humankind, however, is distinguished by its ability to care about others–altruism–and to develop meaningful relationships. Only three types of behavior separate us (mammals) from them (reptiles and other vertebrates): tending to and caring for our children, using our voices to make contact between mother and child, and playful behavior.

Power of Touch

A study published in *Science* in 1980 drew a great deal of attention. A specific type of rabbit was bred to develop hardening of the arteries (arteriosclerosis). The animals were then fed a high-fat diet to speed up the disease process. At the end of the study, however, researchers found that 15 percent of the rabbits had almost no hardening of the arteries at all – their blood vessels were in excellent condition. The group was puzzled until it was found that the female graduate student who fed the animals had cuddled and played with the rabbits that remained healthy. The results were so extraordinary that the study was repeated several times – with identical results every time.

"Touch is the most important of our senses," says Dr. Saul Schanberg, a neurologist at Duke University in North Carolina. "Touch has a unique biological function that is ten times stronger than both words and emotions."

Schanberg has studied psychosocial dwarfism – cases of children who stop growing because they live in emotionally destructive homes. Not even hormone injections can stimulate growth. Growth resumes, however, when the child enters an environment with loving and nurturing treatment. Mental and physical touch therefore appear to be crucial for a good start in life. Skin contact is highly significant for development and maturity in both children and adults. Indeed, touch is just as necessary as sunlight.

In biological terms, touch is our oldest sense. Our all-enveloping skin contains a multitude of sensors for receiving signals from the world around us. They provide us with information on touch, pain, feeling, pressure, and temperature. Sensitivity varies in different parts of the body; for example, the fingertips and tongue are more sensitive than the back. In some cultures people say "the skin has eyes," because you can use touch to "see" different properties: thin, soft, hard, rough, sticky, and porous. This skin "eye" is more developed in the visually impaired, who can even feel the differences between colors. When you enter a room you can often tell whether a complete stranger is friendly or aggressive. You can even sense this with your eyes closed; indeed, you are probably even more sensitive without visual interference.

The skin is the body's largest organ and accounts for as much as 15 to 20 percent of our body weight. It is a barrier – and a bridge – between the world and us. Touch between people has three primary functions. It has a biological value, since it is necessary for contact and communication between parent and child. Touch also has a psychological significance, as it is necessary for establishing a self-identity, self-confidence, and an acceptable body image. Finally, it is highly significant in social experiences, which develop our social skills and competencies.

Many studies have confirmed the biological value of touch and physical stimuli in the newborn. The child's mental, physical, and even social development are dependent on early touch – if infants are not touched enough they may literally "curl up and die." This condition is known as marasmus, which means that the person simply wastes away and it was first identified in orphanages during World War II. The infants who survived were those that had been kept in rooms where they were held and cuddled by the personnel. Since the early 1900s child care had been based on the advice of Dr. Holt's *Care and Feeding of Children* (1894): throw out the cradle, don't pick up the child when it cries, feed it according to a schedule, avoid spoiling the child by touching it any more than is necessary for feeding, bathing, etc. In the 1960s, this form of "child care" was still recommended in some countries. Children were often isolated for a few days after birth to avoid infections. Pediatricians and professionals knew best, and mothers meekly followed the rules. Most infants were bottle-fed on a four hour schedule, and those mothers who nursed their babies only did so for a couple of months at best. No wonder there is such a fixation on breasts in America.

Touch is important even before birth. It is the first sense to develop in the embryo. During its nine months in its mother's womb, the embryo's skin is stimulated continuously by the rhythmic impressions transferred by the fluid surrounding it. Whenever the mother walks, the child is rocked – as if it were in a hammock. Nerves on the child's skin are stimulated as it makes the passage through the narrow birth canal. This beneficial massage should be continued even after the child is born. Touch and face-to-face contact with the mother are both vital for the newborn. If this contact decreases, attachment and the emotional bond between mother and child are also reduced. This applies to both people and animals. Touch is an important channel through which the child can signal its needs, at the same time that it enhances the sense of security and well-being.

Premature infants are particularly prone to suffer from a range of developmental problems. People used to believe that it was best for these infants to be kept isolated in incubators to avoid infection. Today, however, these children receive plenty of touching and massages in their incubators. If labor and delivery is painful, protracted, and complicated, it can leave its marks later in life. A Swedish study at Karolinska hospital's Department of Obstetrics showed that male adults who had had a difficult birth were more likely to commit suicide violently than their siblings. This suggests that a child's start in life is of crucial importance.

Touching, massaging, and carrying a small child provide stimulation and accelerate development. In many primitive cultures the mother holds the child close throughout the day and night. She carries it on her back or in her arms as she walks, cooks, or works. Moreover, aunts, cousins, and grandparents often live close by and help care for the child. In Africa there is a saying that "it takes a village to raise a child." Infants who are massaged increase in weight 50 percent faster than those who are not massaged. These children become more alert, active, and aware of their surroundings. They find noise less disturbing and they have greater emotional control. Babies who are massaged cry less and are better at calming and comforting themselves. When the massaged children grow older they perform better when mental and motor skills are tested than their peers who did not receive massage. Research has shown that the incidence of theft, murder, and rape is considerably lower in cultures that lavish physical attention and affection on their infants.

It is important to hug all children – both girls and boys. Girls and boys receive just as many hugs at the age of twelve months, but by age five boys only receive one fifth as many hugs as girls, even though their need for tenderness is the same! At the same time, more toys are made available for boys than for girls. The message is clear: boys should concern themselves with things and girls should focus on relationships. For example, in 1996, Swedish parents spent twice as much on Christmas toys for boys between the ages of six and nine than for girls of the same age. Such signals have naturally influenced the shaping of male-female attitudes in our western society.

Just as the body can demonstrate nutritional deficiency, people can suffer from emotional deficiency. This can be expressed in different ways. Behavioral scientists say the skin "hungers" if it is not touched enough. Many people who have lived alone for a long time know what it means when the body cries out for physical contact and intimacy. Hugging yourself doesn't help, though a therapeutic massage can alleviate the condition.

Children must receive tender loving care and physical contact – there can be no compromise on this. They need to be touched in order to survive, and some children may prefer to be beaten to not being touched at all. Experiments with monkeys have shown that after a short period of isolation from their mothers, babies experience changes in their sleep, heartbeat, body temperature, EEG pattern, and immune system. When the babies were allowed to return to their mothers, their behavior quickly returned to normal. Yet the physical stress remained, manifesting itself in symptoms such as an increased tendency for infection. The experiment showed that even after reversing the negative effects of isolation, there could still be long-term damage. Subsequent studies on monkeys have shown that partial or total isolation leads to brain damage.

Strong emotions touch us deeply. If people are not touched enough in childhood their cerebral centers related to touch, movement, and loving emotions can be damaged or fail to develop completely. Children who don't receive enough loving care and touch during the first six years of life also run a greater risk of developing physical weaknesses in childhood. Later in life they are more vulnerable to psychosomatic diseases.

Increasing attention is being given to the way in which children are treated as a possible explanation for illness and premature death in adulthood. Researchers used to believe that higher morbidity and mortality among people with lower socioeconomic status was the result of a poor lifestyle. However, more recent data has shown a different perspective. A University of Michigan research group has carried out the largest study to date of the relationship between socioeconomic conditions and healthy behavior. Researchers have found that lifestyle (smoking, obesity, alcohol, diet, and exercise habits) only accounts for 12 to 13 percent of excess mortality. Rather, it is the difficult psychosocial conditions that create higher mortality, which in Sweden is twice as high among low-paid workers as among people with higher salaries. Difficult conditions during childhood lead to chronic negative stress, which together with pessimism, low self-esteem, lack of trust, and an inadequate network of friends and relatives contributes to increased morbidity. The medical explanation could be that low birth weight, premature birth, and malnutrition in childhood lead to stunted growth and impaired resistance to disease. These children need much more love, care, and nurturing.

For some time psychologists have known that people who beat children were themselves beaten when they were children. Child abusers usually have low tolerance for frustration and a short temper. They are more hostile toward their surroundings and feel isolated. They are afraid of and incapable of intimacy. The behavior of abusive parents is reminiscent of the results found in the 1950s and 1960s, when researchers studied baby monkeys who were isolated from their mothers for extended periods. The babies were given a wire doll instead of their mothers, and fed formula from a bottle. Some monkeys became listless, while others became hyperactive or even violent. When these isolated monkeys grew up and had babies they often had to be stopped from hitting their young. They became social misfits, and often sat rocking and hugging themselves. Sadly, the horrifying accounts from Romanian and Chinese orphanages confirm that the results are the same for isolated children. The Romanian children found in the 1990s were physically and mentally underdeveloped, largely because they had hardly been touched or stimulated.

In the 1970s James Prescott studied forty-nine different cultures with native populations and found a correlation between a low level of affection toward small children and a high level of violence in society. Theft, slavery, impotence, wife-purchase, exhibitionist dancing, and killing enemies are features of primitive societies that forbid or punish early touching and premarital sexual expression. The lack of natural physical satisfaction through positive touching probably leads to frustration. People look for other sources of stimulation. Children who are not held and caressed enough can develop a certain resistance to being touched or touching someone else in adulthood. They may find it difficult to experience pleasure and to give pleasure to someone else. The ability to enjoy life is not exactly obvious, but the skill can be learned.

Violence in our society is ever-present and became even more noticeable in the 1990s. Touching and showing affection for children was not accepted during most of the twentieth century. We still live in a low-touch culture and it is worth reflecting on the implications this has had on our society.

Healing Touch

We need warm human emotions—contact and touch—in order to grow and thrive. This is important in childhood, but intimacy and positive physical contact after an individual reaches adulthood can counter childhood deficiencies. Through touch and massage people can experience self-esteem and self-realization. Increased physical awareness promotes an understanding of the connection between emotions and physical problems. A healing process can thereby be started on both an emotional and physical level.

The Touch Research Institute in Florida has carried out research on the effects of massage since 1982. In one study of depressed women, their anxiety levels and the amount of the stress hormone cortisol in their blood dropped after massage. Studies have shown that the health of children with different physical diseases improves significantly if their parents massage them. Children with asthma have fewer attacks and greater lung capacity, glucose levels fall for children with diabetes, and pain decreases in children with rheumatoid arthritis.

The positive effects of massage are probably the result of increased levels of the hormone oxytocin, which raises the pain threshold, activates gastrointestinal motility, and lowers blood pressure. Professor

Take a moment to reflect on how much touching you receive daily. How many hugs? Who do you touch most – your children, partner, friends, or strangers? Do you give more touching than you receive? What stops you from giving more? Which emotions are stimulated by touch for you? Would you like to be touched more, and how can you accomplish this? What kind of touching is taboo for you?

Kerstin Uvnäs Moberg at Karolinska Institutet has found that touch, the right temperature, and certain types of electrical stimulants increase the release of oxytocin in animals. The more often we are massaged, the more positive the effects. This is because the hormone oxytocin works like a two-stage rocket with both short- and long-term effects. People have varying levels of oxytocin, and we can probably influence our own levels.

Professor Uvnäs Moberg found that rats that receive oxytocin injections become stronger and less sensitive to pain as adults. Children who often complain about stomachaches, without having anything wrong medically, frequently have low oxytocin levels. A gentle massage on their stomach will increase the levels of oxytocin. Oxytocin is released in the nursing mother and is significant for the bond not only between mother and child but also between couples. Frequent hugging, touching, and massaging in a relationship strengthens the emotional bond.

Axelsons gymnastiska institut [Axelson's Institute of Gymnastics] in Stockholm has carried out the campaign "Fredlig beröring år 2002" [Peaceful touch 2002] for several years. The campaign slogan is "massage against violence," and preschool teachers and personnel, among others, are trained in massage. The children who receive massage are calmer in school, more focused, and less aggressive toward one another.

Verbal Abuse

When we speak of touch, we generally think of things like hugs, kisses, massage, caresses, and holding hands. But there is also verbal touch – words and statements that touch other people. This includes comments on their appearance, how they dress, their intelligence, personality traits, physical appeal, and talents. Positive verbal touch helps people thrive and builds up their self-confidence. But just as physical touch can be negative (beating, abuse, violence), verbal touch can also be harmful. Negative judgments and insults create a "toxic" environment. Putting people down makes them "shrink" and feel sad – that is verbal abuse.

Words can do just as much harm as a physical blow, if not more because they cut deep and damage our self-image. Since prison sentences for wife-beating are tougher than ever in the United States, there is a tendency for men who previously used physical abuse to engage instead in verbal abuse – a more intangible form of aggression for which few convictions have passed. Of course, women can also engage in verbal abuse.

Children are especially vulnerable to verbal abuse, since they still do not have an independent identity and believe what adults tell them is true. They absorb the words like sponges and develop a self-image based on false premises. This is one reason that many people wear masks. They have constructed a negative self-image and do not believe they are good enough as they are. They may also have learned to show one side to the world, while another side exists internally.

A team of physicians in England carried out a study in which parents were secretly videotaped with their children. The staff was forced to interrupt filming and intervene when they saw infants and older children being abused. Several of the nurses were so upset by what they saw that they needed crisis assistance. This hidden monitoring showed that in a matter of seconds, several apparently loving, confidence-inspiring parents could become cruel and sadistic when left alone with their children. These parents had a remarkable ability to deceive professionals into believing they were good parents, though they actually had personality disorders. This shows how difficult it can be to discover which children are abused.

The way we treat our children determines the kind of society we will see in the future. Unfortunately, the law still provides the least protection for the smallest children. Who listens to a three-year old who is badly treated but lacks the words to express this? The manner in which children are treated also decides how they treat themselves–and others–as adults. Not until we learn to listen and respect the needs of children will our society become more humane.

The Muted Child

For the newborn infant, its voice is proof that of its own existence. It cries to receive attention and let its parents know that it needs food, warmth, touch, and security. A child's cries may not be understood by a mother who was not permitted to show anger and cannot tolerate crying. She may find many ways to distract or ignore the child. When no one responds to the infant's cries, the child eventually becomes quiet. As a result the child may believe that its emotions are forbidden or repressed. For the child this is the same as being unloved, because it cannot understand that it is only its emotional expression that is rejected.

A child who is met with a lack of love time after time eventually learns to shut out its own needs. This may lead to the child screening itself off and becoming a human robot, for whom others decide how it should be, act, and feel. If we deny our emotions we deny ourselves and become cut off from our true inner being. If we lack contact with our intuitive empathetic self we will hunger after love, affection, and confirmation. People who deny themselves tend to dissociate themselves from living, feeling, and being healthy. The child who is not accepted develops poor self-esteem.

Going through life without being yourself and constantly adapting to others can result in lifelong inner stress. This may be expressed as a deeply buried sorrow over not having been accepted for what you are. Some people may not even be aware of this. Denial of life can be manifested as a desire to disappear and die or a desire to have power over others – to oppress and kill.

The natural (loved) child is secure, loving, and gives of itself. It is straightforward and direct, validates itself and others. It feels emotions, including anger when appropriate. The loved child trusts in life and is free to grow. The denied child, however, is tense, frightened, and withholds itself and its emotions. The unloved child avoids loving treatment, exercises strong self-control, and withdraws. This child becomes a jealous, critical perfectionist who idealizes specific people and is totally unaware of its own behavior. We can only do so much to break these patterns.

Health and Emotions

Aristotle was the first to propose a correlation between mood and health over 2000 years ago. Not until the early twentieth century, however, have we had the tools to study this link scientifically.

For example, our emotional health can influence whether or not we come down with a cold. Viruses use the same receptors as neuropeptides to enter a cell. They compete for the same targets, and if more peptides are present it is harder for the virus to reach the receptor. Since the molecules of emotion are involved in the infectious process of the virus, it is logical to assume that the condition of our emotional health affects our tendency to get infections.

The immune system's cells produce peptides that can both increase or decrease thickening in the heart's coronary vessel walls. Even if the role played by emotions is unknown, epidemiological evidence suggests a correlation. For example, it is well documented that people suffer myocardial infarctions more often on Monday mornings than on any other weekday. Moreover, there is a rise in the number of people who suffer myocardial infarctions during the days following Christmas (for Christians) and Chinese New Year (for the Chinese). Both of these holidays often have a strong emotional undertone.

At a major cardiology conference held in the early 1990s it was reported that the common cold underlies the developed world's leading cause of death – heart disease. "Ordinary" infections can develop into heart trouble, and this may be the link to the peptides and receptors associated with emotions.

Some researchers claim that negative emotions may pose as great a health risk as smoking. A repressed or chaotic emotional life demands too much energy, resulting in internal battles to hold certain emotions under control. With less energy left for external use, the ability to stay on track and complete tasks may be greatly compromised.

Why hasn't more attention been paid to the relationship between emotions and health? Probably because this cannot be learned from books. The only way to acquire such understanding is to explore your own emotions. You need to develop a fundamental understanding of yourself by training your emotional intelligence. You can do this by *confronting your emotions* – which is the same as confronting yourself first. You cannot accomplish this in haste or through schooling. It takes time and requires patience, but it is highly rewarding.

Intellectualizing things can be akin to an illness: it results in the continual rejection of emotional expression. People rationalize everything into something understandable, to compensate for emotions that they do not want to know about or cannot handle. Intellectual understanding is a completely different process from emotional understanding. The latter delves deeper and is more revolutionary. Intellectualizing is often an effective method of avoiding personal emotions or the emotions of others; it helps you stay focused on the task at hand and it is an excellent defense against being overwhelmed by emotions – but it is unwise to rely on it in the long run. Used properly, this defense preserves both the emotions and the self.

> *Think about a recent emotional conflict. How did you solve it? By rationalizing your emotions or by making someone else a scapegoat. Or did you turn your emotions inward? Bring the emotions from the conflict to the surface and experience them once again. How do they feel? In what part of the body do you feel them? How would you like to take care of them and express them?*
>
> *A good way to solve conflicts is to use the "I" message. Say for example that "I experience the situation as follows and would like to…" or "I get sad when you say that to me and ask that you…" or "I would be happier if we could wait with…". Practice expressing your emotions with straight "I" messages, and you will appear more clearly defined to both yourself and those around you.*

Relationships

Several research studies have shown that intimate relationships or a large social circle are highly beneficial to the immune system. There is a direct correlation between social ties and longevity. It is important to have a network of close friends and loved ones for both mental and physical well-being. Researchers Janice Kiecolt-Glaser and Ronald Glaser have shown that a happy marriage is of significant benefit to the immune system. The opposite effect occurs when disharmony is present in a personal relationship. It taxes the immune system and people become more prone to infection.

Similarly, isolated living or excessive loneliness is associated with a substantially increased mortality rate. Actually, no one knows *why* people who have close relationships and friends live longer, except that the immune system becomes stronger. We are probably not wired to lead a life with too much solitude; we need to belong to a "tribe" or family. We have to belong to a community for well-being, whether we choose it or are born to it. The "extended family" is a wonderful concept that describes those you care about and call to share both joyful and difficult times.

Social community is indeed of great significance for survival, while social isolation is extremely stressful for body and soul. For example, there is a strong correlation between the lack of social support and low HDL-cholesterol (the good kind), which cannot be explained by age, diet, smoking, exercise, alcohol, or hormonal balance. In his book *Love and Survival*, Dr. Dean Ornish summarizes the importance of love and intimacy: " I am not aware of any other factor in medicine--not diet, not smoking, not exercise, not stress, not genetics, not drugs, not surgery--that has a greater impact on our quality of life, incidence of illness, and premature death from all causes." Dr. Ornish has studied cardiovascular disease for twenty years, and has shown that lifestyle changes can cause serious cardiovascular disease to heal without the help of medications or surgery.

"If a new medication had the same effect, all physicians would recommend it to their patients," says Dr. Ornish, who founded and heads the Preventive Medicine Research Institute, a non-profit organization in Sausalito, California.

Researchers at the Institute observed that while diet and exercise were important, even more important were the support groups formed to relieve doctors of some of their workload. Dr. Ornish therefore stresses the significance of social support, emotions, and a sense of community: "It is healthy to have emotional defenses but the problem today is that most people have no place where they feel safe enough to let down these defenses." If you have nowhere to do this, your defenses are always up, and instead of protecting you, they will insulate you. Paradoxically, the defensive walls that we build to protect ourselves inhibit our ability to survive instead. By creating secure relationships, such as in a support group, people can begin to peel off the defensive layers that inhibit emotional expression.

Studies have shown that the immune system is much stronger in people who feel secure with others. Closeness and touch also play a large role. Moreover, love can have a purely physiological stimulating function. Without love we would wither away; it is as essential as the air we breathe and the food we eat.

Can people use love as a medicine? For many years, Stanford-trained Dr. Leonard Laskow has studied the relationship between emotions and health. His research on herpes showed five key patterns that preserve a poor state of health or disease within the body. These concern difficulties with trust, forgiving, receiving love, experiencing pleasure, and expressing and releasing anger. Problems handling any or all of these emotions can often be traced to the way people were treated as children. Each of these five patterns blocks the energy flow and creates an imbalance that weakens the immune system.

Laskow believes it is important for people to identify the pattern in which they are trapped for healing to occur. He developed a method using love as a transforming force in healing that he calls "holoenergetic" (holistic healing with energy). It is based on identifying the emotional patterns that need to be released, and then confronting them and actively releasing them using breathing and energy healing. Forgiving and reconciliation are important elements of this process, releasing old, undesirable emotional patterns. Unconditional self-acceptance is a form of love of self. Indeed, we need heightened awareness of ourselves and our emotional patterns to convert a pattern of illness into one of health. According to nutritionist David L. Watts, each illness has an emotional equivalent.

The cure comes from medicine and the art of medicine has its origin in neighborly love. From this it follows that healing is not the result of faith but of compassion. Medicine's true basis is love.

Paracelsus

Emotional Repression

It appears that a basic premise of our society is that people are inadequate. Many people, perhaps most, feel that no matter what they do, it isn't enough - they are not good enough. Deep inside, people seem to be ashamed of who they are and consequently hide their true identities. People feel the need to be better than what they already are. They wear a mask in which clothing, expression, and gestures become integral to the disguise. The façade becomes important and people become terrified that their true identity will be uncovered. Some people go through life without ever revealing themselves.

Just as sad as it is unnecessary, to a large extent this attitude is rooted in the way children are treated in our western civilization. If their true emotional expression is denied and their differentiation into independent individuals is restricted, emotional development will also be stunted.

The inability to access our emotions puts us at a disadvantage. We are less in touch with ourselves; we become more dependent on external factors, and are thereby easier to control. It is easy to understand why society became structured this way, as it benefits a hierarchical system.

Moreover, through disguises and masks, large quantities of energy are devoted to actively pursuing *not* being ourselves. Hiding emotions—or hiding the self—correlates with high blood pressure. It often seems as though people have "forgotten" the reason for emotions and find it difficult to get in touch with them. Emotions may then be expressed through the body instead of verbally or consciously. But giving honest expression to yourself provides energy in return.

Children need to be treated with respect and validated by their surroundings. This means that people need to listen to them. Children's emotional expressions have to be accepted and they need to experience a secure emotional environment that will allow them to grow up into mature adults. Today there are far too many three-year-olds hiding in adult bodies, their early emotional development having been inhibited. I have thought about why grandparents often treat their grandchildren much better than they treated their own children. Perhaps they have become wiser with the years, but I believe it is more likely that it is because they do not "own" their grandchildren. You can treat and speak to your own children just about any way you like, for they have nowhere else to go. But you have to treat your grandchildren well if you want to keep seeing them. Although pessimistic, this view is supported by extensive experience.

The drive to turn to parents is strong and as a result children are forced to accept practically all conditions, even if this includes being treated without any respect, beatings, or even incest. People have largely forgotten or repressed how vulnerable they were as children, and how they were at the mercy of adults. As long as we continue to collectively deny how deeply sensitive and vulnerable we are, society cannot be changed.

Denying emotions leads to self-denial, and the strangling of our mental energy. We must listen to our deepest feelings and give them expression, preferably by speaking, painting, dancing, writing, or singing. Allowing creative energy to flow greatly benefits and fortifies our health, giving us the chance to keep alive the child within.

Living With Feelings

Our emotions are the path to our inner selves, to getting in touch with our souls, intuition, and higher intelligence. We can heal anything that we can feel. Thus Descartes and the mechanistic view exit from the stage, and in comes Candace Pert, Daniel Goleman, Dean Ornish, and others with their human view. The conclusion: we all need access to our emotions in order to function, heal, and thrive. Otherwise we die from the inside – suffering psychosclerosis and becoming numbed in soul and thought.

Unexpressed emotions lead to unfulfilled people. But with the knowledge, wisdom, and courage of people like Candace Pert, change can be implemented. She has a stable scientific foundation for her assertion that emotions are the bridge between body and soul. She has paved the way for these positive changes, and we are on the road to a completely new view of humankind— emotional and physical liberation are milestones on the road to the realization of spiritual existence.

> *Everything that promotes a feeling of intimacy,*
> *a sense of community and belonging, can have a healing effect.*
> Dean Ornish, physician and researcher

Imagine being surrounded by people of exceptional emotional intelligence (with a very high EQ). The chances are it would be a warm, accepting, and open atmosphere. You would be accepted just as you are. Those around you would attach less importance to your clothing and appearance – though these factors might still have some relevance.

People would listen to you and respect you, openly receiving your ideas and thoughts. Setbacks would not be seen as dead ends; you would find alternative routes instead. People would view the future optimistically and move with the flow. No one would care about prestige, there would be no traditional hierarchy, and you would be your own boss. Each person would find their area of interest and unique talent, and act in accordance with this niche. The path would be open for taking the initiative, allowing for personal growth. No diffuse emotions would be simmering beneath the surface; instead, people would find the words to describe what is happening. People would deal with minor clashes before they became major conflicts. Not feeling well one day? Someone would care and listen to you. An open exchange of positive emotions would help everyone strengthen each other, with direct communication and completely open praise. People would touch each other as a way of saying "I see you, you exist" or "you mean something to me." The aim would be to grow strong together – not to assert yourself at someone else's expense. This leads to a creative environment, increased self-confidence, and an open, warm atmosphere.

Who wouldn't want such an environment? With luck, this is what our human environment could look like in the near future. It is up to you and me to create it.

What can I do to increase my emotional intelligence?

- Increase your self-knowledge by coming in contact with your emotions and becoming acquainted with your emotional reactions. To accomplish this you have to spend some time on your own, and also develop your emotions in the company of others.
- Increase the flow in your life by practicing getting in touch with your emotions.
- Make a place for creative, pleasurable activities in your everyday life. This could include anything from painting, dancing, writing, acting, listening to music, singing, learning to play an instrument, etc.
- Practice communicating with other people.

8.
The Creative Power of the Mind and Thought

Our thoughts can help influence the life processes in our bodies. We can change our pulse, raise our temperature, and alter our sleep patterns. Our general attitude also has a crucial effect on health: pessimism and a sense of impotence impair immunity, while optimism strengthens it. Thoughts come first; you might say that we shape our reality with our patterns of thinking. By becoming friendly with our thoughts we can make them more consistent with who and what we are, and thus alter our lives. This sets the stage for healing and bio-balance.

Close your eyes, and think about a slice of lemon and feel the increased salivation. Then, concentrate on a time when you were filled with joy and happiness – you will find it also makes you feel happier. Your thoughts affect your mood and that affects your body. You can only think about one thing at a time and by becoming more aware of your thoughts—about where you place your energy—you can implement changes in your life. It's called "mind over matter" in conventional wisdom, symbolically explaining the power of thought.

Research over the past thirty years has shown the significant role played by the mind in the body's healing processes. As a result, methods such as meditation, biofeedback, and support groups are now more widely accepted and there is an increased confidence in human ability to control health.

On page 42 we saw that humankind can be classified into three energy levels. Thoughts and emotions both occupy the second level. The mind is indeed an energy form that is "greater" than the physical body. Though less tangible, it is nonetheless effective. The idea that thoughts are more potent than physical reality, however, collides head-on with conventional western thinking – and it could take time for people to get used to this idea.

"Thoughts" and "consciousness" are abstract words, but if consciousness were a garden, the thoughts would be its plants. What would the garden look like? It all depends on what you plant – roses or thistles. Other people may already have sown the seeds of thistles and thorn bushes, and the garden needs to be tended and weeded constantly. We may not be our thoughts, but they are our tools of communication and understanding. Increasing our awareness of the thoughts controlling our lives is an important step on the path to becoming a self-healing person.

*If you want to see what your thoughts were like yesterday,
then look at your body today.
If you want to see what your body will look like tomorrow,
look at your thoughts today.*
Old Indian proverb

Limited and Unlimited Individuals

Thoughts are one of our greatest assets, but they can also be our greatest limitation. Our view of the world depends upon what we "see," those impressions we capture, and what we see depends on what we expect. Our expectations are shaped from an early age by the way we interpret our experiences of the world around us. True reality cannot be defined; rather, our brain and our senses interpret our perception of reality for us. This varies from one person to the next. If a group of people goes to see the same movie, each one will interpret it differently.

Our previous experiences and thoughts filter the information we receive in the present and this places limits on our thoughts. The result is the same as if you were wearing tinted glasses – you can see some things, but not others. If you are feeling sad or dejected, you will tend to see many depressed people. A pregnant woman suddenly notices expectant mothers wherever she goes. When you feel happy and strong, the entire world has a friendly smile for you, but sadly, if you feel like a victim you are all too likely to become one.

We are also limited by the system of beliefs or convictions we inherit in childhood. The messages imposed on us by the adult world when we are small shape our understanding of the world, other people, and our own abilities. They place a filter in front of our eyes. A child often regards its parents as all-knowing – everything they say is absolute truth. People whose parents were critical when they were young may very well "happen to have" critical managers later in life. People who have a poor self-image in childhood are usually plagued by it throughout their lives. Children who feel worthless and unloved are hardly motivated to achieve anything for themselves. This early imprinting leaves its mark for life, and from their earliest observations children learn from the adults' way of looking at the world.

A Swedish concept called *jantelagen* – an unspoken "law" or rule that says people must not think too highly of themselves – provides a good description of the way people behave in countries influenced by Protestantism. Do not do anything that makes you stand out, but instead remember your own inadequacies. Some of this is reflected in Ingmar Bergman's movies. The rule applies not only to individuals but even affects the foundation on which society is built. This has created a negative, reductionistic approach in which limitations become more apparent than possibilities. Disease is stressed more than health and the self-healing potential of humankind. The media focus on war, turbulence, violence, economic problems, and natural catastrophes. This is detrimental, for *if food nourishes the body, thoughts nourish the soul.* As the Roman emperor Marcus Aurelius said: "Such as are your habitual thoughts, such also will be the character of your mind; for the soul is dyed by the thoughts."

This preoccupation with the negative, the limitations, and feeding ourselves mental junk, will affect our innermost beings. It is not only junk food but "junk thoughts" that steal our energy.

Researchers usually say that people only use between 10 and 30 percent of their brains. This is also true of the way we limit our thoughts, using only a small part of our consciousness. Most people will think the same thoughts tomorrow, or next week, as they did today. Yet the reality is that we are unrestricted, since our souls are bound by neither time nor space and our thoughts are open to change.

Like a piece in a puzzle, each new experience is processed by the brain, compared instantaneously with previous information and sorted to find the right fit. Consequently each day's experiences are filtered through the lessons of prior knowledge, and thus affect all future

Start the day by looking at the world with fresh eyes! Forget about who you are, your experience, your problems, and your personal baggage. Look around you and experience each person and impression as if you didn't already have a routine box in which to classify them. Look at everything as though you'd never seen it before – and what do you see? How do you experience your immediate world and how do you experience yourself?

A 27-year-old woman was on the point of committing suicide because she thought nothing held any meaning. Like many others, she was burdened by her past. But she tried this exercise and in just one day she successfully turned her unbearable despair into positive emotions and became cautiously optimistic toward life – because she dared to see the world with "new eyes."

decisions. We plan our future based on our analysis of past events. And as long as people remain unaware of this, it is difficult to speak about past, present, and future, since the three flow together and interact. Our experiences and their associated thought processes are highly relative. This also means they can be influenced, as they are neither fixed nor stationary.

Indeed, we can use our thoughts to create something new. Thoughts can be self-fulfilling: first comes the thought, then its expression. This happens all the time. When we want something we create an image of the object of our desire. We think about it, absorb new impressions, and consider the emotional aspects. An internal three-dimensional image gradually emerges, after which we find the object of our search. Indeed something first takes shape in our thoughts, our consciousness, before it appears in physical reality.

You could say that our thoughts create our reality, and if we dare to let our thoughts travel on unexplored highways, we could also create another reality. This applies equally to our health and our relationships with other people.

We have within us a vast unrealized potential to benefit society. Once we learn to tap into our inherent capabilities–our thoughts and inner energy–large, positive forces can be released, which may also have a healing effect on the individual and on society. Just as a small number of people can exert a destructive influence on many, so too can a few people have a positive and healing effect on the majority.

The Power of the Mind

Computers that can be controlled by thoughts alone are one example of the power of the mind. This phenomenon is being studied by Princeton Engineering Anomaly Research (PEAR), an interdisciplinary group at Princeton University in New Jersey. Researchers are trying to see whether the human mind can influence computers controlling tasks such as the swing of a pendulum, the height of a water jet, or the movements of a robot. The results of almost twenty years of work clearly prove that the mind can affect computers in a way that greatly exceeds statistical probability. How is this possible?

Because thoughts and human consciousness are far more powerful than conventional science chooses to admit. Consciousness is not only an exchange of electrical signals; our consciousness and the physical world around us are also actually one and the same. Albert Einstein was the first to propound the theory that mass and energy are two sides of the same coin. In other words, something can appear both in physical form (as particles) and as energy (waves), and we can choose to perceive the world as either a physical reality or as energy.

"The subjects who succeeded best at influencing the computer are probably best at 'getting on the same wavelength' as it," says Professor Robert Jahn at PEAR. Computers are digital and use binary communication – infinite combinations of the numbers 1 and 0. It is only at this simple level of binary communication combinations that electronics has proven to be receptive to human influence. You could say that human consciousness reasons with the computer, where waves of consciousness can transfer communication according to a binary pattern. But far too little is yet known about the exact nature of how this works.

According to research from the PEAR laboratory, women are better than men at using their thoughts to influence computers. Large groups of people who concentrate together have greater impact than individuals. The combination of two people who love each other is also very good. Perhaps people who are in love have higher energy levels and are more in touch with their energies and thereby their consciousness. It is clear that amplified energy tends to affect computers more readily. If you've ever wondered why computers won't work just when you're most stressed, this could be the answer!

Synchronization is another fascinating example of how the power of the mind can influence events. Many people have thought of someone, only to meet this person or receive a phone call just a short while later. How does this happen? It is difficult to understand the exact process; perhaps the contact goes via the consciousness. Or, maybe you can "see" what others cannot. Carl Jung calls this "the ability to see around the corner," and it is very similar to intuition. Physicist and healer Barbara Ann Brennan calls it HSP, or "higher sense perception," referring to the ability to receive spiritual perceptions. Some people may hear, see, or feel things that no one else can. This aspect of humankind has hardly been explored – yet it does exist.

Any activity that people pursue gives them energy, thus generating even more energy. For example, we have far more diseases now than forty years ago – despite the fact that over 90 percent of our healthcare budget is spent studying and fighting disease, rather than on preventing disease. Yet the very cause of this phenomenon may lie with this emphasis: if our society had only dedicated the same energy and resources to strengthening healthy processes, we might have fewer diseases today.

It is therefore important to consider the object of your thoughts and energy. Do you spend your time on activities toward which you *really* want to devote your energy? A meaningless job may be spiritually destructive, while a meaningful one can be mentally invigorating. Finding something that brings meaning to your life, and devoting your energy to it, generates still more energy and that helps to heal the entire being. You can gain a wealth of energy from devoting yourself to actions and thoughts that bring positive content to your life, as many prominent men and women have realized. Working for a cause in which you believe provides energy and strength.

We are complex beings in which emotions, thoughts, attitudes, and experience interact. Our frame of reference defines how we perceive our lives and what we do with them, as the following anecdote illustrates.

Three stonemasons building a medieval cathedral were asked what they were doing. The first snapped angrily: "Can't you see, I'm cutting stone." The second answered: "I'm earning a living for myself and for my family." And the third joyfully replied: "I'm building a marvelous cathedral!" All three were doing exactly the same thing – cutting stones. One was bored and had a sense of meaninglessness, one had a personal goal, and one had true understanding. He knew that each stone he cut was important for the beautiful cathedral.

A person's outlook on life can also play a role in recovery. A cold or an illness can be perceived as punishment to someone who is already feeling unhappy. The word "*dis-ease*" itself is a good description of this imbalance or disharmony between the three energy levels: body, mind/emotion, and spirit.

Different cultures also vary in how they cope with illness. A study into reactions to pain, carried out in the 1950s, showed that English Protestants tended to be stoic and deny its existence, while Italians were more expressive and sought to alleviate their pain. Jewish patients also reacted emotionally but were more concerned about what caused the pain and its implications for the future.

In our Judeo-Christian culture, with its strong emphasis on sin and guilt, disease can easily be viewed as a punishment for something you've done wrong. But an illness—or crisis—is actually a natural part of life, designed to help you become more aware, raising your level of consciousness so that when you recover and return to a balanced state, it is on a higher level of satisfaction, self-fulfillment, and creativity. It is also important to remember that healing and human maturation are processes that both take time.

Maybe the real reason people have stomach problems is because they need to learn to take care of themselves. Or perhaps people become seriously ill in order to understand the amazing gift of life. When you are healthy it is easy to take life for granted, and the joy of being healthy, of being able to walk or run, is easily forgotten.

A man once visited his doctor because of a problem that had bothered him for some time. The doctor prescribed some tablets, and gave clear instructions on how the patient should eat, sleep, and take care of himself. Six months later the man was fully recovered. Delighted, he asked the doctor what was in the marvelous tablets he had prescribed, so he could recommend them to others. The doctor replied that the pill had no effect at all: it was the instructions on proper care that had cured the patient.

Think about it. If it were up to you – would you want to become healthy because of a pill, or your own actions? How long are you willing to wait to become healthy? In our fast-paced world everything has to happen now – fast food, breaking news, instant coffee, and meals gulped down in the car. We demand instant gratification; we believe waiting wastes our time. Even when we're sick. Nor do we have time to wait for our body's healing energy, so we take "healing drugs" to treat and eliminate the symptoms – right now. And in the long run, the body's healing ability is undermined because the strong tablets disrupt the bio-balance. Not only do these pills alter our pH and intestinal bacterial flora, they also burden the detoxification system. Short-term solutions create long-term problems. Our health deteriorates – though we haven't got time to be sick.

Becoming sick is often a natural part of life. Children need to suffer various illnesses to build up their immunity. Similarly, an illness or physical problem can be viewed as a natural challenge that life throws into our path to force us to stop and listen – and make changes. People should consider the consequences of their actions first – and dare to change, before the problems pile up. Whether we like it or not, change is part of human nature; it is the basis of our survival.

Fear of Change

What is change? It is opening yourself to something new. In most cases, the healing process involves changing something in life: letting go of certain habits and people, and receiving something new. Changes often stir up fears, covering the gamut from minor concern to paralyzing dread. Many people do not dare to become healthy because they are afraid of what might happen. Even if they are unhappy with their current situation, they don't dare to believe that something better is around the corner.

An artist may not wish to work through his psychosomatic problems for fear of losing his creativity and creative power. This is understandable, since resolution of psychosomatic problems always involves some form of change. But you can never lose your creativity; it can

Take out a large piece of paper and crayons or markers. Select a feeling–from your body or your mind–and let it flow onto the paper. Draw, paint, or write whatever comes spontaneously. Don't hold anything back. Think about your creation, write down the emotions it awakens, and name it. Then close your eyes, and imagine that you are calling it by name, and embrace it. Imagine that you are hugging it, giving it your full support and all your love. Then open your eyes and sit there for a while. Let yourself feel; think about your reaction and what was actually awakened.

only grow stronger as the creative flow becomes more accessible. Priorities may change, however, and you may choose to devote your energy elsewhere.

Some people choose their professions in an unconscious attempt to work through their problems. They choose their mission in life based on a complex–the unprocessed emotional experience(s) that they internalize–not on who they really are. The artist described above would be able to create using his soul and not his complex if he worked through his problems. It takes time to find out who you are, and recognizing that psychosomatic problems are a warning sign is an important victory. Your symptoms want to tell you something; you can't just wish them away. On the contrary, they will grow even stronger as you feed them more energy, through your thoughts. Your troubles and problems will only disappear if you confront them, one by one. Not until you recognize their existence will they vanish completely.

Humans are creatures of habit and changes in life are a common cause of stress. The greater the change, the more stress it creates. Emotional and physical stress can stem from either "good" or "bad" incidents in life: being hired or losing a job, getting married or divorced, starting school or graduating. Any situation that requires change is a potential stress factor. This also applies to changes in the lives of close friends or relatives because they place new demands on you.

The degree of change in life is directly linked to the risk of deteriorating health and well-being. Research has shown that the risk of becoming ill is greatest within the three months following a major change or crisis. The severity of the illness depends on the stress level caused by the incident. Could it be that unresolved crises actually lead to illness? All mammals, including humans, are programmed to react to threats against their biological existence, such as the loss of a loved one or a reduction in territory (work, home, marriage, or custody of children). In the 1980s, German oncologist Dr. Geerd Ryke Hamer studied CT scans of the brain and postulated that unresolved crises cause changes in the brain which he called "hot spots." People undergoing a crisis experience impaired circulation, cold hands and feet, sleep disturbance, and weight-loss, at the same time that they are constantly preoccupied with the crisis, both emotionally and mentally. During this phase cell changes or inflammations may appear in the organs that are linked to the hyperactive area of the brain. Hamer believes that if the biological crisis is not resolved, the hot spots of tension in the brain could trigger cancer in areas of the body controlled by that part of the brain.

This theory is consistent with findings published by James Pennebaker, an American professor of psychology, in the 1990s. Pennebaker studied people who had been involved in violent and unpleasant experiences, such as muggings or car accidents. People who had not worked through their experiences by speaking about them suffered more often from colds, influenza, cancer, and heart disease than those who had processed their emotions. Pennebaker has also shown that "people who write about their deepest thoughts and feelings regarding upsetting events have stronger immunity... than those who only write about trivial events." Everyone undergoes major changes in life such as sorrow and loss, but if we do not process these emotions, there is greater risk of illness.

Other research has shown that people who are able to adapt to new situations have the best resistance to the stress caused by such situations. They are better equipped for handling crises, which is good insurance for health later in life. By changing our attitudes to events we change our perception of the situation and thereby make the outcome completely different. What was first viewed as stressful may be perceived as a challenge instead, a task that helps us grow. Remember, stress can be positive too – we need challenges!

Tension and Relaxation

In its normal state, the body has a certain residual tension, called tonus, which allows it to react rapidly to its surroundings. Without normal tonus, the body would be like cooked spaghetti, or a slab of meat. Indeed, tension plays an important role in our lives, but there is a distinction between adapted and maladapted tension.

Adapted tension is the body's effective response to a threatening situation. It becomes tense, and relaxes naturally again once the threat has passed. If you see a child run into the street your pulse and respiration immediately accelerate. Your instantaneous reaction is a mixture of fear, tension, and worry. The central nervous system triggers the tension by sending hormones, such as noradrenaline, into the bloodstream to enable you to move quickly and correct the situation. Once the child is safe, your inner alarm system calms down and you feel relaxed and relieved once again. Your body returns to its normal state of rest and tonus. Thus the body functions in a dynamic balance – by raising and lowering tension and emotional worry.

People adapt to every situation to which they are exposed. If we experience tension and strain we respond by contracting our muscles. If we do not relax, however, but constantly have inappropriate muscle tension, a pattern is created that will lead to injuries in the long run. This is known as maladapted tension. The physical symptoms may cause us to react with fear, worry, anger, or depression. We become trapped in the downward spiral created by these emotions, and become even more out of balance. We feel victimized by the unfortunate circumstances and wonder: "Why me?"

Many people who experience this begin taking tranquilizers, sleeping pills, muscle relaxants, or painkillers for headaches. These are the pharmaceutical industry's top sellers – drugs that diminish or alleviate our common complaints, the maladapted tensions to which we have grown accustomed. You may become used to springtime asthma and allergies, headaches after a stressful day, menstrual cramps, sleepless nights, or recurrent stomach problems; but have you forgotten how it feels to wake up in the morning–refreshed and rested, energetic and enthusiastic–to greet the new day?

In this vicious cycle you may wonder what has happened to your body's natural ability to be healed and maintain a wholesome balance.

Most of us never learned how to use this skill. You can't build a bookcase if you've left your hammer in the toolbox and you can't use your body's healing powers if they lie untouched in a corner, gathering dust. The vicious cycle of tensions must be broken. Try this exercise to release your tensions:

Relax and focus on your head or neck. Tighten one hand until the tension is as great as that in your neck or head. Stay that way until your hand becomes tired. Now imagine that your hand is your neck muscles, and start relaxing your hand. Feel the blood circulating in your hand; it's becoming warm and relaxed. Continue until your hand is completely relaxed and now notice what has happened to the muscles in your neck or head.

Powerlessness is Hazardous For Your Health

If you find yourself in a situation over which you have no control for an extended period, it will weaken your immune system. We need to feel that we are in charge of our existence and that we can influence what happens in our lives. Psychologist Aaron Antonovsky believes that good mental health can only be achieved through a sense of coherence in one's existence: he believes that our existence needs to be comprehensible, manageable, and meaningful.

The opposite–finding yourself in a confusing and overwhelming situation–can lead to feelings of helplessness. Conditioned helplessness may be the result of situations that are beyond your control or influence, no matter what you do. If you experience this as a child, or for an extended period of time, you may learn a pattern of powerlessness that can harm your health. In one scientific experiment, a rat was placed in a cage that was wired so that the animal received electric shocks through the floor. The clever rat quickly learned to turn off the power by pressing a pedal. Then another rat was placed in the cage, but it could not reach the pedal; instead, the first rat turned off the power every time. Researchers implanted tumors in the two animals, and the rat that could not control the current in the floor eventually died of cancer, while the other one survived. This unpleasant experiment shows just how dangerous it is not to be able to influence or control your life. It inhibits immunity, with potentially dire consequences.

Living under stress for a long time is a form of powerlessness. Research has shown that chronic stress impairs the immune system. Stress inhibits the normal repair process of cellular DNA, our genes, which in the long run can lead to cancer. Feelings of powerlessness often involve depression, which in turn is associated with higher levels of the stress hormone cortisol, and this hormone inhibits the immune system. Researchers have also found that people who are depressed and despondent have a less healthy lifestyle: their diet contains too much fat and sugar, they drink too much alcohol, and they exercise too infrequently.

Depression and mental illness are a general risk factor for premature death. In a study conducted by the Swedish National Board of Health and Welfare's epidemiological center, researchers found that the mortality rate for the thirty thousand men and women admitted with a psychiatric diagnosis during the first half of the 1980s was four times higher than for the rest of Stockholm county's population through 1990. According to the researchers at the National Board of Health and Welfare, the most common causes of death included suicide, accident, and illness – all of which are preventable. In another study of two thousand men employed by Western Electric in Chicago, researchers found that men who were depressed were more likely to die of cancer. But they also found that having a history of emotional problems did not necessarily affect future health. *The way we cope with our problems may be more important than the problems themselves.* A patient's emotional state, however, affects the progress of the tumor once it has started growing.

Research has shown that people who find it difficult to adapt to their surroundings, have given up hope, and have difficulties in interpersonal relationships, are not as well-equipped to fight cancer. Thus it is crucial to have hope, confidence, and a supportive network of friends.

People who feel victimized by circumstances blame others for what happens to them in life. Assuming the role of victim can give an illusory sense of security, offering certain advantages. A middle-aged woman might not want to recover completely from her physical complaints because this would force her to accept responsibility for her life and she could no longer hide behind the mask of disease. A thirty-five year old man might not want a promotion at work in order to avoid the demands that might be placed on him if he had a higher salary. And people would no longer feel sorry for him because of his low income. Most people can actually produce good reasons for staying in their ruts.

But how do you escape the role of victim? By looking at your own role in what is happening and taking greater responsibility for your actions. People will only have power over you if you give it to them. It is also a question of adapting your attitude by distancing yourself from events. You experience and take note of your feelings, but there is no need to identify with them. We are so much more than just the feeling we have at any given moment. Not everyone can divorce themselves from their emotions, but this ability can be learned through meditation when thoughts, images, and emotions are ignored. Pay no attention as these distractions pass through your consciousness, and focus on your core to maintain your calm and contact with your inner self – no matter what happens. In this way you will no longer be a victim of circumstance but an active participant in shaping your life.

An inspiring example of this is the Englishman, James Partridge, whose face was badly burned when he was in a car accident at the age of eighteen. The trauma and the scars it left behind affected his personality and his relationships with other people, but after analyzing his behavior he saw a pattern. If he was passive he became isolated and lonely, since people did not dare to establish a relationship with him because of his appearance. But when he took the initiative and radiated self-confidence, no one cared about the way he looked. Indeed, by switching from passive to active behavior he was able to change the way others responded to him and thereby influence his well-being – and he is now teaching this to others.

There is more than one way to escape the role of victim. Be bold and courageous – view change as a challenge, not as a threat. Research has shown that this can be protective. Rather than becoming afraid and defensive, you are open to new solutions and accept responsibility for yourself and your actions.

To sum up: if you believe you can control your life, you will do it, too! And this positive attitude protects against illness.

Reduce Stress

Since tension and anxiety are underlying factors in most diseases, taking time every day to relax is important. Whether you walk, meditate, take a bath, or listen to music, having personal time is essential – to let go of your stress, problems, and external demands. We are more than just what we do, at home and at work – we are human beings, entitled to enjoy just living!

I was exposed to an overload of stress when I worked in research at the Scripps Research Institute in San Diego, California, in the early 1990s. Picture a large group of international researchers crowded together in a small area, surrounded by noisy machines and equipment. Everyone worked long hours and weekends in this highly competitive atmosphere. We were expected to achieve world-class, independent research. And, at the same time most of us were adjusting to living and working in a new place in a new country. All these factors involved stress that was positive at times, but frequently also robbed us of energy. Deep down, many of us probably weren't feeling very well. Whenever the lab environment grew too stressful I would drive to the ocean and take long walks on the beach. This worked well; the nauseating feelings of stress vanished, and I regained my inner balance. And good ideas for my research always came to me as I wandered.

Long walks are a proven method of combatting stress. Author August Strindberg, who was exposed to considerable stress and pressure in his life, took long walks every day. A walk gradually changes your rhythm. The swinging movements of your arms are soothing, synchronizing the two halves of your brain. Or you might have a special, peaceful place to which you can retreat, perhaps somewhere in nature where you can go to calm down and gather your thoughts.

Research has shown that city dwellers who spend time in "green" surroundings every day feel much better than those who do so more seldom. During winter I enjoy visiting the Butterfly House in the national park, Hagaparken, in Stockholm. I can relax there and recharge my batteries amid the exotic birds and plants and butterflies. Maybe it would be a good idea for large workplaces to create winter gardens as stress-reducers.

Being Present

We are increasingly surrounded by stimuli from mass communication. We are inundated with news, movies, radio, videos, advertising, television, magazines, newspapers, the Internet, and cell phones. The constant noise affects our consciousness. Little wonder that tinnitus is so common today. How are we to hear our own, unique signals against this bombardment of impressions? How can you shut out the noise to avoid being swamped by it?

Sometimes it seems as though we are owned by our thoughts: they occupy our waking time with plans and work. We spend our time either in the past or in the future, and less and less in the present. We live too much "inside our heads" and need to come down into our bodies. Life is a series of moments; it will just pass us by if we are not present as they occur. Relax and focus on either physical perceptions or sensual impressions to keep your attention in the present. Take the time to smell, listen, and observe your surroundings, and before long you will experience a strong sense of presence. Hug your loved one, let yourself be filled by the intimacy and the wonderful feeling of touch. Or soak in a hot tub by candlelight and keep your entire self– your thoughts and emotions–right there. Centering in the present infuses both the task and yourself with power and energy. After a while, this focus brings energy, probably because you have entered into the flow (see p. 294).

Thoughts travel on anything but a linear and logical path. It is important to put your tasks aside occasionally, and do something that occupies other parts of your brain. The best ideas generally come when you are totally relaxed, or when you are running, riding a bike, or doing the dishes. Take some time for yourself and let your thoughts go; this will allow your knowledge to be synthesized and stimulate the flow of ideas. Archimedes is supposed to have come upon his principle of buoyancy while lying in the bathtub, and Newton first devised his theory of gravity while sitting beneath an apple tree watching an apple fall down. So take a break, let your inspiration flow; don't try to accomplish anything – just be.

Being present is no longer a given in our stressed society – it requires a conscious effort. For thousands of years Buddhists have focused on breathing as an effective method of escaping from the yoke of their thoughts. You can unwind by taking deep slow breaths (abdominal breathing). Thoughts tend to run off in different directions like unruly children, but by taking the time to do the appropriate exercises your thoughts can achieve peace and calm.

We devote our lives to superficiality, forgetting about inner values. Something has been lost along the way: the art of being. Lying in bed early on a weekday morning and listening to the church bells ring… Just being; let your thoughts come and go, but do nothing about them. Slide into a pleasant state of non-existence where you can leave your physical dimension behind for just a while, and take a journey in another dimension. This blessed state awaits us all – you have only to seek it out.

> *Sometimes you have to wait for your soul*
> *to catch up with your body.*
> Chinese proverb

Inner Practice

Studies carried out by various research groups have shown that meditation, relaxation, visualization, or biofeedback substantially improve the immune system. Each conscious or unconscious emotional change is accompanied by a physical change, whether you are aware of it or not. Conversely, each physical change is accompanied by a corresponding emotional change. Thoughts associated with negative emotions drag the energy level down, but energy is boosted by thoughts associated with positive emotions.

Meditation is an excellent way of getting in touch with both your inner self and the life force. The method may vary but the basic principle is to relax and forget the everyday. Shut out external signals, turn your focus inward, and enter into a relaxed state. The brain's electrical activity changes to more relaxed waves, measured by EEG. Set aside a time for meditation every day or, even better, start living more meditatively, with many small meditation breaks throughout the day.

As you meditate "you move toward the middle," at the same time that you get in touch with something much larger. By directing your attention inward every day, toward your core, you can recharge your energy from within. You will become more aware of your needs, emotions, intuition, and your true self. It provides strength and energy. You can meditate at home or in a tranquil setting outdoors, or even while walking, by focusing on each step and being present in the now. Use your senses and let the smells, light, or sound help you transcend into a meditative state.

Meditation dissolves stress and can thus prevent and counteract physical and mental illness. Dr. Larry Dossey believes that thirty minutes of meditation is as effective at reducing stress as thirty minutes of jogging. Thousands of scientific studies have shown that regular mental relaxation and visualization lead to improved physical and mental health. Job satisfaction grows, life becomes more enjoyable, and people develop a more positive outlook in general. The quality of everything improves, as does performance at school or work, and even social relationships benefit, say the researchers. Such changes lead to greater self-esteem and self-confidence.

Why do these changes take place? Honing mental skills sharpens inner awareness. Perhaps a large portion of mental energy was previously put to negative use. Regular relaxation exercises and meditation can disrupt these negative thought patterns, and improve your life. Physically, the body responds to meditation with falling blood pressure, slower breathing, deeper sleep, and a better oxygen supply. Good mental health also guarantees good physical health later in life.

Meditation extends into a region that lies somewhere "between" the thoughts, the emotions and the body. There are subtle forces and subtle energies residing within us that can be contacted and activated with meditation, mobilizing our inner healing powers. This aspect of meditation has a mystical side to it, and mystics, healers, and shamans throughout the ages have devoted themselves to meditation. In societies where people believe in shamans, health means being in harmony with the whole picture. Healing is a result of the establishment of this harmony. Entering into a changed state of consciousness can be part of this process.

Biofeedback enables people to control their heartbeat and skin temperature, the size of their pupils, the flow of gastric acid, and sperm production. By relaxing and experimenting with different mental images, most people can learn to alter their inner emotional levels and thereby influence their physical reactions. Slow alpha waves are generated in the brain when people are in a relaxed and conscious state.

Using electrodes linked to the brain (EEG) in a lab setting you can learn to relax by generating healing alpha waves. In a state of relaxation people are also more sensitive to inner events, thereby setting the stage for a natural response to the body's signals.

Visualization creates inner images of situations and incidents that we would like to happen. In a relaxed, meditative state we can journey to both past and future; we can change our emotional reaction to something that has happened, and create an image of what we would like to happen. It is important to pay attention to spontaneous images that come to us such as dreams, as they reveal what might be possible. Visualizing is like releasing dreams into daylight. Be patient, eventually they will appear.

Hope is an "antitoxin" to fear and powerlessness. A hopeful attitude to life is the same as trusting: an attitude that permeates life, making it easier to overcome difficult times. Professor Töres Theorell, from the Swedish Government Institute for Psychosocial Environmental Medicine, has found that hopefulness and optimism can build a barrier against the rapid onset of AIDS in HIV patients. Author and president Václav Havel has said: "Hope is not optimism, nor is it a conviction that something will go well. Rather, it is the certainty that something has meaning – regardless of its outcome." Hope is an essential ingredient in a self-healing person, something you can work on using methods such as affirmation.

Try the following exercise the next time you are stressed out or afraid, anxious, worried, ashamed, or aggressive:
- *Take a moment to breathe calmly, and observe your emotions "from the outside."*
- *Express in words what it is that bothers you.*
- *Focus your attention on your heart center.*
- *Now think about something cheerful and positive, an occasion when you felt strong and happy, and stay with that emotion.*
- *Think about someone or something that makes you feel loved and appreciated just as you are, perhaps a child or a pet, and hold on to the emotion for a while.*
- *Finally, notice your success in breaking the downward spiral of negativity.*

Supportive therapy and self-hypnosis with *affirmations* have been shown to increase survival among women with breast cancer. Affirming involves repeating positively-charged words and meanings so that they are synthesized and become part of subconscious thinking. A negatively-charged mental cassette is replaced with a more positive one. Affirmations work like a mantra that is custom-designed to meet your specific needs. You get more of whatever you think about. The affirmations have to be positively designed, without any negations, for the subconscious to understand the content. Examples of affirmations are "I accept all of me, I am satisfied with myself, I set good limits, I am loved." Affirming is very close to prayer. A prayer for love, guidance, and energy can function just as well as an affirmation – the important common element is the sincerity of your words.

A *placebo* is a pill which has no effect on the body, but the *placebo effect* occurs when a patient experiences a medical effect from such a tablet. This is probably the most common example of the power of mind over matter: we have an inherent healing energy that can be activated psychologically. In drug testing, about 30 percent of subjects experience the placebo effect, but in pain management this number can be as high as 55 percent. This means that more than every other person gets pain relief from an inactive drug (sugar pills). Not everyone is equally susceptible to the placebo effect, but if your expectations are positive, and you have faith, will-power, and commitment, this effect will be stronger, demonstrating the significance of thoughts in the healing process.

Expectations of a treatment play a crucial role for the outcome. If you believe in the treatment and care-givers treat you in a way that reinforces your belief that you will recover, this can account for up to 60 percent of the therapeutic effect. Conventional medicine neither takes this seriously nor capitalizes on it. On the contrary, the placebo effect is seen as distorting the results of tests on a new medication. Why not strengthen the placebo effect–the personal inner healing energy–in medical therapy? It is simple, inexpensive, and builds up people's faith in their own abilities.

It is in the realm of thought that changes are molded, only to be expressed later. Faith plays a major role – whether you call it religion, affirmation, or the placebo effect.

Heal your thoughts and you can heal yourself.
Almitra

How to Manage Life

Why are some people able to cope with everything that comes their way? What sets them apart? The ability to handle different situations in life depends on the "tools" available. The more "coping" tools you possess, the greater your flexibility and the more options you can choose from to escape from a given situation. Below are some examples of these tools.

- The basic ability to trust in yourself, to trust your resources, and to believe that in the end, everything will turn out for the best. This ability is founded on an underlying faith in the good forces of life, otherwise known as a hopeful attitude.
- We can all cope with our lives when we feel healthy in mind and body. In times of poor health, however, it is important to either have or develop the ability to care for ourselves, to recognize our bodies' signals and respond appropriately. As long as they dare to meet the challenge, people can grow when confronted with trials. Basic trust helps. Crises exist to foster personal and spiritual growth. As a result crisis management skills are crucial for coping in life, and should be taught in the earliest school years.
- The ability to calm down when life heats up – to stop, breathe calmly, and wait for the right moment before acting. Sometimes doing nothing is better than reacting impulsively in response to personal fear. Fears can cause a range of reactions from laying smoke screens to panicking – but remember: we are not our emotions. They exist only as warning signals to keep us alert. Experiencing fear is natural, but it does not need to control us.
- The ability to judge people in such a way that destructive situations can be avoided. Common sense is one key element, but you also have to be able to surround yourself with supportive people, or seek the help you need. Avoiding bad situations saves energy that can better be used to achieve your goals.

Luxuriate in Joy

True joy opens us to positive energy, drives away our fears and woes, and aids healing. It is impossible to be happy and afraid at one and the same time. Joy is accompanied by positive emotions that boost energy levels and stimulate immunity. It improves our thought processes and enhances our intuitive skills, making it easier for us to make the right decisions. Humor, which also has a protective and beneficial effect on health, works the same way. A sense of humor makes it easier to accept that you cannot control everything.

We are all born with joy. Small children express joy with their entire being, with smiling faces and bodies "quivering" with happiness. A child will laugh over the smallest things. People who are filled with true joy transfer healing powers to others in their surroundings and raise the energy level in a room. The Dalai Lama calls this "smiling with the heart." He believes that many westerners have lost the ability to experience true joy. We smile behind a mask. Perhaps we are afraid to reveal our true emotions for fear of rejection, or maybe we have just forgotten how to be happy.

True joy grows and thrives in a loving and accepting environment, but atrophies in an environment that is censoring, jealous, and critical. Our culture has long been characterized by control and obedience to authority. This is based on a fear of losing control over people; fear that they will become lazy, deceitful, or–worse–that they might even rebel. This is a rather damning view of humanity. To remain obediently under control, people learn to repress their true feelings, and instead find outlets that bring artificial happiness – sex, drugs, clothing, alcohol, comfort eating, and new gadgets. Unfortunately these do not bring true joy, but merely a fleeting high. One good method of recognizing true joy: it doesn't give a hangover.

Joy is contagious and helps people strengthen the ties between them. It is a strong driving force that pushes away fears, expands consciousness, and opens us to a world of love, wisdom, intimacy, and creativity. Awaken the joy within by stimulating it with your senses. Surround yourself with people you like and with whom you enjoy spending time. Stop to admire and smell the beautiful flowers. Do what you enjoy, and surround yourself with beautiful objects. Beauty is a source of true joy. Do three things every day that bring you joy and fill you with well-being. Joy flourishes when we accept ourselves just as we are. Dare to show your emotions. Discover how liberating it can be to allow yourself to be as silly or nasty as you sometimes feel. Dare to be yourself, remove the mask, and be spontaneous. Life offers far more paths than those you have learned. Dare to release your inner joy and wisdom. Whatever fills you with joy gives you energy. Let joy be your guide in your healing and life processes.

Personal Transformation

We waste far too much time trying to change other people when we can only change ourselves. And there is nothing as frustrating as trying to change someone else.

The only requirement for change within is the will to do so. We can realize or strengthen our willpower quite simply by using it, creating a benevolent cycle – willpower generates more willpower. Desire or will manifests itself in actions: energy, control, clear focus, decisiveness, perseverance, courage, and organizational ability.

When human development is well-balanced and healthy, it extends in every direction – more like an expanding sphere than a straight line. The process involves:

- developing the desire and ability for self-determination
- learning to find joy in beauty
- allowing the imagination to flourish
- stimulating intuition
- finding love
- discovering the Self and its goals

Self-esteem is the foundation of life. Self-esteem is knowing that I am someone, that what I think and do has its foundation deep within me. Self-esteem exists within us all, searching for a site where it can take hold and grow.

We have learned so much – but how much have we learned about ourselves? Consider your relationship to yourself just like the one you have with your best friend. Would your best friend accept that you spend as little time together as you do with yourself? If your friend needs you, would you say: "I don't have time to see you because I'm going to watch the news"? We don't even take half an hour a day for ourselves – even though television, the news, newspapers, magazines, and other demands may occupy hours of our time. How do you think your inner self perceives this? As a sign that you are valuable, popular, and appreciated? Hardly. Your best friend would probably berate you for acting that way or simply cease to be your best friend any longer. Yet you treat yourself so nonchalantly...

You can spend time with yourself in many ways. Make a date with yourself and enjoy a good dinner at home, or go to the movies. Or set aside time every day for an activity that you consider to be fun and that fills you with joy, such as exercising – not because you want to make yourself attractive to others, but just because it's fun. Getting to know someone else is a slow process, so why should you devote less time getting to know yourself? It is important to have a good relationship with yourself: after all, *you* are the one with whom you have to spend the rest of your life.

How do I increase my self-esteem? Externally, you have to take responsibility for yourself, for your actions, and for your reactions. If you blame other people for things, you are denying that responsibility. Avoiding decision-making means letting other people do things for you, which is bad for your self-esteem.

All change takes place from the inside and out. Find your direction in life first – then pick up speed. Most people try to devise a mission in life based on their actions, rather than basing their actions on their mission.

Changing your thoughts is a very effective way of achieving change. You can go from one form to another, to a form and an expression that is more consistent with who you are. This is the very nature of the healing process: to heal the form (mind and body) and continue on to the next form.

> *We are what we think.*
> *Everything we are is found within our thoughts.*
> *With our thoughts, we make the world.*
> Buddha

9.
Healing Detoxification

Never before has the use of both stimulants and sedatives been as widespread as today. What makes it so easy to become physically addicted, and how do we break these vicious cycles? More and more people are troubled by a number of vague mental or physical complaints indicating a bio-imbalance. Is it easier to become addicted when your body is out of balance? Has the drastic change in our lifestyle burdened–poisoned–us more than ever before? People can develop allergic and toxic reactions to ordinary food or to food additives. To regain its balance the body must be detoxified. What does this mean?

We have been taught that a quick cure is available whenever we don't feel well – tablets for headaches, depression, sore throats, sleeping problems, and stomachaches. With our limited patience, it is hard to accept that building a healthy, physically fit body takes time. Perhaps, preferring the quick fix, we have not realized until now that the body can suffer from adverse side effects. Choices include candy, ice cream, coffee, alcohol, tobacco, aspirin, Valium, Prozac, heroin, hashish, ecstasy – a drug for every emotion and need. We can manipulate our minds and our emotions as much as we like, but just what are the consequences for mind and body?

Effort and reward are the very basis of self-esteem. Unless we first raise dopamine levels by making an effort, the reward (elevated serotonin levels) cannot lead to a "bio-balanced" brain. This is a biological fact. Quite simply, it means that without some form of hardship and tension a reward is biologically destructive. It is therefore crucial to feel that you have a meaningful task in order to establish the conditions necessary for bio-balance.

When we use the body's reward system without first making an effort, we disconnect ourselves from the system – our bodies become accustomed to receiving chemicals that disrupt our ability to achieve biochemical balance. For example, the use of substances that inhibit the body's production of noradrenaline, adrenalin, and dopamine reduces its ability for self-stimulation. This is a high price to pay: it sets the body's normal feedback system out of commission, confusing the signals to the body. In effect, we diminish or destroy our natural bio-balance while sacrificing our inherited energy and ability. We are weakened as individuals.

Degenerative diseases and mental and emotional instability have risen sharply as this mentality has taken hold in society, especially during the 1990s. This benefits companies that seek to sell addictive products without taking responsibility for long-term consequences: Today, 46 percent of Americans use at least one prescription drug daily and on average each US resident has 11 prescriptions (in 2001). Tablets for symptomatic relief and industrially-produced "candymeals"–sweet and easy-to-chew–might almost be called the new opium of the people.

On closer examination, it is illogical that some products are legal while others are banned. All drugs have adverse effects; indeed, there is no biochemical difference – so why should the profits from some be more acceptable than from others? Candy, drugs, and alcohol are all attempts at self-medication by people who don't feel well. In the long run, however, they are all doomed to failure.

In summary – legal and illegal drugs are everywhere, aimed at dulling, calming, or producing a high. Why do we live in a culture that so clearly encourages drug use?

The Oral Society

For many years we have been inundated with messages telling us that we only have to put something in our mouths when we're feeling in a bad mood, tired, depressed, or out of balance. The advertisements say when you feel the urge – why wait? Images of joyous, active young people send out a clear message: have some chocolate and find true happiness! We have been programmed to put something in our mouths in response to different feelings – convinced that this is the best way to quell feelings of dis-ease. Whether it's candy or headache tablets doesn't matter – just take something.

The companies don't care if the advertising is deceptive or distorts reality, provided it sells the product. One example is the claim that a chocolate bar provides energy and improves performance. It may boost blood sugar levels temporarily, but it supplies no nutrients for energy or endurance. And the new "energy" drinks, like "Red Bull," contain four sugar cubes and almost the same amount of caffeine as a cup of coffee – are they really good for our children and teenagers? Children go through an oral phase some time between the ages of six months and two years. Everything goes into their mouths for exploration as a natural part of their discovery of the world. Have we collectively become arrested in our development at this stage, where oral stimulation gives security and takes priority over all else?

Perhaps negative emotions are not considered "acceptable" in contemporary society, and that is why we have a tablet for every mood and occasion. Each feeling has its place, however, and if we are to live life to the fullest we need the full emotional spectrum.

Unhealed emotions, which are repressed and not synthesized or released through verbal or other processing, create discomfort in the body. Trauma and stress block the nerve connections throughout the body, interrupting the flow of information. It may seem as though you are "trapped" in your emotions, or that these emotions are unhealed – chronic fear, sorrow, anger, frustration, and bitterness. In such situations we try to avoid emotions perceived as disturbing and unacceptable by eating chocolate, smoking a cigarette, or taking a drink. We use artificial substances all the time to escape from anything that feels unpleasant to something that is calming and comforting – albeit momentarily.

Why not pay attention to our emotions instead and take them seriously for once? Then we would have to take ourselves seriously, too. Maybe we need to express a feeling, or we need to feel better. Our feelings are the path to our selves and to healing, but if we anesthetize them, we anesthetize our essence. Is the widespread use of drugs nowadays a desperate plea for help? Do we choose to poison ourselves to escape living in the now?

Consider the underlying patterns in society. Why do we create a drug-centered society instead of a love-centered society? Perhaps because there is a shortage of love – of caring, touching, empathy, tenderness, and intimacy. Maybe we use different drugs to replace that missing love. Sugar is the good mother who comforts us, who is always there when we need her. The abuser is a child in an adult body

– never having been permitted to be a child, nor receiving the emotions children need. This may also be an expression of loneliness and lack of confidence. As one recovered bulimic said: "The refrigerator was the only friend I could trust." Food, medicine, or alcohol may be the only things that give you the emotion you lack. Sadly, the feeling is but fleeting.

Although we live in a peaceful and relatively secure society, the focus is on self-destructiveness. Why? More acts of genocide were committed during the twentieth century than ever before in human history; we developed atomic bombs capable of destroying the earth many times over. One reason for this self-destructiveness could be that a strong lid was placed over all pain, death, and suffering in the aftermath of World War II. No one wanted to listen and no emotions were processed; instead, people were encouraged to look ahead, remain silent about what had happened, and help build the welfare society. Material success was a common security blanket, a façade behind which angst, despair, and loneliness remained hidden. They say it takes three generations to raise a gentleman – or a drug addict. Three generations have passed since the war, and perhaps we are paying the price in the form of disease, chemical addiction, and violence.

Bad Food Habits

I once asked a representative from the Swedish National Food Administration why advertising cigarettes and alcohol is banned, but advertising foods known to be harmful to the body and teeth–such as chips, junk food, candy, soft drinks–is acceptable. She looked at me in dismay and said it wouldn't be right to interfere with people's eating habits that way. A strange argument, indeed: our society permits some poisons, but bans others. Sugar can be as addictive as heroin and nicotine; yet advertising aimed at young people that glorifies chips, candy, and soft drinks is considered justifiable. How does this reflect on adult responsibility? We aren't dealing with a natural physiological need, but a contrived dependency on processed products.

Sales of candy, chocolate, and ice cream in Sweden and many other countries have increased tenfold since the early 1960s – mainly because of widespread advertising. Children and teenagers are influenced by the association of candy and fast food with sports, sex appeal, popularity, and success. One of the world's best selling ice cream brands cleverly changed its logo to something resembling an emblem for the heart foundation. Obviously associating ice cream with a healthy heart is misleading, since neither sugar nor chemically manipulated fats and starches are beneficial to your heart or your arteries.

The late William Dufty wrote in his objective humorous bestseller, Sugar Blues, about his meeting in 1965 with a Japanese philosopher, who had just returned from Saigon and said: "If you Americans really want to conquer North Vietnam just drop sugar, candy, and Coca-Cola on them. This will destroy them much faster than bombs." North Vietnam was not conquered by the US militarily, but studies now show that sugar consumption has risen sharply in China, India, and Southeast Asia. These countries are also the major growth markets for the soft drink industry. Pepsi and Coca-Cola use pop groups and models and clear allusions to sex, youth, and beautiful bodies to sell their products, and there are always new markets with young people to conquer.

In summary: the more urbanized and "civilized" the developing world becomes, the higher the rate of sugar consumption. Since the fifteenth century sugar has been a sign of economic prosperity in which only the upper classes could indulge. But over the past century the industry has changed this by making various sugar products available to everyone. And today sugar is no longer associated with wealth, but with a surge in degenerative diseases.

A 33-cl soft drink contains the equivalent of about ten sugar cubes. As a result soft drinks have to be served ice cold, or they would taste like sugared water. Coca-Cola also contains large quantities of phosphoric acid, with the same acidity as vinegar. The sweetness masks the low pH; you have no idea that you're drinking such a concoction of sugar, caffeine, coloring, flavoring, and phosphoric acid. While it doesn't quench thirst, it is a diuretic because of the high sugar level and low pH. Rising consumption of soft drinks and sugar changes the bacterial flora in the mouth, leading to tooth decay. Unfortunately, when young people become used to drinking soft drinks in large amounts they may also be paving the way for future alcohol dependency.

Chemical Addiction

Drugs affect the body by imitating or influencing the body's own "drug system." Morphine provides pain relief and feelings of euphoria since it attaches itself to the receptors of the natural endorphins. What, then, is the difference between the drugs we take and the drugs we make within our own bodies?

The latter are part of a complicated, sensitive biosystem with a built-in feedback mechanism. The body has neurotransmitters, such as endorphins, that are released in different places in the brain at different times and in very small quantities, while drugs such as morphine or heroin affect multiple areas in the brain simultaneously. The body's receptors become flooded and "swim" in these chemicals. As you become accustomed to the higher quantities, you become less sensitive to normal levels. The number of receptors drops, and you need larger and larger doses to match the original high. Various adverse effects occur, such as elevated blood pressure and an altered perception of reality (though, of course, this may be exactly what people want).

While nicotine or morphine imitate the body's own substances, cocaine prevents noradrenaline from breaking down. This tricks the body into believing you are in a stressful situation, increasing alertness so you can stay awake longer. Amphetamines have a similar effect, releasing excess noradrenaline and dopamine, and preventing their reabsorption. The drug Ecstasy works by releasing a large quantity of serotonin in the brain. In natural quantities, serotonin has a soothing and pleasant effect. In large quantities, however, it dramatically affects our metabolism and body temperature, producing euphoria and hyperactivity.

We all have a natural ability to relax, reduce pain, and experience sensual pleasure and euphoria – without chemical drugs. If we take external drugs, however, they control us. The body's bio-balance is disturbed and in the end, we lose the ability to achieve the sensual pleasure and well-being that we so desire.

Could the drug society we have created also be an expression of our changed biochemistry? This in turn may be the result of the changing food selection and eating habits we have seen over the past few decades, combined with the constant flood of advertising promising easy access to "uppers" and "downers."

People have varying needs for strong emotional experiences–rushes–in life. Individuals with low levels of MAO (monoaminoxidase, an enzyme that accelerates dopamine metabolism) tend to seek out excitement in order to achieve surges of adrenaline, one of the most addictive substances in the body. People under constant stress receive intense hormonal rushes, which also prevent them from experiencing their emotions. Indeed, you can teach your body to expect these rushes as part of your "normal" state. Or if you eat a large quantity of fast carbohydrates, blood sugar levels soar, bringing an energy boost and possibly causing hyperactivity. Such elevated blood sugar levels, however, soon drop to a level below the starting point. The sugar craving returns and indeed before long your body becomes dependent on rapid carbohydrates in the form of soft drinks, chocolate, cookies, ice cream, or candy, creating a yo-yo effect from which it is difficult to escape. In a sense, using one drug promotes the use of another, since your body has learned to function in a drug-dependent manner. Research has shown, for example, that ex-alcoholics drink more sweet drinks than non-alcoholics.

Neurotransmitters work by adhering to receptors on the cellular surface, which triggers a signal that is fired into the receptor-bearing cell. The body can deal with excess neurotransmitters in a variety of ways. First, they may be broken down using enzymes, but in cases where there is a substantial transmitter surplus, the number of receptors on the receiving cell decreases (downgrades). This second method is the mechanism underlying the development of tolerance toward a specific substance.

A third method for the brain to recover is by means of withdrawal symptoms. When people develop a physical addiction to substances such as sugar, coffee, alcohol, or morphine, they have also modified their inner biochemical "landscape." The brain becomes habituated to these substances and demands them. When these demands are not met, the brain creates physical discomfort in the form of withdrawal symptoms such as irritability, headache, joint pain, diarrhea, or other flu-like symptoms. If you give the brain what it wants, you will immediately feel better – but only for a little while; the receptors soon crave replenishment.

A clear sign of physical addiction is that you feel better as soon as you give the body what it craves. Moreover, the addiction often occupies a large portion of your mentation; you miss the substance and make plans to include it in your life.

Even relatively well-adjusted people may have a chemical addiction. They rely on an external energy source to satisfy their needs, but in the long run this can be undermining. Chemical dependence shields their emotional lives like a translucent barrier, preventing healthy interaction with their intuition.

Dopamine and Serotonin

Dopamine and serotonin are important for our response to stress or stimuli in the environment. They work both as neurotransmitters and as neuromodulators. A neurotransmitter changes the frequency and intensity of the message that is sent. This means that the greater the quantity of neurotransmitters, the stronger the signal. A neuromodulator works as a filter that permits processing of various amounts of information. Dopamine and serotonin are believed to sculpt the chemical landscape that links the external world to our hormones. Levels of these substances influence both our ability to convert sensory impressions to perceptions and our response to the surroundings.

Nerve cells containing dopamine and serotonin are diffusely scattered, enabling them to affect a large area. They respond slowly and act as if it were important to maintain levels of dopamine and serotonin within specific limits, just as the body's temperature stays within a specific interval. The dopamine and serotonin system is also optimized to determine how information shall be processed. These levels change during temporary stress and soon return to base level, but in chronic stress that cannot be relieved, the change in level is maintained.

Dopamine and serotonin have completely different effects on us. High dopamine levels in the brain sharpen thinking and improve concentration. Amphetamines, for example, raise dopamine levels, enabling us to remain focused and stay awake longer. At the end of a long, stressful, and stimulating day most of the dopamine is used up, causing us to feel exhausted. Our brain replenishes the dopamine storage sites while we sleep, allowing us to awaken, bright-eyed and bushy-tailed, for the new day.

People with low levels of dopamine are depressed and fuzzy-brained; they can neither think clearly nor block out external signals. This explains why it is harder to concentrate as the day comes to an end, yet everything feels easier after a good night's sleep. Dopamine also drives the motor system.

Serotonin, on the other hand, decreases the flow and controls the quantity of information processed. Social behavior improves, and fears and worries fade when serotonin levels are high. It is the elevated serotonin levels that are responsible for the sensual pleasure experienced after a good meal.

Dopamine and serotonin control our "needs" system: dopamine signals that we "must have it" and serotonin signals that we "have received it." When we crave basic needs–food, sex, and security–dopamine levels rise to keep us alert and focused, while muscle activity increases to enable us to fulfill our desire. At the same time, serotonin levels drop to facilitate our ability to actively satisfy our needs. Subsequently, serotonin levels climb, notifying the brain that our needs have been met. The sense of satisfaction–that you received what you wanted–leads to a stage with high levels of both dopamine and serotonin. The brain is then in a state of bio-balance and the pain or craving has ceased – we are content.

Although a chronically stressful environment can raise or lower dopamine levels, serotonin levels always fall. If they drop to abnormally low levels the result could be unprovoked anger, aggression, or impulsive behavior, with suggested links to obesity, carb cravings, alcoholism, and depression. If all serotonin is eliminated from a rat's brain it leads to compulsive sexual activity and a insatiable voracious appetite for food.

The brain protects us from overload in dangerous situations by raising serotonin levels. This explains why in an accident situation, events seem to occur in slow motion. Extremely high levels may result in nausea and vomiting, and we may become paralyzed with fear because the serotonin inhibits the dopamine's movement-promoting activity. Typically, we remember very little of such traumatic experiences.

The Craving Brain

Under normal circumstances, the pain that drives us is minimal and we derive great satisfaction from a completed task. But the brain does not work that way for people trapped in cravings or in some form of addiction. Their dopamine levels remain high, while serotonin levels are low and do not increase even after their needs are met. Under such conditions, neither food nor sex offers any relief because the brain's craving never lets up. Quite simply, such people become trapped in their addiction and it is difficult to escape the pain or the craving. In essence, addictions such as alcohol, gambling, pornography, or bingo can completely take over people's lives.

Some substances raise both dopamine and serotonin levels. Nicotine and heroin can do this for a short time, resulting in temporary cessation of the craving – so people may smoke cigarettes to feel simultaneously calm and alert. In truth, nothing changes, and the craving returns as soon as the substances have left the brain. Coffee, sugar, and cigarettes can all raise dopamine levels. Consequently, they lay the foundation for the craving brain.

For people whose brain is controlled by cravings (because of genetics, habits, hormones, or constant stress) the mere thought of alcohol –or any other substance or compulsive activity–can cause dopamine levels to skyrocket. They must have the object of their addiction. The alternative is to attain bio-balance by raising serotonin levels. This can be achieved in different ways, writes Dr. Ronald A. Ruden from the Biobalance Center of New York in *The Craving Brain*. At Alcoholics Anonymous, for example, feelings of solidarity and group security are produced, thereby raising participants' serotonin levels. Other methods include taking St. John's Wort, meditating, or performing some loving action for another person. The latter brings a physical feeling of pleasure, accompanied by warmth and increased energy. Another option is to eat food containing tryptophan, the amino acid that is the precursor to serotonin. High levels of tryptophan can be found in beef, chicken, tuna, tofu, cottage cheese, whole grain pasta, and soy protein powder.

Buddha understood that people would find no peace unless their cravings were removed. He advocated meditation to calm the mind – a reasonable proposition, since meditation leads to a conditioned elevation of serotonin levels and a restriction of nerve impulses. High serotonin levels decrease the flow of signals in the brain, enabling us to "empty" our minds and in this way, meditation brings a sense of pleasure combined with peace of mind. What Buddhists call "nirvana" is really a state of detachment associated with naturally high levels of serotonin and dopamine – in other words, a state of bio-balance.

Ronald Ruden believes people can bio-balance the brain by decreasing stress, while at the same time boosting serotonin, and many people have found success in his method. He maintains that the body should remember and reactivate the positive feedback system lost during years of substance abuse.

Consciously reducing stress will indeed decrease chemical dependency, since chronic stress lowers serotonin levels. In 1971 drug abuse was rampant among American soldiers in Viet Nam. When they returned home, 43 percent admitted to drug use in Viet Nam and half of them felt they were addicted. After some time stateside, however, the number of drug-users dropped to 10 percent, and only 7 percent remained addicted. Escaping from a chronically stressful situation automatically alters the inner chemical landscape, making it easier to overcome addiction.

Sugar Sensitivity

Sugar has a contradictory effect on the body. Like alcohol, sugar leads to the release of beta-endorphins, which are responsible for pain relief. But beta-endorphins also generate feelings of happiness and contribute to emotional self-confidence and self-esteem. Eating sugar can therefore make people feel "high" and diminish perceived physical and emotional pain. Once the body becomes accustomed to repeated intake of sugar products, receptors become desensitized, and more sugar is needed to achieve the same sense of well-being – which makes it easy to become physically addicted to candy, ice cream, cookies, and baked goods. We don't feel well after these constant sugar highs; we become tired and anxious – in effect, we experience withdrawal symptoms. Moreover, these symptoms may lead to poor self-esteem and lay the foundation for a "relapse."

Hormones react to everything we eat, which is crucial for weight, energy level, and well-being. Insulin ensures that surplus glucose in food is absorbed from the blood and fat storage is increased, while glucagon transforms fat into glucose, which can be distributed when needed. With the right food choices you can balance these two hormones to maintain the right levels of satisfactory weight and energy.

Many books, such as Barry Sears' *Mastering the Zone*, advocate stabilizing blood sugar by eating fat, protein, and carbohydrates in the right proportion. Unfortunately, the types of food that lower glucose levels also lower the amount of serotonin. Moreover, these diets worsen the symptoms associated with low levels of beta-endorphins, as addiction researcher Kathleen DesMaisons notes this in her book *Potatoes – not Prozac*. DesMaisons claims that millions of people–including those who are depressed–are *sugar sensitive*. Sweets bring temporary emotional satisfaction, but they really only lead to renewed craving for more. Blood sugar levels rise faster but they also drop faster, and the end result is sensitivity to low blood sugar – hypoglycemia. Since sugar is such a strong and common drug in our society, we are constantly satisfying the craving created by the addictive brain. Americans eat about one hundred fifty pounds of sugar per person per year, with many harmful and stressful physical effects as a result.

People who are sugar sensitive have a bio-imbalance between their glucose levels and the brain's levels of beta-endorphins and serotonin. Since the brain's only nutrient is sugar in the form of glucose, these imbalances affect our entire way of acting, thinking, and feeling. Describing the symptoms of someone with sugar sensitivity is like reading *Bridget Jones' Diary*. Bridget shows all the symptoms of this condition: impulsiveness, low self-confidence, and inexplicable mood swings. Sometimes she is blocked and scatterbrained, troubled and tired, all at once. These are the same symptoms as those associated with low blood sugar, serotonin, and beta-endorphin levels.

There is definitely a correlation between the sharp rise in sugar consumption (30 percent since 1980) and the increasing incidence of depression in the developed world. During the 1990s the proportion of women aged twenty-five to thirty-five suffering from angst, worry, and anxiety doubled and prescriptions for antidepressants tripled.

Sugar Dependency

As noted earlier, sugar can be just as addictive as heroin and nicotine. You can be "sweetoholic" with a constant craving for sweets. Children of even one alcoholic or sugar-addicted parent are more likely to suffer from hypoglycemia. A surplus of beta-endorphin receptors results in a stronger reaction to fast carbohydrates. Such people love bread, sweets, candy, baked goods, and pasta. They may also have problems with alcohol or drugs, and often feel depressed or overreact to stress.

Researchers have shown a correlation between sugar and other types of addiction. Lab rats quickly become addicted to alcohol if you accustom them to drinking sugar solution first, and then gradually increase the amount of alcohol in the solution. Sober alcoholics also prefer drinks with a higher level of sugar than a normal group does.

If you consume large amounts of sugar and candy as a child, the brain is restructured so it is "ready" for nicotie. Consequently, people easily become hooked on smoking, which in turn rewires the brain even more so that when they have their first taste of alcohol, they've never felt better. This makes it very easy to become addicted to alcohol – and hard to stop using drugs. International figures show a full 90 percent of all alcoholics are smokers, compared with 30–35 percent of the normal population. Starting smoking at an early age also increases the risk of alcoholism or other addictions. Children of parents who have been alcoholics or addicted to sugar are also at greater risk of developing sugar dependency. *Sensitization* occurs when the stimulating effects of a drug are reinforced after repeated intake, thus increasing the risk of relapse. Stressful situations easily trigger the desire for something sweet, a cigarette, or a drink. When one drug or stimulus reinforces the response of another drug, it is called cross-sensitization, and those who are sensitive to sugar are particularly susceptible to this.

High sugar consumption makes our body's reward system shut down, resulting in an addicted brain and a number of physical imbalances. The result is a strong addiction that demands external stimulation to feel good, from substances such as sugar, food, alcohol, or smoking. Today, concrete, professional help is available, based on a completely different understanding of the problem. Research in psychology and neurobiology has made it possible to develop individualized treatment programs.

There are three rehabilitation centers in the world that specialize in treating people with multiple addictions caused by an inborn sensitivity to carbohydrates and sugar. You can admit yourself for regular detoxification to break the sugar addiction cycle. Studies in the United States show an 80 percent success rate when therapy is based on this neurobiochemical approach, compared with 20–30 percent for ordinary detoxification centers. Only one center uses a truly holistic approach with diet and nutritional changes, spirituality (the AA program), and functional medicine: the Bitten Jonsson Center in Hudiksvall in northern Sweden. Their team of medical and nutrition experts work together to help people overcome a wide range of addictions–including drugs, sugar, alcohol, bulimia, and anorexia–based on treating the dependency on sugar.

"We teach the patients how food affects them, how their brains function, and what triggers their periods of lack of control. We work holistically with body, mind, and soul," says Bitten Jonsson, R.N. and addicition specialist.

To cure sugar sensitivity, eliminate simple sugars from your diet and instead eat complex carbohydrates (with a low glycemic index, see p. 127). Indeed, you need to cut back on sugar intake drastically, or completely eliminate the many products containing sugar if you have a sugar dependency. Fructose is an acceptable sweetener, however, because of its low glycemic index. Also, make sure you get enough protein at each meal, and eat some carbohydrates three hours after eating protein to help the tryptophan reach the brain, where it is converted into serotonin. DesMaisons recommends eating three nutritious meals a day and eliminating junk food, which only heightens the craving for sugar and causes mood swings, depression, and compulsive behavior. We need to balance our blood sugar, serotonin, and beta-endorphin levels in order to work well and feel good.

The Caffeine Effect

Many depend on their coffee to get through the day. The caffeine found in coffee and soft drinks is temporarily stimulating, and it increases the heartbeat and gastric secretions. Since caffeine reduces blood flow to the brain it can prevent headaches. Coffee is also a diuretic and stimulates intestinal motility. Although this may seem beneficial, unfortunately several somatopsychic problems are associated with caffeine. The effect on the body's biochemistry may even be sufficient to cause psychiatric symptoms.

Caffeine also raises blood sugar levels by stimulating the adrenals to secrete noradrenaline and adrenaline. The heartbeat races and the liver releases sugar (glucose), which is stored in the form of glycogen, raising blood sugar levels and providing the energy boost most people experience when they drink coffee. This stimulates the pancreas, which produces the insulin that brings the level back to normal. If your body has become used to coffee, however, when the insulin is released blood sugar levels will quickly drop below normal, causing fatigue once again. In the long-term this process may contribute to exhaustion of the pancreas.

Caffeine also affects several neurotransmitters in the brain. It blocks the adenosine receptor (adenosine has a calming effect) and stimulates the release of noradrenaline and dopamine to boost your energy. Dopamine also stimulates the brain's reward center, enhancing your sense of well-being. The amount of caffeine in the brain is directly proportional to the amount of coffee consumed, and the maximum caffeine level is achieved after thirty to forty-five minutes. After one cup of coffee it takes hours before the body's biochemistry returns to normal and the caffeine leaves the body. Over time you develop tolerance and need to drink more to feel good. Clearly with such profound physical effects, caffeine is a highly addictive drug. And once you are addicted, you no longer experience the same rush, but instead drink it to avoid withdrawal symptoms such as headache, fatigue, jitters, nausea, irritation, lack of energy, and concentration problems. Just as with sugar addiction, people vary in their response to the effects of caffeine.

High caffeine consumption–like alcohol–causes a number of nervous symptoms. Coffee drinkers may suffer from symptoms similar to those experienced by people with anxiety and neuroses. Caffeine alters the levels of cyclical AMP, a substance needed to produce protein. Laboratory experiments have shown that caffeine raises cholesterol and inhibits cells in the immune system. It uses up B vitamins and some minerals, and increases urinary calcium secretion. Drinking coffee immediately after a meal prevents the uptake of essential nutrients;

Drink	caffeine (mg)
Drip coffee	150
Instant coffee	82
Decaffeinated coffee	2
Espresso (1/8 cup)	71
Double espresso, (1/4 cup)	142
Tea	50
Hot chocolate	8
Coca-Cola, diet (1 can)	50
Coca-Cola (1 can)	45
Pepsi (1 can)	37
Red Bull, energy drink	80

One cup unless stated otherwise   (Source K. DesMaisons, Potatoes Not Prozac)

for example, the tannic acid in coffee binds iron and thereby impairs its absorption. In fact, more energy is required to detoxify the body from caffeine than is actually provided by the coffee itself.

If you decide to eliminate caffeine from your diet, don't go cold turkey: cut back slowly to avoid suffering withdrawal symptoms. Detoxify the body from caffeine addiction gradually by diluting regular coffee with decaffeinated coffee. A fifty-fifty mixture cuts caffeine intake in half and allows you to reduce coffee consumption to an acceptable level, or even quit completely. Alternatively, you can replace your coffee break with a ten-minute walk and get an energy boost from exercise and fresh air. Other alternatives to coffee include the many fruit or herbal teas available or even fresh-squeezed fruit or berry juice.

Stress, Hormones, and Addiction

Eight endocrine glands, as well as the liver and kidneys, secrete hormones into the blood. The glands with the strongest impact on the mind and the emotions are the adrenal, pineal, reproductive, and pituitary glands. The pineal and pituitary glands are located in the brain. The pineal gland produces melatonin, which is needed for sleep, and the pituitary gland secretes several hormones that affect other glands and organs.

The thumb-sized adrenal glands are located above the kidneys. The adrenals produce hormones that we require for energy, enthusiasm, and efficiency. Chronic stress and careless diet (nutritional deficiency) can impair adrenal function, as can chronic emotional stress from either internal or external stimuli. Feeling out of control or being trapped in an addiction are forms of chronic stress. If the adrenals are not doing their job, you may experience fatigue, have difficulties getting started in the morning without coffee, and need sweets and coffee to make it through the day. Though you may be dead-tired, sleep remains elusive because of the thoughts racing through your mind. In many people who experience chronic fatigue and lack of energy, the adrenals have quite simply become exhausted.

The adrenals produce substances such as adrenaline, cortisol, and DHEA (dehydroepiandrosterone). Adrenaline drives the body's "all-or-nothing" response, thereby producing alertness. In normal situations, the stress hormone cortisol has a number of beneficial effects; it maintains emotional stability and counteracts allergies and inflammation. But excessive cortisol levels initiate muscle breakdown, diminish reproductive hormones, inhibit the immune system, and raise cholesterol. Furthermore, as Dr. Dharma Singh Khalsa writes in his book *Brain Longevity*, elevated cortisol levels over prolonged periods of time are harmful for memory function. The ability to concentrate drops and people suffer from reduced energy and premature memory loss. Indeed, reactions to stress can have several devastating effects. Dr. Khalsa recommends a forty-day program to vitalize the brain through diet modification, stress management (using meditation), exercise, and cautious use of medication.

The hormone DHEA is the body's own protective mechanism against the negative effects of stress. The balance between cortisol and DHEA is especially important for achieving good health. DHEA can improve brain function, memory, and immunity, and counteract muscle weakness and osteoporosis. DHEA is therefore believed to counteract aging and to be the leading marker for vitality.

DHEA is a precursor to androgens as well as the estrogens and testosterone that are important for sex drive. Chronic stress is therefore especially harmful for women as it can disrupt the menstrual cycle, decrease sex drive, and make it difficult for them to become pregnant (even if they are menstruating normally). Progesterone also helps

> *Health is more than the absence of illness and disease. It is a resource for a good life. How we feel is related to our living conditions, environment, lifestyle, and genetic makeup. Generally the better the living conditions and opportunities, the better our health – and vice versa.*
> The Swedish National Institute of Public Health

balance the effects of excess cortisol, and using a salve containing natural progesterone may help. An early bedtime and getting a few hours sleep before midnight also help the adrenals to recover before the next day.

High insulin levels inhibit DHEA production while chromium stimulates such production. Thus consumption of sugar–which stimulates insulin secretion and uses up chromium–increases the negative effects of stress.

Studies have shown that methods such as meditation stimulate our natural ability to produce DHEA. People who meditate also have higher levels of DHEA than those who don't. This not only counteracts aging, but also has a rejuvenating effect. By recognizing and interrupting stressful situations before they affect us, we can take control of our stress before it takes control of our emotions and our stress hormones. By performing the exercise on p. 239 every day, you can raise your DHEA levels and stabilize your cortisol and adrenalin levels.

Stress in modern society is the result of many factors. One important one is our changed internal biochemistry; people who are out of balance are under increased stress, leading to even greater bio-imbalance, and so the cycle is perpetuated. Unavoidably this results in negative feedback, and before long people forget how it feels to be in balance (bio-balanced). Widespread use of sugar from an early age is a contributing factor to the development of the drug society. Even babies consume sugar in fruit juices and jarred baby food which contain inverted sugar (fructose and glucose). The glucose is absorbed into the blood faster than ordinary sugar (saccharose). Research has also shown that high consumption of soft drinks by teenagers "prepares" the body for wine, beer, and alcoholic beverages. There is little difference between these substances – the foundation is already laid for the transition from sugar addiction to alcohol addiction. The teens are a high-risk period for sowing the seeds of addiction. Ninety percent of smokers have their first cigarette before the age of eighteen. Although most believe they will no longer be smoking in five to ten years, their cigarettes are still burning.

What conclusions can we draw? We have a sophisticated reward mechanism designed to help us enjoy life. Whether or not it works, however, is up to us, and this depends on how we care for it. If we use legal or illegal drugs to artificially supply these emotions, it is easy to become trapped in an external dependency. Receptors become saturated, dosages must be increased – the adverse effects soon outweigh the original benefits. Withdrawal symptoms transform what was initially positive into a burden – delight becomes plight. This is the Achilles' heel in a very clever biological system, developed to ensure our survival.

Dependency is part of human nature: it is a force both powerful and essential. You cannot develop a loving relationship without becoming dependent on the other person. This does not mean that you cannot survive without them, but that you are happier when you are together – provided, of course, that it is a positive dependence; an *addition*. If you exercise regularly you develop the need to exercise, and become restless if you skip a day. This form of positive dependence improves physical fitness, though it can become abusive with over-exercise. Negative dependence–*addiction*–steals energy and creates imbalance. When a negative dependence (work, food, drugs, sex, candy, gambling, alcohol, etc.) becomes a drug, it undermines our personal energy, leaving a shell behind. In contrast, a positive dependence furnishes energy and builds self-esteem and personal strength. That is a major difference.

Autogenous Stimulation

How do you escape from negative dependence – yet still experience pleasure in life? Remember, everything we do has a bearing on our mental state. Nothing changes if we stay in bed feeling tired. Instead, getting up and moving about while repeating how wide-awake we feel helps us become alert. Give your body and brain a kick-start; replace listlessness and lassitude with energy and enthusiasm by getting out for a walk, a run, or a swim. If you are nervous or preoccupied, seek solitude, breathe calmly and deeply for five minutes, and focus on your *qi* point. Your worries will be replaced by an inner peace as you enter a state of bio-balance.

We can also help each other to thrive by displaying love, emotions, appreciation, and consideration. Touch, intimacy, and visible presence can be highly stimulating and pleasurable. Hugging, kissing, and cuddling with someone you care for offer a wealth of positive, pleasurable feelings. If you want love and attention from your surroundings, do not simply expect this to happen. Take control–reach out and touch someone–say a few friendly words. Emit the energy and emotions in which you would like to be immersed to shape an environment that you will enjoy. Surround yourself in harmony. Caring for a dog, cat, or other pet also creates beneficial emotions that enrich our health and well-being.

One alternative to drug addiction is to learn how to evoke the sought-after emotions of pleasure, sensuality, stimulation, concentration, and relaxation. Tune in to your own inner network of sensual pleasure and delight; make active use of your knowledge and your body. In *Molecules of Emotion*, Candace Pert describes how, while in a relaxed state, she focused on the pituitary gland, which has the greatest number of beta-endorphins in the brain. When Pert used the power of her mind to release the endorphins, she immediately experienced a strong feeling of pleasure. We can do this for ourselves – without drugs. Beta-endorphins are stimulated by music, yoga, exercise, orgasm, meditation, good food, and by spending time with people or even animals that you like. Similarly, you can achieve your own pain relief by breathing in *qi*–life energy–and then visualizing that you are exhaling the pain from the place that hurts. Keep breathing deeply and calmly until the unpleasant feeling is gone.

In *Access Your Brain's Joy Center*, Pete Sanders, an honors graduate from MIT who studied the human brain, describes how we can learn to trigger the brain's natural mechanisms for well-being. In the middle of the brain there is an area (the *septum pellucidum*) that, when stimulated, gives a pleasant, relaxed feeling best described as an inner smile. The area is tucked away above most of the limbic system and is connected with the hypothalamus, serving as the system command center. As early as the 1950s researchers were able to show that electric stimulation of this area in a seriously depressed patient resulted in feelings of happiness. Pete Sanders has successfully used this method to help people lose weight, stop smoking, or decrease alcohol and drug addiction. This self-stimulation can also be used to experience increased sexual pleasure and to control pain (such as migraine headaches) and irritability.

Practice stimulating the septum pellucidum of your brain by placing the middle finger of your left hand on a point about one and a half inches above the level of your eyebrows (about where the third eye sits). At the same time place your thumb on the left side of your head and imagine a line projecting inwards from each one and intersecting in the middle of your brain. Then visualize this point in the brain and "caress" it with your thought, as you would stroke an animal's fur. If you found the right place you will experience immediate pleasure and inner relaxation. This creates a strong physiological reaction that can be strengthened with practice.

Global Detoxification

In the late 1960s, sex and drugs were set free. This may have been a reaction to the ultraconservatism of the fifties. People wanted to celebrate life, youth, and freedom. The younger generation replaced the culture of their parents with rock and roll, feminism, and college life. An enterprising spirit and expansive thinking prevailed, and material wealth was boundless. During the yuppie era of the 1980s, accumulating wealth was not only "allowed" but even considered admirable. Financial barons ruled over a decade during which shopping evolved into a cult, acquiring an inherent value. Many rode the crest of the economic boom. This was followed by a short recession of the early nineties, after which the US economy have continued to do well until the terrorist attacks in 2001.

But it was during the nineties that a search for other, deeper values evolved. After a few decades of experimentation people learned that neither sex nor drugs, nor even money, could bring happiness. People quietly began focusing on personal development: reading, meeting, attending courses, and participating in counseling. New age-phenomena beckoned and people's curiosity led them to seek a different definition of reality. We saw the cautious opening of spiritual channels.

In truth, searching has been the hallmark of the past forty years. Many of the pop and rock legends of the 1960s and 1970s now lead sober lives, despite once being keen advocates of taking drugs. The great spiritual and existential search that has simmered beneath the surface will emerge into the light during the first decade of the twenty-first century. A new wave will sweep our culture in which presence, intimacy, and inner meaning will be the guiding principles. It will be fashionable to be free from drugs and chemical dependencies. We are on the way toward a gigantic global detoxification.

Humankind is part of a biological system – a biosystem. We have polluted our environment and ourselves far too long. Not only are we out of balance ourselves – we have engendered the same situation in the earth. The global bio-imbalance is evident in the extreme weather changes, known as El Niño and La Niña, which brought extreme heat and cold during 1998. That same year natural disasters struck repeatedly in, with earthquakes, floods, and tropical storms. In the first six months of the year over twenty thousand people died, and damage cost insurance companies about $20 billion – more than the total figure for all of the previous year. Elevated water temperatures caused as much as 80 percent of all coral in the tropical belt to die, significantly impacting people who depend on fishing in coral reefs for their livelihood. Ever more extreme weather has a correlation with the greenhouse effect and the destruction of the ozone layer. CFCs are eating away the protective ozone layer, and the ozone hole over the Antarctic has been large for several years. Many experts feel these strong weather variations are here to stay. Indeed, we have successfully established a bio-imbalance not only within ourselves, but also in our entire planet.

But now a reawakening to a detoxification process encompassing both mind and body is underway, on both an inner and outer plane. We are washing away poisons and pollution, liberating ourselves from toxic thoughts and the role of victim. After a transitional phase we will abandon the massive use of external poisons such as drugs, pharmaceuticals (except in urgent situations), and junk food. "Social drug" use–alcohol, coffee, and sugar–will also decline. Healthy alternatives with a positive stimulating effect will be developed. As we become aware of the consequences, it will be impossible to continue to poison ourselves and our earth.

Food as Drug and Allergen

It is not widely appreciated that food can actually lead to pharmacological activity with both mental and physical effects. Food can be the cause of physical changes that result in a bio-imbalance; what we eat can affect everything from mood and concentration to muscle pain and joint inflammations. Natural elements and chemical additives in food both affect us, as does the resultant bacterial flora. Everything we swallow must be processed, metabolized, and in most cases treated by the body's detoxification system before it can be eliminated. Symptoms of poisoning or overload include fatigue, worry, runny nose, irritant cough, labile mood, and eczema.

A healthy external appearance can hide a toxic burden for a long time. In *Detoxification and Healing*, Dr. Sidney MacDonald Baker describes a patient who had long tried to become pregnant, and had even made several unsuccessful attempts at artificial insemination. She was just over thirty, educated, successful, and athletic. All lab results indicated that she was in perfect health. The only clues were the many cavities in her teeth and the high level of sugar in her diet. Excess sugar, combined with medicines such as antibiotics and oral contraceptives, exposes the body to the risk of an overgrowth of yeast. A thorough stool analysis also showed abnormal intestinal flora and an amino acid deficiency, both of which can have a significant bearing on the body's detoxification process. Once this situation was corrected, the woman became pregnant within just a few months.

As we have seen, food can indeed act as a drug leading to problems caused by the food intake itself or withdrawal symptoms. For example, sugar withdrawal is linked to symptoms such as angst, nervous problems, irritability, dizziness, trembling, depression, headache, and insomnia. Certain foods contain substances with a direct effect on receptors in the brain. Chocolate contains phenylalanine, which has an amphetamine-like effect on the body. Milk and flour have been shown to contain exorphins, with an effect similar to that of endorphins, and cow milk has even been found to contain small quantities of morphine. Protein-rich food provides the amino acids tryptophan and tyrosin, with anti-depressant like qualities.

Enzyme deficiency also plays a role in many allergies. Lactose intolerance is probably the best known and is caused by either an insufficiency or total lack of the lactase enzyme. Enzymes facilitate countless chemical reactions throughout the body, including the brain and the gastrointestinal tract. Unfortunately, a shortage of functioning enzymes is all too common in our fast-paced toxic world. For example, the pancreas is extremely sensitive to stress, and if you don't relax before, during, and after a meal, it will fail to produce enzymes properly. Mercury or aluminum poisoning always results in digestion problems.

But food itself may also cause allergic reactions. Migraine can be an allergic reaction to tyramine–a substance occurring naturally in foods such as aged cheese, wine (especially Chianti), and chocolate. Food allergies–even those which have not been identified–are a constant burden on the liver; they can block digestion and hamper absorption of nutrients. They can also cause leakage in the intestine, resulting in problems elsewhere in the body and placing a strain on both the immune and the detoxification systems.

Food Allergies

Allergic reactions to food can affect both your mind and your body. Such reactions lead to histamine release from the immune system's "mast cells." Histamines have many effects on the body, which can manifest themselves as classic allergic reactions: sneezing, itching, and breathing difficulties. But histamine can also be released in those parts of the brain that affect sleep, mood, appetite, and emotions. Consequently food allergies can result in worry, fatigue, slow thinking, irritability, aggression, anxiety, depression, hyperactivity, and learning disabilities. The most common allergy-inducing foods include eggs, grains, peanuts, citrus fruits, and dairy products. Increased sensitivity to various substances in foods, such as coloring or additives, can also result in unpleasant reactions.

Some foods also inherently contain histamine, which can induce reactions in people with histamine sensitivity. They may experience headaches, diarrhea, and a runny nose from just one glass of wine or beer, or even a piece of cheese. The solution is to avoid histamine-containing food. In one research study one hundred people with food allergies followed a histamine-free diet for four weeks. Fifty-seven noticed considerable improvement, and fifteen of them no longer experienced any problems at all. An analysis of the histamine content of fifty-two wines showed that a liter of white wine contained between 3 and 120 micrograms of histamine, but the same amount of red wine contained 60 to 3800 micrograms. Wouldn't it be helpful to state the histamine content of wine on the label? Cheap red wines have also been known to contain ochratoxin, a toxic mold that can induce allergy-like reactions.

The intestinal region, where exposure to foreign substances is greatest, contains a full 80 percent of the immune system's cells. In about 85 percent of food allergies, the IgG-antibodies bind with food to trigger an allergic reaction, which can begin as late as twenty-four hours following food intake. Symptoms include headache (often migraine), fatigue, joint pain, depression, diarrhea, constipation, breathing difficulties, or chronic digestive problems. Eating too much food or the same food all the time, can also produce such symptoms. The stressed digestive process impairs enzyme production, wasting large amounts of energy.

Thus an allergy may cause mental imbalance. This may be appropriately investigated by eliminating the more common allergens from the diet over a period of time. Later, reintroduce the suspect allergens one by one to see whether any of them provokes a reaction. It can also be specifically measured in a Food Allergy test performed on a blood sample. This will reveal not only IgE- but also IgG-reactivity to different foods, which can then be eliminated from the diet.

However, there are many types of food intolerance. In celiac disease (gluten intolerance), the peptides from gluten or gliadin found in flour are toxic to the intestinal mucous membrane because they bind to surface molecules in the cells. Commonly, IgA- and often, IgG-antibodies are directed against these peptides. This results in injury to the body because the immune system reacts to foreign substances attached to the body's own tissues: in other words, a type of autoimmune reaction. But it is important to confirm celiac disease through an intestinal biopsy, since only about ten percent of those who have the disease demonstrate typical symptomatology.

Dairy and Gluten Intolerance

Proteins are built up of a large number of amino acids that are combined in different ways. Digestion breaks down proteins into smaller fragments and individual amino acids that are absorbed by the blood. These are used to build up thymus hormones, different neurotransmitters, and a number of essential messengers in the body. If the proteins are not broken down completely and/or the intestinal wall leaks, smaller protein fragments (peptides) can be absorbed into the blood, causing considerable problems if they happen to resemble any of the body's own transmitters.

Actually, some of the most troublesome poisons are those that resemble friendly molecules and consequently remain undiscovered until they cause problems. The body absorbs these toxins, and they assume a place in important biochemical processes, which may lead to hypersensitivity or other dysfunction. Such changes are inconspicuous at first and increase gradually, making them difficult to detect. Cleansing can therefore be appropriate to help rid the body of stored toxins.

Gluten is a central protein in flour and other grains, and casein is the dominant type of protein in mammalian milk. Peptides from gluten and casein can be especially problematic, producing undesirable endorphin-like effects. Some children change from being hyperactive and confused to completely normal after a few weeks of following a diet free of gluten and casein.

The first articles identifying autism as a biological imbalance that resembles poisoning were published in the 1960s. Although this condition may also have other causes, a correlation does exist between autism and impairment of the detoxification system that neutralizes hormones and neurotransmitters. As a result, the brain tends to confuse the different senses. Visual, sensory, and hearing impulses are not perceived normally.

In times past, many people believed that serious mental disorders were related to diet. In the seventeenth century, excessive consumption of milk and dairy products was thought to cause "melancholia." In the late nineteenth century, vitamin B deficiency (pellagra) was the leading diagnosis in patients admitted to psychiatric hospitals. The symptoms of untreated celiac disease may include psychosis and even on occasion depression. These dietary connections, however, have been downplayed in favor of psychological explanations ever since Freud encouraged doctors to search for causes in childhood experience. For example, until fairly recently, doctors believed that autism was the consequence of an unloving mother or a difficult childhood. Still, the psychological environment cannot serve as the sole explanation, since siblings frequently turn out to be entirely normal.

Karl Reichelt, M.D., a researcher at Oslo's Rigshospitalet, has formulated a theory on why children with autism, hyperactivity, and other mental disorders are unable to tolerate ordinary dairy and gluten products. These children lack certain enzymes that prevent the proteins in flour (gluten) and milk (casein) from breaking down normally. Instead, opiate-like peptides are formed that affect the brain in a way similar to opium.

Reichelt investigated the peptide concentrations in urine among people with autism, anorexia, and schizophrenia and found that they were higher than in healthy individuals. The opiate peptides affect the body, resulting in a chronic "high," which in time results in serious brain damage. Scientists estimate that one or two percent of the population have these defective enzymes: for them, flour and milk are pure poison. Although the quantities of these incompletely broken-down peptides may be small, with time they accumulate and produce psychoactive effects. These findings are supported by some forty similar findings in Norway, Italy, Great Britain, and the United States.

Children with these problems require a strict gluten-free, casein-free (GFCF) diet to return to health. According to Dr. Karl Reichelt, it takes twenty-eight weeks of detoxification to eliminate the gluten peptides from the urine of autistic children. If they are exposed to gluten again, 60 percent of these children develop epilepsy.

In his interesting and thought-provoking book *Detoxification and Healing*, Dr. Sidney MacDonald Baker predicts that over the next decade, we will most probably discover an increasing number of peptides that cause problems for human biochemistry because they resemble normal peptides and are mistaken by the body for the real thing. This leads to either a neutralizing effect on the normal peptides or uncontrollable activity.

In the 1930s, Norwegian physician Asbjörn Fölling noted that many children whose mental development lagged behind had an enzyme defect. A special diet enabled these children to develop normally, thereby preventing retardation. Today all newborns are tested for phenylketonuria (PKU) and perhaps we need to consider testing for other enzyme deficiencies to prevent the development of autism, schizophrenia, or other psychiatric conditions.

Primary Allergy

Food allergens may also strongly impact the immune system. Milk, or any food allergen, can decrease the number of leukocytes circulating in the blood by about 40 percent in susceptible people, since they remain in the body at the site of irritation. As a result, other parts of the body, such as the tonsils, sinuses, or ears, become more vulnerable to infection. Such infections disappear in many children when they stop eating milk and cheese.

Proponents of the "primary allergy" theory believe children become sensitive to milk and gluten products if they are exposed to these basic foods too early or in excessive amounts. "Primary allergy" falls under the clinical ecology movement in the United States and the food intolerance movement in Great Britain. All adult food is actually foreign to our species but we have developed protective mechanisms to deal with it. However, an infant's immune system is tolerant because it is undeveloped, and therefore needs to be nourished with the species-specific milk. Replacing breast milk with other foods, such as cow's milk and flour, in too high levels or too early, causes the child's immune system to incorrectly perceive those substances given prematurely as species-specific. While a properly trained immune system would stop the nutrients at the intestinal barrier, an incorrectly trained immune system permits these substances to pass through the protective barrier. After this occurs, the nutrients can harm the body by binding to normal tissue, thus altering the tissues and triggering an immune response – and possibly even an autoimmune reaction.

Such non-species specific foods may also injure the embryo via the blood and the infant via breast milk, thus triggering a primary allergy. Proponents of the primary allergy theory therefore recommend that pregnant and nursing mothers eliminate milk, grain, yeast, and food with gluten from their diet. They also recommend that mothers nurse at least six months without other dietary supplements to stave off recurrent colds, mental disease, allergies, cardiovascular disease, and other chronic complaints in their children. The European regional office of the WHO recommends avoiding cow's milk until the infant reaches ten to twelve months of age. The organization also refers to research showing that introducing cow's milk prematurely may result in gastrointestinal bleeding. Finnish studies have shown that infants should not receive cow's milk until the age of nine months in order to avert the risk of allergies and infections later in life.

Recurrent colds and fragile health are the result of an incorrectly programmed and overactive immune system. Food allergy tests can show whether IgG antibodies toward ordinary food products are present in the blood.

In 1993, Dr. Frank Oski published *Don't Drink Your Milk*, documenting the correlation between dairy products and children's allergies, eczema, bedwetting, and ear infections. Dr. Oski, former chairman of pediatrics at Johns Hopkins University, believes that many children with recurrent ear infections receive antibiotics unnecessarily, since their problems would disappear if they stopped drinking milk. Ear infections afflict two thirds of all children under the age of two and are the leading cause of hearing impairment in children. Infections of the ear, nose, and throat are also among the most common diagnoses for outpatient visits.

A study from Georgetown University School of Medicine, Washington D.C., confirms the relationship between food allergies and recurrent ear problems. A full 81 of the 104 children with recurrent ear infections were allergic to everyday foods. After excluding milk and flour products, 86 percent of these 81 children showed clear improvement. When milk and flour were re-introduced into their diet, 94 percent suffered from ear infections. In conclusion, it is well worth investigating whether any food allergies are present, which otherwise may heavily burden the body. For example, chronic sinusitis is the most commonly reported chronic disease, affecting 12.6 percent of people (approximately 38 million) in the United States in 1996.

Why are there such differences in how foods are tolerated? One explanation could be the differences in our blood type, where the four blood groups have different receptors on the cell surface. These receptors may or may not bind to the huge variety of glycoproteins in food. In *Eat Right for Your Type*, naturopath Peter J. D'Adamo describes how people with different blood types react to different foods.

For thousands of generations, people have been scattered around the world and have adapted to different diets. The oldest blood type O–the hunter and collector–thrives on meat, fish, and intense physical activity, but should avoid wheat and be cautious with dairy products. Some 42 percent of the world's population has this blood type, which has existed for over 40,000 years.

Fifteen thousand years ago the A blood type developed in the new agricultural societies. It is found mainly in Japan, Italy, and the Mediterranean region. People in this group tolerate vegetarian protein better than animal protein, and characteristically have sensitive digestive tracts. Dairy products often lead to mucous formation, nasal stuffiness, and breathing difficulties. Around 40 percent of the world's population belongs to this blood type.

Five thousand years ago, many people were forced to move and adapt to new areas, and the result was the new B blood type. This group is the most balanced, with a strong immune system and a tolerant digestive system, though these individuals often have problems breaking down dairy products. About 12 percent of the population has this blood group, found mainly in Eastern Europe, Germany, Austria, India, China, and Southeast Asia.

Finally, 6 percent of the world's population has the "youngest" blood type, AB, which evolved between five hundred and one thousand years ago when the Mongols overran large parts of Europe mingling Asian B-type blood with the native Caucasian A type. This chameleon-like blood group easily adapts to changes in the environment and diet. But these individuals tend to have a sensitive digestive tract, an overactive immune system, and can easily become infected by microorganisms.

Food and Autoimmunity

Over the past twenty years, many studies have shown that fasting can alleviate swelling, tenderness, and inflammation of the joints. Professor Bo Ringertz's research group at Karolinska Institutet in Stockholm has shown that fasting results in a clear improvement in patients suffering from rheumatoid arthritis. In the summer of 2002, an article in the Journal of Alternative Therapies described how six people with various autoimmune diseases showed considerable improvement after water fasting for one to three weeks, followed by a vegan diet. The patients, who suffered from rheumatoid arthritis, fibromyalgia, and SLE (systemic lupus erythematosus), became symptom-free or their symptoms were reduced to a minimum.

Researchers have shown that there is a correlation between early exposure to the lactalbumin in milk, the formation of antibodies to this substance, and subsequent autoimmunity as a cause of Type 1 diabetes. They believe that the antibody to lactalbumin cross-reacts with acute phase proteins that form on the surface of the beta cells of the pancreas. The incidence of autoimmune disease is also higher in people with celiac disease.

If we look at all the findings of this research into food allergies and intolerances, a new picture begins to emerge. From an immunologic perspective, it would seem that autoimmune diseases arise step by step as a reaction to ordinary food. One reason could be that some people are deficient in the enzymes that are needed to break down ordinary proteins from flour and dairy products. These deficiencies may be genetic, or they may be caused or worsened by an imbalance in the intestinal flora. The incompletely broken-down peptides trigger the immune system to form IgG and IgA antibodies. Peptides attach to the intestinal wall, which is damaged when the immune system tries to eliminate them. This damage enables the peptides to pass easily through the wall of the intestine, after which they are absorbed into the blood and circulate where they can bind with normal cells throughout the body. Thus the cells are changed in such a way that the immune system perceives them as foreign and the circulating IgG antibodies bind to the peptides on the surface of the cell, causing inflammation.

And so the body's tissue is broken down in an effort to eliminate the foreign peptides – with devastating consequences. As long as the individual eats this food, the immune system is chronically activated, which amplifies the processes of inflammation and tissue breakdown. This attracts pathogenic bacteria, such as our ordinary skin bacteria, staphylococci, which in turn survive by further breaking down the tissue. The staphylococci produce more inflammatory substances, bringing the vicious cycle full circle (see Bio-balance versus Inflammation page 318–321).

Many people have recovered from autoimmune diseases such as lupus and multiple sclerosis by following advice based on the concept of primary allergy. They have reduced or completely eliminated pain, inflammatory conditions, and infections by eliminating poorly tolerated foods from their diet. They have improved their health and quality of life considerably by making wise dietary choices. The more we take our tolerances (genetic or environmental) into account when deciding what to eat, the more we help our self-healing power to function at maximum strength.

What makes it so hard for us to stop eating food that clearly injures our bodies? It may be because a single gluten molecule contains fifteen opiate-like peptides and the brain quite simply becomes dependent on this opium-like impact. Moreover, the inflammation releases histamine and adrenaline, which also have a strong addictive effect. The fact is that the body must also be detoxified from the substances it does not tolerate.

Food and Mental Imbalance

Fast carbohydrates may provoke temperamental outbursts, which can spin out of control under the influence of alcohol. Most violent acts are also committed by people who have been drinking. An extensive study was carried out in the 1980s involving eight thousand participants in fourteen American juvenile correction facilities. By lowering the amount of refined sugar in the food served in prison, violence and antisocial behavior were reduced to half that of the control group. Interestingly though, reducing sugar did not affect behavior in female inmates of juvenile correction facilities. Several studies in the US and Finland have shown that young inmates are particularly prone to strong reactions to sugar. After rising rapidly, the blood sugar then plummets, resulting in extreme fatigue, depression, aggression, or self-destructive behavior.

Professor Stephen Schoentaler at California State University has found that young criminals clearly suffer from nutritional deficiencies – especially of folic acid, vitamin B_1, and vitamin C. Deficiencies in zinc, calcium, magnesium, selenium, and essential fatty acids have also been shown to be associated with violent behavior. Researchers found that low levels of iron can impair judgment, control of impulses, and other functions governed by the left half of the brain (scientific and mathematical talent as well as speech and writing ability).

Alexander Schauss has long studied the effect of nutrition on the mind. He found elevated levels of lead, copper, and cadmium in violent, antisocial adults as compared with normal adults. Cadmium pollutants are most frequently the result of cigarette smoking. Zinc supplements counteract the effect of the toxins and modify behavior.

British police commissioner Peter Bennett uses an "ecological" approach. He has shown in several studies that the aggressive and antisocial behavior of young criminals disappears with proper nutrition and elimination of environmental toxins such as metals. In a joint study with the English National Society for Research into Allergy, ten juvenile criminals (average age eleven) were given an antiallergy diet and balanced nutrition. Eight of these ten hyperactive and aggressive children completed treatment. Their problem behavior decreased dramatically, and in five the problems were completely resolved.

Mental disruptions and imbalances can be caused by several factors. Food allergies are rarely an isolated phenomenon, but are frequently accompanied by malnutrition and low blood sugar (hypoglycemia). Therefore it is important to investigate such possible causes first – before considering sedatives or electric shock treatment. In addition, our system tends to blame criminality on social factors, while ignoring physical factors such as nutritional imbalances.

Since the early twentieth century researchers have known that aggression can be the result of an allergic reaction. The belief is that allergens (via histamines) affect the central nervous system, possibly causing swelling of the brain. Many violent and destructive people could be manifesting the effects of food allergies, low blood sugar, or nutritional deficiency. A full 70 to 90 percent of violent young criminals have a previous history of behavioral disturbances such as aggression, impulsiveness, destructiveness, or antisocial behavior. As we mentioned before, dyslexia is associated with a deficiency of the essential omega-3- and omega-6-fatty acids, and it is five times as common among criminals as in the normal population. Considering nutritional rehabilitation for prison inmates could be a step in the right direction. But it would be even better to implement such health initiatives at an early age, before the debut of criminal behavior.

Our Most Common Toxins

When blood sugar levels are consistently elevated, protein molecules in the blood are glycosylated into AGE-complex (see p. 119), inhibiting the normal function of the proteins. Eliminating these complexes is difficult because a hard chemical compound is formed. The AGE complex becomes trapped in tissues throughout the body, potentially resulting in problems such as kidney failure and compromised immunity.

Not only food but also medications have to be processed by the detoxification system before being eliminated. Medications can therefore have serious adverse effects. For example, taking painkillers too often may make you sick, possibly causing hormonal problems as well as adverse effects in the detoxification organs: the liver and the kidneys. Older people who take an unnecessarily large number of medications may suffer from pseudodementia, but after detoxification the dementia symptoms disappear.

We can also be exposed to toxins via inhalation of substances such as the moldy dust found in the air on farms, around sawmills, or in houses with mold problems. The toxins from the mold (mycotoxins) are absorbed directly into the blood via the lungs, and in time can cause serious poisoning symptoms.

We humans are responsible for the problems associated with this increased toxicity. We refine substances and then redistribute them elsewhere. Lead in gasoline, for example, can result in lead poisoning in both animals and people. PCBs, which have been used in quantity in transmission oil, softeners, solvents, and insulation for refrigerators and freezers, are highly volatile and can be carried away by the wind, falling back to the ground in colder areas. As a result PCB concentrations are found in the Arctic and the Antarctic regions. Indeed, we have created a situation in which toxins are now found in places they never existed before.

Another example is aluminum, one of the most common substances in the bedrock. Metallic aluminum was essentially unknown to life on this planet before the twentieth century. Now we consume aluminum from canned food and from food prepared in aluminum pots. This light metal is especially prone to adhering to DNA and staying there. Getting rid of it is very difficult, and it is stored in the liver and central nervous system. Research has found a correlation between elevated aluminum levels in the brain and the incidence of Alzheimer's disease.

Heavy metals such as lead, mercury, and cadmium are highly toxic for living organisms, and our bodies must work hard to protect us from them. These metals are preferentially stored in fatty tissue in order to facilitate their rapid removal from the circulation. They are stored in protective fats surrounding the organs, as well as in fatty tissues within the nervous system and hormone-producing glands. The body constantly filters and cleanses its fluids, and as a result all detoxifying organs (liver, kidneys, lungs, and gastrointestinal tract) become collection sites.

If amalgam were a new material for dental fillings today, mercury would never be permitted to be used so close to the brain. The Swedish Council for Planning and Coordination of Research (FRN) evaluated the risks associated with amalgam in the teeth on behalf of the government, and found that mercury exposure far exceeded the levels previously assumed: an average of ten micrograms of mercury per day, rising in many cases up to one hundred micrograms per day, affecting between fifty thousand and five hundred thousand people. It has also been established that various organs from the embryo absorb the mercury that leaks out of its mother's amalgam fillings, and mercury is also transferred through breast milk during nursing. Pregnant women and nursing mothers need to be aware of the risks of dental procedures during this time.

Some people leach more mercury than permitted by the maximum limits for industrial environments. This applies especially to gum chewers and teeth grinders. Mercury can also interfere with the immune system, and act as an allergen. Individual responses may vary due to hereditary factors such as the effectiveness of the detoxification system. Considerable time may pass before problems appear, as mercury in the body reaches disruptive levels.

In his book *Putting It All Together: The New Orthomolecular Medicine*, Dr. Abram Hoffer describes a successful CEO who suffered from a broad range of symptoms such as headache, back pain, and episodes of weakness and trembling. At the age of forty-six his diagnosis was "nervous problems created by the tensions and demands of working life." First he was treated with antidepressants, and subsequently with electric shock therapy. He failed to improve and sought help from many different physicians. Purely by chance he met a doctor who practiced orthomolecular medicine. His laboratory workup included a hair mineral analysis, which showed that he had mercury poisoning – a correctable condition.

Two of the world's largest mercury producers have posted warnings on the Internet about the use of their products for dental purposes. A Swedish study carried out by Karolinska Institute's Department of Public Health on two hundred eighty people, showed that eight out of ten felt better when their amalgam fillings were replaced. They had all suffered from various symptoms for over ten years. Since the inception of the Amalgam Unit at University Hospital in Uppsala in 1991 over one thousand people have been referred for amalgam and metal replacement. A year after replacement of their fillings, 90 percent of patients experienced clear improvement in their health. There is growing support for the claim that most people enter a long-term phase of improvement after switching to metal-free alternatives. Mercury detoxification may take from six months to several years, depending on the strength of the bond.

Effective protective measures are required to detoxify our systems and our teeth. Take antioxidants for one month before undergoing the detoxification protocol, and use a special toothpaste that counteracts mercury leaching. Selenium is particularly valuable as it helps detoxify mercury. Find a dentist who practices mercury-free dentistry and is familiar with the mercury detoxification protocol. A method was developed in Finland to replace all amalgam fillings in one session, though not all countries are that advanced in dealing with this problem. Books on the subject are available for more information.

Detoxification of the Body

Toxins can enter the body by absorption though the skin, inhalation, or oral ingestion. The skin, lungs, liver, and gastrointestinal system therefore constitute the main detoxification organs. Their job is to remove not only drugs and foreign chemicals, but also substances that the body produces itself, such as hormones, cholesterol, and fatty acids.

Since we cannot avoid ingesting toxins or allergens–from bacteria, food, or chemical additives and spraying–we need to supply the substances our bodies require for detoxification. Cleansing undesired substances from our systems is our most energy-demanding activity, because detoxification primarily consists of the synthesis (formation) of new molecules. A large part of our energy goes to building new molecules, and detoxification of the body demands at least 80 percent of an adult's energy. Consider this in context: 10 percent of new synthesis takes place in the brain and 5 percent in the immune system.

The liver is the main detoxification organ; if provided with the right nutrients, it can build the new molecules that tissues need and also handle detoxification. A detoxification system that is not fully operational is one common cause of poor sleep. The system uses an abundance of energy, and the body is burdened by any remaining toxins. People may respond by taking sedatives or sleeping pills, while the true problem remains unaddressed: it is the liver that needs help.

Detoxification is a two-step process. In the first phase, toxic molecules are transformed to facilitate their capture, becoming electrified and "sticky." Cytochrome 450 is an enzyme system that activates leftover or toxic molecules. Unable to travel in the body, these activated molecules quickly bind to different "carrier molecules." This is phase two, when the undesired substances are "packaged" in preparation for transport out of the body. Two of the most important carrier molecules are sugar and sulfur, since both are "sticky" and can carry foreign substances out of the body. Glucaronic acid is an oxidized sugar molecule and the amino acid glycine is sweet and sticky like sugar. Sulfur enters the body mainly through the amino acids methionine and cystein, into which it is naturally incorporated. With an inadequate sulfur supply both detoxification and the buildup of molecules and new tissue will be impaired.

Twelve-day detoxification program

Two to three weeks ahead of time: Eat more fresh fruit and vegetables than usual, and take antioxidants (Vitamin C and E, bioflavonoids, selenium, glutathione, etc.) to boost the body's detoxification resources.

Day 1–2: Prepare your body by cutting out coffee, black tea, and alcohol. Drink mineral water, green tea, and herbal tea instead. Eliminate all products containing flour, sugar, and potatoes. Eat large salads or steamed vegetables with low-fat protein in the form of fish, beans, tofu, lentils, skinless chicken, cottage cheese, and mozzarella cheese. Buy fresh bean sprouts or grow your own at home. Take two tablespoons of virgin olive oil every day in your food, and two teaspoons of flaxseed oil per day throughout the treatment. For more efficient cleansing also take bentonite (a special volcanic ash) with psyllium husk or a silica mineral supplement morning and evening every day (available in health food stores). Drink at least two liters of fresh springwater daily.

Day 3–4: Start the detoxification with a two-day fruit fast, since fruits are base-forming, easily digested, and provide enzymes that help clear the system. For example, mango, pineapple, and papaya are especially good for digestion, and kiwi is a diuretic. Since you may have reactions to the cleansing and feel tired and irritable, it is best to schedule the fruit fast for a weekend. Make sure you get plenty of fresh air and daylight, walk or jog, and a sauna would be wonderful.

Day 5–9: Continue with only fruit for breakfast. For lunch and dinner eat fresh lettuce, sprouts, plenty of raw vegetables, lightly stir-fried, steamed, or pickled vegetables, and roots – depending on personal taste, season, and tolerance. Add garlic and ginger for extra spice.

Day 10–12: Now add whole-grain products and protein (see day 1–2) to slowly accustom your stomach to more substantial food. For example, have a large salad with tuna for lunch and brown rice with broccoli for dinner. Continue to eat one serving of grated raw vegetables every day, which provide plenty of fiber, every day. Take note of how you feel, physically and mentally, after even this short cleansing period.

Ingesting agents that are less specific about the toxins they absorb in the intestines facilitates the detoxification process. Carbon, silicon, and germanium have a special ability to bind metals and other environmental pollutants. Active carbon adheres to any molecule it encounters and absorbs both gas and toxic substances in the gastrointestinal system. Bentonite contains a large amount of silicon and therefore has a high capacity for absorbing both toxic microorganisms and harmful products from the intestines. But it also makes detoxification easier in other parts of the body, probably by reducing the toxic burden on the intestines. But don't forget that carbon and silicon should not be taken in combination with food, medications, vitamins, or mineral supplements.

We tend to become mildly acidic when we are ill. The byproducts of metabolism need to be eliminated every day and excess acid is almost always formed in the process, causing detoxification problems. When the body is out of balance and becomes mildly acidic, alkaline supplementation is recommended. Alkaline salts containing sodium- and potassium carbonates are excellent agents for resetting the pH balance.

Antioxidants protect against free radicals and therefore play a major role in detoxification. If left alone, the free radicals attack the tissues and create toxic products. Glutathione, one of the most active antioxidants, is a small peptide composed of three amino acids that also participates in detoxification by binding toxins and guiding them out of the body. Glutathione is reused after disposing of toxins that are byproducts of our metabolism, but the antioxidant is lost after transporting foreign poisons out of the body. We thus lose a vital component of our detoxification system and need to replenish our supply. Glutathione is found in fresh fruit and vegetables, such as avocado, asparagus, grapefruit, and tomatoes, as well as in veal. It is heat-sensitive, however, and easily destroyed when cooked. A diet rich in fresh vegetables and ripe fruit is vital for our self-healing system, ensuring a supply of antioxidants and nutrients for detoxification and vitality.

Our lifestyle today encourages depression, chemical dependency, and degenerative disease. This afflicts not only those individuals trapped in the addiction, but even their friends and relatives. For example, 10–15 percent of children have a parent who has problems with alcohol.

In our society, happiness is the ultimate goal. We are expected to live well: to have happy marriages and children, and to succeed both socially and at work. Although meeting these demands for happiness is a stressful process, most people comply while repressing their unhappiness. Problems are swept under the rug lest this sign of failure be revealed. Yet, how many people are truly happy? Perhaps happiness should no longer be held as the norm and we should live life as it comes. Being content with the way we are today rather than living with the utopian ideal, "when I achieve ... then I will ...," since this attitude only generates dissatisfaction and inner stress. Stop hiding emotions behind the shield of various dependencies – and all that this entails. Others may not perceive us as being quite so fabulous as they do now, but we will be more genuine and true – to ourselves and to those around us. And it might even make us healthier ...

Chemical dependency means handing over control of your life. It encourages feelings of helplessness that, in the long run, feed hopelessness. But we have the power to alter this by making conscious lifestyle changes. An intact detoxification system is a necessity for further human development. Indeed, we need to protect ourselves against visible and invisible toxins – both internal and external. We have to ensure that our most essential cells in the immune, endocrine, and central nervous systems receive appropriate nutrients and are protected from toxic substances. Otherwise these toxins will linger in our bodies and inhibit our mental and physical processes and functions. In short: drugs, toxins, and allergens prevent us from achieving our full potential – intellectually, emotionally, and spiritually.

10.
Consciousness and Spirituality

The human consciousness is the largest untapped potential in the western world today. This as yet unexplored gold mine is one reason for my optimistic view of the future. The twentieth century may have been the century of the exact sciences (physics, biomedicine, genetic engineering), but the twenty-first century will see breakthroughs in the science of psychobiology and human consciousness. This field will expand as we raise our consciousness, both individually and collectively.

We have seen that a number of substances affect the brain and behavior. Could consciousness be the result of the "cocktail" of transmitters temporarily flooding the brain? This description may be apt in purely biological terms, but fortunately there is more to us than mere biology. Our consciousness is vast, at the same time both limited and infinite. Researchers believe that we only use a small fraction of our mental capacity, but I prefer to say that we use less than one per mille of a percent of our consciousness. Human capacity has tremendous potential for growth.

We have extremely limited knowledge of how consciousness works. Buddhists say there are one hundred sixty different states of consciousness – though we hardly use any of them. According to western thought, we may be more or less alert during the awake state, asleep, or indulging in daydreams and fantasies.

Why have we paid so little attention to such an important part of our beings? Perhaps because the study of human consciousness builds on subjective experience and consequently it has fallen more within the realm of the church. To date, western research has investigated areas in which we can produce objective facts, and the human consciousness is therefore just an invisible speck on the map. To learn more about our consciousness we can turn to the wisdom accumulated over thousands of years by the eastern world. It is at the junction of these two philosophies and cultures that something new will take shape. In the first decades of the new millennium we will see a breakthrough in knowledge of the human consciousness, personality, and soul.

Consciousness can be discussed on various planes – for example, a superficial or deeper consciousness of the body, thoughts, emotions, and a higher spiritual consciousness.

We have much to gain by learning more about human consciousness and, in the process, about ourselves too. Moving into an altered state of consciousness enables us to communicate with different parts of our bodies and levels of consciousness. We can also tap into knowledge and wisdom from external sources, in a process similar to "channeling." This phenomenon has been reported in all cultures since the beginning of time; the best-known example may be the oracle of Delphi. Remarkably, the deeper you delve, the clearer it becomes. Since a developed consciousness requires a brain, this is a suitable location to begin our adventure into consciousness.

Consider the development of the brain since the time of the oldest human ancestors (Australopithecus afarensis) three to four million years ago; it is immediately clear that the trend is to move toward more complex systems and a higher consciousness.

I did not discover relativity by rational thought alone.
Albert Einstein

The Ingenious Brain

The brain serves as the central command post for our experiences and actions. To get an idea of its amazing ability, consider that there are more possible pathways for nerve signals in the brain than there are atoms in the entire known universe. The brain can also make new neurosynaptic connections throughout life, thereby further expanding its information network. We require this to interpret the constant bombardment of noise, scents, and visual impressions that are part of our ongoing communication with the outside world. The brain coordinates the information flowing through the senses and controls our response in the form of movement.

The unique aspect of brain function is that only creatures that can move have brains. Still life forms such as plants and trees don't need a brain, whereas all animals are "animated" in the strict sense of the word. The Latin word *animus* means consciousness, and in order to move you need a brain that gives you some form of awareness of the surroundings. Even a simple multicellular organism that moves has a brain, albeit primitive. The cerebellum, located just above the point where the skull is attached to the neck, is responsible for automatic movements and may be considered to be the brain's autopilot. Initially, new movements require an intentional thought process, but after some practice they occur automatically, so they can move into the unconscious realm (this happens with learning to ride a bike, for example). In summary, we need the brain to move and to process impressions from our surroundings.

Is the brain necessary for consciousness? Since the brain develops slowly and gradually, perhaps consciousness does, too. A fetus has a consciousness, though not as developed as in an adult or a newborn. An infant is its body, and unless it experiences touching from the people around it the child will feel rejected, unloved, and it will not thrive. We can assume that the simpler the brain, the lower the degree of consciousness. The brain of the chimpanzee is very similar to the human brain at birth, but subsequently they develop differently. In apes, most development takes place during the fetal stage, but in humans it occurs after birth. This may be the distinguishing feature that makes our consciousness differ from that of our cousins the apes. Unlike chimpanzees, for example, we have an amazing ability to adapt to our surroundings as our brain develops. As a result we have advanced farther than the chimpanzees, even though 99 percent of our genes are identical.

You could say that the human brain and its development during the fetal stage have remained unchanged for the past thirty thousand years – dating to the time of early Cro-Magnon man. They are considered to be the first modern humans with a body similar to ours, and a high, dome-shaped cranium. They used tools, wore jewelry, and left a legacy of cave paintings. There is no doubt, either, that they had a sophisticated language. In fact, if a Cro-Magnon child were born today it would have no problem learning to use a computer.

The challenge for the young brain is to develop and mature based on the stimulation or limitations found in the environment. The newborn brain grows rapidly as nerves extend like the roots of a tree, making contact with other nerves. This establishes countless communication lines between the nerves, laying the foundation for more advanced functions. Our surroundings leave their mark on us at an early age, and our experiences shape the brain's "circuit board." Our unique development depends on the stimulation (and nutrients) we receive as children. In a restrictive (reductionist) society in which children are told about their shortcomings a hundred times more often than about their strengths, they learn to see their limitations rather than their assets and potential.

Some parts of the brain can be honed to perfection, such as the ability for learning and abstract thinking, while other parts remain untapped. Maturation and emotional development can come to a standstill, while other regions become overdeveloped. This situation can create a very limited and targeted consciousness; quite naturally, it affects a person's view of the world. After all, how can we understand anything we have not yet experienced?

You can influence another individual's consciousness and self-image, and the earlier you begin, the greater the impact. In India, baby elephants are tied to a large tree with a thick rope. No matter how hard they try, they cannot escape. As the elephants grow up they are tied to smaller and smaller trees. Eventually a thin rope is used to tie the full-grown elephants to small trees, but they never try to escape – because they don't believe it is possible. Similarly, we may become so conditioned as children that our perception of our selves and the world is inconsistent with who we are. The adventure is to explore our personal reality and rid ourselves of conditioned patterns and pictures that don't fit. We have to expand and integrate our various aspects to elevate our consciousness.

The mere expansion of consciousness has no value –
unless we have found our inner center...
Lama Govinda

Consciousness and Awareness

We create our consciousness using our thoughts, emotions, memories, and senses – the elements that define who we are. Our level of awareness rises as we use more and more of our potential. Just as the universe is boundless, so also there is no limit to human consciousness. Equally important is the need to discover your defining center–your innermost center of gravity and who you are–to be able to expand your consciousness. True strength is not a lack of weakness, but derives from being in touch with your inner self, your core.

Exactly how large is consciousness? Consider a comparison to the seas; two thirds of the earth is covered in ocean, over seven miles deep in places. Understandably, only a fraction of life in the seas has been investigated. The ocean is as deep as the highest mountain on earth: almost six miles. All that is hidden in our own depths–the things we are unaware of or wish to remain unaware of–that is our unconscious. The greater our unawareness, the less our ability to achieve our potential.

Only if we are aware of something, can we do anything about it but, like it or not, all that is hidden in our unconscious affects us. We are vulnerable to needs and desires we are not even aware of, and this may have undesirable consequences. The unconscious communicates through symbols and images, leading to actions evoked by unconscious thoughts, desires, and emotions. Life becomes a stage on which we play the lead in our own personal dramas.

Living consciously means taking responsibility for our actions. Victims no more, we can proactively choose attitudes toward our selves and toward the world around us. We create our own lives – in harmony with our surroundings. Life presents choices, and when we do not choose for ourselves we empower others to do so.

Becoming conscious involves modifying convictions that guide our lives. We may question our roots and background, and we may require time for solitude and reflection. Such introspection might not be compatible with today's "efficient" society, yet there are no shortcuts. To know ourselves better, we must spend time with ourselves. We might lose friends along the way, but we will find new and better friends more suited to our true selves.

Being conscious is synonymous with the will to grow. The urge to create something new is part of the foundation of life. Look around in nature; everything is in a constant process of growth and change – and changes are inherent in life. But what inhibits our growth? Often it is our own fear and ignorance.

How do we expand our consciousness? By getting to know ourselves: our motives, goals, hopes, fears, dreams, emotions, and yearnings. To understand ourselves we must pause and reflect on our feelings, our actions, and the early conditioning that controls our reactions. As children we accepted those roles and behaviors that rewarded us with energy in the form of appreciation, ensuring that we were seen and perhaps even loved. Some people believe they will receive more attention–in other words, more energy–for unusual or difficult behavior, while others succeed in all their endeavors, and receive affirmation for this type of behavior. Some remain silent and well-adjusted as a means of gaining appreciation. But we only see a small part of ourselves as illuminated by the reactions of our parents, teachers, and friends; the rest remains in darkness until someone or something sheds light on it. The diamond hiding within us all must be polished before its true beauty can be revealed.

How do we do this? Keep a journal, or talk to others; counseling has helped many people find their way. The ultimate goal is to develop a good relationship with your self – you must live with yourself throughout your entire life. Learn to integrate your various aspects–those that are denied or affirmed. Expanding personal awareness is a lifelong journey; its length is up to us. Not everyone will become an enlightened guru, sitting atop a remote mountain. You need to find your own path, for only you can find the way to higher consciousness.

The path to increased awareness is often more attractive in theory than in practice; it's a rocky road at best. Along the way you will learn about personality traits and facets you'd rather not know about, encounter emotions you'd rather forget, and dare to see yourself in a new light. Life would be so much easier if someone told you who you are, but that is impossible – only you have the answer, and it lies within yourself.

Changing takes courage, energy, and will-power, and requires mental preparation of varying duration. We may need to take classes and read books before daring to venture out on our own. Psychotherapy can be a step along the way. Waiting in the spiritual sense means waiting on your soul, while taking simple steps to encourage it. The soul speaks through symbols or intuition, but we must listen, lest a lifetime pass without our hearing the message.

The Infinite Human

The "mind" is not located behind the frontal bone – it is infinite. Consciousness is more than just the exchange of electrical signals; in fact, consciousness and the physical world around us are one and the same. This is what the pioneers of quantum physics believed – Planck, Bohr, Heisenberg, and Schrödinger. Max Planck wondered whether it was logically possible to imagine self-awareness that is independent of nature. Albert Einstein suggested that mass and energy are two sides of the same coin and our consciousness works in the same way: the world around us can be perceived either as energy or as a physical reality. We filter reality through our brains and our senses in order to make it comprehensible. By developing our "wave filter" we can move onto the same wavelength as the world around us, but this requires a dedicated effort.

Try tying this in with the concept of the three levels of human existence (see p. 42). First we exist as a physical body. The material world itself is restricted by dualism (classification into opposites such as spirit and matter). The subtle body is the second level and includes emotions and thoughts – energy and movement. Our soul or spirit constitutes the third level. We exist on all three levels simultaneously. Our ability to use them depends on how well integrated we are: how conscious we are.

The soul or spirit has neither beginning nor end; by definition it is infinite and formless. It is also connected to the universal consciousness or the universal knowledge, which works as a type of mental Internet from which we retrieve knowledge about things that we otherwise would not know. We can ask a question and get an answer. When the universal knowledge speaks to you in your waking hours, it is intuition; when you are asleep, it is called dreaming. Many scientists have received their most brilliant ideas in a dream or through a sudden, inexplicable inspiration. There are numerous examples of people who have exhibited profound knowledge under hypnosis of things they know nothing of when awake. During meditation we "dial in" directly to this global consciousness and "surf" the unlimited knowledge. We can train ourselves to communicate at the different levels of consciousness.

This form of ESP (Extra Sensory Perception) is probably the same as "the sixth sense." ESP includes clairvoyance: the ability to sense an incident or predict future incidents without using the traditional five senses. For example, the phone rings and you know who it is before answering, or you think about someone and the person appears a while later. Sometimes when we need something it is suddenly there, without any explanation. Clearly we can affect material phenomena mentally. But this is also telepathy, involving direct interpersonal communication. Telepathy is based on the premise that the greater the emotional bond between two people, the greater the likelihood they will understand messages from one another. This phenomenon is especially common between mother and child and between twins. This process is inexplicable if we only take physical aspects into account, but becomes comprehensible if we are prepared to look at other properties.

"True dreams" and warnings have been reported to be more common among people who have epilepsy. I have a friend who, in connection with her rare migraines, experiences images and premonitions of future events – which later come true. This phenomenon occurs especially in connection with her aura (flashes before her eyes), a symptom that can also precede an epilepsy attack.

One possible explanation is that minerals in the body with electrical properties can function as recipients for signals. Events can be perceived in advance because the concept of time does not exist on the spiritual level in the traditional sense. The signals are converted into chemical energy in order to be understood. Indeed we require a certain quantity of minerals to receive signals and "conduct" electricity. This is one reason that acupuncture, for example, does not work as well in people who have mineral deficiency.

Researchers have shown that collagen molecules have piezoelectric properties because they contain the mineral silicon. These molecules can convert pressure or sound waves into electricity and vice versa. This piezoelectric effect in silicon allows quartz crystals to be used in microphones, radios, and quartz watches. Silicon is used in the manu-

My ex-husband and I used to communicate through our thoughts. I called him at work just to find that he was about to call me, or vice versa. Sometimes the lines were busy because we were calling each other at the same time. We "felt" things and communicated wordlessly and we still do. A remarkable example occurred once while I was on the way home after a lecture and stopped at a gas station. After paying for the gas, I was about to leave when I noticed a stand with a new type of orange-flavored chocolate. I paused and felt a strong craving, but I decided not to buy any since it contained a large amount of sugar, and subsequently put it out of my mind. This happened at about ten to six. Later that evening my ex-husband asked me to taste a new chocolate with 70 percent cocoa that he had purchased, but I wasn't in the mood and declined. Nevertheless he persisted and to my surprise it was: orange-flavored chocolate. I asked him when he had bought it. Right before six he had walked into a chocolate store on a sudden inspiration and bought this orange-flavored chocolate just for me. This had never happened before...

facture of microchips (circuit boards) that have made today's small computers possible and was a contributing factor in the IT revolution that spawned Silicon Valley.

Collagen is the dominant protein in humans, comprising about 25 percent of the total amount of protein. Consequently a person weighing 155 pounds has a full 6.5 pounds of collagen in their skin, bones, blood vessels, connective tissue, internal organs, tendons and ligaments, as well as in the lens of the eye. Collagen contains an abundance of silicon, which is essential for its formation. The highest silicon concentrations are found in the skin, hair, and aorta (the outbound artery of the heart). It is also found in bones and teeth, where it is needed for mineralization.

In summary our bodies contain silicon molecules that can receive and convert energy from one form to another. The abundance of silicon in collagen may explain our ability to receive and send non-verbal energy. Certain internal organs and glands, like the pineal gland, contain collagen (and silicon molecules) capable of receiving external signals and converting them into chemical signals. This exciting concept and this new view of humankind suggest previously inconceivable possibilities. To date we have focused mainly on the effects of chemical energy on the body; specifically, the effects of various molecules (matter). Soon scientists will be investigating the effects of other types of energy on the metabolism and the synthesis of new molecules.

Although more and more people receive light therapy to counteract winter depression, most are still treated with chemical energy (medication). But if we were also to utilize our energy potential, treatment with massage, acupressure or acupuncture, aromatherapy, sound waves (music), or light waves (low- or moderate intensity laser) would be considered routine. Doctors would prescribe medical *qigong* or music therapy. Words of kindness and love would be viewed as a method of treatment.

The Flow

Finding ourselves in the flow is emotional intelligence at its best, for then we are open and in a positive energy-rich state. Characteristic of the flow are spontaneous joy and feelings of mild ecstasy. We become focused and are at one with our task. We lose track of time and our work flows automatically. In such a state we are connected to the universal consciousness through our spirit.

We all share this feeling and may be immersed in it to a varying extent. Everyone, from authors to athletes, tries to enter the flow to achieve peak performance. It is easier to enter the flow when engaged in an activity that consumes us – or when expanding our abilities to perform beyond our limits. Quite simply, we forget about ourselves and enter a state where we leave the ego behind and become part of something larger.

In contrast, if we are trapped in depression or upset and anxious, the flow stops and it is difficult to reenter. Some people use alcohol and other drugs to get around such barriers. This may provide temporary relief, but generally has the opposite long-term effect because the blockages are made permanent, rather than being resolved. This is yet another reason for dealing with unconscious emotions deep within – they impede the creative flow.

You can enter the flow in a number of ways. A state of intense concentration is characteristic of flow and one excellent way of achieving this is to stay completely in the present, attentive to the task at hand. Indeed we require effort and discipline to focus and insulate ourselves against emotional turbulence. Once we are engaged by our task and sufficiently focused, the ability to concentrate is self-perpetuating. At that point we are in the flow and can experience spontaneous joy. American professor Mihaly Csikszentmihalyi notes in his book *Flow – The Psychology of Optimal Experience* that people concentrate best when a task is challenging and they have to make a greater effort than usual. People become bored unless sufficiently challenged, whereas too much pressure creates anxiety. Flow occurs in the space that lies between these emotional levels.

Learning becomes easier when we are in the flow. This motivates us from within rather than by means of threats and/or promises of rewards. Well-being and subtle ecstasy come naturally when we are focused on the here and now. By embracing the principles of flow we create a positive upward spiral and sharpen our sense of focus, presence, and creativity. The process becomes self-generating.

Raised Consciousness

The individual cell has its own consciousness: cells in the body possess memory–a reaction pattern–which lingers even after new cells have replaced them. Just a year ago almost all the atoms in your body today did not exist. Nearly your entire body has been replaced, yet the cell's reaction pattern remains because of the knowledge transferred from one cell generation to the next. For example, a whiff of hay triggers a memory of childhood summer, though not one molecule from that time remains within you. A certain touch can also release memories, transporting us instantly to another time and place. Our bodies possess a far deeper memory than modern science can understand or measure. Like a wound in the body, an injury to our consciousness requires healing. In effect, the first stumbling steps toward raising our consciousness may remind us of pain, anger and sorrow we would prefer to forget.

No one gets through life without problems and we often wall off our wounds in response. But in the process we also screen off contact with our inner, deeper core. Since creativity is born from within, it can be blocked. In effect, we shut off our deeper selves and lose contact with our consciousness and the outside world. If this process is allowed to go unchecked, we ultimately lose contact with our unconscious being.

As time passes we mask our true identity. Wearing such a mask consumes energy – not being, doing, or living as our true selves. So how do you know what to do? By taking the time to listen to your inner voice and do whatever comes naturally – in daylight or in dreams, during meditation or long walks. For example, the introductory riff to the song "Satisfaction" came to Keith Richards while he was asleep; all he had to do was listen. If we take the time to develop as individuals while being honest with ourselves we will be well-rewarded.

Within us is the self, an energy center that tells us what to do. *Intuition* can be perceived as a message from the self, enabling us to connect with our inner knowledge. It can act as a beacon in our lives, guiding our decisions. We may often receive a premonition that something is about to happen or that we should choose a certain path. By being attentive to the inner signals we establish inner communication, further facilitating our access to intuition. An attentive ear is vital to our self-development. But the more we depend on external objective measurements, the less we rely on our senses and our extrasensory abilities. We must exercise our intuition lest we lose the ability to do so. Dare to trust and listen to your intuition, and it will provide answers and guidance in life.

Many eastern cultures use *breathing* as a method of achieving elevated consciousness. Since breathing can be perceived as the link between body and soul, changes in our breathing patterns can influence our unconscious. By developing the ability to consciously change our breathing cycle we alter our energy field and open ourselves to an expanded state of consciousness. To put it in somewhat simplified form, deep breathing affects the heart rate, which in turn alters the body's circulation, oxygenation, neuropeptide secretion, and the distribution of charged particles – resulting in a change in the body's electromagnetic field.

Meditation is a method of elevating our consciousness by entering into an altered state of consciousness. In his book *Wherever You Go,*

One of my friends needed to get away from her daily routine and ponder her situation and a difficult relationship. She traveled far away to Mexico and lived for a month in a cabin overlooking the sea. One night she was awakened by a dream, filled with a stronger feeling of love than she had ever before experienced. In her dream she saw a man who loved her, who wanted to spend his life with her, and they would have children together. She learned his age, that he was Swedish, about his job, and his appearance. That night she woke up, wrote down the details of her dream, and fell back to sleep. The following morning she was elated and hopeful about the dream, and it brought her happiness for days. In time the memory faded. Three months later she was at a dinner where she met a man to whom she was instantly attracted. The feeling was mutual–a spiritual encounter as he called it–and they became deeply engaged in conversation. They fell in love, were engaged three months later, and were married after a year. One month after their first meeting she suddenly remembered her dream. When she reread the description of the loving man in the dream, it exactly matched the man she had met...

There You Are stress researcher Jon Kabat-Zinn, M.D. says that when we meditate we direct our energies inward, only to discover that we contain the entire world within our own consciousness and body. In other words: enter your own microcosm if you want to discover the macrocosm.

During meditation the body produces various substances such as beta-endorphin, DHEA, and serotonin, which counteract stress and provide pleasant relaxation. Electrical activity in the brain also changes. Similarly, *sleep* can be considered to be an altered state of consciousness. The neurons in the limbic system contain serotonin. When these neurons discharge, the slow brain waves–characteristic of sleep–are generated. In animal experiments, substances that deplete the brain of serotonin result in insomnia. Sleep normalizes when these animals are given the amino acid tryptophan, which restores brain serotonin levels.

Dreams can be viewed as messengers from the unconscious. We

can use our dreams as a powerful tool to gain greater self-knowledge. Making the effort to record your dreams and interpret the symbolism can be rewarding. Sometimes dreams can even portend the future.

Healing Prayer

A 1996 Time/CNN poll found that 82 percent of the American population believes that personal prayer has the power to heal. Three quarters believe that prayer helps other people to get well.

What significance does prayer have for accelerating the healing process? In a research study, Professor Randolph Byrd at San Francisco General Hospital, divided 393 cardiac patients into two groups. One group was the object of intercessory prayer by home prayer groups, while the other group did not receive such prayers. Naturally neither the hospital staff nor the patients knew who belonged to which group. Catholic and Protestant prayer groups consisting of five to seven participants were recruited from across the country. The group was told the patient's name and condition and prayed daily for that person. The results showed that patients in the "prayer group" were five times less likely to require antibiotics than those in the control group. Patients in the prayer group were three times less likely to develop pulmonary edema than people in the control group. No one in the prayer group needed help from a respirator, compared with twelve in the other group, and fewer patients died in the group that received prayer.

Researchers also found that longer prayers were more effective, and that general prayer–praying for the general health and well-being of the patient–was more powerful than directed prayer. A problem with directed prayer is that neither the person praying nor the patient knows what to visualize. Other experiments suggest that undirected prayer influences the living being to move toward an optimal condition of health. The person praying does not need to know what is best – the important thing is to pray.

The San Francisco study received substantial attention but also considerable criticism. It stirred Dr. Larry Dossey's interest, however, and in reviewing the literature he found over one hundred thirty published studies showing the effect of prayer on living cells, bacteria, plants, people, and animals. Half of these studies showed statistically significant results. This inspired Dr. Dossey to study the neglected field of telesomatic healing, or the power of prayer, over a period of more than five years. His results were published in *Healing Words*. Dr. Dossey concluded that prayer is an effective and humane method of treatment. Moreover, prayer works and heals because it fosters the faith, endurance, and energy needed to handle illness and crisis. Prayer resembles meditation and also has much in common with parapsychology. You have to find your own prayer style – no single approach suits everyone.

In late 2001, a pair of New York hospitals published a study conducted at a Korean fertility clinic that received considerable attention. The findings were that twice as many women who received "prayer therapy" from a distance became pregnant than those who were not supported by such a prayer group. Groups of religious people prayed for a patient whom they had never seen; all they knew was the patient's name. Moreover, this was a triple-blind study: not even the doctors at the clinic knew about it. Dr. Dossey calls this form of healing–or distance healing–"non-local medicine." He believes that it belongs to the third era of medicine; the first era is the physically oriented modern medicine, and the second is mind-body medicine. The two first eras work "locally."

The medical community has responded to Dr. Dossey's results in different ways: one public and one private. No one is willing to comment publicly, but after his lectures many express their interest and relate their own experiences. Most admit they are afraid of losing their positions, the respect of their colleagues, and their research grants if they openly support his findings. Dr. Dossey, a former co-chair of the Office of Alternative Medicine, National Institutes of Health, is the current executive editor of the journal *Alternative Therapies in Health and Medicine*.

Interest in spirituality and healing has, however, mushroomed in recent years. Seven years ago, only three US medical schools included courses in spirituality and health in the curriculum; today such courses are offered at almost ninety of the one hundred twenty-five US medical schools. Evidently women find it easier to embrace the new approach and think non-locally; that is, they are not limited by time and place. According to Dossey, the fact that half of all medical school graduates are women plays a major role in the rapid acceptance of the third era of medicine. Medical science is undergoing a change: we are opening ourselves to new dimensions and renouncing old limitations.

Telepathic and telesomatic phenomena can be measured scientifically and the results of Randolph Byrd's study and other research show that neither geographic distance nor the number of people prayed for seems to be of significance. How is this possible? One conclusion Dr. Dossey drew from his studies is that electromagnetic energy is not involved: because it is a local phenomenon, it would weaken as the distance from the source increased. Researchers have shown that two people in separate rooms who are empathically linked synchronize their EEGs when they communicate telepathically with each other. Since there is a unified consciousness, the question becomes not how the signal travels from one consciousness to another, but how each brain communicates through that consciousness. Nobel Prize laureate Erwin Schrödinger studied this phenomenon in the 1920s and 1930s and concluded: "The mind is a singular reality in which the total quantity of consciousness is one."

Consciousness is non-local and it is not bound by time or space. Consequently, Dr. Dossey believes that telepathic and telesomatic effects do not involve subtle energy, as is commonly thought, but instead it is a question of consciousness. It involves an as yet undiscovered law of nature that exists – even though we have yet to define it.

One possible explanation is that prayer works through the universal consciousness, which may be related to the concept of God. All major religions concur that God is not localized to just one place. God is everywhere and we can reach Her through prayer no matter where we are. Consciousness is the divine infinite in time and space and unity at the deepest level. Indeed the divine resides within each of us. Or as Khalil Gibran prophesied in 1923: "The Universe's soul and God are identical and they are both also identical with man's divine higher self."

During the past ten years, neuroresearchers have shown that the brain has a center that is involved in deeper spiritual experiences. Quite simply, we are "wired" for spirituality. According to neurotheologists, evolution has programmed the human brain so that we experience pleasure when we move beyond–transcend–the limits of the self and feel that we are part of the universe. After half an hour of meditation or total rest, we feel relaxed and rejuvenated. Researchers used a method called SPECT (Single Photon Emission Computed Tomography) to measure the brain activity of meditating Buddhists and praying nuns and found an area in the upper, posterior part of the brain that becomes totally inactive during a transcendental experience. This part of the brain processes information about time and space and the body's three-dimensional orientation; it decides where the body ends and the rest of the world begins. If this area is injured, you cannot even navigate through a room to sit on a chair. If you block sensory impressions to this area through deep meditation, the delineation between the self and the rest of the world disappears. You feel cosmic unity and some people call this area the "God area" of the brain.

However, it is not possible to determine whether the brain generates the neurologic changes registered during spiritual experiences – or the brain perceives a spiritual reality.

During the early history of the ancient Greeks the gods and faith-healers each had a role in treating the sick. Faith-healing was a special profession whose practitioners were chosen and became recognized and praised. Gradually special temples were built to the healing gods, the most famous of whom was Asclepias. Indeed a form of religious medicine was practiced, in which healing and the spiritual coexisted. Herbs and natural extracts were also widely used. Helping to heal someone is the same as becoming whole, which is very close to the holy.

Healing Relationships

Humankind's third level–the soul or the universal consciousness–has to be considered in order to understand the unsolved mystery that has long baffled researchers: the placebo effect (see page 232). This has been viewed as undesirable when testing new pharmaceuticals and has therefore been dismissed as unimportant. But, now it has climbed to higher levels of biomedical research. In November 2000, the National Institute of Health (NIH) held a conference about the Science of Placebo. This was a landmark event, indicating that mainstream researchers are studying the mechanism of the placebo effect. However, in the spring of 2001, the New England Journal of Medicine published an article stating that the placebo effect is a myth. After evaluating 114 published articles about the placebo effect, a Danish research group drew the conclusion that it is merely the result of day-to-day variations in the disease process, and that patients become better spontaneously. The report received considerable attention since it questioned accepted dogma, but it actually supports the belief that pills just don't matter when we have a self-healing ability and that can be guided in the proper direction.

The new evolving philosophy says that the healing response is because, based on a supportive relationship, you send the appropriate message to your body's "inner pharmacy." Dr. Howard Brody, a family practitioner and professor, describes this in his book *The Placebo Response*. The Danish researchers do not contradict this, but feel that a placebo is a foolish method of delivering such messages.

The conclusion is that we are capable of producing all we need to function and heal, and that the care provider is paramount for successful results. Several studies show that a positive and supportive attitude is a crucial aspect of the physician or therapist's skills. An encouraging pat on the shoulder and a confidence-inspiring conversation can be invaluable. Holistic medicine proponents also believe that unconditional love and acceptance are the most powerful of all medicines – the factor that best promotes the healing process. Consequently, holistic care focuses on generating a good and healing environment and relationship between patient and care provider.

But what is it that is transferred in a doctor-patient relationship that causes such remarkable healing? It probably involves a philosophical definition of the innermost core of medicine and healing. Today's medical care has isolated the physical from the metaphysical, and as Dr. Herbert Benson, Professor of Medicine at Harvard Medical School, said in his book *Timeless Healing*: "Western medicine still makes a clear distinction between mental, emotional, and physical causes of diseases, even though most research shows that the body, soul, and mind are so interwoven that such differences are clearly unscientific." The key seems to be to reach in and influence our inner pharmacy with words or some other form of energy. Good relationships strengthen the immune system and health; the same is true for positive and hopeful thoughts or words.

"Your ability to envision what is possible also determines what happens," says Dr. Larry Dossey. He considers the mind to be a factor in healing, both within the individual and between people.

A growing number of physicians and researchers are starting to talk about the significance of creating a healing relationship in which patients trust their care provider. In this relationship, a transfer to the non-physical level also takes place. Kind words, a warm tone of voice, eye contact, and the ability to listen – these factors make things happen. Healing relationships are a key factor for good health and spontaneous healing. Tieraona Low Dog, a US physician and an expert in botanical medicine, says: "Those of us who connect on a deeper level are healers; the rest are just practitioners."

A Spiritual Awakening

Most of us have experienced feelings of being connected to something greater at one time or another. More people than we think have had experiences that can't be explained by our current worldview. Gallup polls in the 1990s found that 53 percent of American adults had experienced "a moment of sudden religious awakening or insight." Reports of mystical experience increase with education, income, and age (most likely between forty and fifty). These "supernatural" experiences refer to ESP: premonitions and dreams that come true, and people who return in the afterlife. A study involving five hundred Swedish college students showed that eight of ten believe in supernatural experiences but barely one of six believed in God.

A study reported in the journal *Nature* in July 1998 showed that the majority of American scientists have no religious beliefs. Among the more successful, very few even believe in God; 93 percent were atheists or agnostics. Superior knowledge, judgment, and experience were the reasons given for the researchers' lack of belief in God. Maybe this is the "official version"; perhaps they believe something else in private. But there seems to be a marked division of opinion about God, spirituality, and "higher forces" between ordinary people and researchers. In my experience, researchers believe everything can be understood through the power of reason. This attitude is inherent in their approach and in itself entails a form of faith – and undeniably, faith in common sense is rooted in Cartesian reasoning.

But this view is restrictive, since we are so much more than our thoughts and reason – all knowledge and experience aside. Professor Pert believes progress in research depends less upon control, analysis, and competition than upon care, unity, intuition, and spontaneity. According to Dr. Pert, there is a spiritual dimension at the core of research: her most profound insights emanate from a mystical process. She says "God whispers in my ear." Surely Dr. Pert is logged on to the global, mental Internet.

In this age of information, we are open to new visions of humankind. In fact, all we need to do is listen attentively and be receptive with our entire beings. On the subject of enlightenment, Franz Kafka writes: "You do not need to leave your room. Remain sitting at your table and listen. Do not even listen, simply wait. Do not even wait, be still and quite solitary. The world will freely offer itself to you to be unmasked, it has no choice, it will roll in ecstasy at your feet." Or as philosopher Ken Wilber says in his *A Brief History of Everything*: "Consciousness unfurls more and more, realizes itself increasingly and manifests itself more and more. Consciousness (the soul) is everywhere."

A concept called spiritual intelligence, SQ, appeared in 2000. Danah Zohar's book *Spiritual Intelligence* defines this as the ability that provides us with meaning and context in life. People who have a highly developed SQ have spiritual strength and a high level of self-awareness; they are flexible and inspired by visions and values. If you have a high SQ, you can tolerate and utilize crises and painful experiences to achieve a higher level of development. You are able to work against convention; you can convert setbacks and problems into lessons learned and positive growth. You tend to see correlations, to search for basic answers in life. Spiritual intelligence is the ability to create meaning in life–no matter what the situation–by living as honestly and consciously as possible. You could say that the opposite of SQ is spiritual isolation.

The existential spiritual movement sweeping across the western world is known as the "New Age." In fact, it is the old age, and harkens back to our spiritual roots. This multi-faceted movement is unified by the search for something different, something deeper and truer than what can be found in our materialistic world.

The growing interest in healing is another sign of this. According to healer and physicist Barbara Brennan, "All healing is a spiritual experience toward awakening, a path of expanding consciousness and awareness."

A growing number of people realize that money in itself does not bring happiness, but is merely a necessary and practical tool. Increasingly, we turn to nature, shamans, and primitive cultures, seeking inner experiences through dance, music, and meditation. There is a growing movement toward spiritual development in the tradition of the old mystics. The New Age is a diverse movement, snowballing from its own energy. Much of its reasoning fits into the new paradigm, and substantial elements of this philosophy are already being embraced by society.

Our Origin

Humankind can be compared to a tree, where the trunk represents both body and core, the crown is our contact with the spiritual, and the roots are our origin. In the process of developing civilization, we lost something essential: the original energy and mystical significance of our being. This essence transcends mere spirituality, extending far deeper. But, just as spirituality is inherent to this essence, so too are our instincts, emotions, intuition, and the context in which we live. We have lost touch with the roots and crown of our tree.

We have become domesticated. We tread on floors and asphalt in hard-heeled shoes. We eat the flesh of artificially bred cows, pigs, and chickens, which have been crowded indoors into cages and stalls. Animals are dosed with antibiotics to increase their weight. There is widespread use of pesticides and chemical fertilizers in the cultivation of fruits and vegetables. Potted herbs purchased at the supermarket have never touched soil until just before shipment. We eat far too much fruit that's been harvested before it's ripe and shipped halfway around the globe. By spraying their crops, growers manipulate the ripening process and can halt or accelerate growth. Mass-produced food has lost its natural characteristics and so have we, victims of the depleted energy.

Today, we tend to see our ultimate goal as being technological advances and development. This may reflect a need to set ourselves apart from the animals and the "animalistic nature" that we share with them. But we still have sex, give birth, and breast-feed our young just as primitively as we did eons ago. Our primitive past is perhaps most profoundly perceived by parents at the birth of their child. The newborn reminds us of all things mystical and draws us closer to life and existence.

Technical development dominates our sophisticated lives in western society, but human development lags far behind. Along the way we have lost our true core: over time we have isolated ourselves from our emotional nature and our innate connection to all things spiritual and mystical.

This loss is a major factor underlying our society's collective depression and neurosis.

Though we are generally blessed with fulfillment of our basic needs, we still do not know happiness. Lulled by gadgets into false security, we believe money makes us worthy. It fictitiously promises success, but instead brings illusory content to our lives. We find ourselves in a global crisis – for we have lost our way.

The new millennium brings a quest for ancient origins. This does not entail a return to prior conditions or a search for a primitive existence. Rather, we are integrating the neglected elements of our forgotten past. The origin represents all that gives us life and soul, our creativity. We are meant to be wise beings, filled with love, insight, and empathy – sensual emotional beings with a well-developed intellect. Isn't it time to accept this, to reaffirm our energy and our entire beings?

We may be afraid of encountering our origins face-to-face because in doing so we bare ourselves to our own emotions. Confronting intense drives and feelings may seem to pose an overwhelming threat and for this reason society has forbidden us from expressing them. But there is no danger in expressing your emotions; rather, the threat lies in the explosion of repressed emotions: aimed at the wrong people, at the wrong time.

The more we feel and express our emotions responsibly, the less likelihood there is of an inappropriate outburst of repressed emotions. That is true emotional intelligence.

Becoming whole means embracing the original energy within us. No other person can achieve this for us, but those who have traveled this path before can be our guides. The journey requires self-reliance, however, and this in turn requires courage.

The choices are many. We can wander in nature, meditate on our origins, express our feelings in dance or creative writing, play drums, or move to the beat of African music. The origin rests in our lower *chakra*, a powerful energy that makes our being flourish. This energy reveals itself to those who reach for it... when they are ready to receive it.

Today society offers little encouragement to seek out our origins. On the contrary, we are supposed to take our place in the mainstream, make the grade, and strive to please others. No wonder we anesthetize our senses with legal or illegal drugs. We repress and deny our energy–and thus ourselves–prematurely.

To achieve a more humane society we need to address these points. What are we doing? Where can we find the truths that apply to us? Global trends point to an awakening and humankind is searching for enlightenment. This reflects the silent revolution that is already underway.

We need to reaffirm the living force within us on a spiritual level: this most valuable commodity for humankind cannot be bought.
There is a world that cannot be measured, touched, or compared to anything else. This world has a divine aspect, and upon entering it we become whole and strong. It is a source of energy, joy, and strength. Judgment is passed on no one, and truth and righteousness prevail; it is as timeless and bottomless as the origins of life. Then there is an alternate world that can be measured in form, size, numbers, and quantity – money, cars, houses, jewelry, and clothing. That world has been our home for far too long and it is high time to move into the first world in order to heal ourselves.

Remembering My True Self

Many people journey through life like the embryo; they never complete their birthing process. All humankind has physical birth in common, but few are able to fulfill their mental and spiritual birth. This requires experiencing pain and intense emotions, with primitive harkenings – only then can the barrier around us and within us, which isolates us from our true being, be dissolved. We must achieve consciousness, discover who we are, and find our mission in life. The struggle for identity involves the heart, mind, emotions, and intuition. Psychosclerosis is the cessation of development, the end of change, but change is part of life. Personal growth and realization are intimately tied to the meaning of life, whether it involves starting a family, getting an education, climbing mountains, or taking care of the elderly. All individuals possess the innate ability to let their essence expand – through the discovery of their true selves, which is often hidden from the world. We have to embark on a treasure hunt for our true identities. Few people know when they set out what treasures they will find within.

Part of life's meaning is searching for both soul and soul mate. It is no mere chance that Hans Christian Andersen's fairy tale "The Ugly Duckling" is so widely read and enjoyed. A world of ugly ducklings awaits transformation into swans.

Sometimes we are unhappy with our lives because we find ourselves in the wrong place. Those around us may not share our values or our basic philosophy. Energy is wasted by constantly adapting to others: it seeps away, weakening our beings and predisposing us to illness.

The search for who we really are takes time and poses a formidable challenge. But nothing is more enriching than being where we belong, surrounded by supportive people, and devoting ourselves to objectives that spring from an inner conviction. This in itself *is* healing.

11.
The Holistic View – the Foundation for Self-healing

> *Increased knowledge of the integration and interplay of the nervous, immune, and endocrine systems have paved the way for a more comprehensive view: the holistic view. The basic premise is the body's ability to produce all we need to feel good and function well, given the appropriate conditions. The self-healing ability can evolve continuously through prevention, wellness maintenance, and a holistic approach. To accomplish this, we have to pay attention to functional deficiencies in our organs long before problems appear as symptoms. But what are the distinguishing characteristics of the self-healing human, and how do we establish the conditions necessary for healing?*

Whole, health, and holy all share a linguistic root, the Saxon word *hal*. These words are also related in meaning. To be healthy is to be whole, and if you become healthy you are "healed."

The word holistic derives from the Greek *holos*, meaning whole. It refers to a paradigm of reality consisting of integrated wholes, the properties of which cannot be reduced to the characteristics of the different components. For example, a person is made up of cells and these consist of molecules, which in turn are composed of atoms, and so forth. But knowledge of atoms brings us no closer to understanding the human organism. The holistic view considers the whole – body, soul, mind, and emotions. This comprehensive view requires integration of all the body's organs, acting in concert with one another. The whole is greater than the sum of its parts, and the problems of no single part can be treated without also considering the cause within the context of the whole. In the holistic view everyone is interconnected, in details both large and small, like a single vast universal organism. Air pollution in Kazakhstan may be a factor in the death of coral reefs in the Caribbean, through a complex interaction involving thinning of the ozone layer, El Niño, and rising oceanic temperatures.

Researchers noted the relationship between mind and body as far back as the 1940s, but only in recent years has the holistic view really taken off. A contributing factor has been the discovery of the great similarity between the immune system and the nervous system. We now recognize that the body is integrated to an extent that we could not have imagined a few decades ago.

All cells in the body are the product of cell division. Sperm unites with the ovum to create this tiny source cell from which the whole human develops. The body consists of one hundred trillion cells (100,000,000,000,000)–divided into at least 210 different cell types– each the stage of a fascinating life drama. All life processes occur within the cells or on their surface: these are the very processes that allow us to live. The cells are constantly renewed throughout our lives; red blood cells have a life span of just three to four months.

However, there are two systems in the body in which the cells remain undivided and unchanged, (except through the aging process) throughout our post-natal life. One is the brain, in which many cells are not replaced but stay the same from infancy to death. The other is the immune system, consisting of various cell lines strategically scattered throughout the body. Lymphocytes (white blood cells) derive from parent cells (stem cells) in the bone marrow, spleen, and liver, and have a life span of days or months. A subgroup of lymphocytes, however, emerges early in development and has the same origin as the nerve cells in the brain. They never undergo cell division but bear the memory of our "I" – the memory cells of the immune system. They stand guard, ready to reject any foreign substance that enters the body. This is why there must be a match between donor and recipient before an organ such as a kidney can be transplanted.

There are other parallels between the immune system and the central nervous system. Both have a long-term memory, a consequence of the long lives of these cells, and both systems can sense their surroundings. If we not could perceive our surroundings we'd have nothing to remember. By means of our senses (smell, taste, touch, hearing, and vision) the brain registers the surrounding world. Similarly, the immune system detects molecules such as those associated with viruses, bacteria, and parasites that may enter our bodies. The first line of defense is composed of the mucous membranes of the nose, mouth, lungs, genitals, and intestines. Any substance perceived as foreign by the immune system which successfully passes this formidable barrier must be ruthlessly rejected. Thus the immune system also senses its surroundings – though on a different level than the brain. In their ability to recognize and remember, the immune and nervous systems may therefore be considered identical.

Psychoneuroimmunology

Only within the last few decades have researchers begun to understand how the immune system works at cellular and molecular levels, and about twenty years ago serious attention was first paid to the interconnectivity of the immune and nervous systems. In 1981, Robert Ader, an experimental psychologist, first coined the term PNI (psychoneuroimmunology). The following year came the dramatic discovery that immune system cells secrete neuropeptides, and particularly endorphins, which according to the classic understanding of the body were secreted only by brain cells. In response, the editorial department of the prestigious scientific journal *Nature* issued a warning to researchers to beware of "radical psychoimmunologists" who might use this discovery as a basis for suggesting that mind and body communicate with one another. Such was the state of affairs some twenty years ago.

Some immunologists experimented by grinding thymus tissue and cultivating the cells they extracted from it. If the liquid from cultured thymus cells was added to fresh new lymphocytes (from the blood or spleen) the lymphocytes began to grow and develop. Researchers tried to identify the factors responsible within the cultivation fluid, but the quantity of active substance was so minute that it was difficult to isolate. As a result, these researchers were viewed with great suspicion and this whole area of research was called into question. It was at this time that I began my postgraduate studies, and one of the areas I studied was how to get B-lymphocyte (a type of leukocyte) cultures in test tubes to mature into cells that would produce antibodies, the final stage in B-cell development. Such cells were later used to produce monoclonal antibodies – a "hot" new technology in the early 1980s (the discoverers received the Nobel Prize in 1984).

By the end of the decade, technology had caught up with theory.

Advances in peptide and gene technology made it possible to produce larger quantities of immune-system cell factors. This research became the latest trend, with startup companies competing to produce these substances, known as "interleukins."

Convincing the scientific community that the immune system and the nervous system are interconnected and communicate, however, was no easy task. In 1985, Candace Pert published a pivotal article in the Journal of Immunology which underscored the fact that a major shift in thinking had occurred in neuroscience. Her research indicated that cerebral function is affected by a variety of chemicals other than classic neurotransmitters. Many of these new substances were neuropeptides that had previously been studied as hormones, growth factors, or intestinal peptides. Furthermore, receptors for neuropeptides were discovered in the mobile immune cells. Pert's article concluded: "Neuropeptides and their receptors thus join the brain, glands, and immune system in a network of communication between brain and body, probably representing the biochemical substrate of emotion."

The new interdisciplinary field of PNI research studies how emotions and thoughts affect the body and health – and vice versa. Researchers have identified about one hundred active substances that send information back and forth between these different systems. The cells in all three systems (nervous, endocrine, and immune) can produce the same types of informational substances as those that create a psychosomatic network. The immune system and the neuroendocrine system can intercommunicate through their common hormones and receptors. In fact, one has to ask whether these well-integrated systems really are separate at all...

An immune response to a foreign substance results in measurable changes in the brain, such as increased nerve activity and changed levels of neurotransmitters. For example, immune cells can produce substances (peptides) that affect our mood and emotions. We can use this to create a conditioned response in the immune system. In a study of adults with autoimmune disease Robert Ader gave a group of subjects an immunosupressant (cyclophosphamide) with a conditioning agent (cod-liver oil). After several doses, he replaced half of the subsequent treatments with pure cod-liver oil, and discovered the results were equivalent to those in the group that had received cyclophosphamide throughout the study. In effect, the immune system had learned a conditioned response to the taste of the cod-liver oil. This feature can be used to fortify the immune system, showing how the body, mind, and emotions are intimately intertwined.

The knowledge that we can use our minds to influence our health is not new, but recent evidence suggests that certain emotional conditions and personality traits are linked to immune system function. For example, the effect of stress on different types of cells and factors in the body can be measured. When the brain becomes overloaded by stress or trauma, communications between the nervous, hormone, and immune systems break down, and the entire "system" becomes unbalanced. This suggests that a disrupted chemical balance in the brain creates a bio-imbalance throughout the body known as "cerebral stress." This condition is becoming increasingly common in today's society, with a consequent reduction in resistance to illness. Put simply, you cannot affect one of the three systems without simultaneously affecting the others. Psychoneuroimmunology provides definitive proof that the body is integrated into a functioning unit.

The Female Immune System

Although we have known for more than a century that hormones affect the immune system, only recently have researchers turned their attention to the female immune system. Indeed this area has hardly been explored. You might wonder why women's health has been given lower priority. A study carried out in 1998 by a Swedish government agency in charge of monitoring pharmaceutical-related issues showed that regardless of illness, physicians prescribed less expensive drugs to women than to men. To date research has treated the male immune system as the norm, and animal experiments have mainly been conducted on male subjects.

Research shows that the female immune system is stronger than the male's; immunologist Dr. Noel Rose suggested that women are immunologically more gifted than men. Estrogen stimulates cellular immunity, but both cell-mediated immunity (which controls T-cell killer cell activity) and humoral immunity (which controls the B-cell's antibody production) are stronger in women. Sex hormones and glands play a major role in regulating the female immune system – and vice versa. The female reproductive and immune systems are so intimately linked that they function as a feedback system. The strength of a woman's immune system varies naturally depending on her age, menstrual cycle, and pregnancy.

The ability to bear children underpins the woman's stronger immune system: in order to become pregnant she must be healthy. In addition, women need the strength to endure the physical and mental stress of the long pregnancy, and following birth they must be able to handle the stress of feeding, nurturing, and protecting the infant.

The woman's estrogen keeps the immune system fit, while the man's androgens tend to inhibit his immune system, which otherwise changes little following puberty. During puberty the woman's immune system becomes stronger. Her cellular immune system is inhibited during pregnancy, but returns to its previously high level following childbirth. The onset of menopause weakens the immune system once again.

The immune defenses oscillate with the menstrual cycle. Prior to ovulation sex hormones stimulate immunity, while immune activity declines during the latter half of the cycle, as estrogen falls and progesterone climbs. This is required to allow the fertilized egg–which to some extent is a foreign body–to attach itself to the uterine mucous membrane. The estrogen level is related to the level of copper (the "female mineral") and people with a high copper-to-zinc ratio or a high estrogen-to-progesterone ratio are more susceptible to viral disease. Women are therefore more susceptible to viral infections before menstruation than after. People with chronic viral illnesses often have high copper levels, which can be counteracted by supplementing their diet with certain antioxidants and vitamins.

Unfortunately, though, there is a downside to the strong female immune system. Women have nearly three times as great a risk of developing autoimmune diseases than men, according to one large-scale American study. Nine of ten patients suffering from SLE are women of childbearing age. Autoimmune diseases have long been believed to shadow infectious diseases, although researchers still know little about the onset of the autoimmune process. Scientists have noted a correlation between infectious disease and autoimmunity: specifically, there is a rise in the production of autoantibodies–which react to the individual's own body tissue–after most viral infections.

Nearly all autoimmune disease is found in patients with slow metabolisms, a more common condition in women than in men. This leads to increased thymus activity and simultaneously impaired adrenal activity, leaving the individual more vulnerable to viral infection. People with rapid metabolisms, combined with copper deficiency, are more vulnerable to bacterial infection. This is particularly true when the iron-to-copper ratio is elevated. A 30 percent decrease in copper diminishes the activity of the important detoxification enzyme superoxide dismutase (SOD), weakening protection against free radicals. In the event of infection the cells in the immune system release superoxide radicals in defense, and if there is not sufficient protection against free radicals, tissues may become seriously damaged.

Thus nature has endowed fertile women with a strong immune system to ensure the survival of the species. These are the very parameters that guide men in choosing their mates; they prefer a youthful and healthy appearance to be able to perpetuate healthy genes: a basic instinct that has worked for tens of thousands of years.

The Challenged Immune System

In the past the most common reason for taking babies to see the pediatrician was fungal diaper rash, which resulted from washing the infants so much that protective oils were removed. Most modern soaps and shampoos contain carcinogens and are made from cheap industrial bulk chemicals (such as sodium lauryl sulphate) that lather well, but in effect this disrupt the beneficial microenvironment of the skin and scalp.

Soaps wash away natural fatty acids, beneficial bacteria, and enzymes found in our skin, altering our microenvironment. Our bodies produce their own antibiotics without which we become more susceptible to disease. Shampoos with natural glycerine are gentler to the scalp and restore volume to our hair. Most toothpastes include synthetic foaming agents that have a negative effect on the microenvironment of the oral mucous membranes. Skin lotions and lip balm often contain mineral oils, produced from crude oil, which paradoxically have a drying effect on your skin and lips. Therefore it is a good idea to examine your skin care and hygiene products and switch to those without chemical foaming agents, acrylamides, and mineral oils. You don't want to harm the sensitive pH, enzymes, bacterial flora, and fatty acid composition in your skin and mucous membranes – our first line of defense against infections. If the barrier is significantly compromised, the body's immune system must deal with the burden of these substances, and if the burden becomes too great it may further tax the already challenged immune system.

The changes we effect in the environment have both positive and negative impact. Asthma was first described as a "new illness among high-born and distinguished gentlemen" – and thus considered a class-related disease. But asthma appears to have a correlation with exaggerated hygiene, according to Hans Wigzell, Professor of Immunology at Karolinska Institutet. Mice with a hereditary predisposition for developing diabetes contract the disease when kept in overly-hygienic cages, but not when released in a dirty barn – regardless of diet. We too are designed to live in nature and not in ultra-clean houses. Good hygiene is fine, but too much of a good thing can be downright harmful. The bottom line is that the presence of healthy bacteria is beneficial and we even need certain types of infections.

A similar argument applies to our interiors – the intestines. We need a healthy intestinal flora that produces both antibiotic and anticarcinogenic substances as well as healthy byproducts for our intestinal mucous membranes and bodies. The intestinal mucous membrane has the same surface area as a tennis court and it is much more permeable in children than in adults. If you suffer from frequent colds, infections, or allergies it may be a sign that your immune system is chronically irritated. Not only your brain requires sleep and rest to work, but also your immune system. The symptoms our bodies display may in fact be caused by overload or toxins that manifest themselves in swollen mucous membranes, upset tummies, increased secretions, and irritated airways.

Over a third of children in the developed world today suffer from allergies or other hypersensitivity disorders, compared with just a few percent thirty to forty years ago. However, in Sweden it has been found that children who attend Waldorf schools have only half the risk of suffering allergies as children in conventional schools. Among families embracing Rudolf Steiner's Waldorf school philosophy, hardly one fifth of children are vaccinated and they take antibiotics less frequently. The children are nursed longer and sixty percent eat food preserved with lactobacilli, which are healthy for the intestinal bacterial flora. As an example, six out of ten children have had measles and it is felt that these natural infections enhance protection against allergies.

Children need to catch diseases to strengthen their immunity – to achieve improved immunocompetence. As long as the necessary nutrients are provided by diet, most childhood diseases are benign and get better on their own. They also generally result in lifelong immunity, whereas the vaccine's immunity may be transient. The new chicken pox vaccine is estimated to have an efficacy of six to ten years: this could mean that people who have been vaccinated as children may contract the disease at a time in life when the chance of dying is twenty times higher. During a flare-up of measles in the late 1980s, half of those who became ill were young people and adults who had been vaccinated as children.

Vaccinating children has become a controversial issue in recent years. Some researchers believe that certain substances in the vaccines are neurotoxins that could injure a small child's undeveloped brain and nerves. Harris Coulter found that in 15 to 20 percent of children, vaccinations result in low-grade encephalitis that may cause neurologic disorders. From 1993 to 1995, three different whooping cough vaccines were tested on 82,900 Swedish children and three physicians monitored the children for a twenty-two month period. Of those who had been fully vaccinated, ninety-five came down with whooping cough. During the first six months after the start of the trial, thirty died, although the cause of death was only listed for four children. In their conclusion, the doctors expressed concern that there might be a risk of serious adverse effects associated with the vaccination. Whooping cough vaccine has been included in routine vaccinations since January 1996, and in that year the Swedish Medical Products Agency received eighty-nine reports of serious adverse effects, of which one hundred nineteen diagnoses were believed to be linked to the vaccination. Many of the vaccines used in the United States still contain mercury, though this has now been removed in countries such as Sweden.

Children are first vaccinated when they are three months old. Marta Granström, Assistant Professor of Clinical Microbiology at Karolinska Hospital, believes that a balance has to be struck between protecting the infant as early as possible and waiting until the immune system is mature (at age two). The position of the medical establishment is that the benefits of vaccinations far outweigh the risks, but that children should not receive more vaccines than are necessary. Swedish children receive the lowest number of vaccinations in Europe. The idea that vaccinations contribute to an increase in childhood allergies is contradicted by the low rate of allergies in former Soviet countries, where vaccinations have long been obligatory. Studies of children in Estonia show that they have a different intestinal flora with more lactobacilli than Swedish children, again suggesting that intestinal flora plays an important role for our health.

In effect, the problem with vaccinations is that they are held up as the sole method of infection prevention. Many retirees are vaccinated against influenza every year because it is felt that complications can be more serious than in younger individuals. However, older people often have nutritional deficiencies and in many cases they could avoid the flu and other diseases by improving their diet, eating preventative herbs (Echinacea), augmenting intestinal flora, practicing *qigong*, and exercising. Presenting the different options encourages people to make up their own minds.

Bio-balance versus Inflammation

Bio-balance means living with the body in balance. People function based on certain given conditions, and this fine-tuned interaction keeps the life processes running. Under these given, natural conditions, the body and mind are self-regulating and self-healing.

But what happens if these given, natural conditions change? Consider the relationship between inflammatory conditions and chronic disease. Researchers have shown that inflammation of the gums, known as periodontitis, increases the risk of developing several systemic diseases such as diabetes, pulmonary disease, and cardiovascular disease. On page 129 we noted that in the 1930s, dentist Weston Price found a correlation between modern diet, poor dental hygiene, and degenerative disease. It was not until the 1980s that the first modern research studies noting the correlation between oral health and general physical health were published in Finland. In the late 1990s,

U.S. research reports were published in which molecular biology and epidemiological studies clearly showed that oral infections affect our general health. The risk of cardiovascular disease increases from twenty-five to several hundred percent in people who have periodontitis. This a serious issue, as periodontitis is a widespread disease found in about 15 percent of the adult population.

Oral health is crucial to physical health in general, but what is the mechanism involved? Bacterial plaque at the edge of the gums causes a local infection, which in turn starts an inflammatory reaction that breaks down the tissue (periodontitis). Bacteria, bacterial substances, and transmitters (cytokines) from the inflamed tissue can enter and spread through the circulatory system. Because these substances act as strong irritants to the immune system, they can cause damage elsewhere, thus increasing the risk of developing systemic diseases.

The transmitters–cytokines–can either promote or inhibit the inflammatory process. Cytokines such as interleukin-1, interleukin-8, and prostaglandin-2, which stimulate this process, are produced in the inflamed pocket along the gumline. The pocket becomes a reservoir that constantly transfers these inflammatory substances into the circulatory system. In fact, its effect is similar to that of a small bump in the road that succeeds in overturning a huge load.

Scientists have found many correlations between inflammation and lifestyle diseases. For example, higher levels of the acute phase C-reactive protein (CRP) have been shown to provide early warning of this damaging inflammatory process and serve as an independent marker for heart disease. The Journal of American Medical Association (JAMA) recently reported that data from the Women's Health Study indicate that women with the highest serum CRP levels are 15.7 times more likely to develop Type 2 diabetes compared with those with the lowest levels. An extensive Dutch study shows that people who have taken anti-inflammatory medications for a long time have a lower rate of Alzheimer's disease. A major study from Karolinska Hospital showed that people with severe psoriasis had twice the risk of dying from cardiovascular disease compared with the rest of the population.

Even depression could be considered to be an inflammatory reaction in the body. Depression doubles the risk of having a new myocardial infarction (MI). A patient who becomes depressed after the first heart attack runs a four to five times greater risk of death from a new infarction within six months of the first MI. Sleep is also important: people who sleeps less run a higher risk of getting diabetes. A recent Japanese study showed that people who work more than 60 hours a week and sleep less than five hours a night were at greater risk of heart disease.

Obesity is a major public health problem that is on the rise. Over half of all adults in the United States are overweight, and the proportion of obese children has doubled in thirty years. People who are overweight are much more likely to get diabetes, and diabetics are three times more likely to get cardiovascular disease than a normal population group. Just over half of all diabetics suffer from coronary heart disease. High blood pressure and depression are other obesity-related diseases.

Evidence now suggests that even obesity might be caused by chronic, low-grade inflammation. Overweight or obese children and adults have elevated blood levels of the same inflammatory substances that are risk factors for cardiovascular disease. Our modern diet provides too little healthy fat and too much chemically processed fat and trans fats, which inhibit natural fat synthesis and hormone production. Scientists at the University of Buffalo observed that a high intake of sugar or of high-fat, high caloric fast food increases the inflammatory markers in the blood and this condition lasts for at least three to four hours after eating this type of food.

A deficiency of essential omega-3-fatty acids has an inflammatory effect on the body. Unhealthy intestinal flora can cause intestinal leakage – nutrients leak out into the body, resulting in inflammation. Other obesity-related factors also help cause constant inflammatory processes, which can be debilitating for the body. Should this hypothesis prove to be true, it could lead to a radical new view of treatment and prophylactic measures for the fastest growing disease in the developed world – obesity.

We have to use a holistic approach to understand many of today's lifestyle diseases. The conventional, segregated medical view treats each body part separately, but the body is interconnected, and all of its parts work together. We need a number of health-promoting substances in order for the different cells and parts of the body to be able to interact as a functioning, healthy whole. Negative stress and an inadequate, low-nutrition diet prevent the body from maintaining its bio-balance, thus encouraging destructive and inflammatory bacteria. Unhealthy bacteria find it easier to flourish, and a negative spiral is created.

The body strives for *homeostasis*, to maintain balance at all times. If it comes out of balance or is exposed to stress, the system contains a built-in mechanism for recovery. Though the process is self-regulating, it is affected if normal conditions come "out of balance." It is a delicate process, since several factors and substances depend on one another to work. Still, our bodies have a strong inherent, self-healing ability that we can strengthen by our actions and choice of lifestyle.

Different Paradigms

If the new paradigm represents information, participation, and interaction, the old one reflects knowledge, specialization, and hierarchy.

Today's medical personnel possess a wealth of knowledge about subjects like emergency care, laboratory analyses, and surgical procedures – but there are limitations. Western medical care is based on allopathic medicine, which applies a mechanical and reductionistic approach. It is pathologically-oriented, based on the principle that diseases have a physical cause and especially that the body is attacked by foreign objects, such as a virus or bacteria. Recently, people have also begun to investigate changes on the genetic level as an explanation for disease. Many doctors seem to have forgotten about trusting their own senses, intuition, and experience. Modern medical care is symptom-oriented and the patient assumes a more passive role. It has also long advocated that we can eat whatever we want, though this attitude has changed in the wake of recent research confirming the effect of diet on health and the disease process.

In contrast, other medical approaches allow that the disease process may have several different causes and that we need to focus on the individual rather than on the symptoms. This is the approach of functional medicine, which encourages interdisciplinary knowledge and collaboration between physicians, dentists, and various types of alternative therapists. To note that disease is present is not of interest in itself; rather, we must find and correct functional flaws. A single symptom can actually have several causes and should be treated in different ways. Naturally, conventional medicine is also needed: the two approaches should be viewed as complementing one another.

Functional medicine was founded in the 1980s in the United States by Dr. Jeffrey Bland, a student of Nobel Prize laureate Dr. Linus Pauling. Dr. Bland believes that we have enough biochemical and medical knowledge to be able to understand what creates health on an individual level.

"We are entering the age of the individual, where we are moving from treating the masses to treating the individual," says Dr. Bland.

The understanding that we are all biochemically unique and that each treatment must be based on the needs of the individual is a true paradigm shift. For example, two people may have the same vitamin B blood level, though the levels within their cells may show up to a fivefold difference. Functional medicine focuses on the cause rather than on inhibiting symptoms, since impaired or increased organ function always occurs long before pathological changes become manifest in the form of symptoms. Illness can be prevented by the early initiation of treatment aimed at its cause – in other words, by correcting the body's bio-imbalances. Several tests have been developed to measure the function of various organs, such as intestinal permeability or the effectiveness of the liver's P450 detoxification system. Other tests include pH, redox potential, and resistance (mineral concentrations) in the blood, urine, and saliva. A hair mineral analysis measures the body's mineral status and hormonal function.

Functional medicine clinics help people who have chronic problems (such as chronic fatigue, hypersensitivity, inexplicable pain, and digestive problems) correct imbalances even before these people notice them. The new functional analyses make it possible to explore new dimensions of health that could not previously be demonstrated in analyses. Vague symptoms are often associated with inadequate function, such as impaired intestinal and liver function, elevated or impaired hormone production, insufficient absorption of nutrients, hypersensitivity to food or environmental factors, nutritional deficiency, and fungal, viral, bacterial, or parasitic infections. According to functional medicine, it is possible to restore better function through a healthy diet, lifestyle changes, and diet supplements.

Briefly, the underlying philosophy of conventional medicine is to suppress, cure, or kill the disease process – while patient-focused medicine and functional medicine aim at locating and correcting functional deficiencies at an early stage. To make a holistic diagnosis using a functional or individual-centered approach, the care provider inquires about the person's background and living conditions, and carries out a physical exam and tests. Without labeling the problem, the therapist should consider what might be missing or should be avoided. Examples of what might be missing include nutrients via diet, or other nutrients such as love, heat, music, sunlight, exercise, emotions, meditation, creative expression, sexuality. Examples of what could be avoided include allergens such as food, dust, mold, pollen, chemicals, and bacteria; toxins such as heavy metals, including biological, synthetic, and petrochemical; or other substances that drain energy from the body such as drugs, pharmaceuticals, processed food, or certain people. The holistic approach involves restoring inadequately performing functions, and correcting excesses, thereby re-establishing the body's bio-balance.

Integrative Medicine

To achieve true healing we need to consider all aspects, the entire picture – and that is integral to the concept of integrative medicine. It encompasses not only the body but also our emotions, thoughts, and the soul. This also includes the "magical" power of the healing relationship – with some kind of interaction in the non-physical world. A physician can take advantage of the belief-system to promote healing.

This means that the current medical system must broaden its view, begin thinking on an interdisciplinary level, and gradually become integrated with the field of complementary and alternative medicine (CAM). Progress is already underway. We need more wellness programs and medical care co-existing, side-by-side. Preventive medicine also has to play a greater role, and the National Policy Dialog (NPD) is working to establish a public agency to promote an integrated health care (IHC) system. The National Center for Complementary and Alternative Medicine, NCAM, plans to change its name to the National Center for Integrative Medicine, NCIM. According to NCAM there are a total of 620 (!) different alternative treatment methods and a 1998 independent Cochrane study showed that there is scientific evidence that 37 percent of these methods work or probably work. The purpose of holistic, integrative medicine is to integrate conventional and alternative forms of therapy in order to promote optimal health and prevent or treat disease. It is an overview that integrates our many facets and also takes our environment into account.

The body's energy system must also be included in the new wellness philosophy. This new field with old roots is known as Frequency Medicine; examples of treatments via the energy body include acupuncture, acupressure, reflexology, *qigong*, kinesiology, color therapy, and treatment with magnets. Modern medicine still ignores our energy body and the fact that you can influence the body's physical health by influencing its energies. Medicine has not yet had its Einstein and therefore continues to plod along on well-trodden paths. In the 1930s, quantum physics came but conventional medicine has not yet embraced this. The purely physical aspects of surgery and chemistry (pharmaceuticals) still prevail in medicine, and the main difference from the nineteenth century is that the methods have become more sophisticated. It's time for a change.

What is the attitude of conventional medical science toward the concepts of the new integrated and functional medicine? These days there is an openness and curiosity that did not exist just five years ago. There are centers for integrative medicine at Duke, Harvard, Stanford, Columbia, and the University of California, San Francisco, and at least two thirds of all medical schools in the United States offer courses in CAM. Today programs for integrative medicine are offered at twelve US universities and the Dean at the University of California, San Francisco Medical School says that: "This movement has the potential to save the soul of medicine."

Professor Hans Wigzell, President of Karolinska Institutet in Stockholm, Sweden, and former chairman for the medicine prize of the Nobel committee, says: "We can draw many ideas from functional medicine. But these new up and coming disciplines that want to gain acceptance by the scientific establishment will achieve results faster if controlled experiments are carried out."

As an example, Wigzell mentions a study conducted by the journal New Scientist aimed at finding out what portion of studies had strict scientific controls, About 5 percent of physics experiments were controlled; in medicine 8–9 percent of clinical trials were correctly controlled; while over 90 percent of parascientific studies were strictly controlled. (Examples of parascience include how to influence objects with the power of thought and prayer.) These findings indicate that higher demands are placed on research studies released for publication in fields where validity has come into question. Controlled research linked to objective studies greatly reduce the amount of time needed for new ideas to gain acceptance.

Dr. Andrew Weil, a well respected author and self-healing pioneer, thinks the field of integrative medicine is positioned well: "It is still a consumer-led movement, but it's gaining a real response from academic medicine. At this point, I think it's unstoppable and that it will result in a transformed system, including the system of medical education. Much needs to happen before that comes to pass, but I clearly see us moving in that direction".

Medical Freedom

Thomas Jefferson–philosopher, president, and social reformer who formulated the Declaration of Independence–advocated both religious and medical freedom. He said: "Enlighten the people generally, and tyranny and oppressions of body and mind will vanish like spirits at the dawn of day." Jefferson also wrote a book on health and personal care and believed that people must have both rights and obligations to protect and strengthen their own health and vitality. He advocated that people should live in such a way that physicians and medical care should be needed as little as possible. This is an excellent time to reflect on his thoughts on medical freedom; though more than two centuries have passed, this issue is more relevant than ever – especially considering the ever-increasing costs for the individual.

The problem with the current US healthcare system is that insurance companies are sitting between the patient and physician or therapist and deciding which referrals and medications should be reimbursed. Insurance companies establish relationships with the pharmaceutical industry and enter into individual agreements for discounts on medications. Different insurance plans cover different drugs, creating a confusing situation for doctors. Moreover, the majority of resources go to medical care, while preventive, counseling, and alternative therapies are largely left outside the system. More expensive insurance plans offer coverage for chiropractors, acupuncture, and massage, but this is not standard; people have to pay for most alternative medical treatment out of pocket. In addition, 30–40 percent of the population is uninsured since medical insurance has become increasingly expensive, and most young people cannot afford it. Another problem in the United States is that the country is so large that people do not have a sense of community and it is more difficult to work together to achieve significant, sweeping improvements in medical care and wellness programs. The major insurance companies also have political clout, and as a result doctors no longer have much influence. And how good is that for the health of the system?

One problem that western doctors have in common is that there is too little time for patients and too much time spent on paperwork. Industrial efficiency measurements have taken over and changed the medical scene into a type of healthcare system never seen before. It has become impersonal and the individual does not matter – and this applies to both patient and provider. The human encounter is not valued. Physicians and nurses are replaceable units in whom reproducibility, efficiency, knowledge, and efficient performance are paramount. The current medical system is harshly criticized by Dr. George E. Lundberg, former editor of JAMA, the Journal of the American Medical Association, for twenty years. He believes that since the 1950s, business has taken over medicine, professional standards have deteriorated, and the traditional doctor-patient relationship has collapsed. Billions are invested in developing new medications while the patient is ignored. Doctors have been among the most vocal critics of the distribution of resources and a rigid, hierarchical thinking in healthcare.

Something must be fundamentally wrong in the current medical care model since more and more people are becoming ill and the cost of medications and insurance keeps rising every year.

There is good reason to consider whether or not the monopoly controlling the philosophy of medical care–the pathology-based approach–actually benefits us. The current medical system should be reformed by implementing an individual-focused, holistic approach in integrative medicine.

We should have a general medical insurance that allows us to choose coverage for preventive healthcare, functional medicine, and nutritional medicine – because we need all of them. Mental and spiritual care (e.g. psychotherapy) should be given equal status with physical care and should likewise be covered by insurance. Spiritual pain is as tangible as physical pain. One third of all people who seek primary care believe that they suffer from mental problems, such as depression, anxiety, and suicidal thoughts. In ordinary cases the family physician must rely on his or her own ability to speak with the patient or prescribe medication or sick leave. Much can be gained from interdisciplinary collaboration. Three primary care centers in Göteborg, Sweden, hired psychologists and achieved excellent results in reducing the length of sick leave, early retirement, and prescribed medications. Sometimes the obvious is the hardest to accept.

Dr. Andrew Weil stated the following at the Alternative Therapies Symposium in San Diego in 2002: "We need to redesign the medical paradigm to get us out of the economic mess and make doctors happy about what they are doing."

But most important are the concrete actions that we can choose to take, starting today, to improve our health and lifestyle. But then it's up to us to gather knowledge – for this is the key to a changed society. Books, the media, and the Internet have made knowledge freely available. Whether the current system wants it or not, we are on the way toward a society in which the individual is gaining greater influence, especially concerning personal health.

By all indications, body and health-related activities and research will occupy fully one third of society's attention. Health and wellness issues are advancing toward a brighter future.

> *Research is to see what everyone else has seen*
> *and to think what no one else has thought.*
> Albert Szent-Györgyi, Nobel Prize laureate 1937

Self-healing

How does science view the phenomenon of self-healing? The stem cells in the immune system are the source cells from which all more specialized immune cells develop, such as leukocytes, macrophages, and mast cells. Stem cells are therefore crucial to the immune system. They lie dormant within the bone marrow, and occasionally they divide into two daughter cells that either return to the resting stage or enter the circulatory system where they mature and develop into the various types of blood cells. They live and fulfill their function, and ultimately they die. However, other types of body cells have their own stem cells.

"The new thinking is that stem cells are present in all human organs, and that there is not a fixed number of cells that simply live and later die," says Hans Wigzell. "Stem cells have even been found in the brain, in the hippocampus (in the limbic system), for example. Excessive stress diminishes the number of cells because fewer new cells are formed and survive. When the stress decreases and you calm down, additional cells are recruited (this has been shown in animal experiments). Self-healing is therefore more widespread within the body and throughout life than previously believed. In effect, even eighty-year olds can harness and fortify their self-healing energy."

A Swedish research group led by Jonas Frisén at Karolinska Institutet succeeded in 1999 in localizing and isolating "pluripotent" stem cells from the adult brain. The implication is that such stem cells have the ability to develop and mature into many different types of nerve cells. An American research group led by A.B. Peck has succeeded in generating stem cells in cell cultures derived from the adult pancreas that mature into insulin-producing cells. These discoveries shed a new and exciting light on human self-healing potential. Although it remains to be seen whether these findings can be applied to medical treatment, we could definitely use this stimulation potential within our own bodies.

A prerequisite for self-healing, however, is that we truly want to be healed and become more whole as people. We must be ready for an improvement, and understand that changing takes will-power and that this is often, but not always, a conscious choice. Healing requires that we be receptive to beneficial, healing energies. Consequently we need to seek an environment that is healing, loving, and accepting. It helps if we recognize that the notion of finite love and finite energy is a misconception. If all the resources of the universe were made available, the energy crisis would be solved once and for all. However, we can continuously draw life energy (*qi*) because its supply is inexhaustible. Love and the life force are available in abundance and there is more than enough for us all. We must actively seek it and retrieve it – through meditation, contemplation, *qigong*, and in our relationships. We need only grasp this concept and open ourselves to the possibilities.

A crisis often signals a need to pause, to reflect on why we are sick, feel bad, or are unhappy with our lives. Finding our own motivation and discovering meaning in what we do are prerequisites for harnessing our inner healing forces.

Every individual can muster a greater or lesser resistance to disease. Howard S. Friedman, Professor of Psychology at the University of California, Riverside, has carried out extensive research in the association between personality types and diseases. The findings included several life factors common to the self-healing personality:

- good self esteem (conscious personality)
- a sense of deeper meaning in life
- a sense of creative self-fulfillment
- a sense of control and keeping options open
- a sense of optimism, combined with faith, will-power, and commitment
- a supportive social network (family and good friends)
- an appropriate level of challenge and excitement

Collectively these factors create a will to live, feel good, and awaken the positive emotions that lie at the core of a wholesome, healthy person. We can influence and develop these factors throughout our lives.

The time we need to achieve good health and vitality depends on our starting point. A new approach in new surroundings brings about personal change. Typically, such changes are relatively stable and relapse is unlikely. It is a question of acquiring good habits and making them part of our daily lives.

Sleep and Rest

Getting enough sleep is crucial for self-healing. The brain usually "knows" when it is time to sleep. The center of the brain contains the pineal gland, which controls the sleep and waking cycles. This gland produces melatonin in varying quantities according to the time of day; when levels are high, we sleep. As a result, this hormone is widely used as a cure for jet lag and sleep disturbances. Melatonin is an endogenous substance that is considered quite benign and is available over the counter at pharmacies.

Despite extensive research into the effects of sleep, we still do not know exactly why it is necessary – although researchers have conducted many experiments showing the consequences of sleep deficit. During sleep the brain produces proteins much faster than when we are awake. These proteins are needed to maintain integrity and function. Sleep gives us a chance to replenish our stores of those biochemicals necessary for cerebral function. This applies to the learning process, memory function, and even the mechanism that governs temperature regulation.

Under normal circumstances we convert only a small portion of the energy derived from food and oxygen (respiration) into heat, while the lion's share is reserved for other vital functions. But if we only sleep three hours per night, many such functions begin to deteriorate within a few days. Without adequate sleep, energy cannot be stored effectively and instead it vanishes as heat. People with sleep deficit burn themselves out – literally. If rats are prevented from sleeping for an extended period of time they require more and more food. Despite their enormous food consumption, in the end they die, exhausted and emaciated. Getting a good night's sleep is essential for the body's vital and self-healing functions.

One of the greatest problems of modern life is that we spend most of our time outside ourselves. In effect, we are not centered within ourselves and are not particularly receptive to our own mental and physical signals. And as a result, either we are not on the same wavelength as others and can't hear anything, or perhaps we don't have time to listen. This in itself may actually be considered a disease.

In our information-intensive society it is all too easy to constantly rely on input from the environment. But if we fail to use our intuitive skills we lose them. For example, if you don't wear a watch you can soon estimate the time with reasonable accuracy. You can even decide what time to wake up each morning. We have a well functioning internal clock – but it will only work if we use it.

Most of us need to hone our skills at being present in the now. One good method is to pause and heed our five senses. See, feel, smell, and hear your surroundings. When eating, take the time to taste your food. Feel its consistency and think about how the food will feel in your stomach. The whole point of eating, after all, is to satisfy your stomach! By sticking closer to the present we derive more from life and from ourselves. Or as Swedish aphorist Stig Johansson said: "All those days that came and went – how was I supposed to know that that was my life."

Our senses are under constant input bombardment and therefore we need to schedule a "mental fast" from time to time. Whether weekday or weekend, I spend these days living in the "now."

Prepare for the fast the night before – don't listen to the news or the weather. Avoid the barrage that our senses are usually exposed to by leaving the TV turned off. Relax with a cup of herbal tea before going to sleep. In the morning linger an extra five to ten minutes and appreciate how comfy your bed is. Awaken your body through gentle stretching, and say good morning to yourself by checking to see how you feel. Proceed with your day as usual, but with the difference that you remain in the present. Forget the morning paper, and instead 'taste' your breakfast. Use your five (six) senses to remain in constant awareness. Establish eye contact when you greet people or speak with them and listen carefully when they tell you how they feel.

Note your reaction to other people – do you become tense or do you breathe freely? Who makes you feel good and who makes you feel unsure of yourself and out of balance? Continue in this way by being attentive to your senses and to your body's signals. In the evening, take the time to contemplate the day and how it affected you. Feel free to record your thoughts and reactions.

Replenish Your Energy

We can view our bodies as an energy complex with a number of subsystems ensuring that it functions as a whole, including the immune, nervous, endocrine, circulatory, lymphatic, musculoskeletal, and gastrointestinal systems. These systems cooperate and are receptive to subtle energies in the form of thoughts, emotions, or consciousness. But they require energy to function.

We are born with a supply of "life energy." The level varies, depending partially on the energy level and lifestyle of our parents. This life energy is our driving force, fueling the body's various processes during development and growth. Children heal more quickly than adults and the young recover faster from overexertion and sleep deficit. But the duration of our life energy depends on how we budget it. In our youth the supply may seem inexhaustible – but this is not the case. Unless replenished, it will run dry. Severe infection, antibiotics, or stress overload cause chronic inflammation that could bring us to the "wall," causing burnout from which it may take years to recover. Today even people in their early twenties may suffer from chronic fatigue syndrome, constant neck and back pain, or stomach problems. Our inherent life energy must be viewed as an asset, a resource – there to be used but never consumed. We need to continuously restore ourselves through nutritious food, exercise, love, and joy.

This could explain why many modes of treatment, which work by raising the level of energy via different channels, may alleviate or cure the same illness. For example, rheumatism can be successfully treated via medical *qigong*, laser therapy, or dietary modification. Though the mechanisms differ, they all raise the body's energy, and this is a radical approach to health and disease. These treatment options are consistent with Ayurvedic and Chinese or Tibetan traditions, even if they are not expressed as such. I would like to advocate an ecological approach to health that also considers the conditions and limitations with which evolution has endowed us. Humankind is a relatively new player on the evolutionary stage and as a result we are more sensitive to flaws in our inner make-up. We are so advanced in body, mind, and soul that our fate now rests in our own hands; if we don't act now we risk catastrophic demise at the mercy of the most "primitive" organisms. Viruses feel no empathy; they just have an inherent drive to multiply and live – just like we have.

Inevitably, we are part of the world around us and it is part of us. If we fail to nurture the cultivated plants and crops that sustain our lives, sooner or later we will all suffer. We rely on the earth's bounty for nourishment. We have to learn to budget our resources – our money, our mental energy, and our bodies. The less care we dedicate to our inner selves, the more susceptible and sensitive we become to disruptions in our external surroundings.

Keep a journal with any information you think might be relevant to your health. Include your test results and interesting articles. Save information on resources such as workshops and new therapies. Record how you feel and how your surroundings affect you. This will be your personal "health diary." By doing so, you will be prioritizing your health, consciously giving it a space in your life.

The Laser Effect

We radiate energy from three energy levels—soul, mind, and emotions—as well as our bodies. If these are in conflict and fail to mesh, the energies interfere with and perhaps cancel each other, and we are unable to generate power. A light bulb emitting light in different directions is ineffective, but if instead the light is emitted with a single wavelength, you will have a laser ray with incredible power, precision, and reach. And so it is when our own energy is synchronized – from the inside out. This generates vast power, enabling us to accomplish the most demanding tasks. Find your niche in life where you love to be and feel loved, and you will thrive like a plant in the right environment. You can work long and hard, sustained by self-generating energy. This is the secret to personal happiness and contentment with your situation.

Living in disharmony, on the other hand, consumes energy. Consider the man whose soul is creative and artistic, yet becomes a systems engineer because of outside demands and expectations. His heart and emotions want him to create, while systematic and analytical thinking occupy his time and physical reality. If he fails to take action he will eventually lose touch with his soul (the self) and deteriorate as his energy fades. Or take the case of a woman whose disposition is geared to empathy and human relationships, but–since her background does not value this–becomes an accountant, involved in endless number-crunching. Her job drains energy rather than generating it, and since this is in conflict with her heart's desire she soon suffers from migraines and stress.

Simply put, harmony–resonance–between our different energy levels results in good health, while disharmony causes energy losses, which in the long run can result in crisis and illness. In effect, harmony and health are one.

Herein lies the explanation for sudden healing. We need to be in frequent contact with our deeper levels. Please feel free to join the "frequent soul program" to get in touch with the *real* you. A psychological condition (caused by an energy disturbance in the mind, soul, or emotions) can be resolved in an hour, but a physiological condition (in which the energy disruption appears in the body) may take weeks, months, or years to heal and disappear.

To effect healing we must nurture all three sides of life – the physical, the spiritual, and the mental and emotional. The first of these is what we usually refer to as the material. It is not enough to focus on only one element, such as eating healthy food while neglecting our feelings – sooner or later we reach a dead end. We need to nurture all three elements, encouraging them to grow and develop, side by side.

Health is a balance between body and soul, thought and deed, physical and mental power. The body contains a built-in plan for the healing processes.
Caroline Myss, Ph.D. in Energy Medicine

Activate Your Self-Healing

How do you initiate the self-healing process? We probably need a basic positive attitude toward ourselves in order to want to take care of our health. We need to believe we are worthy. And when we care for our own health we benefit not only ourselves but also our surroundings. This is a powerful motivator in itself! Indeed, all change begins with our acceptance of our current situation.

How do we develop healthy habits? Most of us know what we should do; the hard part is doing it. I believe that desire and joy are the strongest driving forces when it comes to change. Here are suggestions to help you get started:

1. Make a *wish list* of what you know you should do or would like to do for your health – but which you don't have the strength for. Imagine that a good fairy magically transforms you into your ideal state. What would you wish for? Write down this wish list and then close your eyes. Imagine how it would feel to be someone who accomplishes these things. What would you look like? Let a picture emerge and visualize yourself in this new stage of higher energy. What emotions do you feel when you're there? How does it feel to be completely healthy? Open your eyes and put your list away or throw it out. But save your inner picture of how you would look when you had done or were doing everything on your wish list.

2. On another piece of paper, write down a few things you would like to add to your life right now to feel better. Think about what you can do to raise your energy and well-being. Maybe eating fresh vegetables and fruit every day, eating more salads, or more fiber (wholegrain bread every morning). Perhaps you want to get more exercise every day (like walking to work, taking the stairs instead of the elevator, or starting to exercise or dance). It may also be a good idea to develop an interest that provides you with exercise naturally, such as getting a dog or going horseback-riding, so that exercise becomes something fun and meaningful and not just a "necessary evil." Or perhaps you need to exercise less and be more sensitive to your body's needs? Would you like to spend more time listening to music, but feel that there's never time – here's your chance! Or maybe you want to be-

come more playful, laugh more, see more entertaining movies. Maybe you want to have a relaxing massage every other week. Do you need to cut back on your inner self-critical voice? Perhaps it is time to take vitamin and mineral supplements, buy virgin olive oil, or enjoy a leisurely weekly bath. Use this method to choose a few items and add them to your current habits.

3. Let some time pass, and then eliminate or cut back on some things or habits you feel you'd be better off without.

Repeat steps two and three every other month. All changes are best achieved when implemented slowly and gradually. It takes at least eight weeks for the body to get rid of a physical addiction, so there is little reason to overdo things at the start. It took a long time for your body to get where it is today, so a gentle transition to healthier and more enjoyable habits is best. Reach in and pull out your visualized ideal from time to time and remind yourself of the feeling of living according to your wish list. When a year has passed, why not review your list if you saved it, or perhaps it is time for a new wish list.

The easiest way to effect change in life is to reach into our unconscious. This also recruits our mental energy – a powerful driving force. Thought always precedes realization in the physical world…

We can achieve visualization in two ways: by creating an image of what we want or by opening ourselves to images that spontaneously emerge from within. The latter entails listening to your unconscious, a source of far deeper knowledge than the self. In effect, this is similar to the principle underlying non-targeted prayer.

Why should you make the effort to change your state of health? Quite simply, you will feel better – your system will feel cleaner and your being lighter. You will be more alert, have greater initiative, and the energy to accomplish more. The good feelings generated by your efforts to improve your health are a driving force in themselves. As a side benefit, you may improve your life in unforeseen ways: by sleeping better, feeling more relaxed, and finding inner strength. You will most likely find love in your life and for your life. Life can take on a new shape – if you are willing to give it a chance. You derive a vast quantity of positive energy by pursuing activities that bring pleasure.

*He who has begun
has half done.
Dare to be wise –
begin!*
                Horace, philosopher

Self Diagnosis

There is a time when you need to stop and take stock of your life. Sort out and discard the unnecessary, distracting, or irrelevant. Stop scattering your energy in different directions and avoid letting your life be dominated by people and things to which you cannot relate. After all, negative energy–whether it's from junk food, toxins, or the wrong people–burdens our bodies and our souls.

Self-diagnosis is therefore a healthy option. We can accomplish this by strengthening our intuition and developing our abilities to analyze the state of health of our energy resources. We need to take the time to recognize whether our activities provide or deplete our energy. Learning to apply this in everyday situations saves energy and makes us stronger.

Self-assessment can make a difference. Discover your true core values, since everyone dedicates their thoughts–and thus their energy–to the basics in which they believe. Here I am not referring to religion, but rather to a way of life and the ethics governing right and wrong. Life is a succession of decisions such as where to live, what work to pursue, whether or not to start a family, and so on.

But are your beliefs rooted in your true self or have you adopted them from others? Abandoning old beliefs can be difficult because the longer we have held them, the more energy we have expended, and the greater the resistance to new thinking – a problem that only worsens with time. We may be forced to sacrifice our position–and much more–to be able to rethink our lives. And there are no guarantees. Many people aren't ready to change unless they can see clear gains. But sometimes you have to venture in hopes of gain – whatever the outcome may be.

We also have to expose the fears that control us and limit our choices in life. Pursuing new activities that expand our horizons often awaken our fears. While this is natural, we can choose not to let fear stop our growth. Fears are simply emotions and do not pose true physical barriers. A good method of expanding our consciousness is to analyze how much responsibility we take for different parts of our lives. Use the bar diagram below for an overview of your life.

How much responsibility do you take for your:

	0	25	50	75	100%
job?					
closest friends and relatives?					
relationships?					
diet?					
exercise?					
emotions?					
personal development?					
life energy supply?					

Draw a line on the scale somewhere between 0 and 100 percent and fill in the bar to the left of your mark. How does it look? Do you have a broad base to stand on or is it top-heavy? Does your life appear to be in balance or do you relinquish responsibility for parts of it to others? The less responsibility you surrender in this overview, the more consciously you live your life.

Self-healing humans are in touch with themselves, their emotions, and their intuition. They have an ability to sense the energy and emotional state of others. It is a choice and a way of life, rather than a specific method. You cannot learn this at a weekend workshop – although that might be a step in the right direction, as people can inspire each other.

Like the plant that flourishes in sunlit, fertile soil, people thrive and evolve in response to a loving environment, nutritious diet, and close contact with their life energy.

- Love is a potent transforming force. Children who suffer emotionally and/or physically may be stunted in their mental development, but begin to grow once again when they are exposed to a loving environment. This also applies to our inner being, and consequently the most important thing we can do for ourselves is to ensure that we are in a supportive, friendly, empathic, and respectful environment – in short, surround ourselves with loving people. If you have been involved in an accident or a traumatic experience, or are ill or addicted, seek out others who have survived similar problems and been healed. You will be able to benefit from their healing energy, which will "set you straight," and speed up the healing process.
- Just as we need to breathe, we need to eat nutritious food with plenty of vitamins, minerals, essential fatty acids, high-quality protein, and slow carbohydrates.
- You can get in touch with your life energy in many ways – through prayer, meditation, or *qigong*.

This modern approach to health awareness means that we must consciously influence our energy in a positive direction. Our emotions and the nourishment found in food are merely different forms of energy that we can use to raise or lower our energy levels.

The energy in our bodies can be viewed as a bank. The more energy we invest in ourselves, the greater the returns. And as a dividend we enjoy greater pleasure in life. As a result we can interact with those around us by giving and receiving ever more. And perhaps this is the key to the greatest source of joy, satisfaction, and good health!

We must try to live as openly and honestly as possible through acts of kindness, while viewing life as an infinite process.

How can you influence your state of health?

1. Believe that you can influence it.
2. Pay attention to your thoughts. What do you *really* believe? Take inventory. Listen to your inner self – your intuition!
3. What is good – what is bad? What do you want to keep, what do you want to discard?
4. Look at the whole picture: diet
   exercise
   thoughts
   the soul (the mind)
   your meaning in life
5. Seek new knowledge.
6. Integrate changes into your life gradually.

The Wholeness

Today's vision results from yesterday's ideas. I have tried to get behind the façade to understand the logic underlying textbook medicine – to see what predominant philosophies have shaped our current healthcare system over the past forty to fifty years. You could label it a "drug solution" since the leit-motif has clearly been "a drug for every symptom" or "a drug for every emotion." This view is based on a certain concept of humankind, but as we have seen it no longer applies.

No longer can we accept the notion that for each symptom there is a patent remedy that fits every person. As individuals, we are biochemically unique and we do ourselves a disservice by failing to acknowledge our amazing complexity. We are where and who we are today as the result of past events. Knowledge of ourselves is the key to discovering the path we must travel toward personal healing. Such knowledge includes simple medical and biochemical facts about our bodies, and also about our minds, emotions, hopes, and dreams – quite simply, to discover who we truly are. From this starting point we can wander through life.

Some people search for a single solution to all their problems; if they find something that works, they tout it as an example for others to follow. I don't believe in this approach. Life is too multifaceted for one universal solution. You must seek your own path. Just as each symptom has several potential solutions, we must explore various approaches to help ourselves,

By nurturing the whole in our lives we create compatibility within ourselves. Just like healing and disease processes, all change takes time, so we must be patient as we set the stage for healing to begin.

By raising our consciousness about our thoughts, feelings, desires, and needs we move closer to unity with our true selves. Through this process we access the positive energy within and we can also live in balance with ourselves, those close to us, and our environment. In the end we become more whole and thus establish contact with life's holiness – the endpoint that we must all seek individually.

We used to be able to make use of knowledge and experience from the past to solve our problems, but this is no longer the case. Now we need to look to the future, become visionaries and explore new ways of thinking to solve these problems. And it helps to be independent and mentally free from tired old patterns of thinking.

We live in an interdisciplinary age, where the borders of the past have been erased. The Internet, media, communications, and global airline networks have created a smaller world. Dance, theater, ballet, singing, and music merge into a single performance. Humanity has become boundless, freeing itself from the barriers of the past – including our views on health and healing. The time has come to tear down the walls separating physician, psychiatrist, psychologist, massage therapist, nutritionist, chiropractor, physical therapist, and others. All share the same goal – to help people toward better health. All try to see, understand, and explain the world from the perspective of their own discipline. The future can be found in interdisciplinary knowledge and research – in an integrated body of knowledge. Humans are far too complex to be explained from a single viewpoint. Be humble and open to other ways of viewing the world than just your own.

> *There is one thing stronger than all the armies in the world,*
> *and that is an idea whose time has come.*
> Victor Hugo

Change has been the recurrent theme of this book – transition from one stage to another. Nothing stands still, except in relation to something else. All aspects of the universe are in constant motion: expansion and contraction, hot and cold, vibrations and cyclical events. Yin and yang flow through all living things and we need only join the dance of life, just as the molecules dance within us.

In studying immunity and health I find that the deeper you look, the more you approach quantum physics and existential research. At their core, healing and health are a spiritual process. Perhaps such insights may lead us to spiritual guides–people with knowledge in psychology, medicine, philosophy, and spirituality–people of great experience. They have a highly developed sense of empathy and can function as catalysts for their fellow human beings, by both facilitating and hastening the development of others. Interest in mystical (divine) experiences will also continue to increase dramatically. Through meditation you can get in touch with the inner essence of existence which helps you understand yourself, others, and life's inner meaning. The more I study and experience healing the more convinced I am that true healing takes place on the spiritual level. Illness and distress occur when we disconnect from our deeper essence, our soul.

Through all the years that I have attempted to understand the mysteries of the immune system, mind, and brain I have continued to feel the same awe and admiration for their beauty. It is as if it were planned from the start, even though we humans may not understand it until afterwards – if at all. There is something inherently magical which remains elusive and which will surely fascinate physicians, therapists, healers, researchers, mystics, and other people throughout all time…

SEVEN THOUGHTS ON HEALING
- We are all endowed with self-healing abilities that can be strengthened.
- There are no quick solutions. Miracles can happen, but for most of us healing is a conscious process requiring time and energy.
- You must focus on the whole.
- All healing takes time.
- A single symptom may have many causes.
- Each person is biochemically and spiritually unique and should be treated as such.
- Many paths lead to healing – no single way is right for everyone. The challenge is to find *your* way.

Postlude
My Path to Self-Healing

I could never have written this book had I not personally been through an extensive healing process on every level: physical, intellectual, emotional, and spiritual. Although I have always been strong and healthy, I have devoted most of my time to learning about self-healing. I spent much of my life running away from my emotions and therefore from myself. Research gave me the perfect excuse to escape my emotions; for years I cultivated the efficient, rational, and intellectual side of my personality, never realizing that this was only taking me farther and farther away from my strength and my inner self.

Healing is a personal process. Although external help, therapy, stimulation, or inspiration can be helpful, it is not the physician or therapist who heals us – we have to do the healing ourselves. No one else can do the job for us, no matter how much we might want this to happen. This is why self-healing is so crucial and it's high time we learned to unleash this natural power. No matter what we've been through or how badly we feel, we are always in a position to begin the healing process – provided we are ready to feel better and take responsibility for our lives.

To heal is to become whole, to be grounded within ourselves. I have achieved this wholeness – this feeling of being "one" on the inside. I am part of a larger flow where life is an exciting process: I love learning, discovering new things, and seeing new correlations. Experiences and encounters are enriching and stimulating. My health is far better than ever before, even though I am nearing 42. My close friends and extended family surround me with love, support, and inspiration. Life is beautiful – a wonderful, enjoyable experience.

I have found my mission in life and this is a great source of joy and satisfaction. My work and my lectures provide me with the opportunity to travel and meet thousands of people. Despite constant commuting between California and Sweden in recent years, I am at home wherever I am because I am at home within myself. "Home is not a place – it's a state of mind"; but reaching this point was no easy task.

The harmony and inner peace that I feel today are far from the disharmony and emotional chaos of my childhood. I spent the first thirty years of my life running away from (and compensating for) anything I could not handle – until the day when absolutely everything was broken and I was finally ready to heal. And I acquired the baggage I lugged through my childhood from previous generations. We inherit not only our genes but also our behavior, which can leave even deeper marks. Dysfunctional parents cannot have whole children; you can only achieve that wholeness yourself, in your own life.

I was born into a family that valued knowledge, research, culture, and nature. Family unity was important and from the outside our parents appeared to have formed the perfect, successful family with three adorable well-behaved children. We children lived up to their expectations: we were successful and obedient, since those were the accomplishments and externalities that were rewarded. Our parents rarely praised us or expressed their appreciation; they didn't want to spoil us. I became the typical over-achiever and was successful in everything I did: school, sports, and friends.

My childhood was rich in material things such as ski trips and family vacations. But something was concealed behind that happy façade: an emotionally deprived childhood, full of uncertainty and insecurity. Our father held us all in his iron grip of dominance and mood swings. We children were held responsible for our parents' emotions and reactions. It was hard, but when you grow up with it you accept it as being the norm. For many children growing up in the 1960s and 1970s, a dysfunctional family seemed to be the norm rather than the exception. It was probably always this way, but it was not until the 1980s and especially the 1990s that, equipped with new tools for delving into hidden areas, people began to talk about the issue. This had previously not been possible because of the shaming inherent to a childhood that focused on what was wrong with an individual rather than what that individual did. We internalized everything, blaming ourselves and preferring not to talk about our problems.

I always wanted a better life; I felt that life held me hostage because I was born in the wrong place, to people who did not understand me. When I was small, my favorite fairy tales were "The Ugly Duckling" and "Sleeping Beauty"; both deal with transformation and awakening.

My awakening came when I began to meditate at the age of 30. I'd been living and working as a researcher in southern California for over a year and in that fresh environment I began to reevaluate some of my old assumptions. I forgot about the demands to achieve; I began to relax and have more fun. The people there were completely different and they valued life in a different way. My interest in people and psychology blossomed; I went for counseling and began reading books on personal development. I learned about psychoneuroimmunology – an exciting new field that studies how our thoughts and emotions, body and soul work together and interact. For me this was a revolutionary discovery, and yet an obvious one: it defined what I had always felt and experienced.

For years I had been feeling poorly without knowing why; how frustrating, when from the outside everything seemed to be so right and to make so much sense. Meditation introduced me to a brand new world–my inner self–and led me to realize that I did not like myself. This was surprising; after all, I seemed to have everything I needed: a good education, an exciting job, friends, a house, a car... But everything I had done was aimed at living up to the requirements and expectations of others. The hard part was that I had no idea know what I wanted, because I had internalized the desires and demands of my surroundings – I did everything to please others and receive a little love and appreciation. But now, step-by-step, I began to untangle the knots and discover things about myself that slowly led to my spiritual awakening.

We all share the experience of a physical birth, but the birth of the soul is up to each one of us. The path to the soul leaves the physical plane via the intellectual and the emotional. However, if you encapsulate your emotions you will never arrive at that place within, but will become increasingly estranged from your core. Physical birth and spiritual birth are both painful experiences, and our unconscious fear of pain holds us back from our awakening. If we are in an environment where such an awakening is possible, then we can make it happen. It is our own choice: we can set ourselves free, or prevent our own liberation. For me, California was the safe and secure place, far from home, where I actually dared to begin to listen to my inner self.

Meditation helped me to get in touch with emotions from long before and I remembered how my father abused me physically and emotionelly when I was a child. This had led to my creating an illusory world of happiness and success, concealing everything that I repressed and did not want to remember. Suddenly I saw my life and the world around me through new eyes. I felt I'd been cheated and deceived all my life – even though I had actually tried to make the best of the situation.

This awakening made me leave the Scripps Research Institute, after twelve years in biomedical research, to stand up and confront my emotions. Now that I knew what was wrong I could fix it and make everything normal. I began to paint, write, and meditate in order to process and take hold of my life and my self. Dealing with all that had been lost and slowly trying to patch my soul back together involved an overwhelming process of grieving.

I no longer wished to be closed in—whether in a laboratory or in a cage of my own making—and I took up activities that challenged me. I began to climb mountains, camped out in the desert, and spent a month traveling on my own in Costa Rica. I've always enjoyed challenges, especially challenging myself; perhaps that's why I specialized in immunology. The immune system needs to be challenged in order to mature and function properly. I am convinced that childhood diseases are important to our physical and mental health in adult life. Surviving trials and confrontations makes you stronger, but you also have to get through them. You have to believe that everything will work out; you have to want to reach beyond safe boundaries. Hope is a strong part of this and the best way out is not always the easiest way. If something frightens me and makes me feel unsure of myself, I will do whatever it takes to overcome my fear and, perhaps, myself. Like the immune system, we need challenges to be able to grow, mature, and develop.

Something within me made me leave California's warm and pleasant climate and return to Sweden in 1993. I did not feel at home; I came down with intestinal candidiasis, and "hit the wall." It often seems that you cannot begin the recovery process until you hit bottom, which acts as a wake-up call and forces you to accept your full responsibility. Sometimes I believe we become sick because we aren't ready to face a new trial, to accept the new challenge that life presents us. Then perhaps we have to stop, bide our time, and take the next train instead. I believe that just as diseases slowly develop over time, unseen, the healing processes also need to develop beneath the surface for a while before we are ready for them.

I was probably responsible for my yeast infection, nutritional deficiencies, and pointless relationships because I wasn't ready to grow up and abandon some of my acquired, destructive behaviors. Perhaps I needed to be small and injured for a while longer. But I remember the day when I decided that I'd finally had enough. I fell on my knees and cried, praying for healing – and then healing entered my path, followed by a positive and loving relationship. I received help through alternative medicine, which in turn fostered my interest in nutritional and complementary medicine. Years of therapy followed and I was helped by counseling, as well as picture, dance, and body therapy, and also by balancing nutrients. I listened to the needs of my inner self.

Along the way, I learned so much that could never be taught in books. My healing process has been a great source of knowledge, giving me a depth that I would never have achieved in any other way. Previously, I had had an exceptionally high IQ, been strictly self-disciplined, and had extensive knowledge about many things, but this emotional and spiritual journey gave me a whole new dimension. You cannot achieve this by studying; the path to this knowledge requires you to work through your emotions and through contact with something on a higher plane. Spiritual awareness is an important element in the healing process and our emotions illuminate the path to the spiritual plane. But it is a heavy-duty job that can be compared to getting down on your hands and knees to scrub the floor, over and over again.

Looking back, I am amazed at the ingenuity of mind and soul: the ability to compensate for, resolve, and work through difficulties. After I completed my PhD at age 27, I underwent an identity crisis. I had no idea what I wanted to do with my life, no defined goals. I was unhappy. I had a postgraduate position lined up in the United States and was engaged to be married when the crisis hit. Suddenly I didn't know where my personal boundaries ended and others' began. I felt sick. I couldn't live on my own; I took a leave of absence from my job and stayed with my parents. My intuition told me to ride my bike around the roads I had known in my childhood. This helped me cut through the knot inside me and find my way home. I put myself back together; I found my boundaries; I was self-healed. And after just a week or so, I was functioning properly once more.

The biggest challenge I ever faced was two years ago when our son died shortly before he was born. I had to give birth to our dead child. The unfathomable pain and sorrow you experience on such an occasion is difficult to describe. Your child should never die before you do; it defies nature. At first, the sorrow was so overwhelming that surviving each day was a trial. But the journey goes up and down; slowly but surely, you get through it. Thank goodness for the wonderful volunteer support groups available in the United States for situations like this. We received invaluable support from other parents whose children had died and from San Diego Hospice. I couldn't understand why this had happened to me after all I'd been through. But the task of working through my sorrow and all the tears shed for Carl Sputnik helped to heal me completely. It put me in contact with spiritual forces I didn't know existed. I see my little angel as a gift; he is with me, albeit on another plane.

I have probably always been a seeker and an incurable optimist. No matter how difficult my life has been, I've always known everything would work out in the end, that it would get better. And so it did – and in my experience, having faith in a higher being will get you through the most difficult experiences. In my nightmare childhood, I read fairy tales about good and evil; I dreamed my way into a lovely world of goodness. I spoke to God and Jesus, who gave me strength and comfort. Although my childhood had neither religion nor spirituality, I have prayed to God when things have been at their worst and always received support. No one told me that I could do this; I found this spiritual support on my own.

The more I learn about the healing process, the better I understand that it takes place on a more profound plane. Therefore you need to be ready for healing, patiently biding your time. Opening yourself to healing means opening yourself to what you are, deep within. Then you live in harmony on the physical, emotional, intellectual, and spiritual planes. Being true to yourself requires you to create the best conditions for healing. Pay attention to your body and your reactions. Listen to your inner voice and do whatever makes your inner self vibrate with joy. Add things that you make you feel good every day; these are "additions," not "addictions." Be kind to yourself and respect your needs. We need more people who are spiritually aware to lead us out of our millennia-long sleep, like so many Sleeping Beauties awakening

– a process now in full swing.

I look through the window, over meadows and fields, beyond the deep blue sea to the horizon. Nature's beauty speaks to me and gives me spiritual power. I feel great joy to have reached where I am in life. And yet, this is just the beginning...

Susanna Ehdin
December 2002

References
(Books and a selection of scientific publications)

General about Health

Clayman, Charles B. (ed.). *American Family Medical Association Medical Guide.* Random House, 1994.

Chopra, Deepak. *Perfect Health – The Complete Mind Body Guide.* New York: Three river press, 2001.

Berman, B.M. "The Cochrane Collaboration and evidence-based complementary medicine." J. Alternative Complementary Medicine 3 (1997): 191–4.

Dickersin, K. and Manheimer, E. "The Cochrane Collaboration: evaluation of health care and services using systematic reviews of the results of randomized controlled trials." Clin. Obstet. Gynecol. 41 (1998): 315–31.

Jahnke, Roger. *The Healer Within – The Four Essential Self-care Methods for Creating Optimal Health.* SanFrancisco: Harper, 1997.

Johansson, Ingvar och Niels Lynöe, *Medicin och Filosofi – En introduktion.* Göteborg: Daidalos, 1997.

Moyers, Bill. *Healing and the Mind.* Main Streets Books, 1995.

Northrup, Christiane. *Women's Bodies, Women's Wisdom – Creating Physical and Emotional Health and Healing.* New York: Bantam books, 1998.

Singer, Charles. *A Short History of Science to the Nineteenth Century.* Mineola: Dover Publ., 1997.

The National Swedish Board of Health and Welfare. "Folkhälsorapport 1997 (Public Health Report), SoS-rapport." 1997:18.

Weil, Andrew. *Spontaneous Healing – How to Discover and Embrace Your Body's Natural Ability to Maintain and Heal Itself.* New York: Ballentine books, 2000.

White, P.J. "Evidence-based medicine for consumers: a role for the Cochrane Collaboration." J. Med. Libr. Assoc. 90, no. 2 (2002): 218–22.

WHO Policy Perspectives on Medicines: *Traditional Medicine – Growing Needs and Potential.*" no. 2, (May 2002).

Energy

Brennan, Barbara Ann. *Light Emerging – The Journey of Personal Healing.* New York: Bantam books, 1993.

Brennan, Barbara Ann. *Hands of Light: A Guide to Healing through the Human Energy Field.* New York: Bantam books, 1993.

Dossey, Larry et al. "Energy Medicine – Subtle Energies, Consciousness and the New Science of Healing." Twelve lectures from ISSSEEM-conferences (the International Sociatey for the Study of Subtle Energies and Energy Medicine), Sounds True Audio, Boulder, CO, 1998.

Dummer, Tom. *Tibetan Medicine – And Other Holistic Health-Care Systems.* London: Routledge, 1988.

Eisenberg, David and Thomas L. Wright. *Qi – Encounters with Qi: Exploring Chinese Medicine.* W.W. Norton & Co., 1985.

Judith, Anodea. *Eastern Body, Western Mind.* Berkeley: Celestial Arts, 1996.

Karu, Tiinu. *The Science of Laser Therapy.* Amsterdam: Gordon and Breach Science Publ., 1998.

Laskow, Leonard. *Healing with Love: A Breakthrough Mind/Body Medical Program for Healing Yourself and Others.* Wholeness press, 1992.

Luger, E.J. et al. "Effect of Low-power Laser irradiation on the Mechanical Properties of Bone Fracture Healing in Rats." Lasers in Surgery & Medicine 22 (1998): 97–102.

Myss, Caroline. *Anatomy of Spirit: the Seven Stages of Power and Healing.* Harmony Books, 1996.

Myss, Caroline. "Energy Anatomy; The Science of Personal Power, Spirituality and Health." Sounds True Audio, Boulder, CO, 1996.

Ozaniec, Naomi. *Chakras for Beginners.* Trafalgar Square, 1999.

Persson, L. and B. Klinge. "Efficacy and Safety of Monochromatic Phototherapy in Patients with Gingivitis." (a report), www.biolight.se.

Ryberg, Karl. *Levande färger – en bok om färgernas dolda psykologi.* ICA bokförlag, 2000.

Schubert, V. "Effects of Phototherapy on Pressure Ulcer Healing in Elderly Patients after a Falling Trauma. A Prospective, Randomized, Controlled study." Photodermatol. Photoimmunol. Photomed. 17 (2001): 32–8.

Siegel, Bernie S. *Love, Medicine and Miracles.* New York: Harper Perennial, 1990.

Selye, Hans. *The Stress of Life.* New York: McGraw Hill, 1978.

Nutritional Medicine

Bergner, Paul. *The Healing Power of Minerals, Special Nutrients and Trace Elements.* Rocklin, CA: Prima Publishing, 1997.

Bland, J.S. "Psychoneuro-Nutritional Medicine: an Advancing Paradigm." Alternative Therapies in Health & Medicine 1 (1995): 22–7.

Bland, Jeffrey S. *Genetic Nutritioneering.* Los Angeles: Keats publishing, 1999.

Braverman, Eric R. et al. *The Healing Nutrients Within,* New Canaan, CT: Keats Publishing, 1997.

Carper, Jean. *Stop aging now!* Harper Perennial, 1996.

Chandra, R.K. "Food hypersensitivity and allergic disease: a selective review." American J. of Clinical Nutrition 66 (1997): 526S–529S.

Hoffer, Abraham & Morton Walker. *Putting It All Together: The New Orthomolecular Nutrition.* New Canaan, CT: Keats Publishing, 1996.

Lee, John R. *What Your Doctor May Not Tell You About Menopause: The Breakthrough Book on Natural Progesterone.* New York: Warner Books, 1996.

Malter, R. "Trace Mineral Analysis and Psychoneuroimmunology." J. of Orthomolecular Medicine 9, no. 2 (1994): 79–73.

Morgan, S.L. et al. "Nutrient Intake Patterns, Body Mass Index, and Vitamin Levels in Patients with Rheumatoid Arthritis." Arthritis Care & Research 10 (1997): 9–17.

Peavy, William S. *Super Nutrition Gardening: How to Grow Your Own Powercharged Foods.* Avery Publishing Group, 1993.

Pike, J. and R.K. Chandra. "Effect of Vitamin and Trace Element Supplementation on Immune Indices in Healthy Elderly." International J. for Vitamin & Nutrition Research 65 (1995): 117–121.

Schauss, Alexander and Carolyn Costin. *Anorexia and Bulimia – A Nutritional Approach to the Deadly Disorders.* New Canaan, CT: Keats Publishing, 1997.

Schauss, Alexander. *Minerals, Trace Elements and Human Health.* Tacoma, WA: Life Science Press, 1998.

Schauss, Alexander. *Nutrition and Behavior.* New Canaan, CT: Keats Publishing, 1985.

Smith, B.L. "Organic Foods vs. Supermarket foods: Element Levels." J. Applied Nutrition 45 (1993): 35–38.

Stanway, Andrew (editor). *Nutritional medicine.* London: Pan Books Ltd, 1987.

Watts, D.L. "Determining Osteoporotic Tendencies from Tissue Mineral Analysis of Human Hair Type I and Type II." Townsend Newsletters for Doctors & Patients Aug./Sept. & Oct. 1986.

Watts, David L. *Trace Elements and Other Essential Nutrients – Clinical Applications of Tissue Mineral Analysis.* Dallas, TX: Writers Block, 1995.

Diet

Campbell, TC and J. Chen. "Diet and Chronic Degenerative Diseases: Perspectives from China." Am. J. Clinical Nutrition 59 (1994): 1153S–1161S.

D'Adamo, Peter J. with Catherine Whitney. *Eat Right for Your Type – The Individualized Diet Solution.* New York: Putnam, 1996.

Eaton, S.B., et al. "Paleolithic Nutrition Revisited: a Twelve-Year Retrospective on its Nature and Implications." European J. of Clinical Nutrition 51 (1997): 207–16.

Ehdin, Susanna. *The Art of Cooking for the Self-Healing Human.* Stockholm, Sweden: Forum, 2000.

Elkins, Rita. *Digestive enzymes – The Key to Good Health and Longevity.* Pleasant Grove, UT: Woodland Publ., 1998.

Fuller, Dicqie. *The Healing Power of Enzymes.* New York: Forbes Publ., 1999.

Lindeberg, S. et al. "Age Relations of Cardiovascular Risk Factors in a Traditional Melanesian Society: the Kitava study." Am. J. of Clinical Nutrition 66 (1997): 845–52.

Montignac, Michel. *Eat yourself slim.* Michel Ange Network Inc., 1999.

Ornish, Dean. *Dr. Dean Ornish's Program for Reversing Heart Disease: The only System Scientifically Proven to Reverse Heart Disease without Drugs or Surgery.* New York: Ivy Books, 1996.

Oski, Frank. *Don't Drink Your Milk.* Chicago: Wyden Books, 1997.

Roizen, Michael and John la Puma. *The Real Age Diet.* (www.realage.com) Harper Collins, 2001.

Ruisniemi, Maija. *Bästa kosten för mage och tarm.* Orsa, Sweden: Energica förlag, 1995.

Schlossers, Eric. *Fast Food Nation.* Houghton Mifflin Co., 2001.

Sears, Barry. *Mastering the Zone.* New York: Regan Books, 1997.

Spake, Amanda. "How McNuggets changed the world." U.S.News & World Report, Jan. 22, 2002.

Walford, Roy L. *The 120 Year Diet.* New York: Simon & Schuster, Pocket Books, 1988.

Walford, Roy L. and Lisa Walford. *The Anti-Aging Plan – Strategies and Recipes* for *Extending Your Healthy Years.* New York: Four Walls Eight Windows, 1994.

Wigmore, Ann. *The Hippocrates Diet and Health Program.* Avery Penguin Putnam, 1986.

Wilhelmsson, Peter. *Friskare liv med rätt kost + vitaminer och mineraler.* Ica bokförlag, 1997.

Willcox, B.J., D. Willcox, and M. Suzuki. *The Okinawa Program.* New York: Potter Publ., 2001.

Willet, Walter C. *Eat, Drink and be Healthy. The Harvard Medical School Guide to Healthy Eating.* New York: Simon & Schuster, 2001.

Sugar

Appleton, Nancy. *Lick the Sugar Habit.* New York: Avery Publishing Group, 1996.

Autio, J. et al. "The effect of two sucrose diets on formation of dentin and predentin in growing rats." Acta Odontologica Scandinavica 55 (1997): 292–5.

Bantle, G.A., et al. "Effects of varying carbohydrate content of diet in patients with non-insulin-dependent diabetes mellitus." JAMA 271 (1994): 1421–8.

Brownlee, M. "Advanced protein glycosylation in diabetes and aging." Annual Review Medicine 46 (1995): 223–34.

Chicco, S.A. et al. "A Sucrose-rich Diet Affects Triglyceride Metabolism Differently in Pregnant and Nonpregnant Rats and has Negative Effects on Fetal Growth." J. Nutrition 126 (1996): 2481–6.

Christensen, L. "The effect of carbohydrates on affect." Nutrition 13 (1997): 503–14.

Cohen, M.P. and F.N. Ziyadeh. "Role of Amadori-modified Nonenzymatically Glycated Serum Proteins in the Pathogenesis of Diabetic Nephropathy [Review]." J. Am. Society Nephrology 7 (1996): 183–90.

Colantuoni, C. et al., "Evidence that Intermittent, Excessive Sugar Intake Causes Endogenous Opoid Dependence." Obesity Research, 10 (2002): 478–88.

Dufty, William. *Sugar Blues.* New York: Warner Books, 1993.

Dyer, D.G. et al. "Accumulation of Maillard Reaction Products in Skin Collagen in Diabetes and Aging." J. Clinical Investigation 91 (1993): 421–422.

Goldman, J. et al. "Behavioral Effects of Sucrose on Preschool Children." J. Abnormal Child Psychology 14 (1986): 567–577.

Grand, E. "Food Allergies and Migraine." Lancet 8126 (1979): 955–959.

Huumonen, S. et al. "Greater Concentration of Dietary Sucrose Decreases Dentin Formation and Increases the Area of Dentinal Caries in Growing Rats." J. Nutrition 127 (1997): 2226–30.

Jones, T.W. et al. "Enhanced Adrenomedullary Response and Increased Susceptibility to Neuroglycopenia: Mechanisms Underlying the Adverse Effects of Sugar Ingestion in Healthy Children." J. Pediatrics 126 (1995): 171–7.

Kampov-Polevoy A. et al. "Evidence of Preference for a High-concentration Sucrose Solution in Alcoholic Men." Am. J. Psychiatry 154 (1997): 269–70.

Lee, A.T. and A. Cerami. "In Vitro and In Vivo Reactions of Nucleic Acids with Reducing Sugars." Mutation Research 238 (1990): 185–91.

Lenders, C.M. "Gestational Age and Infant Size at Birth are Associated with Dietary Sugar Intake Among Pregnant Adolescents." J. Nutrition 127 (1997): 1113–7.

Lonsdale, D. "A Sugar Sensitive Athlete: Case Report." J. Advancement Medicine 7 (1994): 51–58.

Matsumoto, M. "Osteopenic Changes in High Sugar Diet-induced Diabetic Rabbits." Diabetes Research 18 (1991): 115–22.

Nash, J. "Health contenders." Essence 23 (1992): 79–81.

Pagliassotti, M.J. Changes in Insulin Action, Triglycerides, and Lipid Composition During Sucrose Feeding in Rats." Am. J. Physiology 271 (1996): R1319–26.

Palinski, W. et al. "Immunological Evidence for the Presence of Advanced Glycosylation End Products in Atherosclerotic Lesions of Euglycemic Rabbits." Arteriosclerosis, Thrombosis & Vascular Biology 15 (1995): 571–82.

Pamploma, R. et al. "Mechanism of Glycation in Atherogenesis." Medical Hypotheses 40 (1990): 174–181.

Preuss, H.G. "Effects of Glucose/insulin Perturbations on Aging and Chronic Disorders of Aging: the Evidence." J. American College of Nutrition 16 (1997): 397–403.

Vlassara, H. "Advanced Glycation End-products and Atherosclerosis." Annals Medicine 28 (1996): 419–26.

Wilhelmsson, P. "Klinisk nutrition vid Parkinsons sjukdom." Näringsråd & Näringsrön 3 (1998): 2–5.

Zernicke, R.F. et al. "Long-term, High-fat-sucrose Diets Alters Rat Femoral Neck and Vertebral Morphology, Bone Mineral Content, and Mechanical Properties." Bone 16 (1995): 25–31.

Zhu, H., et al. "Effect of Different Diets on Oral Bacteria and Caries Activity in Sprague-Dawley Rats." Microbios. 91 (1997): 105–20.

The Intestinal Flora

Alm, Johan. *Atopy in Children: Association to Life Style.* Stockholm, Sweden: Doctoral dissertation, Karolinska Institutet, 2001.

Asp, N.G. "Resistant Starch – An Update on its Physiological Effects." Advances Experimental Medicine & Biology 427 (1997): 20110.

Crook, William G. *The Yeast Connection: A Medical Breakthrough.* New York: Vintage Books, 1986.

Cummings, J.H. et al. "A New Look at Dietary Carbohydrate: Chemistry, Physiology and Health. Paris Carbohydrate Group." Eur. J. Clinical Nutrition 51 (1997): 417–23.

Cummings, J.T. and G.T. Macfarlane. "Role of Intestinal Bacteria in Nutrient Metabolism." J. of Parenteral Enteral Nutrition 21 (1997): 357–65.

Macfarlane, G.T. and S. Macfarlane. "Human Colonic Microbiota: Ecology, Physiology and Metabolic Potential of Intestinal Bacteria." Scand. J. Gastroenterology - Suppl. 222 (1997): 3–9.

Majamaa, H. and A. Isolauri. "Probiotics: A Novel Approach in the Management of Food Allergy." J. Allergy Clinical Immunology 99 (1997): 179–85.

Peltonen, R. et al. "Faecal Microbial Flora and Disease Activity in Rheumatoid Arthritis During a Vegan diet." Br. J. Rheumatology 36 (1997): 64–8.

Popovich, D.G. et al. "The Western Lowland Gorilla Diet has Implications for the Health of Humans and Other Hominoids." J. Nutrition 127 (1997): 2000–5.

Roberfroid, M.B. "Health Benefits of Non-Digestible Oligosaccharides." Adv. Experimental Medicine Biology 427 (1997): 211-9.

Schneeman, B.O. "Carbohydrates: Significance for Energy Balance and Gastrointestinal Function." J. Nutrition 124 (1994): 1747S-1753S.

The Body and the Mind

Davis, Phyllis K. *The Power of Touch.* Carson, CA: Hay House, 1991

Dewhurst-Maddock, Olivea. *The Book of Sound Therapy; Heal Yourself with Music and Voice.* Fireside, 1993.

Downing, George. *Kroppen och ordet, Kroppsorienterad psykoterapi – teoretisk bakgrund och klinisk tillämpning,* Stockholm, Sweden: Natur och Kultur, 1997.

Feldenkrais, Moshe. *Awareness Through Movement.* San Francisco: Harper, 1991.

Friedman, Howard S. *The Self-Healing Personality*. New York: Plume, 1992.

Greenfield, Susan A. *The Human Brain – A Guided Tour*. New York: Basic books, 1997.

Landgren, M., B. Kjellman, and C. Gillberg. "Attention Deficit Disorder with Developmental Coordination Disorders." Arch. Disease Childhood 79 (1998): 207–212.

Minett, Gunnel. *Andningen som helande kraft* (The healing power of breathing). Orsa, Sweden: Energica förlag, 1994.

Shapiro, Debbie. *Your Body Speaks Your Mind*, Freedom, CA: Crossing Press, 1997.

Singh Khalsa, Dharma. *Brain Longevity: The Breakthrough Medical Program that Improves Your Mind and Memory*. Warner books, 1999.

Singh Khalsa, Dharma. *The Pain Cure: The Proven Medical Program that Helps End Your Chronic Pain*. Warner books, 2000.

Sutherland, Caroline M. *The Body "Knows"– How to Tune in to Your Body and Improve Your Health*. Carlsbad, CA: Hay House, 2001.

Uchino, B.N., J.T. Cacioppo, and J.K. Kiecolt-Glaser. "The Relationship Between Social Support and Physiological Processes: a Review with Emphasis on Underlying Mechanisms and Implications for Health." Psychological Bulletin 119 (1996): 488–531.

Emotions and the Mind

Berry, D.S. and J.W. Pennebaker. "Nonverbal and verbal emotional expression and health." Psychotherapy & Psychosomatics 59 (1993): 11–9.

Childre, Doc and Howard Martin. *The Heartmath Solution*, SanFrancisco: HarperCollins, 2000.

Dohmar, Alice and Henry Dreher. *Self-nurture: Learning to Take Care of Yourself as Effectively as for Everyone Else*. New York: Viking press, 1999.

Goleman, Daniel. *Emotional Intelligence*, Bantam Books, 1997.

Ornish, Dean. *Love and Survival*. San Francisco: HarperCollins, USA, 1999.

Pennebaker, James W., editor. "*Emotion, Disclosure, & Health*." American Psychological Association, 1995.

Pert, Candace B. et el. "Neuropeptides and Their Receptors: A Psychosomatic Network." J. Immunology 135 (1985): 820s–826s.

Pert, Candace B. *Molecules of Emotion – Why You Feel the Way You Feel*. New York: Schribner, 1997.

Sanders, Pete A. *Access Your Brains Joy Center.* Sedona, AZ: Free Soul, 1996.

Steiner, Claude. *Achieving Emotional Literacy – A Personal Program to Increase Your Emotional Intelligence.* New York: Avon Books, 1998.

Stevens, Anthony. *Private myths: Dreams and Dreaming,* Harvard Univ. Press, 1997.

Theorell, T., K. Konarski et al. "Treatment of Patients with Chronic Somatic Symptoms by Means of Art Psychotherapy: A Process Description." Psychotherapy & Psychosomatics 67 (1998): 50–6.

The Immune System

Beisel, W.R. "Nutrition and Immune Function: Overview." J. Nutrition 126 (1996): 2611S–2615S.

Biondi, M. and L.G. Zannino. "Psychological Stress, Neuroimmunomodulation, and Susceptibility to Infectious Diseases in Animals and Man: A Review." Psychotherapy & Psychosomatics 66 (1997): 3–26.

Buhlin, K., et el. "Oral health and cardiovascular disease in Sweden." J. Clin. Periodontol. 29 (2002): 254–9.

Carlsten, Hans. "Kvinn-o-hälsa." Svenska Läkaresällskapet och Spri, 46 (1995): 76–85.

Cohen, N., J.A. Moynihan, and R. Ader. "Pavlovian Conditioning of the Immune System." Int. Arch. Allergy Immunology 105 (1994): 101–6.

Das, U.N. "Is Obesity an Inflammatory Condition?" Nutrition, 17 (2001): 953–66.

Dubos, R.J. *Louis Pasteur, Free Lance of Science,* Da Capo Press, 1986.

Johansson, C.B. et al. "Identification of Neural Stem Cell in the Adult Mammalian Central Nervous System." Cell 96 (1999): 25–34.

Legato M.J. "Women's health: not for women only." (Review) Int. J. Fertility Womens Medicine. 43 (1998): 65–72.

Levy, Elinor and Tom Monte. *The Ten Best Tools To Boost Your Immune System.* Mariner Books, 1997.

Maier, S.F. and L.R. Watkins. "Cytokines for Psychologists: Implications of Bidirectional Immune-to-brain Communication for Understanding Behavior, Mood, and Cognition." Psych. Review 105 (1998): 83–107.

Muller, N., and M. Ackenheil. "Psychoneuroimmunology and the Cytokine Action in the CNS: Implications for Psychiatric Disorders." Progr. Neuro-Psychopharmacology & Biological Psychiatry 22 (1998): 1–33.

Nathanielsz, Peter W. *Life in the Womb – the Origin of Health and Disease.* Ithaca, NY: Promethean Press, 1999.

Plutzky, J. "Inflammatory Pathways in Atherosclerosis and Acute Coronary Syndromes." Am. J. Cardiol. 18;88 (2001): 10K–15K.

Rose, N.R . "The Role of Infection in the Pathogenesis of Autoimmune Disease." (Review) Seminars in Immunology 10 (1998): 5–13.

Toxins and Detoxification

Bland, Jeffrey with Sara Benum. *The 20-day Rejuvenation Diet Program*. New Canaan, CT: Keats Publishing, 1997.

DesMaisons, Kathleen. *Potatoes Not Prozac*. New York: Simon & Schuster, 1998.

Engel J.A., et al. "Neurochemical and Behavioral Studies on Ethanol and Nicotine Interactions." In: Interactive Monoaminergic Basis of Brain Disorders (Eds: T Palomo, RJ Beninger and T Archer), Madrid: Editorial Sintesis, 231–247, 1999.

Gobbi, G. et al. "Coeliac Disease, Epilepsy and Cerebral Calcifications." The Lancet 340 (1992): 439–443.

Hansen, D. et al. "High Prevalence of Coeliac Disease in Danish Children with Type I Diabetes Mellitus." Acta Paediatr 90 (2001): 1238–43.

Jarisch, R. and F. Wantke "Wine and Headache." Int. Arch. Allergy Immunol. 110 (1996): 7–12.

Karjalainen, J. et al. "Bovine Albumin Peptide as a Possible Trigger of Insulin-dependent Diabetes Mellitus." New. Eng. J. Med. 327 (1992): 302–307.

Kenton, Leslie. *Leslie Kenton's 10 Day Clean-Up Plan*, London: Vermilion, 1998.

Knivsberg, A.M., K.L. Reichelt, et al., A Randomised, Controlled Study of Dietary Intervention in Autistic Syndromes." Nutr. Neurosci. 5 (2002): 251–61.

Krohn, J., et al. *Natural Detoxification – The Complete Guide to Clearing Your Body of Toxins*. Point Roberts, WN: Hartley & Marks, 1996.

MacDonald Baker, Sidney, *Detoxification and Healing – The Key to Optimal Health*, New Canaan, CT: Keats Publishing, 1997.

Murray, J. "The Widening Spectrum of Celiac Disease." Am. J. Clinical Nutrition 69 (1999): 354–63.

Reichelt, K.L. et al. "The Effect of a Gluten Free Diet on Glycoprotein Associated Urinary Peptide Excretion in Schizophrenia." J. Orthomolec. Med. 5 (1990): 223-239.

Reichelt, W.H., et al. "Peptide Excretion in Celiac Disease." J. Pediatr. Gastroenterol. Nutr. 26 (1998): 305–9.

Ruden, Ronald A. *The Craving Brain.* New York: HarperCollins, 1997.

Spirituality and Consciousness

Begley, Sharon. "Religion and the Brain." Newsweek, May 7 (2001): 50–58.

Benson, Herbert and Marg Stark. *Timeless Healing: The Power and Biology of Belief.* New York: Schribner, 1996.

Brody, Howard. *The Placebo Response – How You Can Release the Body's Inner Pharmacy for a Better Health.* Cliff Street Books, 2000.

Bischofsberger, Erwin. *Mäster Eckharts Andliga Undervisning.* Stockholm, Sweden: Katolska bokförlaget, 1994.

Campbell, Joseph. *The Power of Myth.* New York: Doubleday, 1988.

Cha, K.Y. et al. "Does Prayer Influence the Success of in Vitro Fertilization-embryo Transfer? Report of a Masked, Randomized Trial." J. Reprod. Medicine 46 (2001): 781–7.

Csíkszentmihályi, Mihály. *Flow: The Psychology of Optimal Experience.* New York: HarperCollins, 1991.

Dossey, Larry. *Healing words: The Power of Prayer and the Practice of Medicine.* Mass Market Paperback, 1992.

Koopman, B.G. and R.A. Blasband. "Two case reports of distant healing: New paradigms at work?" Alt. Therapies in Health and Medicine, 8 (2002).

Larry Dossey. *Reinventing Medicine – beyond mind-body to a new area of healing*, SanFrancisco: HarperCollins, 1999.

Einhorn, Stefan. *A hidden Good: About Religion, Science and the Search for Good.* In press (Swedish edition 1998).

Jahn R.G. "Information, Consciousness, and Health." Alt. Therapies in Health & Medicine 2 (1996): 32–8.

Kabat-Zinn, Jon. *Wherever You Go, There You Are: Mindfulness Meditation in Everyday Life.* Hyperion, 1995.

Murphy, Joseph. *The Power of Your Subconsscious Mind*, New York: Bantam Books 1982.

Newberg, A.B., E.G. d'Aquili, and V.P. Rause. *Why god won't go away. Brain Science and the biology of belief.* New York: Ballantine Publ. 2001.

Wilber, Ken. *A Brief History of Everything*, Boston: Shambhala, 1996.

Zohar, Danah and Ian Marshall. *SQ: Connecting With Our Spiritual Intelligence.* Bloomsbury Pub Plc, 2000.

Index

A

abuse, verbal 211–212
acid-base balance 136–138
acupuncture 62–63, 292
addiction 250–252
    alternative 264
    stress 260–263
addition 263
ADHD 114
Ader, Robert 311, 312
Adlercreutz, Herman 157
adrenaline 63, 92, 104, 121, 245, 258,
adrenals 81–82, 261
affirmations 240
AGE-complex 119–120,
alexithymia 196
alcoholism 95, 250, 254–255,
    sugar dependency 257–258
allergy, food 268–271
    behaviour
    children 115
    intestinal flora 150–151
    primary 272–274
    reducing the risk 316
Almitra 241
alpha waves 239
alternative medicine 21–22, 299, 323, 347
Alzheimer 45, 191, 279, 319
aluminium 97, 279
amino acids 105
amphetamine 250
anatomy of energy 64–65
animus 287
anger 195
anorexia 95, 258, 271
anti-aging 142–144
antibiotics 158
antibodies 51, 269, 273, 275
antioxidants 75, 99–100
antiserum 20
Antonovsky, Aaron 232
amalgam 97, 279-281
amygdala 189
Aristotle 213
asthma 56, 150, 210, 316
Atkins, Robert C. 127
autism 271
autogen stimulation 263–265
autoimmune diseases 20, 275–276, 314–315
autonomic nervous system 82, 190
awareness 289–294
    body 170–172
    meditation 296–297

B

Bacon, Francis 18
Baker, Sidney MacDonald 108, 267, 271
Beck, Robert 69
Bennet, Peter 277
Benson, Herbert 302
being present 236–237
Bergnerm Paul 74
beta carotene 77, 100
beta endorphins 169, 181, 284, 297
    and sugar sensitivity 255–258
bio-balance 25, 27, 49–50, 228, 250, 252, 254-255, 264, 318-321
    brain 245
bioenergy fireld 67
biofeedback 238
bio-imbalance 26-28, 51, 67, 83, 98, 192, 256, 262, 331, 322
    global 266
biological age 132
biochemical energy 56
biochemically unique 21, 322, 340

bioflavonoids 77, 100
Bitten Jonsson Center 258
biofeedback 221
Bland, Jeffrey 322
blood sugar levels 106,
    120–121, 255–259
blood type 274
BMI 125
body awareness 170–172
Bohm, David 67
breast cancer 136, 158, 161
breathing 164–168
    consciousness 296
Brennan, Barbara 67–68, 226, 307
Bridget Jones Diary 256
Brody, Howard 302
Buddha 143, 244, 254
Buddism 23, 24, 42, 138
Burkitt, Dennis 157
Byrd, Randolph 298

C

caffeine 258–260
calcium 73, 81, 84–86, 118
CAM 21–22, 323–324
Campbell, Colin 131
Campbell, Joseph 178
cancer 131
candida 153–156
    oral 155
carbon compounds 36
carbon dioxide 34
cardiovascular disease 26,
    47, 86, 131, 213
    cure 215
    fatty acids 98
    magnesium 92
    margarine 110
    sugar 118
chakra 62-63
Chandra, Ranjit K. 102
chemical addiction 250–252
chlorophyll 34
chromium 73, 117
cholesterol 77, 156, 188

cortisol 261
    elevated 113, 118, 259
    HDL 215
    insulin 120
    LDL 110, 121
    lowered 77, 80, 112, 162, 180
Chopra, Deepak 139
cobalt 73
Coca-Cola 249
cold 70
color therapy 54–56
communication 59
compassion 217
consciousness 36, 59, 239,
    285–294, 295–297
coping 241
cortisol 63, 92, 191
copper 73, 78, 88, 96, 101
cravings 254–255
crisis, unresolved 230
Cro.Magnon man 287
crystals 58
curry lines 37–38
cytochrome P 450 281, 322

D

D'Adamo, Peter 274
Dalai Lama 23
dance 174–175
Darwin, Charles 184
Daoism 42
degenerative diseases 246
depression 26, 76, 83
    allergy 127, 268–71
    emotions 200, 233
    inflammation 319–320
    intestinal flora 92, 151, 154
    life style 283
    light 54–56
    nutrition 76, 80, 96
    seratonin 256–258
    sugar 118, 268–269, 271
Descartes, René 18, 185-7, 218
DesMaisons, Kathleen 256–258
detoxification 28, 266

global 265–267
mechanism 75
mineral and vitamins 101–102
twelve day program 282
diabetes 26, 45, 47, 113–115,
 118, 120–121, 275
bacteria 316
gestational 114
reduced risk 132, 157, 209
Diana, Princess 95, 153
dieting 117
digestive system 104, 146–147
DHEA 261–262
DNA 45, 71, 99
mutations 72
Dohmar, Alice 166
Doleman, Daniel 183
dopamine 245, 252–253
Dossey, Larry 238, 298–300, 303
Downing, George 195
dreams 193-194, 297
Dufty, William 249

E
earth energy 37-40
earth radiation 37–39
Eaton, Boyd 125
Ecstasy 250
Edelson, Stephen B. 155
EEG 193
Ehrlich, Paul 20
Einhorn, Stefan 59
Einstein, Albert 19, 37, 67, 225,
 286 (quotation), 291, 324
electromagnetic radiation 39
empathy 183
emotion 18, 182–185
 to live with
 health 213–214
 food 140–141
 living without 196–199
 memory 190–192
 molecular base 187–190
 relationships 215–216
 repression 217–218
 unconscious 191–194
 unhealed 247
emotional intelligence 183–184, 220
emotional repression 217-218
endocrine glands 190
endorphins 63, 148, 169, 179,
 181, 188, 250, 255–257, 264
energy centers 62-63
energy meridians 61
"energy vampires" 65
enzymes 133–135
 deficiency 268
EQ (emotional intelligence) 185
estrogen 64, 73, 76, 85–85
 false 154
 immune system 313–314
exercise 169–170
existence on three levels 42
extended family 215
euphoria 250

F
Faraday, Michael 70
fast food industry 123–125
fat for life 110-113
fatigue 56
fatty acids, essential 111–113
fear of change 228–230
feelings, value of 184-185
Feng Shui 39
fetus, health status 113–116
fibromyalgia 275
flaxseed oil 112
flow 294–295
folk medicine 19
food, balancing 138.140
 consumption (in US) 124
 emotions 140–141
food industry 108–110, 123–124
free radicals 71, 98–99
Friedman, Howard S. 49, 329
Frisén, Jonas 328
Fry, William 179
functional foods 159–163
functional medicine 322–323

fungal infection 153–156
    genital 154
Følling, Asbjørn 272

G
Galilei, Galileo 18
garlic 161
Gauthier-Hernberg, Gabrielle 61
geopathic stress 38
geomagnetism 38
Gibran, Khalil 300
ginger 161
glycemic index 127
glutathione 75, 282–283
gluten-free 273
gluten intolerance 270–274
God area 301
Granström, Marta 317
grapefruit seed extract 161
green tea 100, 144, 158, 282
Gustafsson, Jan–Åke 56

H
hair mineral analysis 80–81
Hamer Ryke, Geerd 230
harmony 57
HDL 215
healing 68, 308, 323, 327–330, 334
    love 68, 215–216,
    music 175–176
    sound 57
    spiritual 23–24
    touch 209-210
health awareness 32
health triangle 43–44
healthy lifestyle 28, 130–133
Hildegard of Bingen 24
hippocampus 189–191, 328
Hippocrates 17, 128
Hoffer, Abram 129, 280
holistic view 309–310
hormones 64
holographic 67–68
HSP 226
Hugo, Victor 341

hyperactivity 95, 114, 250–251
    food allergies 268–271
hypnosis 194

I
immune system 51–52, 313–317
immunotherapy 20
information technology 35
inner essence 342
intestinal bacteria
    allergies 150–151
    healthy 145, 148–149
    infection 152–153
    leakage 149
instant gratification 228
insulin 120–121
intuition 18, 23, 61, 238, 243, 252,
    291, 296, 304, 321, 337, 340, 347
integrative medicine 22, 323-325
internal ecology 25
iodine 73
iron 73, 78, 80
isoflavones 135–136, 158–159

J
Jahn, Robert 225
jantelagen 223
Jefferson, Thomas 325
Johansson, Catarina 171
Jonsson, Bitten 258
joy 241–243
Jung Carl 226

K
Kabat-Zinn, Jon 297
Kafka, Fanz 304
Kandell, Eric 190
Khalsa, Dharma Singh 261
Konarski, Kristoffer 48, 197

L
Lama Govinda (quotation) 288
Laskow, Leonard 68, 216
Lee, John R. 85

life energy 41-42, 332
lifestyle 28 130–133
light 53–56
limbic stress 203-204
limbic system 184, 189
Lindeberg, Staffan 125
Linnaeus, Carl von 19
living force 34
love 24, 33, 63, 69, 142,
    180–181, 190, 195, 201,
    203 215–217, 339
Low Dog, Tieraona 303
Lundberg, George E. 326
Lundegårdh, Bengt 75

M
MacDonald, Sidney 269
MacLean, Paul 189, 203
macrobiotic 139
magnetic field 69
magnesium 73, 118, 191
mantra 177–178
MAO 251
marasmus 205
massage 206
Mayer, John 183
Meister Eckhart 24
medical freedom 325-326
meditation 13, 23–24, 41, 60, 61,
    132
        and hormones 262, 264, 297
        practice 234, 237–238, 292
        sound 178
memory and emotions 190-193
mental illness 233
meridians 23
metabolism 81–84
migraine 56, 80, 118, 127
minerals 72–94
mitochondria 44–46, 54
monochromatic light 55–56
Montignac, Michel 127
music, healing 175–176
muted child 212-213
Myss, Caroline 64

mystical 176, 178, 238,
    304–306
    experience 303, 342
mysticism 24

N
nerve bundels 190
new age 304
Newton, Isaac 18, 236
nicotine 250
nirvana 255
noradrenaline 63, 81, 92, 121, 231,
    245, 250, 258
Northrup, Christiane 54

O
obesity 26–27
    juvenile 115
    inflammation 320
olive oil 112
omega-3-fatty acids 111–113
opoid system 118
organic food 74–75
orgasm 180, 264
Ornish, Dean 131, 215–216, 219
ortomolecular medicine 79–80
osteoporosis 84–86, 118
Oski, Frank 275
Overton, Donald 191
oxidation 81, 98
oxytocin 209–210

P
paradigm 15, 18–20, 29,
    305, 309, 321–22, 329
Partridge, James 234
Pasteur, Louis 20, 128, 130
Pauling, Linus 79, 129, 322
pathological 20, 102, 108, 321, 322
Penfield, Wilder 189
Pennebaker, James 230
personal transformation 243–244
personal power 28
Pert, Candace 187–188, 192, 264
pharmacological 19, 267

phosphorous 73
piezoelectric effect 58, 292
placebo effect 240, 302–303
Pontius, Annelise 205
potassium 73
power of touch 204-209
power, personal 28, 234
powerlessness 232-235
Paracelsus 41
PMS 80, 93, 112, 127, 166
prana 41
prayer 240, 298–301, 325, 336, 339
pregnancy 113–116
Prescott, James 208
preverbal therapy 196
Pribam, Karl 67
Price, Weston 129
progesteron 85–86, 314
pseudonormal 198
psycoanalysis 195
psychoimmunity 65–66
psychoneuroimmunology 30, 311–312
psychosclerosis 34, 308
psychosocial dwafism 204
psychosomatic 24, 48
    network 190
psychotherapy 141, 195, 199, 290, 327
psychotic seixure 203
Pythagorus 41

Q
qi 61–63
qigong 61–62, 332, 339
quantum physics 291

R
reductionism 18, 21
relaxation 231, 238
REM-sleep 193
relationships 215–217
Reichelt, Karl 273
rheumatoid arthritis 156, 275

Ringertz, Bo 275
Rose, Noel 313
Rosen, Marion 195
Ruden, Ronald A. 254–255
Ruismiemi, Maija 156
Rumi 24
Ryberg, Karl 56

S
Salovey, Peter 183
Sanders, Pete 264
Schanberg, Saul 204
Schauss, Alexander G. 95, 277
Scent-Györgyi, Albert (quotation) 327
Schlosser, Eric 123
schizophrenics 79, 271
Schoentaler, Stephen 277
Schopenhauer, A. 102
Schuman waves 69
Sears, Barry 127, 256
selenium 73
self-confidence 256
self-diagnosis 337–340
self-esteem 243
self-healing personality 329
Semmelweis, Ignaz 129
senses 52
senzitation 257
seratonin 253–254
sexuality 180–181, 266
Selye, Hans 89–90
Shealy, Norman 64
Siegel, Bernie 33
silicon 56, 58, 73, 97, 100, 283, 292-293
    bone formation 86–87
sinuitis 275
skin products 315–316
SLE (systemic lupus erythematosus) 275
sleep 105, 330–331
smoking 100, 213
soy products 87, 105, 162
    isoflavones 135–136, 158–159

seratonin boost 254
spiritual 42, 226, 342
    awakening 303–305
    birth 309
    channels 266
    energy 46
    growth processes 31, 241, 290
    healing 23–24
    pain 327
    sound 178
spirituality 41, 44, 59, 63, 258, 289, 305, 342
SQ (spiritual intelligence) 304
St. John's Wort 254
Steiner Claude, 200
stem cells 30, 327–328
Stevens, Anthony 186
stone age diet 126--127
stress,
    cycle 90
    hormones 92
    nutrition 89–91
    reduce 235

sugar 117–120, 255–257
    dependency 257--258
    sensitivity 255–256

sulfur 73, 100, 137, 281
support group 216
sweets, desire 118
synchronization 226
syntesthesia 52

T

teenage eating habits 106, 116–117
tension and relaxation 231
Theorell, Töres 239
thought, creative power 221-227
Tibet 23
Touch 204– 210
Toxic fats 109–110
toxins 258, 271, 278–280
    metals 97, 277
transformation, personal 243–244

triune brain 189

U

Uvnäs Moberg, Kerstin 210

V

vaccination 317-318
verbal abuse 213–214
violence 209, 211
viral infection 51
visualisation 22
vitamins 76–81

W

Waerland, Are 157
Waldorf schools 316
Walford, Roy 142
water, energized 69
    drinking 88
Watts, David 81, 216
Weil, Andrew 170, 325, 327
wellness process 48
Western medicine
WHO 39, 107
wholeness 340
Wigmore, Ann 156
Wigzell, Hans 316, 328
Wilber, Ken 304
Willett, Walter C. 135
Williams, Roger 81

Y

yin and yang 38, 60
    food 139
yoga 61, 167, 173, 184, 264
    breathing 194

Z

Zinc 73, 88, 91–95
    immune system 80
Zohar, Danah 304

About the Author

Dr. Susanna Ehdin has a Ph.D. in Immunology with three bestselling books in Sweden on holistic health, self-healing, and healthy foods.

Dr. Ehdin works as a lecturer and consultant in the fields of psychoneuroimmunology (PNI), holistic health, nutrition, and consciousness. In October 2002, she was designated Sweden's most popular lecturer by the Swedish weekly business magazine *Veckans Affärer*. She is an independent scientist and author who frequently appears in the media in Sweden. An independent scientist is free to do research, write, and formulate new ideas.

Susanna Ehdin recieved a Ph.D. in Immunology at Lund University, Sweden, (1988) and has done research at Scripps Research Institute in La Jolla, California (1989–92). She is on the advisory board for the *Nordic Journal of Biological Medicine* and a member of the board of Biogaia AB, a Swedish-based international functional food company. For the past few years she has written a biweekly personal health column for Dagens Industri, Scandinavia's leading business newspaper.

Dr. Ehdin has published four books that have sold 250,000 copies in Sweden. Presently The Self-Healing Human has been translated into six languages and the book is under consideration for translation into more languages. She divides her time between southern Sweden and southern California.